PONTIFICAL INSTITUTE OF MEDIAEVAL STUDIES

STUDIES AND TEXTS

15

PRINTED BY UNIVERSA — WETTEREN — BELGIUM

EXCOMMUNICATION AND THE SECULAR ARM IN MEDIEVAL ENGLAND

A STUDY IN LEGAL PROCEDURE FROM THE THIRTEENTH TO THE SIXTEENTH CENTURY

F. DONALD LOGAN

TORONTO

PONTIFICAL INSTITUTE OF MEDIAEVAL STUDIES

1968

Of cursyng oghte ech gilty man him drede,
For curs wol slee right as assoillyng savith,
And also war hym of a *Significavit*.

Canterbury Tales, General Prologue, lines 660-62.

To Richard Cardinal Cushing

PREFACE

THIS present study grew out of research on the medieval court of the Arches. In seeking out source material on the Arches, my attention was drawn to the files of significations of excommunication in the archives of the Public Record Office, London. The Arches material was gleaned from them at that time, and my investigation suggested that these files would merit closer study in their own right at a later date. A few months later I was wisely advised by Professor Stephan Kuttner, now of Yale University, to turn to the significations straight away; this study owes its beginning and much more to that most humane scholar. Taking as my starting point these files of episcopal requests for secular assistance, I have tried to treat the whole question of the use of secular power to coerce the return of excommunicates to the church in medieval England.

Much valuable research has been conducted in recent years in defining, on the level of political theory, the relationship between "church and state" (to use the anachronistic terms, which are still fashionable). It is hoped that this study might show in one limited area the actual cooperation which existed in practice between these two spheres of medieval society. It is my conviction that examination of the many points at which interaction took place will reveal the actually existing relationship, which may or may not concur with the formulations of the theorists.

Work on this study has been spread over several years and several countries, and in the process I have become immensely indebted to many scholars trans-Atlantic, cis-Atlantic, and, that new breed of the jet age, mid-Atlantic. Considerable help and advice were generously given me by Dr A. B. Emden and Mr J. W. Gray, and I benefited greatly from information supplied me by Dr Robert W. Dunning, the Reverend Dr Keith Egan, O. Carm., Dr John Fines, Dr E. B. Fryde, Dr Ralph A. Griffiths, the Reverend Dr T. L. Hogan, S. J., Dr Michael Kelly, Miss Jane E. Sayers, the Reverend Professor Michael M. Sheehan, C.S.B., Professor Niels Skyum-Nielsen, and Reverend Professor J. R. O'Donnell, C.S.B.

Professor F. R. H. DuBoulay read a considerable part in manuscript; for this and much else besides, including the opportunity to present some of this material in an early stage before his seminar at the Institute of Historical Research, University of London, I stand very much in his debt. This book has been much improved and saved from many errors thanks

to the Reverend Professor Leonard E. Boyle, O.P., of the Pontifical Institute of Mediaeval Studies, Toronto, who gave the entire manuscript the
benefit of his broad erudition and clear judgment. To no scholar do I owe
more than to Dr Helena M. Chew, formerly of Queen Mary College,
University of London, who encouraged this work from the start, who read
it at several early stages, and who read it once again in proof; her assistance
was always generously given and will always be deeply appreciated.
I value the suggestions of these scholars very much indeed and have de-
parted from them only infrequently and then, I fear, to my own peril.

The officers and staffs of libraries and archival depositories have greatly
facilitated my work: the Public Record Office, in particular Miss D. Giffard;
the Institute of Historical Research; the British Museum; Lambeth Palace
Library; the library of the Pontifical Institute of Mediaeval Studies, in
particular the Reverend Harold B. Gardner, C.S.B., Transcripts of Crown-
copyright records in the Public Record Office appear by permission of the
Controller of H. M. Stationery Office.

The tedious task of easing the passage of this study through the press
has been cheerfully borne by my friend, the Reverend Professor J. Am-
brose Raftis, C.S.B., of the Pontifical Institute of Mediaeval Studies. It is
a pleasure to thank Miss Karen A. Corsano and Miss Deborah A. Field,
students at Emmanuel College, Boston, for their help at a crucial stage in
proof-reading, and Miss Paula Duggan and Miss Judith B. Willard, also
of Emmanuel College, for assisting in the compiling of the index.

The reader will encounter frequently in the pages which follow medieval
bishops fulminating sanctions on their subjects. This work owes its com-
pletion to the interest, encouragement, and support of a modern bishop
in the mold not of the fulminator but of the pastor of souls and patron of
learning. The dedication all too inadequately expresses my gratitude to
Richard Cardinal Cushing, archbishop of Boston.

Boston, Massachusetts   F.D.L.
Easter, 1967.

TABLE OF CONTENTS

PREFACE 7

LIST OF ABBREVIATIONS 11

INTRODUCTION 13

Chapter I — THE POWER TO SIGNIFY EXCOMMUNICATED PERSONS   25
    I. The Power of Bishops 26
    II. The Power of Papal Officials . . . 30
    III. The Power of Lesser Prelates . . . 33
    IV. The Question of Jurisdiction . . . 35

Chapter II — PERSONS SUBJECT TO SIGNIFICATION . . . 43
    I. Contumacy, Excommunication, and the
      Secular Arm 44
    II. Clerical Subsidies and the Secular Arm . 53
    III. Types of Persons Signified for Arrest . . 61
    IV. The Number of Excommunicates Signified
      to the Secular Arm for Arrest . . 66
    V. Heretics and the Secular Arm . . . 68

Chapter III — THE SIGNIFICATION PROCEDURE 72
    I. Procedure in the Ecclesiastical Court . 72
    II. The Bishop's Request for Secular Aid . 79
    III. The Action of the Royal Chancery . . 86
      A. Writ de cursu 86
      B. Issuance of the Writ 91
      C. Chancery Fees 97
    IV. Delivery of the Writ 99
    V. Execution by the Sheriff 102
    VI. Effectiveness of the Signification Procedure . 110
    VII. Note on Wales and the Counties Palatine . 112

Chapter IV — The Effect of Appeal   116
    I. Canonical Provisions for Appeal .   . 116
    II. The Use of Appeal to Avoid Capture . 120
    III. The Argument Against the Action of Chan-
    cery 134

Chapter V — Absolution and Reconciliation 137
    I. The Nature and Procedure of Absolution   137
    II. Delivery of the Excommunicate from Prison 145
    III. The Writ *de cautione admittenda* .   .   . 150
    IV. The Number of Imprisoned Excommuni-
    cates Absolved 154

Epilogue   156

Appendices   159
  A. An Early Description of the Signification Procedure   . 161
  B. Selected Significations of Excommunication   .   .   . 162
  C. Signification of Excommunication from Non-Episcopal
    Jurisdictions 176
  D. The Secular Arm and the Collection of Clerical Subsidies 187
  E. The Use of the Secular Arm Against Heretics   .   . 189
  F. Selected writs *de excommunicato capiendo*   .   .   . 195
  G. Description by the Sheriff of Sussex of the Capture of the
    Excommunicate Vincent Fynche, 1430 198
  H. Selected Documents Concerning Appeals   .   .   . 201
  I. Selected Documents Concerning Absolution   .   .   . 205
  J. Registers of Writs and Excommunication   .   .   . 211

Select Bibliography   217

Index   225

ABBREVIATIONS

Ann. Mon.	*Annales Monastici* (ed. H. R. Luard; R. S., London, 1864-69).
BM	British Museum.
Bracton, *De Legibus*	Henry de Bracton, *De Legibus et Consuetudinibus Angliae* (ed. G. E. Woodbine; 4 vols.; New Haven, 1915-1942).
BIHR	*Bulletin of the Institute of Historical Research.*
Cal. Chanc. Warr.	*Calendar of Chancery Warrants.* (Public Record Office, London, 1927).
Cal. Chart. Rolls	*Calendar of the Charter Rolls* (Public Record Office, London, 1903-1927).
Cal. Fine Rolls	*Calendar of the Fine Rolls* (Public Record Office, London, 1911-).
CCR	*Calendar of the Close Rolls* (Public Record Office, London, 1902-).
Cole, *Documents*	*Documents Illustrative of English History in the Thirteenth and Fourteenth Centuries* (ed. Henry Cole; London, 1844).
Conc. oec. decr.	*Conciliorum oecumenicorum decreta* (eds. J. Alberigo *et al.*; Freiburg, 1962).
Councils 2	*Councils and Synods with other documents relating to the English Church*, vol. 2, *A.D. 1205-1313* (ed. F. M. Powicke and C. R. Cheney; Oxford, 1964).
CPR	*Calendar of the Patent Rolls* (Public Record Office, London, 1901-).
Curia Regis Rolls	*Curia Regis Rolls* (Public Record Office, London, 1922-).
EHR	*English Historical Review.*
Foedera	*Foedera, conventiones, literae* etc. (ed. Thomas Rymer; re-ed. Adam Clark; Record Commission, London, 1816-30).
Jaffé	*Regesta pontificum Romanorum ab condita ecclesia ad annum post Christum natum MCXCVIII* (ed. P. Jaffé; Leipzig, 1885-88).
Lyndwood	William Lyndwood, *Provinciale (seu Constitutiones Angliae)* (Oxford, 1679).
Mansi	*Sacrorum conciliorum et nova et amplissima collectio* (ed. J. D. Mansi *et al.*; Florence, Venice, Paris, Leipzig, 1759-1927).
PL	J. P. Migne, *Patrologiae cursus completus... Series latina* (Paris, 1844-1864).
Pollock and Maitland	F. Pollock and F. W. Maitland, *The History of English Law before the Time of Edward I* (2nd ed.; Cambridge, 1911).
Potthast	*Regesta pontificum Romanorum inde ab a. post Christum natum MCXCVIII ad a. MCCIV* (ed. A. Potthast; Berlin. 1874-75).
Prynne	William Prynne, *The History of King John, King Henry III, and the most illustrious King Edward the I* (London, 1670).
Reg. —	Abbreviations for those bishops' registers which have been published by private societies contain the surname of the bishop and the name of his diocese; the full reference can

	be found by consulting the index to *Texts and Calendars: An Analytical Guide to Serial Publications* (London, 1958) by E. L. C. Mullins.
Reg. Epp. Peckham	*Registrum epistolarum fratris Johannis Peckham, archiepiscopi Cantuariensis* (ed. C. T. Martin; R. S., London, 1882-85).
Reg. omn. brev.	*Registrum omnium brevium* (London, 1634).
Rot. Parl.	*Rotuli Parliamentorum* (London, 1783-1832).
RS	[Roll Series] *Rerum Britannicarum medii aevi scriptores, or, Chronicles and Memorials of Great Britain and Ireland during the Middle Ages.* Published under the direction of the Master of the Rolls, 1858-1911.
Salter	*Snappe's Formulary and other Records* (ed. H. E. Salter; Oxford Historical Society, vol. 80, 1924).
Salzman	L. F. Salzman, "Sussex Excommunicates," *Sussex Archaeological Collections* 82 (1941) 124-140.
Select Charters	*Select Charters and other Illustrations of English Constitutional History* (ed. William Stubbs; 9th ed.; Oxford, 1913).
Statutes	*The Statutes of the Realm* (eds. A. Luders *et al.*; London, 1810-1828).
Tract. univ. iur.	*Tractatus universi iuris, duce, et auspice Gregorio XIII* (Venice, 1584-86).
TRHS	*Transactions of the Royal Historical Society.*
VCH	*Victoria County Histories.*
Wahrmund	*Quellen zur Geschichte des römisch-kanonischen Processes im Mittelalter* (ed. L. Wahrmund; Innsbruck, Heidelberg, 1905-1931).
Wilkins	*Concilia Magnae Britanniae et Hiberniae,* A.D. 446-1718 (ed. D. Wilkins; 4 vols.; London, 1737).
Year Book	*Les Reports del Cases en Ley* (London, 1679).

All archival references, unless otherwise identified, are to the Public Record Office, London.

For canonical works the abbreviations which have been proposed as standard by the Institute of Medieval Canon Law have been used (see *Traditio* 15 (1959) 452-64); thus, e.g., X stands for the *Decretals of Gregory IX.*

The standard abbreviations for the counties of England are used (e.g., Lincs. for Lincolnshire).

INTRODUCTION

THE exclusion of a person from normal society constituted in medieval Europe a penalty inflicted by both secular and ecclesiastical authorities. The excommunication used by the church was analogous to the imperial ban and to the outlawry of the common law.[1] Radically, excommunication severed a person from the Christian community; it removed him from the communion of the faithful. In a unitary Christian society this amounted, at least in theory, to nearly complete ostracism. Amidst the dashing of candles and the tolling of bells he was cursed and cut off from the church's body as a scandalizing member, henceforth to be treated as a pagan.[2] The essential element in excommunication was this separation from the faithful — *separatio a communione fidelium*.[3]

This separation allowed of degrees: from exclusion merely from the reception of some of the sacraments to exclusion even from one's own

---

[1] Maitland calls excommunication "an ecclesiastical outlawry" (Pollock and Maitland 1. 478).

[2] The element of the curse in excommunication has been stressed by Julius Goebel, *Felony and Misdemeanor* (New York, 1937), pp. 263-65. In the rite of excommunication the bishop proclaimed, "Membrum putridum et insanabile... ferro excommunicationis a corpore Ecclesiae abscidamus," and the rubric directed him to announce to the people that the excommunicate was hereafter to be held "non pro christiano, sed pro pagano" (see the *Ordo excommunicationis* in *PL* 138. 1123-25). For seven other forms of solemn excommunication see *De antiquis ecclesiae ritibus libri*, lib. 3, cap. 4 (ed. Edmund Martène; Antwerp, 1736-38, vol. 2, cols. 903-912). For English examples see *Die Gesetze der Angelsachsen* (ed. F. Liebermann; Halle, 1903-16), 1. 432-441.

[3] Not much modern work has been done on the history of excommunication. In his introduction to Le *"Liber de excommunicatione" du Cardinal Bérenger-Frédol* (Paris, 1912) E. Vernay gives a useful summary of the canonical teaching on excommunication. See also Hinschius 5. 1-492, and Peter Huizing, "The Earliest Development of Excommunication *Latae Sententiae* by Gratian and the Earliest Decretists," *Studia Gratiana* 3 (1955) 277-320. The relation of excommunication to penance has been traced by François Russo, "Pénitence et excommunication: Étude historique sur les rapports entre la théologie et le droit canon dans le domaine pénitentiel du ixᵉ au xiiiᵉ siècle," *Recherches de science religieuse* 33 (1946) 257-279, 431-461. For the views of two medieval thinkers see Jean Leclercq, "L'interdit et l'excommunication d'après les lettres de Fulbert de Chartres," *Revue historique de droit français et étranger*, 4th ser., 1944, pp. 67-77; Nicholas M. Haring, "Peter Cantor's View on Ecclesiastical Excommunication and Its Practical Consequences," *Mediaeval Studies* 11 (1949) 100-112. For problems related to excommunication in England see Miss R. M. T. Hill, "Public Penance: Some Problems of a Thirteenth-Century Bishop," *History* 36 (1951) 213-226; *eadem*, "The Theory and Practice of Excommunication in Medieval England," *History* 42 (1957) 1-11. The effects of excommunication on membership in the church have been treated historically by Alfons Gommenginger, "Bedeutet die Exkommunikation Verlust der Kirchengliedschaft?" *Zeitschrift für katholische Theologie* 73 (1951) 1-71.

familia. The basic distinction made by the canonists from the thirteenth century onwards was between minor and major excommunication, a distinction based on degree of separation. Minor excommunication separated a person from reception of the Eucharist, from celebration of Mass and possibly even from attendance at Mass; such a one, although he could validly take part in elections, could not validly be elected. This penalty — assimilated by many authors to mortal sin — constituted a very minor weapon in the church's arsenal of penalties. It could be imposed and removed by any priest with jurisdiction in the internal forum (i.e., in the forum of conscience).

Of far greater significance was the censure of major excommunication, which separated the excommunicate not only from the Eucharistic Body of Christ but also from the Mystical Body of Christ; it was excommunication in its strict sense.[4] It left the excommunicate dispossessed of all religious rights. He was excluded from entry into church, from the company of the faithful, from pleading in secular and ecclesiastical courts,[5] from the enjoyment of a benefice, and from all legitimate ecclesiastical acts; and after death his body was even denied ecclesiastical burial. Although he had lost his rights, the excommunicate was still bound to keep his obligations (e.g., a priest must still recite the divine office). By the thirteenth century canonical teaching had reserved the power to impose major excommunications to certain prelates having jurisdiction (i.e. to bishops, archdeacons, deans of cathedral chapters, and abbots) and to judges acting by their commission.[6] Thus, clerics or monks not in priest's orders who had this jurisdiction (e.g., as archdeacons or abbots) could excommunicate; laymen — but never women, not even abbesses — acting as ecclesiastical judges had the power to excommunicate. If to a canon was added a clause excommunicating all violators of the canon, then their

[4] The distinction between anathema and major excommunication was not always clearly stated. The difference, according to Hostiensis (Henry de Segusio, died 1271), was that major excommunication refers to the simple imposition of the penalty (e.g., by an ecclesiastical judge) whereas anathema refers to its solemn imposition by a bishop and twelve priests (*Summa* (Lyons, 1542) 5. de sententia excommunicationis. 2). When used by itself the expression "major excommunication" does not exclude anathema but stresses the judicial rather than the ritualistic aspect of the penalty.

[5] The dictum was "excommunicatus non habet personam standi in iudicio." Excommunication became a standard exception admissable in the common law courts; see Anthony Fitzherbert, *La Graunde Abridgement* (London, 1565), v. *excommengement.*

[6] Hostiensis allowed parish priests to fulminate *ipso iure* excommunications and to impose minor excommunications in the internal forum (*Summa* 5. de sententia excommunicationis. 5). This never became common teaching and was not the English custom. With regard to commissions to judges the phrase commonly employed in English commissions was "cum cuiuslibet cohercionis canonice exequendique que in hac parte decreueritis potestate."

excommunication was said to be *a iure*; if an excommunication was inflicted as a judicial sentence or as an individual precept, then it was said to be *ab homine*. In excommunications *latae sententiae* the mere performance of the forbidden act gave rise to an automatic excommunication: Titus strikes a cleric and is *ipso facto* excommunicated. In excommunications *ferendae sententiae* a positive sentence *post factum* imposed the penalty: Titus contumaciously refuses to answer a citation and is declared excommunicate by the judge. So grave were the effects of major excommunication that previous warnings were required before it could be imposed. In excommunications *latae sententiae* the law or precept contained the warning. In penalties *ferendae sententiae* three warnings or one peremptory, at the judge's discretion, had first to be issued.

Not all excommunications imposed in the middle ages, not even those carried out with solemn anathemas, were necessarily valid. Many legal reasons could have been alleged in proof of invalidity. Perhaps the excommunication had been issued by a person having no competence (e.g., by a bishop against someone not his subject in a matter not of his cognizance) or by a judge after a legitimate appeal; or perhaps the person had not been guilty of mortal sin.[7] In view of this common teaching of the canonists concerning the possible invalidity of sentences of excommunication it would be uncritical to assume in every case that excommunicates who remained unmoved by their excommunications were in fact contemning the keys of the church: many indeed may have been convinced of the invalidity of their excommunications.

Excommunication was a censure, its purpose medicinal. Separation from the company of the faithful was intended to induce the excommunicate to seek absolution, reconciliation to the church, and restoration to his place in society. As a spiritual penalty, admittedly with social consequences, excommunication did not always succeed in effecting the desired repentance and consequently the obdurate excommunicate was not an unfamiliar figure. If the penalty of excommunication failed to achieve its desired effect, the church, having used her ultimate weapon, had no further penalty to inflict. It is not surprising that in such circumstances the church sought the aid of the secular power, for the church insisted on the general duty of temporal rulers to lend support to the church whenever the good of society required. Thus, just as the secular arm of society used its *vis coactiva* for the recapture of the Holy Land and for the punishment of heretics, so it used this same *vis* to coerce obdurate excommunicates to repentance.

---

[7] No mortal sin, no crime; no crime, no penalty. The imposition of an excommunication established a presumption of crime and sin.

From as early as the fourth century ecclesiastical synods claimed that the secular power should assist the church against such obdurates.[8] Merovingian and Carolingian legislation restated the role of the secular power in his respect.[9] By the twelfth century some form of secular action was in use in most parts of western Europe. In the German part of the empire the imperial ban was imposed on those who remained excommunicate for six weeks and, conversely, the church imposed excommunication on those who remained under imperial ban for the same period; by the end of the thirteenth century the period had been extended to a year and a day, where it became fixed.[10] In Italy the ban was likewise used in this connection.[11] The procedure in much of France was influenced by the Albigensian troubles: those who remained excommunicate for more than a year were assimilated to the state of heresy or suspicion of heresy and were subject to the confiscation of their movables and immovables and perhaps to arrest.[12] In Aragon the death penalty was threatened if fines did not suc-

---

[8] See Maurice Morel, *L'Excommunication et le pouvoir civil en France du droit canonique classique au commencement du XVe siècle* (Paris, 1926), pp. 5-12.

[9] Hinschius 5. 375-76.

[10] *Ibid.*, pp. 391-94. On 26 April 1220 Frederick II included this chapter in his privileges to the ecclesiastical princes: "Et quia gladius materialis constitutus est in subsidium gladii spiritualis, excommunicationem, si excommunicatos in ea ultra sex septimanas perstitisse predictorum modorum aliquo nobis constiterit, nostra proscriptio subsequatur, non revocanda, nisi prius excommunicatio revocetur" (*Monumenta Germaniae Historica, Constitutiones* 2. 90) On 22 November of that same year he issued an edictal law touching the same matter: "Item quecumque communitas vel persona per annum in excommunicatione propter libertatem Ecclesie facta perstiterit ipso jure imperiali banno subjaceat a quo nullatenus extrahatur nisi prius ab Ecclesia beneficio absolutionis obtento" (*Historia diplomatica Friderici secundi* (ed. J. L. A. Huillard-Bréholles; Paris, 1856-1861), 2. 1. p. 4). The earlier privilege required a *denuntiatio* and a royal sentence in each case, whereas by this later law the imperial ban was incurred automatically after a year (see Stephan Kuttner and Antonio Garcia y Carcia, "A New Eyewitness Account of the Fourth Lateran Council," *Traditio* 20 (1964) 167-171). The sword-helping-sword image reappears frequently in connection with secular constraint of excommunicates; see Pseudo-Edward (*infra* p.20,n.28), Bracton (4.327), the statutes of Peter Quinel, bishop of Exeter, in 1287 (*Councils* 2. 1031), and the statutes of John Stratford, archbishop of Canterbury, about 1342 (Wilkins 2. 708).

[11] See Hinschius 5. 593; Goebel, *Felony and Misdemeanor*, p. 266.

[12] The royal ordinance *Cupientes* (1228) addressed to various cities and dioceses in Languedoc provided for seizure of goods by the bailiff after a year (*Recueil général des anciennes lois françaises* (eds. F. A. Isambert *et al.*; Paris, 1822-1833) 1. 230-33; see Morel, pp. 69-78, and Hinschius 5. 396-97). Curialis, a cleric in northwest France, wrote in his *Summa* in the third quarter of the thirteenth century that after a year an excommunicate should be imprisoned and his goods sequestrated (Wahrmund 1. 3. pp. 7-8). The Council of Melun, called by the archbishop of Sens in 1216, legislated the punishment of the body and property of those remaining excommunicate for over a year (Mansi 22. 1087). For the use of the secular arm against heretics see Julien Havet, *L'Hérésie et le bras séculier au moyen âge jusqu'au treizième siècle* (Paris, 1881).

ceed.[13] According to the Danish church laws a person remaining ex-communicated for a year and a day could be placed under ban.[14] It was, then, in local custom and legislation and not in the general canon law that practices of secular coercion of excommunicates had their foundation.

In England by the early thirteenth century records begin to appear which reveal a well-established procedure of secular aid against obdurate excommunicates. Briefly, by this procedure the royal chancery at the request of a residential bishop would issue to the local sheriff a writ for the capture and detention, until absolved, of any person who had remained excommunicate for more than forty days.[15] This system was used through-out the rest of the middle ages, survived the religious changes of the sixteenth century, and fell into desuetude only in the early seventeenth century. The present study seeks to describe in detail this procedure from the time of its appearance in records of the thirteenth century until the time of the reforming statutes of Henry VIII in the 1530's.

This practice of using the secular arm against excommunicated persons which made its appearance in the records of the thirteenth century owes its origin to the provisions made by William the Conqueror regarding the ecclesiastical courts (1072 × 1076). This ordinance secured the establish-ment of canon law as the basis for ecclesiastical discipline. To this end, the Conqueror removed ecclesiastical cases from the hundred courts (i) by forbidding archdeacons and bishops either to hear ecclesiastical cases in the hundred court or to take such cases to lay judges and (ii) by command-ing persons involved in these cases to come to the place designated by the bishop, where they will receive justice "non secundum hundret, sed se-cundum canones et episcopales leges."[16] The question of the existence of

---

[13] Hinschius 5. 398.

[14] *Skånske lov, Anders Sunesøns parafrase, Skånske kirkelov* (eds. Sv. Aakjaer *et al.*; *Danmarks gamle Landskabslove med Kirkelovene*, vol. 1, pt. 1; Copenhagen, 1933), pp. 904-912. I am grateful to Mr. Peter King and to Professor Niels Skyum-Nielsen for their kindness in calling these reference to my attention; see N. Skyum-Nielsen, *Blodbadet i Stockholm* (Copenhagen, 1964), p. 188, n. 21.

[15] For brief descriptions of this procedure see Pollock and Maitland 1. 478; R. C. Fowler, "Secular Aid for Excommunication," *TRHS*, 3rd ser., 8 (1914) 113-117; Irene J. Churchill, *Canterbury Administration* (London, 1933) 1. 521-23; Brian L. Woodcock, *Medieval Ecclesiastical Courts in the Diocese of Canterbury* (London, 1952), pp. 95-97; Carson I. A. Ritchie, *The Ecclesiastical Courts of York* (Arbroath, 1956), pp. 105-110. Reference should be made to the introductions to the calendars by Salter and Salzman (see *supra* abbreviations).

[16] "Propterea mando et regia auctoritate precipio, ut nullus episcopus uel archidiaconus de legibus episcopalibus amplius in hundret placita teneant, nec causam que ad regimen animarum pertinet ad iudicium secularium hominum adducant, sed quicumque secundum episcopales leges de quacumque causa uel culpa interpellatus fuerit, ad locum, quem ad hoc episcopus elegerit et nominauerit, ueniat ibique de causa uel culpa sua respondeat, et non secundum hundret, sed

formally constituted ecclesiastical courts in pre-Conquest England —
as distinct from the bishop making judgments in *ad hoc* disciplinary matters
— has not yet been settled,[17] but it is certainly difficult in the light of this
legislation to imagine previously existing a highly institutionalized system
of ecclesiastical courts.[18] What can be said with certitude is that these
provisions were intended to establish the discipline of the church under its
own laws and procedures and to sever its link with English law and procedure.

King William, realizing that ecclesiastical discipline would be no
stronger than the ability of the authorities of the church to secure respect
for it, made two provisions in this same ordinance to deal with those who
after three citations were unwilling to appear. First, they should be excommunicated. Secondly, if it proved necessary, the strength and justice
of the king or sheriff should be used for their correction.[19] Thus, the
penalty for contumacy was to be excommunication; this the bishops were
soon to confirm at the Council of Winchester.[20] For William, the secular

secundum canones et episcopales leges rectum Deo et episcopo suo faciat" (*Die Gesetze der Angelsachsen* (ed. F. Liebermann; Halle, 1903-1916) 1. 485; *Select Charters*, pp. 99-100). For the date
see Curtis H. Walker, "The Date of the Conqueror's Ordinance Separating the Ecclesiastical
and Lay Courts," *EHR* 39 (1924) 399-400.

[17] The argument in favor of the existence of ecclesiastical courts before the conquest has been
recently stated by Professor R. R. Darlington in the 1962 Creighton Lecture (*The Norman Conquest*,
London, 1963) and by Professor Frank Barlow (*The English Church, 1000-1066*, London, 1963),
both intent to show the essential continuity between pre-conquest and post-conquest England,
but they have not convincingly refuted the position of Makower who, while allowing that "purely
ecclesiastical courts to determine disputed questions existed in the Anglo-Saxon period," concluded
that "there was no division between the judicial and administrative authorities nor can a sharp
line be drawn between the two forms of activity exercised by one and the same authority" (Felix
Makower, *The Constitutional History and Constitution of the Church of England* (Eng. trans.; London,
1895), pp. 388-89).

[18] It is significant that the Conqueror introduced this legislation by commenting on the previous
lack of observance of episcopal laws and that the remedy which he provided was the removal of
ecclesiastical cases from the hundred courts.

[19] "Si uero aliquis per superbiam elatus ad iustitiam episcopalem uenire contempserit uel
noluerit, uocetur semel et secundo et tertio. Quodsi nec sic ad emendationem uenerit, excommunicetur; et si opus fuerit ad hoc uindicandum fortitudo et iustitia regis uel uicecomitis adhi-
beatur. Ille autem qui uocatus ad iustitiam episcopi uenire noluerit, pro unaquaque uocatione
legem episcopalem emendabit" (see *supra* n. 16).

[20] The Council of Winchester, probably in 1076, threatened excommunication as a penalty
for contumacy in criminal cases: "Laici vero, si de crimine suo accusati fuerint, et episcopo suo
obedire noluerint, vocentur semel, et iterum, et tertio: si post tertiam vocationem emendari
noluerint, excommunicentur; si autem post excommunicationem ad satisfactionem venerint, foris-
facturam suam, quae Anglice vocatur oferhyrnesse seu lahslite, pro unaque vocatione episcopo
suo reddant" (Matthew Parker, *De antiquitate ecclesiae et privilegiis ecclesiae Cantuariensis cum archie-*

arm was to be used only if the spiritual penalty failed. It was left apparently to the discretion of the bishop whether he would invoke the assistance of the king or the sheriff. It should be noted, too, that left unspecified was the exact nature of the secular aid.

Provisions can be found in Anglo-Saxon laws for the use of secular constraint (e.g., exile, loss of property) against excommunicates.[21] This is hardly surprising in a legal structure which failed to distinguish secular and spiritual jurisdictions: one can scarcely speak of the secular arm lending its support to the ecclesiastical.[22] In his ordinance William the Conqueror was not restating this Anglo-Saxon provision. His provision for secular constraint against excommunicates was only part of a major innovation, namely, the establishment of separate ecclesiastical courts. In order to insure respect for the citations of these ecclesiastical courts, William made available to the church the power of the secular arm against those excommunicated for failure to obey such citations. William was clearly not continuing an Anglo-Saxon practice.

One can look with greater confidence to an origin in William's general conception of the cooperation between the ecclesiastical and secular jurisdictions. He had entrusted the enforcement of the truce of God in Normandy to the bishops, who were to use excommunication as a penalty against violators.[23] At the Council of Lillebonne in 1080 he made further provision that, should excommunication fail, the bishops should invoke the aid of the local lord or, if that were not given, the aid of the ducal viscount to bring the person to the bishop's justice.[24] True it is that no

---

piscopis eiusdem lxx (Lambeth, 1572), p. 98; also, but with errors, Wilkins 1. 367); see Heinrich Böhmer, *Kirche und Staat in England und in der Normandie in XI und XII Jahrhundert* (Leipzig, 1899), p. 93, n. 1; Makower, *Constitutional History and Constitution of the Church of England*, p. 392, n. 2.

[21] 2 Cnut 4. 1 and 2 Cnut 66. 1 (Liebermann, *Die Gesetze* 1. 311, 353).

[22] Professor Barlow states that "defiant excommunicates would be constrained by the lay power to stand trial at the shire court, and there, if found guilty, they would receive an ecclesiastical penalty, and sometimes a secular penalty as well, at the discretion of the episcopal judge" (*The English Church, 1000-1066*, p. 259), yet the evidence presented fails to support so organized a procedure.

[23] See especially the Council of Caen (1047) in *Concilia Rothomagensis provinciae* (ed. G. Bessin; Rouen, 1717), p. 39 and in Mansi 19. 597. For a general treatment of the truce of God in Normandy see Goebel, *Felony and Misdemeanor*, pp. 297-328, and Charles H. Haskins, *Norman Institutions* (Cambridge, Mass., 1925), p. 37. For the relationship of William to ecclesiastical councils in Normandy see Böhmer, *Kirche und Staat*, pp. 32-33.

[24] "Pax Dei, quae vulgo Trevia dicitur, sicut ipse Princeps Guilelmus eam initio constituerat, firmiter teneatur, et per singulas Parochias dictis excommunicationibus removetur. Qui vero servare contempserint vel aliquatenus fregerint, Episcopi, secundum quod prius statutum est, eos judicando justitiam faciant. Si quis vero Episcopo suo inobediens fuerit, Domino in cujus

trace of a practice exactly like that provided for England in William's ordinance can be found in the very sparse records of the Norman church before the conquest of England, yet according to the ancient custumal of Normandy, which was compiled in the early thirteenth century but which reflected a much earlier practice, any man (the ducal household was excepted) remaining excommunicate for a year and a day would have his goods subject to the mercy of the duke.[25] In Normandy, then, from the time of Duke William the secular arm was used with respect to excommunicates. Subsequent Norman practice is difficult to isolate from possible English influences, yet it is clear that in the duchy a procedure very similar to the English procedure for the secular punishment of excommunicates was in use by the thirteenth century and provides at least a parallel to English practice if not the certain continuation of a custom which gave rise to the English practice.[26]

In England itself after King William's time, the practice next appears in the spurious *Leges Edwardi Confessoris*, a compilation belonging probably to the early twelfth century.[27] These "laws" permitted the bishop to invoke the king's aid in exacting satisfaction from wrongdoers.[28] They further

terra habitat Episcopus hoc demonstret, et ille subdat eum Episcopali justitiae. Quod si et Dominus facere contempserint, Regis Vice-Comes per Episcopum inde requisitus omni remota excusatione faciat" (Bessin, *Concilia*, p. 67).

[25] "Si aliqui vero aliorum hominum exommunicati fuerint et excommunicationis vinculo per annum et diem negligenter subjaceant, omnes rei in misericordia Ducis erunt" (*Le très ancien coutumier de Normandie* (ed. E. J. Tardif; Société de l'histoire de Normandie, Rouen, 1881), p. 2).

[26] In 1217 Philip Augustus ordered the bailiffs of Normandy to follow the custom of justicing excommunicates when so requested by the archbishop of Rouen or his suffragans (*Cartulaire Normand de Philippe Auguste, Louis VIII, Saint Louis et Philippe-le-Hardi* (ed. Léopold Delisle; *Mémoires de la Société des antiquaires de Normandie*, ser. 2, vol. 6), no. 253). For an example of the Norman custom in practice in 1223 see *ibid.*, no. 1130. In 1254 Innocent IV in his decretal letter *Venerabilibus* to the bishops of the province of Rouen referred to the Norman custom whereby the sheriff at the bishop's request seizes and detains the goods and body of any person remaining excommunicate for forty days (Potthast 15454; the text of the letter is printed as a note in the Richter-Friedberg edition of the *Corpus Iuris Canonici* (Leipzig, 1879-1881) 2. 1096-1100. An inquest, perhaps contemporary with this papal letter, was held to determine the custom in the *bailage* of Caux concerning civil constraint against excommunicates (Morel, *L'Excommunication et le pouvoir civil en France*, pp. 98-99, 196-200). Thirteen of those interviewed were clerics, of whom eight said that it was not the custom, two said that it was and gave examples of it, and three others thought it was but were not certain. A nobleman and a *bourgeois* both declared it to be the custom but that they had never seen an example of it. Eight other answers were given, ranging from denials to affirmations with much difference in detail.

[27] On Pseudo-Edward see Pollock and Maitland 1. 103-04; F. Liebermann, *Über die Leges Edwardi Confessoris* (Halle, 1896).

[28] "Quodsi aliquis sibi forisfecerit, episcopus faciat suam iustitiam. Et si pro iustitia episcopi emendare noluerit, ostendat regi; et rex constringet forisfactorem, ut emendet cui forisfecit, et episcopo et sibi. Et sic iuste gladius gladium iuuabit" (*Die Gesetze* (ed. Liebermann) 1. 629).

provided that the secular arm could demand gage and pledge until satisfaction from anyone who disregarded a bishop's sentence for forty days;
if he failed to appear within the next thirty-one days, he was to be outlawed.[29] Distraint of property and outlawry may well have been the form
which the secular punishment generally took at this time.[30] If canon
five of Archbishop Theobald's legatine council reflected English practice
in 1151, then at that time a person who remained excommunicate for a
year became infamous and was subject to disherison by the secular arm.[31]
It is not clear when imprisonment began to be employed as a secular
penalty against excommunicates; as a common punitive measure it cannot
be traced back earlier than Henry II, who had jails built in every county.[32]

During the second half of the twelfth century nothing further is heard
of the secular punishment of excommunicated persons. Mention of the
practice is found neither in the royal writs nor in Glanvill's treatise.[33]
Procedure during the last part of the twelfth century may very well have
operated directly from the bishop to the sheriff without reference to the
king's central administration, for the ordinance of William the Conqueror
allowed action by mandate either to the king or to the sheriff. According
to the terms of the charter of Beverley Minster, confirmed in 1202, signification of obdurate excommunicates could be made directly by the clergy

[29] "Et si eorum sententiam defugiendo uel superbe contempnendo paruipenderit, ad regem de
eo clamor deferetur post dies XL; et iusticia regis mittet eum per uadimonium et per plegios, si
habere poterit, usque dum Deo primitus et regi postea satisfaciat.

"Et si infra triginta et unum diem per amicos suos seu per iusticiam regis reperiri non poterit,
ore suo utlagabit eum rex.

"Et si postea repertus fuerit et teneri possit uiuus, regi reddetur, uel caput ipsius, si sese de-
fenderit" (*Die Gesetze* 1. 631). Goebel concludes that "the matter is so circumstantially described
in the *Leges Edwardi* that its authenticity is not open to serious doubt" (*Felony and Misdemeanor*,
p. 316).

[30] Goebel suggests that at this early period secular constraint took the form of outlawry (*ibid.*,
p. 315).

[31] "Sanctorum patrum vestigia secuti precipimus ut hii qui anathematis sententia condemnantur, si per annum integrum in ea pertinaciter perseverent infames et detestabiles habeantur, ut
neque in testimoniis neque in causis audiantur, et in principis sit potestate ipsos exheredare"
(Avrom Saltman, *Theobald, Archbishop of Canterbury* (London, 1956), p. 548; also printed in
Mansi 21. 750). In the second half of the twelfth century in England disherison meant "cutting
off a man's heirs from succession as a matter of law so that the property devolves as if there were
in fact no heirs" (Goebel, p. 253, n. 136).

[32] See Pollock and Maitland 2. 516; R. B. Pugh, "The King's Prisons before 1250," *TRHS*,
5th ser., 5 (1955) 1-22.

[33] Dr. R. C. van Caenegem does not mention any such writs in his volume, *Royal Writs in
England from the Conquest to Glanvill* (Selden Soc., 77, 1958-59) ; I am indebted to him for the
personal assurance that no writ of this kind came to his attention during his research on twelfth-
century writs.

of Beverley to the sheriff of Yorkshire, who would then capture the ex-communicates "non expectato alio mandato secundum consuetudinem regni nostri."[34] The subsequent practice of direct signification to places where the king's writ did not run and the occasional practice of direct certification of absolution were probably continuations of an earlier practice of direct recourse of bishop to sheriff.[35]

By 1201 recourse was being made in at least some instances to the central administration,[36] but clear evidence of procedure by royal writ does not appear until 1212,[37] although it may be possible to infer from the Beverley Minster charter that such royal mandates were being issued by 1202. The writ came into use, then, sometime between Glanvill (*ca.* 1189) and 1212 or possibly 1202. In 1222 Langton's Oxford synod excommunicated those who refused to execute this writ.[38] Five years later the writ appears in the earliest extant register of writs.[39] And in that same year Henry III wrote to his justiciar in Ireland describing this procedure.[40]

[34] *Cal. Chart. Rolls* 3. 141-42.

[35] See *infra* pp. 101-02, 147-48.

[36] On the pipe roll for Michaelmas 3 John (1201) was entered a letter from the archbishop of York to the chief justiciar Geoffrey fitz Peter, earl of Exeter, requesting the use of the secular power against certain persons who had remained excommunicate for the better part of a year (*The Great Roll of the Pipe for the Third Year of the Reign of King John, Michaelmas 1201* (ed. Doris M. Stenton; Pipe Roll Soc., n. s., vol. 14, 1936), p. 243). In 1203 the official of the archdeacon of Richmond wrote the justices of the *Curia Regis* for the use of the secular arm against the excommunicate Hugh de Saberge (*Curia Regis Rolls* 2. 298). Two years later the pipe roll carried an entry that the archdeacon of Richmond paid one palfrey for the capture of certain excommunicates (*The Great Roll of the Pipe for the Seventh Year of the Reign of King John, Michaelmas 1205* (ed. Sidney Smith; Pipe Roll Soc., n.s., vol. 19, 1941), p. 58).

[37] "...qui non fecit preceptum regis de capiendo quodam excommunicato" (*Curia Regis Rolls* 6. 252). Unfortunately the roll is defective and further information is lacking.

[38] "Excommunicamus etiam omnes illos qui gratia lucri, vel odii, vel alias malitiose contempnunt exequi domini regis mandatum contra excommunicatos editum claves ecclesie contempnentes" (*Councils* 2. 107).

[39] "Si uero archiepiscopus uel episcopus uel iudex ecclesiasticus mandauerit domino regi per literas patentes quod excommunicatus noluerit iustificari per censuram ecclesiasticam, tunc fiat illi tale breue:

"Rex uicecomiti salutem. Significauit nobis dominus episcopus de N. quod R. propter manifestam contumaciam suam excommunicatus est nec uult per ecclesiasticam censuram iusticiari. Quoniam uero potestas regia sacrosancte ecclesie in querelis suis deesse non debet, tibi precipimus quod predictum R. per corpus suum iusticiari quousque sacrosancte ecclesie tam de contemptu quam de aliis iniuriis ab eo fuerit satisfactum. Teste etc." (London, BM, Cotton Ms. Julius D. II, f. 147ᵛ). For more information on this register sent to Ireland by Henry III in 1227, see F. W. Maitland, "The History of the Register of Original Writs," *The Collected Papers of Frederick William Maitland* (ed. H. A. L. Fisher; Cambridge, 1911) 2. 130-37; originally in the *Harvard Law Review* 3 (1889-1890) 113-115, 167-69.

[40] For transcription see *infra* Appendix A, p. 161.

When the great canonist Henricus de Segusia (Hostiensis) came to England probably about 1236 he found in operation this customary practice of secular assistance against excommunicates.[41] It is clear, then, that when the practice appears in the records of the early thirteenth century the secular penalty was imprisonment and procedure was by royal writ.

The principal records, the significations of excommunication, begin to appear at this time.[42] The significations were the episcopal requests for the aid of the secular arm which were sent to the royal chancery and there kept on file. The bishop "signified" the name of the excommunicate, and the writ which was issued began "Significauit." The usual medieval term for the request, however, was *littera captionis*, and in the very late medieval period, by the process of extending the name of the writ to apply to the request for that writ, the request was called alternatively a *significavit*. The earliest surviving significations of excommunication are undated but come from the reign of Henry III (1216-1272) and the pontificate of William of Sainte-Mère-Église, bishop of London (1199-1221) and consequently can be dated 1216 × 1221.[43] The chancery files of significations from the bishops of other dioceses have all begun by 1265.[44]

[41] "Vel dic, et melius, quod hic loquitur secundum consuetudinem Angliae, secundum quam, ex quo est aliquis excommunicatus ab ordinario et per xl dies mansit in excommunicatione, curia regia ad requisitionem ordinarii qui excommunicavit capit eum et tenet detrusum in carcere, quousque satisfaciat vel satisdet in manu ordinarii de parendo" (*In V decretalium libros commentaria* X 2.28.17, v. *ordine iudiciario* (no. 2); cf., *ibid.* X 2.28.45, v. *appellatione interposita*; also *Summa* 2. de iureiurando. 5). For a study of Hostiensis' years in England see Noël Didier, "Henri de Suse en Angleterre (1236 ?-1244)," *Studi in Onore di Vincenzo Arangio-Ruiz* (Naples, [1953 ?]) 2. 333-351. Professor Stephan Kuttner has very kindly drawn my attention to these references by Hostiensis.

[42] The requests of the bishops for the secular arm against excommunicates are to be found in London, the Public Record Office, Chancery, *Significations of Excommunication etc.*; the present number for this class is C.85; for a brief description see *Guide to the Contents of the Public Record Office* (London, 1963) 1. 42. This class contains in addition to the requests of the bishops concerning excommunicates a small number of requests for other writs such as *de vi laica amovenda*. It is presently arranged by province: the metropolitan see first and then each suffragan see in alphabetical order (save that the four Welsh sees are put together after the other suffragan sees of Canterbury). The files of each diocese are in roughly chronological sequence. Post-Reformation bishoprics, peculiar jurisdictions with the power to invoke the secular arm, and miscellaneous files complete the class.

Calendars have been published of the requests made by the bishops of Chichester (L. F. Salzman, "Sussex Excommunicates," *Sussex Archaeological Collections* 82 (1941) 124-140), by the chancellors of the University of Oxford (H. E. Salter, *Snappe's Formulary* (Oxford Historical Soc., 1923), pp. 23-39), and by Robert Grosseteste, bishop of Lincoln (*Rotuli Roberti Grosseteste, Episcopi Lincolniensis, 1235-1253* (Canterbury and York Soc., 10, 1913), pp. 504-07).

[43] C. 85/117/1-3. For a transcription of no. 1 see *infra* Appendix B, p. 162.

[44] York probably in 1237 (C. 85/145/25), St. Asaph in 1241 (C. 85/167/1), Bath and Wells by 1242 (C. 85/33/33), Lincoln (C. 85/97/4) and Winchester (C. 85/153/2) in 1243, Coventrv and

For the period up to the Reformation about 7,600 significations of excommunication survive, of which about 2,800 — roughly one-third of the
total — date from the thirteenth century. These records are without
parallel in western Europe, just as, it would appear, the English procedure
against excommunicates as a highly formalized and institutionalized
procedure was itself without parallel. What they reveal is a practical
area in which close cooperation — not wholly without irritants — characterized the relations of the ecclesiastical and secular jurisdictions.

Lichfield in 1244 (C. 85/52/16), Canterbury in 1245 (C. 85/1/1-2), Norwich in 1246 (C.85/130/3),
Ely (C. 85/66/1) and Chichester (C. 85/43/1; Salzman, pp. 125-26) in 1247, Hereford (C. 85/85/2)
and St. Davids (C. 85/167/5) in 1249, Worcester in 1250 (C. 85/159/1), Salisbury in 1252 (C.85/
145/1), Rochester (C. 85/143/2) and Durham (C. 85/118/2) in 1253, Llandaff in 1254 (C. 85/
167/7), Carlisle in 1260 (C. 85/194/3), and Exeter in 1265 (C. 85/71/7). Only one signification of
excommunication to the royal chancery survives for the diocese of Bangor, and it is dated 1396
(C. 85/167/33). For the significations which were made from non-episcopal jurisdictions see
infra Appendix C, pp. 76-82.

CHAPTER I

THE POWER TO SIGNIFY
EXCOMMUNICATED PERSONS

NOT every man who had the power to excommunicate could request the capture of excommunicated persons. The possession of the former did not imply the latter. The power to excommunicate belonged to bishops, archdeacons, and abbots, and also to judges acting by their commission. In practice every ecclesiastical judge could excommunicate. On the other hand, the ability to signify excommunicates to the royal chancery for arrest was severely restricted: it belonged properly to the residential bishops of England and Wales, and then solely in respect to persons subject to their jurisdiction.[1] If other prelates and judges wished to secure the capture of obdurate excommunicates and had no special royal privilege to signify, they had to petition their bishop to send a signification to chancery; if he refused, recourse could be had to the metropolitan.[2]

---

[1] The bishops of Ireland, according to a mandate of Henry III in 1227, could write to the royal chancery of England for the writ *de excommunicato capiendo* and the justiciar of Ireland would be responsible for the capture (see *infra* Appendix A, p. 161). For an example see *Calendar of Documents relating to Ireland, 1171-1251* (London, 1875), no. 2377. No such requests survive in the chancery signification files. By 1377, however, the bishops of Ireland had to request these writs from the chancellor of Ireland, who would issue them under the seal of Ireland (*CCR, 1374-77*, pp. 481-82).

With respect to Scotland, a provincial synod of 1225 provided in a general way that excommunicated persons should be coerced after forty days by having their *loca* placed under interdict and, if necessary, by invoking the aid of the secular arm: "Et ut divinus timor incutiatur fortius obstinatis, ad excommunicatorum insolentiam reprimendum, si necesse fuerit, brachii secularis auxilium, prout catholicorum regum temporibus fieri consuevit, et de jure debuit, invocetur" (Wilkins 1. 613).

[2] *Provinciale* 5.17.c. Praeterea contingit, v. *praelatorum* (ed., p. 350): "i.e., Episcoporum: nam ad rogatum Praelatorum Inferiorum Rex non consuevit scribere pro captione Excommunicatorum. Unde si aliquis fuerit Excommunicatus ab Inferiori Episcopo, utputa, Decano vel Archidiacono, invocatio Regiae Majestatis fieri debet per Episcopum: nam inferiores Episcopis non possunt invocare brachium saeculare ... sed Episcopi exequentur eorum sententias .... Quod si Episcopi hoc facere noluerint ad hoc compelli possunt per Archiepiscopum." See also *ibid.*, 3.2.c. Ut clericalis ordinis, v. *brachium seculare* (ed., p. 127).

I. THE POWER OF BISHOPS

As soon as he was elected, a bishop acquired the customary right of bishops in England to request a royal writ for the capture of excommunicated persons. This meant that even before his consecration a bishop-elect could, and in some cases did, signify excommunicates. Henry Newark as archbishop-elect of York did so in 1297,[3] as did George Nevill, bishop-elect of Exeter, in 1457.[4] From at least the time of Edward III registers of writs are found which contain the form of the writ *Significavit* requested by a bishop-elect.[5] Alternatively, the vicar of the bishop-elect could signify for him. In 1296 the dean of Lichfield signified in the name of Walter Langton, bishop-elect of Coventry and Lichfield.[6] A consecrated bishop in full possession of the spiritualities and temporalities of his see could likewise delegate this power to his vicar-general when he absented himself from his diocese. This was not an uncommon practice. Examples could be cited covering all periods and from most English dioceses. Again, registers of writs from at least the time of Edward III recognize requests from "gerens vices." There is no reason to believe that a bishop had to get special royal permission for his vicar-general to signify in his absence, although in 1284 Edward I granted by special favor that writs for the capture of excommunicates would be issued at the request of the vicar of the archbishop of York during the latter's absence.[7] It is quite likely that Archbishop Wickwane, while requesting the king's license to go to Rome, likewise requested that writs be issued at the mandate of his vicar-general.

In the overwhelming majority of cases it was the bishop himself who sought the secular aid. For the validity of the writ *de excommunicato capiendo* it was necessary that the bishop who requested the writ be living at the moment the great seal was affixed to the writ. His prior death would render the writ null, and another request would have to be sent during the vacancy by the keeper of the spirituality or subsequently by the new bishop.[8] The royal justice Henry de Spigurnel in the eyre of Kent of

---

[3] C.85/176/21-24.

[4] C.85/81/1.

[5] See, e.g., London, BM, Harl. MS. 947, f. 200ᵛ; this same form is found in the printed *Reg. omn. brev.*, f. 65ʳ.

[6] C.85/56/1. Likewise, in 1306 Richard de Neuport, vicar-general of the bishop-elect of London, sent a *littera captionis* to chancery (C. 85/119/1).

[7] Prynne, p. 324.

[8] For example, in 1443 Archbishop Stratford requested the capture of four persons who had been excommunicated under his predecessor Archbishop Chichele (C. 85/17/3,5,6; for a transcrip-

1313 observed that a *Significavit* would not be issued upon the request of a deceased archbishop: "Cest breue ne vous put valer pur ceo qe lerceuesque est mort qar tele breue apres sa mort homme ne grantera nul capcion."[9] During vacancies, however, the power of signifying was regularly exercised by the keepers of the spirituality in the various dioceses, who either requested the metropolitan to signify for him[10] or sent the request directly to chancery himself. The latter was probably the more common way. From the time of Edward I registers of writs began to include this writ granted at the request of the keeper of the spirituality *sede vacante.*[11]

Even in a bishop's lifetime, the official of a bishop could himself signify excommunicated persons, at least during the reign of Henry III.[12] Allow-

---

tion of no. 5 see *infra* Appendix B, p. 170). It was recognized, too, in the king's courts that the death of an archbishop did not nullify the excommunications which he had imposed (cf., *Year Books of the Reign of King Edward the Third. Year XIV* (ed. L. O. Pike; R. S., London, 1888), pp. 226-29).

[9] *Year Books of Edward II*, vol. 7, *The Eyre of Kent, 6 and 7 Edward II* (ed. W. C. Bolland, Selden Soc., vol. 27, 1912), pp. 185-86.

[10] E.g., during the vacancy of Llandaff in 1386 a signification was sent by the archbishop of Canterbury, "ad quem omnis et omnimoda iurisdiccio ecclesiastica ciuitatis et diocesis Landauensis sede ibidem uacante dinoscitur pertinere" (C. 85/11/24).

[11] See, e.g., London, BM, Add. MS. 11557, f. 19^r, and Harl. MS. 1608, f. 27^{r-v}; cf., *Reg. omn. brev.*, f. 65^r. For an example of such a request see *infra* Appendix B, pp. 168-169. In May 1265 the chancery refused to accept a signification from the chapter of York *sede vacante* ("non conceditur nisi per literas officialis sede uacante" — C. 85/169/44 dorse). Although, in fact, the next signification in October of that year was from the official, the chapter appears to have exercised the right during the rest of that vacancy (C. 85/169/47-51). During the vacancy of 1279 the official again issued significations but thereafter the dean and chapter or one of its officers seem to have done so regularly. During the vacancy of 1315-17 the dean and chapter of York sent 51 significations of excommunication and eight significations of absolution, although the new archbishop had already been elected; they were described as acting *sede vacante* and not as vicars of the archbishop-elect (C. 85/180).

[12] Master Hugh de Mortimer, official of the archbishop of Canterbury, did so in ten cases in 1247, 1249, 1254-56 (C. 85/1/5-7, 13-19); John de Hubrug (?), official of the bishop of Bath and Wells, in two cases in 1251 (C. 85/33/2-3); Master Lawrence de Sumercot, official of the bishop of Chichester, in one case in 1247 (C. 85/43/1; Salzman, p. 125); R. de Leycester, official of the bishop of Ely, in one case probably in 1258 (C. 85/66/7); Master Peter de Solerio, official of the bishop of Hereford, in 3 cases in 1254 and one case in 1257 (C. 85/85/6-8, 11); Master Simon de Radenover, official of the bishop of Hereford, in 8 cases in 1265 to 1268 (*ibid.*, nos. 24-31); Master Robert de Marisco, official of Lincoln, in 2 cases in 1245 and 1250 (C. 85/97/23-24); the official of the bishop of London in one case in 1268 (C. 85/117/26); the official of the bishop of Rochester in one case in 1257 (C. 85/143/3); Master H. de Withebroc, official of the bishop of Worcester, in 2 cases in 1250 (C. 85/159/1-2; he may have been the same person as Master Henry de Withebrohc, *BRUO* 3. 2066); Master William Fresel, official of the bishop of Carlisle, in one case involving 24 persons in 1260 (C. 85/194/3). It is most likely that in all of these cases the officials were acting on behalf of absent bishops. For an example of a signification from an official see *infra* Appendix B, p. 167.

ance was made for such a practice probably by the earliest extant register of writs[13] and certainly by Bracton.[14] The practice was short-lived: no trace of it appears after 1268. In any event, during this brief period when the official signified excommunicates, he was acting not by ordinary authority but by authority delegated by the bishop, the only authority he possessed.

Vicars-general, keepers of the spiritualities, and officials exercised the power to signify excommunicates only *loco episcopi*. This power belonged properly only to the bishop and was exercised principally by him. Why was the proper possession of this power restricted to bishops ? One cannot assume that the reasons given by lawyers of the last three centuries of the middle ages constitute anything other than attempts to rationalize an existing practice. The restriction of this power to bishops seems to have formed part of the general conception of William the Conqueror. In the ordinance which removed spiritual cases from the hundred court William provided that offenders of *episcopal* law should appear at the place assigned by the *bishop*, where they would do what is just to the church and to the *bishop* according to the canons and the *episcopal* laws; excommunication and the secular arm were to be used against anyone refusing to come to *episcopal* justice. The emphasis clearly was on the jurisdiction of the bishop.[15] The contemporary council of Winchester (1076) referred only to the bishop when it established excommunication as the penalty for contumacy.[16] Further, Pseudo-Edward explicitly stated that it was the bishop who should invoke the king's aid against contumacious persons.[17] Although the reason for restricting the practice to bishops was not stated in these early texts, William's ordinance clearly implies a conception of the church's polity in which it was the bishop who exercised justice.

---

[13] See *supra* p. 22, n. 39. The "iudex ecclesiasticus" spoken of in this text must refer to the judge of the archbishop or bishop (i.e., his official). If it referred to ecclesiastical judges in general, there would have existed the absurdity of judges possessing a power not possessed by archdeacons and abbots.

[14] "Ubi quis rite fuerit excommunicatus et in excommunicatione pertinaciter perseveraverit per quadraginta dies, claves ecclesiae contemnendo, tunc ut gladius gladium adiuvet ad mandatum episcopi vel eius officialis capiatur excommunicatus. Sed numquam capietur aliquis ad mandatum iudicum delegatorum nec archidiaconi vel alterius iudicis inferioris, quia rex in episcopis coertionem habet propter baroniam" (*De legibus* 4. 327). For the date of this treatise see H. Kantorowicz, *Bractonian Problems* (Glasgow, 1941), pp. 22-36, who concluded that it was written before 1239, and H. G. Richardson, "Azo, Drogheda, and Bracton," *EHR* 59 (1944) 22-47, who argued that it could not have been written before 1254 at the earliest.

[15] See *supra* pp. 17-18, nn. 16, 19. It should be noted that the only mention made in this ordinance concerning the archdeacon was that he should withdraw from the hundred court.

[16] See *supra*, p. 18, n. 20.

[17] See *supra* p. 20, n. 28.

The lawyers of the common law from the time of Bracton did not look to the internal governance of the church for the reason for the restriction of the power of signifying excommunicates to bishops; rather, their rationalization turned on the relationship of the bishop to the king. For Bracton, the bishops had this power, while others did not, because the king had coercive power over the bishops 'propter baroniam.'[18] Bishops possessed temporalities held from the king, which the king could seize if a bishop refused to obey the king's order to absolve an imprisoned excommunicate; this the king could not do to the pope or to an archdeacon.[19] Although in many respects the royal courts and the royal chancery used different criteria for the admissibility of certificates of excommunication,[20] they were at one in requiring that such certificates must come from the bishop.[21]

The canonists agreed with the common lawyers and chancery practice by denying to lesser prelates the power of signifying excommunicates, but not for the same reason. From at least the thirteenth century the canonists held it as a general principle that those below the rank of bishop could not invoke the secular arm in any matter. The *Decretals of Gregory IX* (1234) clearly acknowledged the right of bishops to invoke the secular arm.[22] Michael de Fano, the author in the third quarter of the thirteenth century of a specialized treatise on the subject, allowed this power only to judges who were ordinaries or who were delegated with special mention of this power in the delegation.[23] To Guido de Baysio

[18] See *supra*, p. 28, n. 14. On the baronial status of bishops see Miss H. M. Chew, *Ecclesiastical Tenants-in-Chief* (Oxford, 1932), chap. 5.

[19] This was made plain as the reason for rejecting an exception of excommunication which was certified by the archdeacon of Chester (*Year Book 8 Henry VI*, no. 8). Also, the royal courts refused to admit as proof of excommunication certificates from a bishop's commissary who was not a commissary of record (*Year Book 11 Henry IV*, P. 16; *Year Book 20 Henry VI*, M. 1; *Year Book 7 Edward IV*, T. 17) and from the abbot of St. Albans (*Year Book 35 Henry VI*, H. 4; *Year Book 12 Edward IV*, M. 18). Analogously, the king's justice refused to accept a certification of absolution from a papal judge-delegate (*Year Books of King Edward the Third. Year XVI* (ed. L. O. Pike; R.S., London, 1896-1900) 1. 148-151).

[20] See *Year Book 20 Henry VI*, no. 12.

[21] *Year Book 11 Henry IV*, no. 16, states that in the time of Sir William Herle, chief justice of common pleas in 1327-29 and again in 1331-37, officials and commissaries of bishops had been able to give testimony of excommunication, but because of mischief caused thereby parliament decided that no one could do this save the bishop alone.

[22] X 1.31.1.

[23] *Tractatus de brachio seu auxilio implorando per iudicem ecclesiasticum a iudice seculari vel e contra* (*Tract. univ. iur.*, vol. 11, pt. 2, Venice, 1584), f. 409ᵛ, which is a misnumbered folio. For Fano see J. F. von Schulte, *Die Geschichte der Quellen und Literatur des canonischen Rechts* (Stuttgart, 1875-1880) 2. 138-39.

(Archdiaconus), writing about 1300, it appeared that inferiors to bishops, even if they possessed ordinary jurisdiction, could not invoke secular aid directly but only through the bishops.[24] On this general question of invoking secular aid Lyndwood was stating the common teaching in requiring that inferiors to bishops should have the bishop make their requests for them.[25] In applying this to the more specific question of invoking secular aid against excommunicates, Lyndwood denied to prelates below the rank of bishop the power of signifying contumacious excommunicates for capture and commented from his knowledge as a practitioner in the ecclesiastical courts that the king was not wont to issue the writ *de excommunicato capiendo* at their request.[26] The canonists, then, although treating this question within a different framework, agreed with the common lawyers that the power to invoke the secular arm against excommunicated persons was limited to bishops.

II. THE POWER OF PAPAL OFFICIALS

The position of papal officials in England, especially judges-delegate, in respect to the capture of excommunicates sentenced by them became at times a source of irritation between the papacy and the crown.[27] Although the canonists may have differed among themselves about the ability of judges-delegate to invoke secular aid,[28] the teaching of the common lawyers and the practice of the king's chancery were clear: a papal judge-

---

[24] Guido de Baysio, *Rosarium* (Lyons, 1516) C.23 q. 5 c. 26.

[25] 3.2 c. Ut clericalis ordinis, v. *brachium seculare* (ed., p. 127).

[26] See *supra* p. 25, n. 2.

[27] For a consideration of judge-delegate procedure in general see George G. Pavloff, *Papal Judge Delegates at the Time of the Corpus Iuris Canonici* (Catholic Univ. of America, Canon Law Studies, no. 426; Washington, 1963). With special reference to England see Pollock and Maitland 1. 114-115; Adrian Morey, *Bartholomew of Exeter, Bishop and Canonist* (Cambridge, 1937), chap. 4; Jane E. Sayers, "A Judge Delegate Formulary from Canterbury," *BIHR* 35 (1962) 198-211; *eadem*, "The Jurisdiction of the Papacy in Cases of Appeal and First Instance in England from 1198 to 1254, with particular reference to the Southern Province" (unpublished B. Litt. thesis, Oxford Univ., 1960); Charles Duggan, *Twelfth-Century Decretal Collections* (London, 1963), pp. 20-21.

[28] In the middle of the thirteenth century Hostiensis affirmed that judges-delegate could invoke secular aid (*In V decretalium Libros commentaria* X 1.29.7), which opinion was later opposed by Archidiaconus in 1300 (*Rosarium* C.22 q.5 c.26). Lyndwood, writing *ca.* 1430 (3.2 c. Ut clericalis ordinis, v. *brachium seculare*), preferred the opinion of Henry Bohic, a Parisian canonist (d. 1350) who held that judges-delegate could invoke the secular arm in cases involving lay persons or lay possessions when ecclesiastical penalties would not have the desired effect (*In quinque decretalium libros commentaria* (Venice, 1576) X 1.29.7).

delegate could not request the capture of excommunicates. According to Bracton, the king never grants this writ at the request of judges-delegate since he has coercive power only over bishops ("propter baroniam").[29] This was consistent with the general position of the pope before the common law courts, where documents under his seal were inadmissable. In practice chancery would not issue writs at the request of judges-delegate.[30]

Attempts were made by the popes to reverse this policy, but to no avail. One of the articles presented by papal nuncios before the Hilary parliament of 1273 bore the title "De excommunicatis per iudices delegatos capiendis."[31] Although the text unfortunately does not survive, it was probably not unlike the complaint made by Pope Clement V in 1309. At that time (28 October 1309) letters were sent by the pope to the archbishop of Canterbury and his suffragans in which he complained *inter alia* that royal officials would not capture excommunicates at the request of papal nuncios and judges.[32] On 14 February 1310 Archbishop Winchelsey received these papal *gravamina*, which he was directed to bring to the attention of the king.[33] This he did on 28 February. The king delayed his initial reply to the archbishop until 31 March because of the internal crisis which required him to appoint the Ordainers. The king promised that he would call a council of the realm and send a detailed reply before the council of Vienne.[34] This promise he repeated in a letter to the pope on 12 July 1310.[35] There the trail seems to end.

There was no urgent reason why papal complaints should have been pressed too far for, in fact, a *modus operandi* did exist. Papal officials would simply request the bishops to make the required signification for them. Actually, the earliest extant signification (1216 × 1221) was for the arrest

---

[29] See *supra* p. 28, n. 14.

[30] Analogously, chancery would not grant the release of captured excommunicates at the request of judges-delegate. In connection with the case of Master William Bloyhou a chancery clerk stated, "Bene scitis quod ad supplicacionem huiusmodi iudicum delegatorum curia non rescribit" (Prynne, p. 1245). For more on this case see *infra* p. 38.

[31] *Councils* 2. 806.

[32] "Excommunicatos quoque sedis auctoritate predicte ad requisicionem nunciorum predictorum seu judicum a sede concessorum eadem dicti officiales et ministri dicti regis capi facere denegant, quamvis ipsi ad instanciam ordinariorum regni predicti eorum auctoritate excommunicacionis sentencia innodatos dummodo sentenciam hujusmodi per quadraginta dies sustinuisse constiterit personaliter pia et laudabili ac religiosa consuetudine capi faciant, et sub carcerali custodia detinere" (*Reg. Winchelsey, Canterbury* 2. 1033; Wilkins 2. 323; for an undated summary in French see *Reg. Winchelsey* 2. 1040).

[33] Wilkins 2. 325-28.

[34] *Reg. Winchelsey* 2. 1042-44; Wilkins 2. 328-29.

[35] *Foedera* 2. 1. 111.

of a person excommunicated "for contempt of decisions of the pope and of
the papal legate."[36] In a letter to Henry III in his ninth regnal year
(1224-25) two judges-delegate in recounting the details of a case stated
that they had commanded the bishop of Lincoln to signify a person whom
they had excommunicated and who had remained obdurate.[37] Occasionally bishops even informed the king in their requests that the person
had been excommunicated by the authority of the apostolic see,[38] by
legatine authority,[39] by a papal nuncio,[40] or even by collectors of the papal
tenth.[41] On 6 October 1275, when the bishop of Salisbury signified two
laymen of his diocese at the request of the abbots of St. Albans and St. Augustine's, Canterbury, who had been deputed by the apostolic see as conservators of the hospital of Jerusalem in England, he stated that all the
bishops of the province of Canterbury had received a papal directive to act
upon such requests.[42] This papal directive could conceivably have been
part of a broader order including all papal officials in England and may
have been related to the apparent rejection of the article of complaint
two years earlier. In any event, there was a *modus operandi* which preserved
the chancery rule and at the same time gave papal judges the advantage of
access, albeit indirect, to secular coercion.[43]

In view of this clear rule and its consistent application in practice, the
developments of the late fifteenth and early sixteenth centuries are most

[36] For the text see *infra* Appendix B, p. 162.

[37] Prynne, p. 67.

[38] From the bishop of London, 1288 (C.85/118/28).

[39] From the bishop of Lincoln, 1268 and 1269 (C.85/98/52, 62). In the latter case the bishop
stated that he had received letters from Master Andrew, canon of St. Paul's, London, who informed
him that, acting as commissary of the cardinal legate, he had excommunicated Thomas Marlowe,
cleric.

[40] The bishop of Bath and Wells on 30 March 1263 signified Master William de Ditton, cleric,
of Ely diocese, who had been excommunicated "per discretum uirum .. cantorem Messanensem
domini pape capellanum et nuncium" (C. 85/33/13).

[41] Robert Wickhampton, bishop of Salisbury, in 1279 signified the excommunication of Henry
de Foghelston at the request of the papal collectors of the tenth for the Holy Land, who had
excommunicated Henry (C. 85/145/52).

[42] "... quia uero dominus papa .. episcopis Cantuariensis prouincie suffraganeis per suas bullatas
litteras mandat et iniungit quod ad denunciacionem conseruatorum eorundem .. prioris et fratrum
pro suis excommunicatis capiendis et per secularem potestatem cohercendis singuli per suas
dioceses scribere debeant" (C.85/145/80).

[43] The same *modus operandi* worked in the case of the absolution of signified excommunicates.
E.g., on 21 Sept. 1291 the archdeacon of Westminster, commissary of a papal judge-delegate,
wrote to the bishop of Norwich, informing him of the absolution of Edmund de Hoo; the bishop
on 7 Dec., quoting the commissary's letter, informed the king of his absolution (C.85/133/4;
for a transcription of this request see *infra* Appendix I. pp. 206-07).

puzzling indeed, for without any apparent explanation chancery began to issue the writ *de excommunicato capiendo* at the request of judges-delegate. On 7 January 1499 the abbot of Bermondsey, a papal judge-delegate, successfully requested a writ for the capture of Thomas Silkestede, prior of Winchester cathedral.[44] This is the earliest such case, and it may not be wholly coincidental that the person at whose instance Silkestede had been excommunicated was the chancellor of the realm himself, Cardinal Morton. This signification was followed by others from judges-delegate in 1500, 1509, 1512, 1520, 1527, and 1530.[45] In a further development, Cardinal Wolsey in his capacity as *legatus a latere* requested in at least twenty cases between 1524 and 1529 the capture or release of persons excommunicated in his legatine court.[46] No theoretical justifications were made for the extension of this power to papal judges-delegate and papal legates: not even Wolsey would have claimed baronial status *ratione legationis*.

III. THE POWER OF LESSER PRELATES

By special royal privilege the power to signify was enjoyed by some prelates below the rank of bishop. In fact, among the earliest references to the capture of excommunicates in the first years of the thirteenth century is found mention that this power was enjoyed by the provost and chapter of Beverley Minster and by the archdeacon of Richmond. The use of significations by lesser prelates continued throughout the rest of the middle ages, but the number of such significations is relatively small: a scant 327 out of about 7,600.[47]

During the thirteenth and early fourteenth centuries the power to signify was held by some of the exempt jurisdictions, probably by reason of their exemption. Frequently significations from these persons would make specific mention of the fact that they were exempt from the jurisdiction of the local bishop and subject directly to Rome. For instance, in a signification of 1314 the abbot of St. Albans described his monastery as "sacrosancte Romane ecclesie immediate subiecti" and his jurisdiction as "ab

---

[44] C.85/207/1.

[45] C.85/200/1; C.85/207/2-5, 7-10.

[46] C.85/188/13-26, 28-33. The excommunicate was frequently described in these significations as "nostre iurisdiccioni legatine subditus et subiectus."

[47] For a full list of persons below the rank of bishop who enjoyed this power, for the years in which they exercised it, and for the royal grants by which they held it see *infra* Appendix C, pp. 176-79.

omni iurisdiccione ordinaria exempta."[48] In this early period the abbots
of the exempt abbeys of Bury St. Edmunds, St. Albans, Westminster,
Waltham, and Evesham exercised this power as did the deans of the royal
free chapels[49] at Penkridge, Shrewsbury, Tettenhall, Stafford, and St. Martin le Grand, London, the archdeacon of the virtually exempt archdeaconry
of Richmond, and the provost and chapter of Beverley Minster.[50] Three
attempts by the prior of Durham in 1291 to signify excommunicates were
rejected in chancery pending a decision of the King's Bench whether the
prior possessed this power.[51] The prior appears to have sent no further
significations.

These lesser prelates who possessed the power of signifying normally
held it by virtue of letters patent from the king, who made the grant either
in perpetuum to the prelate and his successors or to him alone during
tenure or for a specified number of years (usually two, three, or five, but
occasionally twenty). It was probably expected that the prelate would
mention in the *littera captionis* the details of the royal grant, and indeed this
was frequently done.[52] It was by letters patent that the privilege of signifying excommunicates was extended during the fourteenth century to
include holders of other jurisdictions. The chancellor of the University of
Oxford as early as 1337 had this privilege and exercised it more or less
continually for two hundred years. Richard II besides renewing it to the
abbot of Westminster, the archdeacon of Richmond, and the chancellor
of Oxford, went further and extended the privilege to certain of his own
clerks who as ecclesiastics held the archdeaconries of Lincoln, Norfolk,
and Ely, the deanery of St. Paul's, London, and the obscure prebend of

----

[48] C.85/212/26. In another but later example, the abbot of Bury St. Edmunds prefaced a
signification: "Cumque nullus preter nos aut Romanum pontificem uel ipsius legatum ab eius
latere missum infra dictam uillam Sancti Edmundi uel quattuor cruces a summo altari dicti
monasterii uno miliario distantes ullam iurisdiccionem ualeat uel debeat ibidem exercere et ob
hoc alterius non interest hoc uestre maiestati regie significare, supplicamus..." (dated 10 March
1435: C.85/213/24).

[49] Pope Innocent IV granted to the royal free chapels of England exemption from the jurisdiction of the ordinary by bull of 21 July 1245 (Potthast 1173; *Foedera* 1. 1. 261). For a general
discussion of the royal free chapels see Mrs. Dorothy Styles, "The Early History of the King's
Chapels in Staffordshire," *Transactions of the Birmingham Archaeological Soc.* 60 (1936) 56-95.

[50] Also, the archdeacon of Taunton signified in one case (1244 × 1263: C.85/214/10).

[51] C.85/175/44 and C.85/214/23-24 bear the same endorsement: "Breuia de excommunicatis
capiendis ad denunciacionem prioris Dunelmensis de cetero non concedantur quousque dis-
cussum fuerit in curia et curia regis fuerit certificata utrum excommunicati capi debeant ad
denunciacionem eiusdem prioris nccne."

[52] See, e.g., *infra* Appendix C, p. 183. On one occasion the chancellor of Oxford excused his
omission of the details of the grant for the sake of brevity (Salter, p. 31).

Thurrock in the royal free chapel at Hastings.[53] What is more, he acceded to the request of his confessor and gave the same favor to the chancellor of Cambridge.

The bishops considered the extension of this privilege by Richard II to be an unbearable usurpation of their authority. In 1391 they protested to the king that the signifying of excommunicates by lesser prelates was "contrary to the laws and liberties of the church, the custom of the realm, and the *cursus* of the royal chancery." The king yielded and on 28 April 1391 he ordered to be revoked all such grants made during his reign saving only those given to the abbot of Westminster and the chancellor of Oxford.[54] Although that seems to have settled the matter at that time, the bishops probably harbored a lingering dislike for the use of signification by lesser prelates. In 1435 John Stafford, chancellor of England and bishop of Bath and Wells, may presumably have been voicing this episcopal feeling when he said that he almost retched at the thought of abbots enjoying this privilege.[55] Yet the practice continued and was exercised in the fifteenth and early sixteenth centuries not only by abbots but by other prelates as well.

IV. The Question of Jurisdiction

The power to signify excommunicates, whether exercised by bishops or by lesser prelates, could not be used indiscriminately. A bishop had the power to signify all and only those whom he had the power to excommunicate. Since a bishop in excommunicating was acting by ordinary authority, his power to excommunicate was restricted to persons belonging to his jurisdiction. The bishop of a residential see had jurisdiction *ratione personae* over everyone domiciled in his diocese and *ratione materiae* over everyone involved in any matter (e.g., a testament or a crime) which came under his

---

[53] Richard Medford, prebendary of Thurrock, received the same privilege when he later became archdeacon of Norfolk.

[54] The episcopal protest was made in the names of all the bishops of both provinces and probably emanated from the convocation which met 17-21 April at St. Paul's, London. Its text unfortunately does not survive; the contents can be reconstructed from the *narratio* of the revocation. It should be noted that the revocation did not include prelates who had received the privilege before the reign of Richard II and still possessed it. For the text of the revocation see *infra* Appendix C, pp. 182-83.

[55] "Illatis in Cancellariam Domini Regis litteris istis, et exhibitis, satis difficilem reddebat se Cancellarius primitus ad scribendum pro captione corporis; pro eo quod parumper stomachanter pertulit, ut Abbas aliquis hujusmodi libertatis privilegio insignitus esset" (*Annales monasterii Sancti Albani a Iohanne Amundesham* (ed. H. T. Riley; R. S., London, 1870-71) 2. 81).

cognizance. For example, if the bishop of Durham excommunicated a man of the Salisbury diocese concerning a matter over which he had no jurisdiction, the excommunication was null. In addition, the metropolitan had jurisdiction over the subjects of his suffragans when they appealed to him *in forma iuris* and when he visited their dioceses. A bishop or a metropolitan, thus, could excommunicate by ordinary authority only those persons who were legally subject to his jurisdiction and only such persons once excommunicated could he signify to chancery for a writ of capture. Quite logically, the same jurisdiction which was required for excommunication was required for signification. Just as the bishop of Durham could not excommunicate the Salisbury man over whom he had no jurisdiction, so too he could not request his capture.

It should come as no surprise that disputes concerning jurisdiction frequently involved the question of the capture of excommunicates. Disputes concerning the exemption of religious houses from the jurisdiction of the local bishop — a recurring theme familiar to students of medieval history — did in the late thirteenth century touch this question. In 1276 despite his protestation of exemption the Cistercian abbot of Forde was excommunicated and signified for capture by the bishop of Exeter. As a consequence, the Cistercian abbots of England petitioned king and council in the Hilary parliament of that year to revoke the capture. The king did not want to become involved and convinced the parties to agree to ecclesiastical arbiters, who found in favor of the bishop.[56] In a similar case during Pecham's pontificate complaints were made by the Premonstratensian abbey of Bayham in Sussex against the archbishop and likewise against the bishop of Chichester to the effect that they had excommunicated and requested the capture of the principal officers of the abbey and their adherents contrary to the abbey's exemption.[57] How the king disposed

---

[56] The case is reported in *Reg. Bronscombe, Exeter*, pp. 84-91.

[57] The controversy concerned the right of presentation to the church of Hailsham (see *VCH, Sussex* 2 (1907) 86-89). The archbishop and the bishop of Chichester both favored the claim of the Augustinian priory of Michelham over that of Bayham. On 2 April 1280 the bishop of Chichester requested the capture of the abbot and 54 others (C.85/43/40; Salzman, p. 129); the archbishop on 22 May of that year signified most of these same persons (C.85/3/17) and repeated the signification again two days later (*ibid.*, no. 13). On 14 April 1281 the bishop of Chichester again signified the principal officers of the abbey and their adherents (C.85/44/1; Salzman, p. 130), as did the archbishop on 7 May (C.85/3/57) and on 29 June (*ibid.*, no. 56). These measures plus the interdict of 19 July (*Reg. Epp. Peckham* 1. 208-09) and the sequestration of 24 July (*ibid.*, 1. 210-11) by the archbishop secured the repentance and absolution of the abbot's party probably in Aug. 1281 (*ibid.*, 1. 220-21). Yet, before 1281 was finished, they had once again been signified as excommunicate by the bishop of Chichester (C.85/44/3; Salzman, p. 130). In March 1288 Pecham issued another request for their capture (C.85/4/30), as did the bishop of Chichester in

of the complaint against the bishop of Chichester does not appear,[58] but by reason of the complaint against the archbishop he caused the writ for capture to be nullified.[59] All these cases raise the same legal point: since a bishop cannot excommunicate subjects of an exempt abbey by his ordinary authority, *a fortiori* he cannot signify them for capture.

The dispute enkindled by Pecham in his metropolitical visitation turned on the question of his jurisdiction over the subjects of his suffragans and whether, having finished visitation in a diocese, he could continue cases begun during visitation.[60] Quite naturally this involved the subject of *captio excommunicatorum*. Nowhere was this truer than at Exeter. The relations between Pecham and Peter Quinel, bishop of Exeter, had been

---

Nov. of the following year (C.85/44/17, 19-20; Salzman, p. 131). The affair continued even into Winchelsey's pontificate. The exact place where the undated pieces quoted in the following two footnotes belong is not easy to determine, but they probably belong to either 1280 or 1281.

[58] The following undated complaints are found among the chancery miscellany:

"Isti sunt articuli contra dominum Cycestrensem episcopum per abbatem et conuentum de Begeham.

"In primis quod iidem religiosi ex dispensacione sedis apostolice specialiter noscantur priuilegiati, adeo quod nec idem dominus episcopus uel quisquis alius prelatus suspensionis, interdicti, uel excommunicacionis sentencias ualeat qualibet aliqua in canonicos seu monasterium ordinis eorum promulgare. Prefatus tamen episcopus contra indulta huiusmodi temere ueniens, que eciam non ignorat, occasione contencionis suborte inter prefatos religiosos et quosdam aduersarios suos sentenciam maioris excommunicacionis in quasdam personas et eis adherentes, quasi auctoritate ordinaria non ex delegacione sedis apostolice, quesiit colore, motu proprio temere promulgauit.

"Item excommunicatos sic de facto, cum de iure non posset, capi procurauit per regiam potestatem.

"Item licet ab eodem episcopo ob premissa canonice fuisset ad sedem apostolicam appellatum, de qua appellacione sibi sufficienter innotuit, cui deferre debuit, quod indebite facere non curauit.

"Item idem dominus consilio, auxilio, opere et opere contra dictos religiosos clam et palam super ecclesiam de Helesham tempore excommunicacionis huiusmodi partem se constituens confouet et confouebat partem aduersam.

"Item dicti religiosi occasione excommunicacionis huiusmodi impediuntur quominus possunt prosequi ut tenentur ius suum in curia domini regis in qua de premissis parati sunt facere plenam fidem" (C.49/2/24).

[59] An undated draft of a royal ordinance: "Ordinatum est per dominum regem et totum consilium suum propter euidencias quas ipse inspexit de exempcione abbatis et suorum quod, quando archiepiscopus certificat curie regie de hiis qui sunt excommunicati et petit breue de capcione et abbas recenter et antequam breue de capcione concedatur certificat curie regie quod omnes illi uel aliqui eorum quos dictus archiepiscopus testatur esse excommunicatos ut predictum est sint de sua exempcione, extunc cessat breue de capcione de illis quos abbas certificat esse exemptos donec aliud inde fuerit prouisum etc." (C.49/67/9).

[60] See Miss Decima Douie, *Archbishop Pecham* (Oxford, 1952), chap. 5. Article 2 of the *gravamina* of the suffragans (1282) complained that the archbishop weakened their authority by continuing cases begun but not completed during his visitation (*Councils* 2. 922).

none too cordial since the archbishop had appointed a dean to Exeter cathedral virtually on the eve of Quinel's consecration.[61] Pecham began his visitation of Exeter in March, 1282, and soon excommunicated Master William Bloyhou, who was a supporter of the bishop in his opposition to the dean and who was alleged to be an intruder into the church of Pound-stock. This church had been held by Reginald le Arcevesk, canon of Exeter and one of the dean's principal supporters.[62] Pecham requested Bloyhou's capture on 25 June and again on 4 December.[63] At about this same time and perhaps as a cover to the latter request the archbishop wrote a letter to the chancellor in which he complained that his visitation of Exeter had been impeded by "enemies of God and of the church," who deserved excommunication and whom he prayed the chancellor to capture.[64] Bloyhou was soon placed in irons by the sheriff of Devon. In a letter of 26 December Bishop Quinel protested to the chancellor that in the past it was not the custom for chancery to issue writs at the request of the archbishop for the capture of persons not of his diocese.[65] The bishop probably won that round, for he secured Bloyhou's release by reason of Bloyhou's appeal to the apostolic see and his subsequent absolution,[66] but the case was to be heard of again.

In an effort to calm the waters ruffled by such jurisdictional disputes chancery ruled in 1286 not to accept significations from the archbishop unless he stated in the signification that the excommunicated person was subject to his jurisdiction. The particular case which gave rise to this ruling was the signification of three supporters of the hapless Master William Bloyhou, whose names Pecham had sent to chancery on 26 October 1286 without identifying them as to diocese or jurisdiction.[67] Hereafter the archbishop must add after the names of the excommunicates the words "nostrae jurisdictionis." Archbishop Pecham objected to these "new words" and woundedly averred that it was unthinkable that he

---

[61] On the dispute over the deanship and its sequel, viz., the murder of the precentor, see Frances Rose-Troup, *Exeter Vignettes* (History of Exeter Research Group, monograph no. 7; Manchester, 1942), pp. 38-57; and *Reg. Bronscombe and Quivel, Exeter*, pp. 438-451.

[62] Arcevesk and the dean were later implicated in the murder of the precentor in 1283 (see preceding note).

[63] C.85/3/65, 70.

[64] Prynne, pp. 1244-45.

[65] "Nec solebant sicut nec deberent, prout audivimus, captiones concedi ad mandatum ipsius domini super alienos parochianos, super quod non credimus (breve) super captione praedicti magistri a vestra consciencia aliquatenus emanasse" (*ibid.*, p. 1245).

[66] See *supra* p. 31, n. 30.

[67] C.85/4/29.

would signify anyone who was not of his jurisdiction.[68] In fact, the words were not new: they or their equivalents had been used by Kilwardby and even by Pecham himself.[69] What really was new was the insistence on their use.

Before 1286 the way in which the bishops described the excommunicated persons depended on the *stylus* of their chanceries. As a result the form varied from diocese to diocese and within each diocese from time to time. For example, as early as 1247 a signification from Canterbury stated that the excommunicate was of the Canterbury diocese,[70] yet in the years immediately following Canterbury significations more frequently than not omitted such a description, and it was not until Kilwardby's pontificate (1273-78) that they mentioned that the excommunication had been imposed by ordinary authority.[71] In the surviving Worcester significations mention that the excommunicate was of that diocese was not made before 1286, and the phrase "auctoritate nostra" was used only three times before 1299.[72] It was even decided in a particular case in the *Curia Regis*, probably during Kilwardby's pontificate, that the signification should not contain

[68] "Frater J., etc., dilecto in Christo filio, etc., domino Willelmo de Hamelton, domini regis Angliae clerico, salutem. Nuper pro captione domini Radulfi Bloyou, Michaelis Bloyou et Walteri de Lyw clerici, quos dudum nos Exoniensem diocesem visitantes, pro suis contumaciis et manifestis offensis majoris excommunicationis sententia innodavimus, in qua per biennium pertinaciter perstiterunt, in certa forma per consilium regium accepta et hactenus usitata, regiae scripsimus majestati. Pro quibus quidem literis nostris ea quae ad curiam regiam in hac parte pertinent, exequi ut dicitur recusatis, nisi quaedam nova verba, scilicet "nostrae jurisdictionis" in literis hujusmodi inserantur, quae hactenus in talibus literis nostris non consueverunt apponi. Super quo, si est ita, non modicum admiramur, praesertim cum non sit verisimile quod nos pro aliquo capiendo, nisi de nostra jurisdictione existeret, scriberemus. Quocirca vos requirimus et rogamus quatenus formam litterarum in casu hujusmodi curiae regiae per nos missam, in ipsa curia approbatam, et hactenus usitatam, admittere velitis, et quod ad curiam regiam pertinet, ut moris est, ulterius exequi in praemissis, quia sub novitate verborum latere posset processu temporis aliquid captiosum. Valete. Datum apud Otteford, iii. idus Novembris, anno Domini M CC octogesimo sexto" (*Reg. Epp. Peckham* 3. 936-37).

[69] Both archbishops frequently identified an excommunicate by stating that he was "of our diocese" or, if of another diocese, the name of that diocese (see C.85/2-3 for examples from the archbishop of Canterbury). In fact, on 27 July 1286, a scant three months before the chancery ruling, Pecham used the words "nostre iurisdiccionis" in signifying an excommunicate (C.85/4/25).

[70] C.85/1/5.

[71] C.85/2. It should be noted that a statute of the Synod of Wells I (?1258) required that archdeacons and their officials, when they requested the bishop to signify an excommunicate, should give the reason for the excommunication and indicate by what authority, ordinary or delegated, he was excommunicated (*Councils* 2. 613). In very similar words Bishop Quinel of Exeter made the same requirement in 1287 (*ibid.*, p. 1031).

[72] C.85/159-162.

such expressions.[73] The chancery ruling of 1286 sought to regularize the form used at least by the archbishop of Canterbury. It probably had a general application or was soon brought to apply to the significations from other bishops as well. From the late thirteenth century the form of the writ *de excommunicato capiendo* in registers of writs stated that the excommunicated person was of the bishop's diocese and had been excommunicated by his ordinary authority. Since it was the practice for the writ to repeat *mutatis mutandis* the words of the request, it is safe to assume that the request which the writ in the registers presupposes likewise contained these words. A register of writs, possibly from the late thirteenth century, spelled out in a *regula* the requirements of form for both archbishops and bishops: mention must be made by the archbishop of the authority by which the person has been excommunicated and each bishop must mention whether the excommunicate is of his diocese unless this fact is otherwise evident.[74] Similarly, in the eyre of Kent, 1313-14, Hervey de Staunton, king's justice, observed that for a *capias* a bishop must not only testify to the excommunication but also must show that the excommunicate belongs to his jurisdiction.[75] The rule was clear: a bishop must affirm his jurisdiction over the person excommunicated. In practice, from the end of the thirteenth century every bishop almost invariably stated (i) that the person

[73] On a scrap of parchment attached to Pecham's request for the capture of the prior of Barnstaple (10 June 1279) a chancery clerk wrote, "Et quia illa eadem uerba scilicet 'de diocesi' et 'auctoritate ordinaria' tempore alterius archiepiscopi in curia regis propter hec fuerunt modo reiecta, non potest capcio impetrari nisi omissis uerbis predictis scilicet 'diocesis' et 'auctoritate ordinaria'" (C.85/3/6). Thus, in a particular case because of peculiar factors the king's court refused to allow capture when the signification contained those phrases. The earlier case may have concerned the same priory of Barnstaple over exemption; in fact, the prior had been excommunicated by the bishop of Exeter shortly before 20 Aug. 1272 (*Reg. Bronscombe, Exeter*, p. 24) but a search of the *Curia Regis* plea rolls has failed to produce any trace of such a dispute.

[74] "Regula. Aliquando contingit quod archiepiscopus scribit regi pro hominibus capiendis racione appellacionis uel auctoritate ordinaria. Et tunc oportet quod fiat mencio in patente archiepiscopi et similiter in breui ut sic: 'Significauit nobis uenerabilis pater I. Cantuariensis archiepiscopus per literas suas patentes quod W. auctoritate ordinaria propter manifestam contumaciam suam excommunicatus est nec se uult etc.'

"Oportet similiter quod fiat mencio in patente et in breui utrum sit parochianus suus necne ut sic: 'Significauit nobis etc. quod W. parochianus suus uel sue iurisdiccionis propter manifestam contumaciam etc.'

"Set si constet euidenter quod sit de diocesi episcopi uel archiepiscopi, tunc non est necesse quod ponatur in breui 'parochianus' uel alio modo set fiat breue in communi forma prout supra patet" (London, BM, Harl. MS. 858, f. 83r).

[75] *Year Book of Edward II*, vol. 8, *The Eyre of Kent 6 and 7 Edward II* (ed. W. C. Bolland; Selden Soc., vol. 29, 1913), p. 163.

was of his diocese or, if he were not, then the reason for his jurisdiction, and (ii) that he had been excommunicated by ordinary authority.[76]

It would take more than the establishing of a chancery rule to put an end to problems of disputed jurisdictions. Such disputes were still to occur and still to touch upon the signification procedure as, for example, in 1302 when the archbishop of Canterbury and the bishop of Worcester attempted to signify the prior and other officials of St. Oswald's, Gloucester, only to be thwarted by the archbishop of York, who claimed in chancery that jurisdiction over the priory pertained to him.[77] Even in cases in which disputed jurisdiction was not a factor, according to a clerical *gravamen* of 1309, chancery upon being told that an excommunicate was not subject to the bishop's jurisdiction would reject the bishop's request for the writ for capture; the clergy even stated that chancery had in the past followed such a practice "per errorem."[78] There is no evidence to suggest that

---

[76] Besides "nostre iurisdiccionis" the expressions "nostre diocesis" and "noster parochianus" were likewise used. Instead of "auctoritate ordinaria" the Hereford significations from 1289 to 1312 used "iuris ordine obseruato" (C.85/88-89). In two cases in 1294 the archbishop of York justified his jurisdiction "racione delicti sui in diocesi nostra commissi" (C.85/175/89-90), and in 1519 one of his successors described an unfortunate Cluniac as "nobis subiectus racione criminis siue delicti fornicacionis per ipsum cum quadam Agnete Waddingham de Radford dicte nostre Eborum diocesis commisi" (C.85/188/4). Also, the bishop of Bath and Wells in 1424 described an excommunicate as "nostre iurisdiccioni racione contractus infra ciuitatem Wellie initi notorie subiecta" (C.85/40/18). Occasionally the archbishop of Canterbury mentioned that he enjoyed jurisdiction because of his metropolitical visitation (e.g., "occasione uisitacionis nostre quam in dicta diocesi iure fecimus metropolitico" — C.85/6/29) or, more frequently, because of appeal to his court: "in quadam causa ad nostram Cantuariensem curiam legitime deuoluta" (e.g., *ibid.*, no. 17).

[77] *Cal. Chanc. Warr.*, p. 157; Prynne, pp. 984, 1026-27. In the following year a dispute arose between the archbishop of Canterbury and the abbot of St. Augustine's, Canterbury, about jurisdiction over appropriated churches. In the case at issue both prelates excommunicated and signified the persons in question. An appeal to Rome resulted in favor of the archbishop, yet the king would not allow chancery to issue the writ on the basis of a signification made before the judgment at Rome (*Cal. Chanc. Warr.*, p. 180). It should be noted that signified excommunicates could use the normal channels of ecclesiastical appeal to challenge the bishop's jurisdiction and that pending the appeal the writ for capture would be superseded; for examples see Prynne, pp. 610, 1291-92.

[78] "Item, petitur ut credatur litteris episcoporum quando scribitur per ipsos episcopos pro captione excommunicatorum post xl dies iuxta consuetudinem regni, ita quod ad assertionem quorumdam dicentium eos non esse subditos excommunicantium non denegetur breve captionis eorumdem, sicut in preteritum per errorem fieri consuevit" (*Councils* 2. 1272). A similar complaint appears among the undated *gravamina* inserted in the register of John de Halton, bishop of Carlisle, following a document of the year 1302: "Licet generaliter sine delectu personarum consueverat scribi pro capcione quorumdam excommunicatorum post xl dies ad suggestionem cujuslibet episcopi suas litteras ad cancellariam domini regis dirigentis, modernis tamen temporibus ad

chancery continued this practice thereafter. But in individual cases chancery did reject significations because the bishop had not indicated that the excommunication had been imposed by ordinary authority. For example, in 1326 the request of Bishop Droxford of Bath and Wells for the capture of certain Wiltshire rioters was rejected because the excommunication had been by delegated and not ordinary authority.[79] Likewise, in 1380 a signification from Archbishop Sudbury against four persons of Exeter which failed to state that they had been excommunicated by ordinary authority was ineffective.[80] Similar omissions were frequently overlooked, which shows that the rule, although not always enforced, was enforceable when enforcement was desired.

The chancery practice underlined the common canonical teaching that a prelate cannot excommunicate a person who is not of his jurisdiction. In requiring that the person signified for capture should belong to the prelate's jurisdiction, chancery was merely seeking assurance that the person had been validly excommunicated.

---

nudam assercionem exemptorum precedencium excommunicatos non esse subditos ordinariorum excommunicancium, denegantur in eadem cancellaria littere capcionis eorundem" (*Reg. Halton, Carlisle* 1. 172).

[79] *Reg. Drokensford, Bath and Wells*, p. 262.

[80] A scribe in the archbishop's chancery glossed the exemplification of the signification in Sudbury's register with the words, "Ista significacio non fuit expedita in cancellaria quia non fuerunt excommunicati auctoritate ordinaria" (London, Lambeth Palace Library, Reg. Sudbury, f. 64ᵛ). Ten years later Archbishop Courtenay signified the same persons, indicating that they had been excommunicated "auctoritate ordinaria," and the signification was duly accepted in the king's chancery (C.85/11/56).

Chapter II

PERSONS SUBJECT TO SIGNIFICATION

IT would be wholly untrue to think that in medieval England the secular arm could have been invoked against every excommunicated person. A great many excommunicates, perhaps the majority, fell outside the provisions of this procedure. Those who incurred this censure *ipso facto*, i.e., by violating a law to which it was attached, were not as such liable to capture.[1] It can be stated in general that the secular arm was used chiefly against those who had been excommunicated for contumacies against ecclesiastical courts. Such a *contumax* may have come under the cognizance of the court because of alleged defamation, unjust possession of a benefice, adultery, mishandling of the administration of a testament, suspicion of heresy, or the like. Yet, whatever may have brought him within the purview of the ecclesiastical court, his excommunication was due to contumacy.

The ordinance of William the Conqueror which provided for the use of the secular arm against excommunicates was clearly directed only towards those persons excommunicated for contumacy committed against ecclesiastical courts.[2] The known facts about instances of the use of the signification procedure show that it was used, save for the possible exception to be treated in the next section, only against persons whose excommunication resulted from proceedings in ecclesiastical courts. The early significations tell little else about an excommunication except, perhaps, that it was incurred because of contumacy, but, as significations became fuller, they frequently indicated the reason for the contumacy ("in non

---

[1] Among the 7,600 extant significations no more than 25 deal with excommunications incurred *ipso facto*. But even in these cases the persons were later declared to be excommunicate by an ecclesiastical court to which they were cited. Their failure to obey the citation or to perform the penance enjoined on them by the court constituted the reason for their being denounced by the court as already excommunicated. In such cases the period of 40 days before the invoking of the secular arm was reckoned not from the day of the excommunication but from the day of the denunciation in court. For example, a signification from the bishop of Ely dated 13 March 1455 informed chancery that William in the Hay *alias* William Taylour of Lichfield had been denounced as an excommunicate because he had laid violent hands on the persons of two Minorites, killing one and maiming the other (C.85/63/12). For another example, see *infra* Appendix B, p. 169.

[2] See *supra* pp. 17-18.

ueniendo coram nostro officiali," "in non parendo mandatis curie nostre,"
"in non peragendo penitenciam," etc.) and not uncommonly were the
names of the litigants given and the matter under dispute stated.[3] The key
to the writ *de excommunicato capiendo* lies clearly in the canonical notion of
contumacy, for this writ could be sued only if a person who was excommunicated for contumacy persevered in his contumacy for forty days
after excommunication.

I. CONTUMACY, EXCOMMUNICATION, AND THE SECULAR ARM

The meaning of contumacy in the period of the classical canon law
differed so markedly from the meaning in the patristic period that it has
been observed that they had in common merely the same word.[4] To the
Fathers *contumacia* signified a deliberate and obstinate opposition to the
very authority of the church and, as such, merited exclusion from the
Christian community. The ecclesiastical reformers of the eleventh and
twelfth centuries began to use excommunication as a means of enforcing
church discipline;[5] since they still required that contumacy must precede
excommunication, it undertook a different meaning. In the high middle
ages *contumacia* was reduced to simple disobedience; it could be incurred
by human weakness and did not imply an offense against faith nor a state
of mind in rebellion against the church's authority itself. The canonists
of the post-Gregorian period, however, based their teaching on contumacy
largely on Roman law.[6] The general lines were set during the twelfth

---

[3] The bishop of Lincoln in a signification of 1206 described a man as excommunicated "propter
manifestam contumaciam" (*Curia Regis Rolls* 4. 182). Although the form of the significations
varied from diocese to diocese and from time to time within the same diocese, nonetheless from
the 1240's onward the overwhelming number of these significations stated explicitly that it was for
contumacy that the excommunication had been incurred. Thus, by 1230 the significations from
Bath and Wells, Chichester, Ely, Hereford, Lincoln, London, Winchester, St. Davids, and St.
Asaph described the excommunicate in this way. By 1280 the significations from every diocese
followed this form save Coventry and Lichfield, which used the alternative *culpis* (or *meritis*) *suis
exigentibus* (C.85/52-55), but this gave way in 1296 to the contumacy form (C.85/56).

[4] Alfons Gommenginger, "Bedeutet die Exkommunikation Verlust der Kirchengliedschaft?",
Zeitschrift für katholische Theologie 73 (1951) 45-46.

[5] This significant change did not go unnoticed and unopposed. In vain did St. Peter Damiani
protest to Alexander II of the use of excommunication as an instrument for the enforcement of
ecclesiastical discipline: "Porro nec beatus papa Gregorius, vel caeteri Patres qui diversis temporibus in apostolicae sedis regimine floruerunt, hunc morem in suis reperiuntur observasse de-
cretis, et vix eorum aliquando statutis anathema subnectitur, nisi cum catholicae fidei clausula
terminatur" (Epp. 1. 12; *PL* 144. 215).

[6] For the Roman law on contumacy, see L. Charvet, "Contumacia, Contumax," *Dictionnaire
de droit canonique* 4. 506-07.

and thirteenth centuries; subsequent centuries saw clarifications, amplifications, but no great advance.[7] A few generalizations applicable to the
period here under review can therefore be made.

The canonists were almost unanimous in relating contumacy to procedure
in ecclesiastical courts. In essence, contumacy was considered to be disobedience to the orders of a court and, ultimately, to the law itself.[8] It
could be committed by failing to come to court when cited, by leaving
before a case was finished, or by refusing to obey the decisions of a court.[9]
Contumacy for failure to appear in court could be incurred not only by

---

[7] For a listing of some of the relevant legal texts, see P. Torquebiau, "Contumacia, Contumax",
ibid., 4. 507-513.

[8] Although Bernard of Pavia (*Summa decretalium* (Regensburg, 1860) 2.10.2) and Hostiensis
(*Summa Hostiensis* (Lyons, 1517) 2. *de contumacia.* 1) define contumacy as disobedience "erga
iudicem vel prelatum," their treatment of contumacy clearly demonstrates that they considered it
in the context of ecclesiastical courts.

[9] This threefold mode of incurring contumacy can be traced back to a text in Gratian which
stated that a person should be excommunicated for refusal to come to a synod after being canonically cited, for not obeying sacerdotal precepts if he does come, and for presuming to leave
before the case is finished (C.11 q.3 c.43, from the council of Tribur, 895). Commenting on this
text in his *Summa*, Huguccio understood it to mean that there are three ways of incurring contumacy and that contumacy is the only reason for excommunication: "uel in principio cause cum
quis uocatus uenire contempnit uel in medio cause ante tempus recedit illicenciatus uel in fine
date sentencie obedire contempnit. Et est pro hiis tribus criminibus id est pro contumacia aliquorum istorum trium modorum procedente de quolibet crimine" (Paris, Bibliothèque Nationale,
Lat. MS. 3892, f. 192^(va)). Raymond of Pennafort and others after him took the Gratian text to
refer to contumacy: "haec autem contumacia inuenitur multiplex: nam alia est in non ueniendo in
iudicium, siue quia peremptoria citatione recepta uenire contemnit, siue quia malitiose seipsum
occultauit, siue quia impedit, ne possit ad eum citatio peruenire. Alia, quando citatus uenit ad
iudicium, sed non uult stare iuri uel ante finitam causae examinationem contumaciter, et illicentiatus recedit. Alia quando offensa eius est manifesta, et iussus a iudice non uult emendare"
(*Summa sancti Raymundi de Peniafort* (Rome, 1602) 3.33.22). The ordinary gloss on the Decretals
was not so broad: "Multis modis committitur contumacia quandoque attenditur respectu non
venientis ... quandoque respectu non restituentis ... quandoque respectu non respondentis, vel
obscure respondentis, quod idem est ac si non responderet ... quandoque respectu non iurantis ...
quandoque respectu non recedentis infecto negotio ... et quandoque respectu non exhibentis"
(X 2.14.2, v. *contumaciter*; see too X 2.6.5, v. *si autem*). This formulation of the gloss was repeated
with little change by Innocent IV (*In V libros decretalium commentaria* X 2.14.2) and later by others
including the fourteenth-century English compiler William of Pagula (*Summa summarum*, London,
BM, Royal MS. 10 D.X, f. 92^(rb)). Similarly, Hostiensis in discussing how contumacy is incurred
stated, "Dicitur ergo contumax, vel quia non venit, vel quia non vult respondere, vel obscure
respondet ..., vel quia non restituit ad preceptum iudicis ..., vel quia non iussus exhibet ..., vel
quia latitat, vel quia procurat, ut citatio ad ipsum pervenire non possit ..., vel quia non iurat ...,
vel quia non defendit" (*Summa aurea* 2. de contumacia. 2). Durandus summed up this matter by
using Gratian's distinction: "Contumax est qui trinis edictis vel uno peremptorio citatus non
venit, vel venit sed non obedit, seu illicentiatus recedit" (*Speculum iuris* (Frankfurt, 1668) 2. 1.
de contumacia 1. 1).

failure to obey a citation but also by hiding so that the citation could not be made or by impeding the citation. This contumacy for non-appearance must surely have been the most common form of contumacy; in fact, some canonical writers limited their discussion of contumacy to it. Innocent III in his decretal letter *Quoniam frequenter*[10] wrote in this manner, but the context shows and the glossator reminds the reader that non-appearance was actually only one kind of contumacy.[11] Thus, a person could be declared a *contumax* just as much by not performing a penance enjoined by the court as by not appearing at all, for it was contempt of authority which constituted the nature of contumacy.

The basic distinction between mere contumacy and offense was first made by Innocent III in the decretal letter *Ex parte* (1205) and was followed by the commentators. According to this, if a person was obstinately disobedient to authority, he was guilty of mere contumacy (*sola contumacia* or *contumacia tantum*), yet if in addition he refused to repair injury done to someone else, he was guilty of offense (*offensa* or *contumacia praegnans*).[12] For example, a person who was adjudged to be in unjust possession of property would commit an offense if he refused to restore it to its true owner. Satisfaction could even be due to a plaintiff who suffered loss by the refusal of the defendant to appear when cited thrice or once peremptorily and who refused to obey the court order to satisfy the plaintiff for his loss. Offense, then, was established by the refusal of a person to make satisfaction to another party; it carried with it, if it were manifest, the necessity of "sufficient caution" before absolution.[13] It was common

---

[10] Potthast 3665; X 2.6.5: "contumax apparuerit is ... sive quia peremptoria citatione recepta venire contemnit, sive quia malitiose se ipsum occultat, sive quia impedit, ne possit ad eum citatio pervenire."

[11] v. *impedit*: "Et sunt tres modi contumaciae, et quocumque illorum aliquis contumax sit, habetur pro contumace. Primum modum habes hic: et alios duos modos contumaciae habes 11. q. 3 certum est [C. 11 q. 3 c. 43.]."

[12] "Credimus distinguendum, utrum in aliquem interdicti vel excommunicationis sententia sit prolata pro contumacia tantum, quia scilicet citatus stare noluit iuri; vel etiam pro offensa, quia videlicet iussus noluit maleficium emendare" (Potthast 2467; X 5.40.23). Commenting on this decretal, Innocent IV explained, "Si excommunicatus sit pro sola contumacia, dummodo constet contumacia, non absolvetur contumax, nisi prius refusis expensis, et alio interesse, quia et tunc potest dici manifesta offensa" (*In quinque libros decretalium commentaria* 5.40.23); see, too, his decretal letter *Venerabilibus* (Potthast 15454; Sext. 5.11.7). Among other commentators see, e.g., Bartholomew of Brescia (*Glos. ord.* C.11 q.3 c.8, v. *minimis*; *De cons.* D.2 c.15, v. *excommunicetur*) and Hostiensis (*Summa* 5. de sententia excommunicationis 7 ; 2. de contumacia 2).

[13] Innocent III made this point in the same decretal *Ex parte*; two years later in *Cum olim* he stated that an offense was manifest when it was legitimately known because of confession or proof or from unassailable evidence (Potthast 3110; X 5.40.24). Concerning the requirements for absolution see *infra* p. 137-44.

teaching from at least the early years of the thirteenth century that contumacy either in the sense of mere contumacy or offense was prerequisite
for major excommunications *ab homine*. The dictum *pro sola contumacia
debet quis excommunicari* was a commonplace among the canonists. This
principle was clearly accepted by Huguccio (*ca.* 1190).[14] Joannes Teutonicus, the glossator of Gratian's *Decretum*, writing *ca.* 1216, dissented
from this by asserting that excommunication could be imposed either for
contumacy or for crime.[15] No other dissident voice was heard, and the
principle enunciated by Huguccio became common teaching.[16] Hence,
excommunication was imposed not as a penalty for a crime which gave
rise to the judicial proceedings (e.g., sacrilege) but as a penalty for contumacy which arose as a result of those proceedings (e.g., non-appearance).

It is one thing to say that excommunication was imposed because of
contumacy and quite another to say that excommunication was the normal
penalty for contumacy, which is not true, for excommunication as a
penalty for contumacy was allowed only a limited role in the common law
of the church. The penalties used against contumacious persons were
largely borrowed from Roman law; their application depended on the type
of case and the point at which the contumacy took place. In criminal
cases, according to the general canon law, excommunication was the
usual penalty for contumacy. In civil cases the usual penalty was *missio in
possessionem* (i.e., the other party was "sent into possession" of that about
which the action devolved, or, if that was impossible, he was "sent into
possession" of its value); in addition, the trial might even continue *parte
absente*. In sum, if the defendant was contumacious in a case concerning
a real matter and if the case had been contested (*post litem contestatam*), the
judge could proceed to sentence or, if the evidence was not clear enough
for that or if the case had not yet been contested (*ante litem contestatam*),
he could allow the plaintiff possession for a year (*missio in possessionem*).
In personal actions the judge could use this latter penalty to the amount
of the declared debt and, if the case had already been contested, he could

---

[14] Continuing his commentary on C.11 q.3 c.43 (see *supra* p. 45, n. 9) he states, "Dico quod sola
contumacia est causa excommunicacionis et cum dico quod quis est excommunicandus pro homici-
dio et furto et sic de quolibet alio mortali peccato set sic intelligitur si nolit satisfacere de illo, hor
est pro contumacia talis uel talis criminis, nisi enim deprehendatur incorrigibilis excommunicaic
non debet." See, too, Huguccio on C.11 q.3 c.8 (f. 189ra) and C.11 q.3 c.41 (f. 192rb). Cf.,
Summa Rufini (Paderborn, 1902), pp. 314-15.

[15] C.11 q.3 c.8, v. *minimis*. "Quandoque excommunicatur aliquis pro contumacia, quandoque
crimine."

[16] In his gloss Lyndwood merely repeated what had been accepted teaching for over two
hundred years: "Causa excommunicationis esse debet non ipsa litis sive dissensionis materia, sed
contumacia non parentis Judicis mandatis sive Juri" (3.28 c. Saeculi principes, v. *pro tali causa*;
ed., p. 265).

decree actual recovery. The contumacy of a plaintiff was rightly considered a yet graver offense since it was he who had initiated the legal action.[17] If the plaintiff did not come after three citations, he was allowed a year in which to appear to resume the case, but resumption was predicated on his payment to the defendant of his expenses. If he failed to come within the year, the judge would hear the arguments and witnesses of the defendant on the principal matter under dispute. If the plaintiff's contumacy occurred after the contestation, the judge could proceed to judgment. At any rate, a contumacious plaintiff was subject to condemnation in the expenses of the adversary unless the latter too was contumacious.

In civil cases, however, where *missio* was not possible, excommunication could be used.[18] Durandus denied that the judge had the option of sending into possession or of excommunicating: rather the judge should begin with a lesser penalty (i.e., *missio*) whenever possible, saving excommunication as a final resort "quia nulla maior poena est in ecclesia."[19] The dictum repeatedly used by the canonists *crescente contumacia crescere debet et pena* applied only to a contumacious person in criminal cases: he was first to be suspended, then excommunicated, then excommunicated with solemnity, and finally, if he was a cleric, he was to be deposed. The curious fact emerges that, although contumacy was demanded as a prerequisite condition for excommunication, this penalty itself was not the only or even the principal penalty for contumacy in the general canon law.

In England a different practice prevailed: excommunication was the usual penalty for contumacies of every kind from at least the mid-thirteenth century. In a context which clearly included civil as well as criminal cases William the Conqueror established excommunication as the penalty to be used against persons refusing to come to an ecclesiastical court after three citations.[20] Examples of *missio in possessionem* do exist for the twelfth century[21] and at least for the first half of the thirteenth century in cases heard by judges-delegate.[22] Although the legatine constitutions of 1237

---

[17] "Maior est contumacia actoris quam rei: etsi actor non venit, qui alium ad iudicium provocavit, presumitur potius contra ipsum quam contra reum absentem" (*Glos. ord.* X 2.14.3, v. *ad domum*).

[18] Innocent III in his decretal *Tuae fraternitatis* of 1206 outlined the penalties for contumacy (Potthast 2656). He was not, however, innovating but was merely stating the current canonical teaching (cf., Bernard of Pavia, *Summa decretalium* (Regensburg, 1860), 2.10.4). For a very detailed exposition of the penalties for contumacy, see *Glos. ord.* X 2.14.3, v. *terminetis*).

[19] *Speculum Iuris* 2.1. de contumacia 3.

[20] See *supra* p. 18, n. 19. The provisions of the Council of Winchester (*ca.* 1076) and of Pseudo-Edward appear to refer to criminal cases.

[21] See, e.g., the cases from England in the Decretals under the title *de dolo et contumacia* (2.14.1-3).

[22] Jane E. Sayers, "The Jurisdiction of the Papacy in Cases of Appeal and First Instance in

made provisions for this penalty,[23] probably only limited use was made of it by the ecclesiastical courts in the late thirteenth century and thereafter.[24] The use of other penalties in cases where one would expect *missio* was left to the discretion of the judge according to William of Drogheda in his *Summa aurea* (1239).[25] An examination of the plea rolls of the *Curia Regis* has already shown that a significant increase in the use of excommunication against contumacious persons occurred in the middle and late years of the thirteenth century.[26]

The evidence yielded by the files of significations shows that contumacious persons were regularly excommunicated both in civil and in criminal cases. Where details of the cases are given in the significations, one sees that excommunication was used against contumacious persons in every type of case over which the ecclesiastical courts enjoyed competence. In some cases lesser penalties may have been invoked first at the judge's discretion, but excommunication was certainly the ultimate weapon of the church against the contumacious.

The significations of excommunication frequently contain information about the case at issue in varying degrees of detail, but more frequently nothing of the case emerges save for the fact of the person's contumacy.[27]

England from 1198 to 1254, with particular reference to the Southern Province" (unpublished B. Litt. thesis, Univ. of Oxford, 1960), pp. 228-229. I am grateful to Miss Sayers for supplying me with this information.

[23] *Councils* 2. 259; text also appears in Wahrmund 2. 2. p. 17. Yet John of Acton in glossing this text (*ca.* 1335) noted, "scias hujusmodi possessionis missionem locum in beneficialibus non habere hodie" (v. in *possessionem mittendum*; *Constitutiones Legatinae* (Oxford, 1679), p. 73).

[24] Pending an exhaustive examination of thirteenth-century ecclesiastical court records the extent of the use of *missio* cannot be fully determined. In a formulary book of the court of the Arches which dates probably from the late thirteenth century the form of the penalty of *missio* for contumacy was included (London, Inner Temple, Petyt MS. 511.3, f. 57v).

[25] "Nec prohibitum est, quin diversam poenam possit iudex imponere" (*Summa aurea*, 31; Wahrmund 2. 2. pp. 35-36). Durandus, however, held that the judge did not have the option either to send into possession or to excommunicate (*Speculum iuris* 2.1. de contumacia 3).

[26] "It is remarkable that between the years 1200 and 1212 only two of the prohibition pleas recorded in the plea rolls bear witness to excommunication for contumacy in court christian; in 1220, but 3 out of 27; in 1230, 2 out of 26. In 1250, however, 8 out of the 17 ecclesiastical suits mentioned have resulted in the excommunication of the defendant; in 1260, 9 out of 14; in 1280, 7 out of 11; and in 1285, 5 out of 10. The rolls of the intervening years confirm the conclusion that there is in the middle and latter part of the thirteenth century a marked tendency to multiply the number of excommunications for contumacy" (G. B. Flahiff, "The Writ of Prohibition to Court Christian in the Thirteenth Century," *Mediaeval Studies* 7 (1945) 243, n. 82).

[27] The significations in the extensive York files contain very little information about the cases involved. Apart from identifying the excommunicate as an executor of a testament on a few occasions, they indicate in only 8 instances the nature of the case (the laying of violent hands on a cleric once each in 1401, 1403, 1514, and 1527; tithes in 1465; sacrilegious fornication in 1519;

4

This variety in the form of the significations does not permit any conclusions about the incidence of particular types of cases in which contumacy arose, excommunication was imposed, and the aid of the secular arm was invoked. Yet the conclusion does emerge that excommunication was used against contumacious persons in all manner of cases without distinction. *Ex officio* cases (i.e., correction cases) are identifiable in 421 cases, *ad instantiam* cases (i.e., civil cases introduced by another party) in 1,005 cases, and *ex officio promoto ad instantiam* (i.e., correction cases introduced by another party) in 28 cases; yet the remaining significations, more than seven thousand, are silent on this matter.[28]

The persons mentioned in the significations were the persons familiar to ecclesiastical judges. There was the cleric who neglected his property or his celibacy,[29] the woman given to concubinage,[30] the thief,[31] the adulterer,[32]

---

marriage in 1529). The significations from other dioceses, however, are more generous. Those from Canterbury, for example, reveal testamentary cases in 39 different years from 1256 to 1525; cases touching benefices in 22 different years from 1280 to 1512; defamation cases in 22 different years from 1326 to 1526; cases of *fideilesio* and perjury in 15 different years from 1337 to 1472; tithes cases in 22 years from 1324 to 1532. The files of the other dioceses are generally more full than York and less full than Canterbury.

[28] Although the general pattern indicates more instance than office cases, the latter appear in the significations from certain dioceses in large numbers. The bishops of Carlisle between 1400 and 1443 issued 49 significations, all of which concerned *ex officio* cases (C.85/196-197). The bishops of Bath and Wells between 1447 and 1512 sent 26 significations to chancery, 22 of which pertained to *ex officio* cases (C.85/41/10 - C.85/42/1).

[29] In a signification dated 16 Jan. 1520 it is noted that Richard Tomlyn of Exeter diocese was excommunicated for contumacies in a case in the audience of the archbishop of Canterbury in connection with his neglect of the fabric of his church (C.85/24/42). On 13 Feb. 1384 the incontinent rector of Whatlington, Chichester diocese, was signified (C.85/45/37; Salzman, p. 135). The unfortunate Thomas Multon, prior of Tiptree, combined both of the above crimes as well as others: "super criminibus delapidacionis et periurii necnon fornicacionis et adulterii" (signification dated 12 Nov. 1389: C.85/122/37).

[30] E.g., in 1524 Anne Gylys and John Lyngen, gentleman, of the parish of Stoke Edith, Hereford diocese, were excommunicated for contumacy in disobeying the warnings of the vicar-general concerning their concubinage (C.85/94/12). In another case, on 25 July 1407 the bishop of Exeter signified Joan Boyle, who had been excommunicated for her refusal to perform the penance imposed on her for the crime of fornication and incontinence with John Rogger, monk of Modbury, which she continued "per decem annos et amplius publice et notorie" (C.85/78/10).

[31] E.g., William Gassyngham, layman, of Norwich diocese was signified on 22 May 1375 by the prior and chapter of Christ Church, Canterbury, *sede vacante*, for contumacies committed in a case concerning his alleged theft of a missal (C.85/10/34).

[32] E.g., the bishop of Coventry and Lichfield signified Richard Hylton, tailor, and Joan Dawes, both of Staffs., on 13 Jan. 1422 on account of their excommunication arising out of an *ex officio* case of adultery (C.85/62/3).

the assaulter of clerics,[33] the defamer,[34] the perjurer,[35] the debtor,[36] the magician,[37] and so forth. There were those cited in suits concerning testaments,[38] tithes,[39] mortuary rights,[40], benefices,[41] marriages,[42] and even

---

[33] Twenty-eight such cases have been noted. E.g., on 11 April and again on 16 June 1402 the bishop of Hereford signified that the layman Henry Wynnesbury had been excommunicated for failure to appear in a case concerning the laying of violent hands on the person of a cleric (C.85/91/37-38). Wynnesbury was captured and imprisoned, but soon was absolved; his deliverance was requested on 24 Oct. 1402 (C.85/91/40). In a case from Bath and Wells diocese Richard Tylly had laid violent hands on Ralph Hyllyng, priest, "to the effusion of blood" (signification dated 26 Feb. 1454: C.85/41/20).

[34] Fifty-nine such cases have been noted in the signification files. E.g., Thomas Colvill of Lincoln was excommunicated and later signified (11. Aug. 1380) in a defamation case with Richard de Weston, chaplain, his adversary (C.85/10/38). He later appealed to the apostolic see and was acquitted *sine die* in King's Bench on the octave of St. Hilary 1381 (C.47/108/10/dorse of piece dated 13 Oct. 1380).

[35] *Fideilesio* and perjury were normally coupled and probably concerned non-payment of debts; see Brian L. Woodcock, *Medieval Ecclesiastical Courts in the Diocese of Canterbury* (London, 1952), pp. 89-92.

[36] In two significations from the chancellor of the University of Oxford (in 1405 and 1407) the excommunicates were referred to specifically as debtors (C.85/209/27, 31; Salter, pp. 37-38).

[37] On 15 July 1387 the chancellor of Oxford signified Thomas Durham, who had been excommunicated for his contumacy in not obeying warnings "super quibusdam artis magice et maliciose diffamacionis articulis" (C.85/208/55; Salter, p. 35).

[38] Testamentary cases constitute the largest single type of identifiable cases in the signification files: 128 with the earliest in 1256. The fact that so many cases appear in the files is due in large part to the practice of identifying excommunicates in testamentary cases as executors of a particular testament. For the use of this procedure in testamentary cases see Michael M. Sheehan, *The Will in Medieval England* (Toronto, 1963), p. 222.

[39] E.g., a signification from the bishop of Hereford dated 14 Dec. 1370 relates that Christine Herd had been excommunicated in connection with a case of spoliation of tithes which were due to the dean and chapter of Hereford (C.85/90/22). In another case, John Wygot of Devon was signified on 23 Dec. 1405 in a case concerning his failure to pay one calf as his tithe to the rector of Cheriton-Fitzpaine (C.85/78/4).

[40] E.g., in 1445 Nicholas Polpayne and Roger Mayse were excommunicated for their contumacy in not appearing before the commissary of the audience of causes of the bishop of Exeter in a case concerning mortuary rights, which had been instanced by William Clegh, vicar of Newlyn (C.85/80/6). In another case, the charge of exhumation was brought against William Newburg, John atte More, and Adam atte Style of the hamlet of Leigh in the parish of Mells, Bath and Wells diocese, for the removal of the body of Isabel atte Putte, parishioner of that church (signification from the archbishop of Canterbury, 7 May 1390: C.85/11/59).

[41] The mere 33 such cases in the signification files are scarcely indicative of the mountain of litigation in the ecclesiastical courts over benefices.

[42] Frequently a married person would be excommunicated for failing to obey the sentence of the court to return to the marriage partner. E.g., Margery Langford, legitimate wife of Richard Clyderowe, esq., was excommunicated by Master William Lyndwood in the court of the Arches for not heeding warnings of the court "in quadam causa siue querele negocio restitucionis obsequiorum coniugalium" (signification dated 21 March 1418: C.85/14/16, and with some variations in *Reg. Chichele, Canterbury* 1. 185).

suspicion of heresy.[43] In the year 1441, for example, there are extant 21 significations, which contain in all the names of 43 excommunicates. In only 6 of these significations was mention made of the case radically at issue: a tithes case and a case concerning adultery from the diocese of Chichester,[44] one perjury case each from Exeter[45] and Salisbury,[46] the case from Salisbury too of seven men who had imposed violent hands on a cleric,[47] and from Exeter the case of the husbandman Hugh Knyght, who blackened the chin and the nose of the image of the Virgin with a burning candle and reviled it with the gibe, "Mable, ware thy berde."[48] In the year 1447 the arrest of 31 excommunicates was requested in the 26 extant significations; in only 10 of these can the type of case be determined: 4 cases of perjury,[49] 3 of adultery,[50] 2 of defamation,[51] and one case of marriage,[52] and one case of the use of the art of necromancy, incantation, and sortilege.[53] Clearly, then, excommunication was regularly imposed

[43] See *infra* pp.

[44] C.85/47/13, 14; Salzman, p. 138.

[45] C.85/79/24.

[46] C.85/149/21.

[47] C.85/149/22.

[48] "Hugo in quadam capella sancti Iohannis Baptiste apud Neweport in parochia de Tawton Episcopi eorundem comitatus et diocesis barbam siue mentum et nasum ymaginis beate Marie cum quadam candela de cera accensa ingrauit cum fumo eiusdem candele sic uulgariter delusorie et contemptibiliter ymaginem ipsam alloquendo 'Mable, ware thy berde" in uilipendium et delusionem ymaginis beate Marie et contra determinacionem ecclesie in materia adoracionis ymaginum salubriter factam" (C.85/79/25). St. Thomas More recounts a not dissimilar incident of a man called Clyffe, "a manne of myne," who in his madness talked to an image of Our Lady on London Bridge, blasphemed it with diabolic words (which "now a daies bloweth out by the mouthes of heretyques"), and, setting his hands on the child in her arms, broke its neck (*The Debellacyon of Salem and Bizance* (English works, London, 1557), p. 935).

[49] Two from the archbishop of Canterbury (C.85/18/2, 13) and two from the bishop of Lincoln (C.85/112/29, 30). The six men of Exeter diocese who were signified by the archbishop on 8 July 1447 (no. 2) were subsequently signified on 15 Apr. 1448 (C.85/18/26) and in 1450 (the day and month have been torn off: C.85/19/11).

[50] Two from the bishop of Lincoln (C.85/112/32, 33) and one from the bishop of Exeter (C.85/80/7).

[51] Roger Swayn *alias* Taylour of Beds. on 23 June 1447 by the bishop of Lincoln (C.85/112/31) and John Hervy of Exeter diocese on 29 Nov. 1447 by the archbishop of Canterbury (C.85/18/5). Hervy's absolution was certified to chancery on 20 Jan. 1448 (*ibid.*, no. 19).

[52] This was the case concerning Anna de la Launde of Lincoln diocese, who was signified by the archbishop of Canterbury on 22 July 1447 (C.85/18/1) and again on the following day (*ibid.*, no. 3). The endorsements indicate that a writ was issued to the sheriff of Lincs. after the first signification and to the sheriff of Notts. after the second. Her absolution was signified on 12 May 1450 (C.85/9/8), but she was subsequently excommunicated by the official of the London consistory and signified for capture by the bishop of London on 4 March 1455 (C.85/125/6).

[53] According to a signification dated 13 July 1447 John Rox had been excommunicated for failure to perform the penance imposed on him for this crime; the writ for his capture was directed to the sheriff of Northampton (C.85/112/34 and dorse).

against contumacious persons regardless of the type of case in which they were involved.

The excommunicated persons who are found in these cases had one thing in common: they had disobeyed the church and as a result were considered contumacious. Their expulsion from the Christian community resulted not from their refusal to pay tithes or from striking a cleric or from their flirtations with heresy or from anything of the like, but rather from placing themselves in obstinate disobedience to the church in her courts.

II. CLERICAL SUBSIDIES AND THE SECULAR ARM

A very large number of the persons against whom the writ *de excommunicato capiendo* was used were persons excommunicated for contumacies contracted for failure to pay clerical subsidies. The practice of the clergy granting special taxes to the popes can be found as early as the late eleventh century. During the thirteenth century the English clergy with papal approval gave subsidies to the king for crusading expeditions. At the end of that century Boniface VIII faced the difficulty posed by the kings of England and France exacting clerical subsidies without his approval. There emerged from the quarrel at that time between Edward I and Archbishop Winchelsey an acceptance of the doctrine of necessity: in actual necessity the clergy could grant subsidies to the crown without papal approval. In practice, the king could still request the subsidy of the pope — as indeed was done by Edward I in his latter years — but increasingly he had recourse to the convocation of the English clergy.[54]

The collectors of these subsidies granted to the king were themselves clerics and were throughout our period empowered to punish defaulters by using ecclesiastical penalties; episcopal registers contain many examples

---

[54] There does not exist a general study of clerical subsidies to the king. For the reign of Edward I, see H. S. Deighton, "Clerical Taxation by Consent, 1279-1301," *EHR* 68 (1953) 161-192. With reference to particular places see W. H. Blaauw, "Subsidy Collected from the Clergy of Sussex, 3 Richard II, 1380," *Sussex Archaeological Soc. Collections* 5 (1852) 229-243; J. E. Brown, "Clerical Subsidies in the Archdeaconry of Bedford, 1390-2, 1400-1," *Beds. Historical Record Soc.* 1 (1913) 27-61; and *A Subsidy Collected in the Diocese of Lincoln in 1526* (ed. H. E. Salter; Oxfordshire Historical Soc., 1913). For the role of convocation see Dr. Dorothy B. Weske, *Convocation of the Clergy* (London, 1937), chap. 5. For subsidies to the pope the work of William E. Lunt is indispensable. See especially *Papal Revenues in the Middle Ages* (2 vols.; New York, 1934) 1. 77-81; *Financial Relations of the Papacy with England to 1327* (Cambridge, Mass., 1937) and its sequel *Financial Relations of the Papacy with England, 1327-1534* (Cambridge, Mass., 1962). The effect of lay subsidies on the clergy is clearly explained by James F. Willard, *Parliamentary Taxes on Personal Property, 1290 to 1334* (Cambridge, Mass., 1934), 93-109.

of the imposition of the penalties of suspension, sequestration, and excommunication.[55] These penalties did not always prove effective, and at times the secular arm was invoked. The papal legate Ottobon in a letter to the archbishop of York in 1268 allowed for recourse to the secular arm after the failure of ecclesiastical censures.[56] Yet from even before 1268 there survives at least one example of the use of the secular arm for the collection of a clerical subsidy: in the course of the collection of the triennial tenth granted by the church in 1250 for the promised crusade to the Holy Land, John Climping, bishop of Chichester, excommunicated the prior of Lewes for ignoring repeated demands for payment and on 20 May 1255 requested his capture.[57]

During the latter years of Edward I and the early years of his successor two forms of secular assistance were available to enforce collection of clerical taxes.[58] In the first place, the bishop could use the procedure of signification already long in use against excommunicates. Archbishop Winchelsey was probably referring to this procedure when in 1301 he told his suffragans to invoke the secular arm, if necessary, against such contemners of the keys of the church.[59] Examples of the use of the signification procedure survive for the years 1279,[60] 1296,[61] 1308[62] 1309,[63] and

---

[55] The registers do not always clearly distinguish the type of subsidy, whether papal or royal, but see, e.g., *Reg. Woodlock, Winchester* 1. 82; *Reg. Charlton, Hereford*, pp. 56-57; *Reg. Giffard, York*, pp. 130-31 ; *Reg. Reynolds, Worcester*, p. 69. Professor Lunt observed that sequestration was not frequently employed (*Financial Relations... to 1327*, p. 329; *idem*, "The Collectors of Clerical Subsidies Granted to the King by the English Clergy," *The English Government at Work, 1327-1336* (eds. W. A. Morris and J. R. Strayer; Cambridge, Mass., 1940-1950) 2. 252).

[56] Wilkins 2. 21; see Lunt, "The Consent of the English Lower Clergy to Taxation during the Reign of Henry III," *Persecution and Liberty : Essays in Honor of George Lincoln Burr* (New York, 1931), p. 138.

[57] C.85/43/6; Salzman, p. 127. For the details concerning this grant, see Lunt, *Financial Relations ... to 1327*, pp. 255-290.

[58] The taxes granted in 1274, 1301, and 1305 were made at the direction of the pope. The greater part of these grants went to the king. See Lunt, *Financial Relations ... to 1327*, pp. 311-346, 366-395. For those granted to Edward I by consent of the clergy, see Leighton, *art. cit., EHR* 68 (1953) 161-192.

[59] *Reg. Winchelsey, Canterbury*, pp. 753-54: "per quamquam severitatem ecclesiasticam per vos et vestros ministros ad hoc deputatos districcius compellatis, contra obstinatos rebelles et claves ecclesie contempnentes invocando si necesse fuerit auxilium brachii secularis."

[60] Henry de Fogheleston was signified by the bishop of Salisbury at the request of the collectors. He had impeded their collection of the sexennial tenth granted for the Holy Land in 1274 (C.85/145/52).

[61] C.85/101/37, 41. This was connected probably with the collection of the tenth granted by the clergy to the king in 1295 and due in two instalments in 1296. Alternatively, it may have been connected with the collection of the arrears on an earlier tax. See Deighton, *art. cit.*, pp. 176-78.

[62] *Reg. Woodlock, Winchester* 1. 241.

[63] *Ibid.*, 1. 360.

1313.[64] Alternatively, the bishops could give the names of defaulters to the local sheriff so that he could attach their goods and require their appearance in the king's courts. In a letter of 6 December 1305 to the bishop of Winchester Edward I promised that the sheriff of Southampton would act in this way if he was so requested by the bishop or his agents.[65] At the end of that same month the bishop of Winchester wrote to five deans of his diocese requesting them to collect the tenth and to send the names of defaulters to the sheriff.[66]

The existing evidence indicates that, when the secular arm was invoked for this purpose during the reign of Edward III, it was in connection with subsidies in support of the war against France. During the years at the beginning of the war when the king was suffering financial difficulties, the signification procedure was used against defaulters: for the years from 1338 to 1346 seven significations containing a total of 37 excommunicates from six dioceses.[67] The king undoubtedly brought pressure on other bishops to seek the capture of defaulters. Simon Montacute, bishop of Ely, told his official in a letter of 3 August 1341 that the king was demanding the names of such defaulters so that he could capture them. Montacute refused to bow to these demands and permitted his official merely to proceed to sequestration — not a surprising response in that year of crisis between Archbishop Stratford and the king.[68]

The mere sprinkling of such cases up to this time turned into a virtual torrent after 1371, which once begun lasted thirty-five years. In 1371 the clergy of both provinces were constrained by the king to grant £50,000 in aid of the renewal of the war in France to be levied even of *minuta beneficia* and of benefices previously exempt from taxation.[69] Clerical

---

[64] *Reg. Greenfield, York* 2. 39.

[65] *Reg. Woodlock, Winchester* 2. 903-04.

[66] *Ibid.*, 1. 82.

[67] From St. Davids the signification of the Cistercian abbot of Strata Florida on 1 Oct. 1338 (C.85/167/22); from Norwich 4 clerics on 17 Feb. 1339 (C.85/134/23) and on 11 May 1345 4 rectors (*ibid.* no. 34); from Worcester 5 persons on 16 Dec. 1339 (C.85/163/29); from Exeter the dean of St. Buryan on 8 Aug. 1341 (C.85/76/35); from Hereford 17 persons including the abbots of Buildwas, Evesham, and Flaxley on 26 Sept. 1343 (C.85/90/15); from London the prior of Hurley and 4 rectors (C.85/120/32).

[68] He wrote to his official that the king "sua nobis direxit breuia pro huiusmodi leuanda decima uicibus repetitis uolens de non soluencium huiusmodi nominibus cercius reddi ut pro capcione eorum manus extendere ualeat sue regie maiestatis"; he was unwilling to yield to the king because "contra eos ad eorum conuicendam maliciam inuocari non oporteat brachium seculare" (Cambridge Univ. Libr., Ely Diocesan Records, Reg. Montacute, f. 73ʳ; calendared by Canon J. H. Crosby, *Ely Diocesan Remembrancer* no. 76 (Sept. 1891), p. 603).

[69] According to the terms of this grant, the levy was to be made of the temporalities and spiritualities of all the prelates and religious of both provinces, of rectors, vicars, and other ecclesiastical

opposition may have been expected by the king in view of the tax which he had imposed on the clergy without their consent in 1370. Such an expectation would have been fully justified by ensuing events. The surviving records indicate that in 1372 the arrest of 90 persons was requested on account of their failure to pay the subsidy; in the following year there were 143 and in 1374 there were 173. And so it continued with regard to the ensuing grants, and before the torrent subsided in 1407 at least 1,500 clerics had been excommunicated and signified for arrest for this reason,[70] containing in their number scores of abbots, priors, and members of the higher clergy, but principally the lower clergy — rectors, vicars, and stipendiary priests.[71] Also included were a few laymen, farmers of ecclesiastical benefices.[72] Although some significations of this kind came to chancery during the ensuing years (9 persons in 1411 and 12 in 1420), the storm was clearly over by 1407.

As early as 1374 the king realized that the subsidy would not be levied

---

persons, whether privileged or not, whether their benefices were usually taxed or not, even those of royal free chapels, also of foreigners as well as natives, and of stipendiary priests. Payment was to be enforced by sequestration and other penalties, and those refusing payment were to appear in King's Bench on the quindene of Michaelmas (London, Lambeth Palace Libr., Reg. Wytleseye, ff. 42v-44v; see also Thomas Walsingham, *Historia Anglicana* (ed. H. T. Riley; R. S., 1863-64) 1. 312-313; Ranulf Higden, *Polychronicon* (eds. C. Babington and J. R. Lumby; R. S., 1865-66) 8. 375-76). Some account of this grant may be seen in Maude Clarke, *Medieval Representation and Consent* (London, 1936), pp. 29-32; Dorothy B. Weske, *Convocation of the Clergy* (London, 1937), pp. 164-65.

[70] This is a conservative total. Many significations had attached lists with the names of the excommunicated defaulters; unfortunately a large number of these lists are now missing. The total arrived at assumes only four names on each missing list, wheras some surviving lists contain 7 or 8 times that number.

[71] Bishop Arundel of Ely on 12 March 1375 requested the arrest of the following excommunicates who had refused to pay the clerical subsidy and had remained excommunicated for sixty days: the abbots of Tilty, Lesnes, Shrewsbury, Notley, S. Valery-sur-Somme, St. Osyth, Wendling, Reading, and Sées; the abbesses of Wilton and Barking; the priors of Rumburgh, Binham, S. Jacu (or Jacet), Panfield, Linton, Castle Acre, Bermondsey, Longueville, Bushmead, Fordham, Ware, Mount Mokelin, Keniworth, St. Botolph's, Colchester, Wellington, Bardney, Swavesey, Royston, St. Neots, Hatfield, and Thetford; the prioresses of Stamford, Goring, and Campsey Ash; the rectors of Swavesey, Duxford, Wickham, and Coates; the vicars of Hauxton, Thremhall House, and Burton Hospital (*Ely Diocesan Remembrancer*, no. 115 (Dec.-Jan., 1894-95), p. 347. In 1386 during the vacancy of the see of Llandaff the archbishop of Canterbury signified defaulters from that diocese including in a single signification 13 abbots, 14 priors, 2 prioresses, the chapter, archdeacon, precentor, treasurer, and chancellor of Llandaff as well as a large number of parsons and vicars (*CCR, 1385-89*, pp. 149-150). The existence of arrears from Welsh sees was not unusual at this time (cf., *Rot. Parl.* 3. 481, 521). I am grateful to Dr. Robert Dunning for calling these last references to my attention.

[72] E.g., the bishop of Chichester invoked the secular arm against seven farmers on 29 Jan. 1404 (C.85/46/12; Salzman, p. 136).

without the aid of the secular arm and, wishing to apply a remedy, he wrote to the sheriffs of the shires in the diocese of Lincoln — he may have written to all his other sheriffs at the same time — ordering them to assist the bishop, whenever required, against defaulters by use of distraint, imprisonment, and otherwise as the bishop would think best.[73] Twelve years later Richard II directed his sheriffs and others of his ministers to be attendant to the collectors "in all things which may hasten the collection."[74] The extent to which the method of direct signification from bishop to sheriff was resorted to does not appear in the records. What is worthy of note is that the king was willing to bypass his chancery in order to enforce collection of the subsidy.

At any time the task of the collectors must have been difficult and fraught with dangers even to physical safety,[75] but in this latter part of the fourteenth century the continued exaction made of the lower clergy despite their poverty could scarcely contribute to the popularity of the collectors and undoubtedly was a factor contributing to the social unrest among the lower clergy which was related to the Peasants' Rising. In fact, in 1381 not long after the Rising had been suppressed, the collectors in the diocese of London would not use the writ *de excommunicato capiendo* against defaulters, because they still feared for their lives.[76] Acting on the petition of these collectors, the king instructed the exchequer not to press them for the taxes of the clergy who had fled to avoid prosecution.[77]

Except for a solitary signification in 1490 from the bishop of Rochester[78] the use of the signification procedure for the enforcement of the collection of subsidies is not seen again after 1420 for over a hundred years. In 1529 Archbishop Warham took the unusual action of requesting the arrest of the prior of Clifford, collector in the archdeaconry of Hereford, because

---

[73] The letter is transcribed *infra* Appendix D, pp. 187-88; see *CCR, 1374-77*, p. 37.

[74] *Cal. Fine Rolls* 10. 133.

[75] According to a writ dated 28 Oct. 1373 William Ellerton, chaplain, Robert Danheney, vicar of Stonesby, and Alexander Trissell, parson of Goadby-Marwood, Lincoln diocese, were outlawed for assaulting the collector of the clerical subsidy (C.47/66/5/146). In the following year the bishop of Coventry and Lichfield complained to the king of the physical abuse accorded to his collectors at Shrewsbury by priests of the royal free chapels (S.C.1/56/3).

[76] "Nepurquant les ditz Coillours n'osent mye leur pursute par Brief de Significavit, n'autrement, pur paour du mort" (*Rot. Parl.* 3. 128).

[77] A. Réville, *Le soulèvement des travailleurs d'Angleterre en 1381* (Paris, 1898), appendix 2, no. 87 (p. 225). Concerning the involvement of the lower clergy in the rising, see the introduction to Réville's work by Petit-Dutaillis, pp. xlix-l (English translation in *Studies and Notes Supplementary to Stubbs' Constitutional History* (Manchester, 1908-1929) 2. 270-72).

[78] Master Roger Tochett, rector of Lakenham, was the defaulter (signification dated 10 March 1490: C.85/144/29).

he had not made his payment on time and was then twenty days overdue.[79] In another unusual event in that same year the abbot of Leiston, a collector for the bishop of Norwich, wrote to the chancery *in his own name* to request the capture of a recalcitrant rector.[80] Both of these incidents were connected with the collection of the fifth which Wolsey in pursuit of a disastrous foreign policy had extracted from the clergy. During 1532 and 1533 the secular arm was invoked by the bishops of Exeter and London for assistance in collecting the subsidy granted to Henry VIII in 1531,[81] but in all less than a hundred clerics were involved and of these most were Welshmen.[82] The Tudor revival of a practice with a long previous history scarcely rivalled the use made of it under Edward III, Richard II, and Henry IV.

How effective was the use of the secular arm as a means of coercing the payment of clerical subsidies to the king ? If the reactions of the clergy of the London diocese in 1374 were representative, then these measures must have been fairly effective. On 10 July 1374 a signification was drawn up in the chancery of the bishop of London; it contained the names of 39 clerics.[83] Before it was sent, one name was deleted. By 20 October 1374 at least 18 others had returned *ad gremium ecclesiae* and had been absolved, presumably after paying their taxes.[84] To correlate the London figures for 1374 with other dioceses cannot be done because of the alternative methods available to bishops for notifying the secular authorities about the absolution of a signified excommunicate.

It would be a mistake to think that the use of the secular arm for the collection of subsidies was employed only in support of subsidies granted for the benefit of the king. It is true that such subsidies accounted for the overwhelming majority of cases of this sort, but the same procedure was turned on occasion to the advantage of the church. Gregory X and Nicholas III as a consequence of the grant of a sexennial tenth for a crusade by the Council of Lyons in 1274 issued instructions which included allowance for recourse to the secular arm,[85] but Boniface VIII in similar in-

---

[79] C.85/25/18.

[80] C.85/213/32.

[81] Wilkins 3. 742-44.

[82] The two significations from the bishop of Exeter are dated 19 April and 23 May 1532 (C.85/82/14, 15). The bishop of London sent one in 1532 (C.85/126/35a) and at least 4 between March and September, 1533, including one with St. Asaph clergy and one with Bangor clergy (*ibid.*, nos. 35b, 37, 38, 40, 40a, 40b).

[83] C.85/121/41.

[84] C.85/121/42-52, 56. Others may have been absolved and their records lost.

[85] The text of the conciliar grants is in *Conc. oec. decr.* (Freiburg, 1962), p. 286. Gregory X issued a set of instructions on 23 Oct. 1274 (Potthast 20947; English translation in Lunt, *Papal*

structions in 1301 required permission of the apostolic see before such recourse was made.[86] Such a restriction does not appear to have been observed in England, and at least by 1330 papal instructions no longer insisted upon it.[87]

Instances can be cited from the reign of Edward I when papal collectors had recourse to secular restraint. Raymond de Nogaret, papal nuncio, in an undated letter (probably of 1274) wrote to the chancellor of the realm requesting that sheriffs be directed to assist him should he require their help.[88] As a result writs to that effect were issued to the sheriffs on 10 September 1274[89] and again in 1275[90] and 1276.[91] In the tenth year of that same reign (1281-82) another papal collector rehearsed to the chancellor his woeful tale of clerics, Hospitallers, Templars, and exempt abbeys, who were unmoved by ecclesiastical penalties. He complained that some even thrashed the corn before he could have it sequestrated. His suggestion for a remedy could scarcely have recommended itself to the king, for he asked the king to direct his sheriffs to assist the collectors by threshing the corn sequestrated in the barns of the defaulters and that the sheriffs act "non tanquam vicecomites, set tanquam ministri ecclesie per ecclesiam convocati."[92] Predictably, nothing further was heard of his suggestion.

The traces of the use of secular force for the collection of subsidies for the church are very slight indeed after Edward I. In 1310 the

Revenues in the Middle Ages (New York, 1934), 2. 167): "None of those not paying, however, will be compelled by the violence of secular power, unless the contumacy or rebellion of the one not paying should be of such nature or so great that deservedly the aid of the secular arm ought to be invoked against him, as would be done in other cases or affairs on account of contempt of ecclesiastical censure." Nicholas III issued another set before Feb. 1279 (text: *idem*, "A Papal Tenth levied in the British Isles from 1274-1289," *EHR* 32 (1917) 86-8; English translation by Lunt in *Papal Revenues* 2. 184). This latter interprets the former, *inter alia*, in respect to secular aid: "There follows: 'None of those not paying shall be compelled by the violence of secular power.' From this declaration many assume the boldness of not paying. Therefore it is expedient to specify particularly contumacy or rebellion for which the secular arm ought to be invoked, and when, namely, after they should stand excommunicated for forty or sixty days." It should be observed that these crusading subsidies were in fact destined to finance Edward I's projected crusade.

[86] 3.7.1 in *Extrav. Comm.*

[87] The papal instruction of 3 Jan. 1330, which the archbishop of Canterbury quoted in a letter to his collector, was satisfied that secular assistance would be used only if necessary (*Literae Cantuarienses* (ed. J. B. Sheppard; R.S., 1887-89), 1. 323-29; translated by Lunt, *Papal Revenues* 2. 106-09).

[88] Prynne, p. 133.

[89] *Ibid.*

[90] *Ibid.*, pp. 160-61.

[91] *Ibid.*, pp. 178-79.

[92] *Ibid.*, pp. 1246-47.

bishop of Winchester provided for signification as an ultimate weapon to be used against those who refused to pay the penny in the mark for the expenses of the inquisitors against the Templars.[93] In another instance, the secular arm was invoked early in 1416 against the dean of Lynn, Norwich diocese, for his continued refusal to contribute to the support of the English delegation at the Council of Constance.[94] On one occasion in 1474 the same procedure was applied against 32 clerics from Exeter diocese who had failed to pay the charitable subsidy granted to Cardinal Bourgchier by convocation in the previous year.[95] Even when it is borne in mind that the church enjoyed some of the revenues raised in England for the crusades, nonetheless it was unquestionably the king who benefited most by this practice of secular constraint against tax defaulters.

Can the contumacy contracted for failure to pay subsidies be related to the ecclesiastical courts? There is no direct evidence that such defaulters were always cited to appear in court or that their contumacy was contracted for failing to come or for some other action subsequent to their coming. An undated chancery memorandum, possibly from the early 1370's, insisted that the secular power was to be used against defaulters only if they were guilty of contumacy and contempt of ecclesiastical censure such as would lead in other matters to the invoking of the secular arm.[96] But were they cited to appear in court before they were excommunicated? Several examples do exist which show such defaulters, already excommunicated, being cited to an ecclesiastical court to show reason why they should not be arrested by the secular arm,[97] but the question here is whether the contumacy which gave rise to the excommunication was *erga iudicem*. The collectors, although their coercive powers gave their office a quasi-judicial aspect, were not ecclesiastical judges. The two collectors who entered Shrewsbury and were thrown into the Severn by an angry crowd of stipendiary priests will bear witness against any supposition that collectors sat, as it were, judicially and waited for the clergy

---

[93] *Reg. Woodlock, Winchester* 1. 489-490, 538.

[94] The collector requested the keeper of the spirituality to signify the dean for capture on 12 Dec. 1415 and the keeper complied on the last day of Jan. 1416 (*Reg. Chichele, Canterbury* 3. 392-94).

[95] C.85/81/25. Innovations had been made in the terms of the subsidy of 1473, including the giving of power of canonical censure to the collectors (see F. R. H. DuBoulay, "Charitable Subsidies Granted to the Archbishops of Canterbury, 1300-1489," *BIHR* 23 (1950) 159-160).

[96] "Nullus autem non soluencium compelletur per secularis uiolenciam potestatis nisi ipsius non soluentis contumacia uel rebellio talis aut tanta fuerit quod merito contra ipsum sicut fieret in aliis casibus seu negociis propter ecclesiastice censure contemptum inuocari debeat auxilium brachii secularis" (C.47/19/3/4).

[97] *Reg. Wykeham, Winchester* 2. 138-140, 142; *Reg. Chichele, Canterbury* 3. 392-93.

to bring their subsidies to them.[98] No doubt in some cases defaulters were cited to appear in court and as a result of their non-appearance were excommunicated, but it cannot be stated that this was general procedure.[99] The contumacies involved in most cases were directed against the collectors and were committed "in non soluendo subsidium." This use of the secular arm against persons in such cases appears to stand as an exception to the general practice of signifying only those excommunicates whose contumacies were related to proceedings in the ecclesiastical courts.

III. Types of Persons Signified for Arrest

An analysis of the persons against whom the writ *de excommunicato capiendo* was issued would reveal a broad cross-section of medieval society. Before the judges of the ecclesiastical courts there appeared persons lay and clerical, men and women, of high and lowly condition. Some were titled; some even mitred; some were scholars. Yet most belonged to the endless army of those who appear only once in the records of history. If any of them acted contumaciously and despite excommunication remained obdurate, he might soon find himself lodged in the king's jail.

Exempt from excommunication and, hence, exempt from the procedure of this writ were tenants-in-chief[100] and royal ministers such as sheriffs.[101] Some persons with a curial or tenurial relationship with the king as feudal lord claimed, according to episcopal complaints, that they enjoyed the privilege of not being cited before ecclesiastical judges outside their village or parish and, thus, if they asserted this privilege in chancery, the request of the bishops for the writ for their capture would be denied. Undated *gravamina*, belonging possibly to 1301, contained such a complaint with reference to "aliqui de curia domini regis."[102] Similar complaints made in 1309 and repeated in 1316 referred to "aliqui de tenura domini regis."[103]

---

[98] S.C.1/56/3.

[99] For an example see *infra* Appendix D, p. 188.

[100] Constitutions of Clarendon, c. 7 (*Select Charters*, p. 165).

[101] This matter was *sub lite* during the thirteenth century. Bishop Grosseteste became involved in a controversy with the king in 1250 by excommunicating the sheriff of Rutland (Matthew of Paris, *Chronica Majora* (ed. H. R. Luard; R. S., 1872-1883) 5. 109). In the Michaelmas parliament of 1279 Archbishop Pecham conceded that the king's ministers should not be excommunicated even if they disobeyed the king's writ to capture excommunicates (*Rot. Parl.* 1.224; Prynne, pp. 235-236; *CCR, 1272-79*, p. 582), although at the Council of Lambeth in 1281 no such explicit exemption was made of the king's ministers (*Councils*, 2. 907).

[102] *Reg. Halton. Carlisle* 1. 172.

[103] *Councils* 2. 1272, and *Statutes* 1. 173. The expression "de curia" in the earlier complaint referred to persons subject to the jurisdiction of the king as their feudal lord, whereas the ex-

To the latter complaint the king replied that the writ had never been denied in such cases and would not be denied in the future.

Among the *excommunicati capiendi* were many members of the higher clergy. In 1459 the archbishop of York requested the arrest of a brother bishop, Robert Wodburn, an Augustinian friar, who was bishop of Hólar in Iceland and had been acting as suffragan to the bishop of Carlisle.[104] The archbishop of Cashel had tried unsuccessfully in 1377 to have writs issued from the royal chancery of England against two of his suffragans, the bishops of Limerick and Waterford and Lismore.[105] In one instance a signified excommunicate later became archbishop of Lyons.[106] Much more common was the request for the capture of excommunicated abbots, at least 80 during our period. The reasons for the excommunications of these abbots are not always clear, but many concerned the collection of the clerical subsidy, resistance to episcopal visitation, and disputes concerning appropriated churches. Although there were Benedictine, Augustinian, and Premonstratensian abbots among them, the largest number were clearly Cistercians. Quite frequently the signification would contain not only the name of the abbot but likewise the names of the senior officers of the monastery. For example, in 1299 Archbishop Winchelsey signified the abbot, prior, subprior, cellarer, sacristan, and almoner of Ramsey Abbey.[107] Against the Cistercian monastery of Sawley the signification

pression "de tenura" in the complaints of 1309 and 1316 referred to persons who were tenants on the royal demesne (and who consequently were *de curia*). Cf., the provisions of Constitutions of Clarendon, c. 10 (*Select Charters*, p. 166). Despite the king's reply it would appear that some such exemption had been implied; Edward I in a chancery warrant of 1302 directed a writ *de excommunicato capiendo* to be issued, noting that the excommunicate "has not yet come to the king's service willingly and is not at present in it" (*Cal. Chanc. Warr.*, p. 152). Perhaps not unrelated was the later action of parliament (1344) which gave to the chancellor cognizance of cases involving chancery clerks or their servants (*Rot. Parl.* 2. 154-55; see H. C. Maxwell-Lyte, *Historical Notes on the Use of the Great Seal of England* (London, 1926), pp. 10-11; B. Wilkinson, *The Chancery under Edward III* (Manchester, 1929), p. 87).

[104] C.85/186/51. He had been provided to Hólar on 27 June 1441 (Francis Roth, *The Earliest Austin Friars, 1249-1538*, vol. 2 Sources (New York, 1961), p. 324). Conrad Eubel (*Hierarchia Catholica Medii et Recentioris Aevi* (2nd ed.; Münster and Padua, 1913-1958) 2, 166) gives the date 14 July 1441. He never gained access to his diocese (see Jón Helgason, *Islands Kirke fra dens Grundlaeggelse til Reformationen* (Copenhagen, 1925), p. 227).

[105] C.85/214/45-46. The request was denied because such writs should issue from the chancery of Ireland under the seal of Ireland (*CCR, 1374-77*, pp. 481-82).

[106] Peter of Savoy (de Sabaudia), dean of St. Martin-le-Grand, London, and dean of Salisbury, was signified as an excommunicate by Archbishop Winchelsey in 33 Edward I (1303-04) (Prynne, p. 1041). He was provided by Clement V to the vacant see of Worcester in 1307 without effect; in the following year he became archbishop of Lyons, which he held until his death in 1332 (see Eubel 1. 316).

[107] C.85/5/28.

from the archbishop of York in 1306 named not only all of these senior officers, save the almoner, but added the subcellarer, subsacristan, master of the *conversi*, bursar, *causator*, porter, guest-master, master of the forest, and the masters of the dependent hospitals at Tadcaster and Berkeley.[108] Strangely enough, the abbot of Evesham, who appears to have enjoyed the power to signify excommunicates from 1332,[109] was himself signified in 1343 for not paying the clerical subsidy.[110] In addition there were many priors of priories and wardens of hospitals as well as abbesses and prioresses against whom the writ was issued. An archdeacon of Lincoln was confined to prison because of his obduracy in excommunication.[111] Deans of such prominent churches as St. Paul's, London,[112] and Lincoln Cathedral[113] were subject to arrest as excommunicates. Even men connected with ecclesiastical courts occasionally suffered excommunication and signification: apparitors (i.e., summoners),[114] notaries public,[115] proctors,[116] and in one instance an ecclesiastical judge.[117] Members of the lower clergy of every office, beneficed and unbeneficed — including such well known names as Master Nicholas Hereford[118] and John Ball[119] — comprise a notable number of the excommunicates.

---

[108] C.85/178/3. There can be no doubt that the abbot of Sawley went to prison due to this writ (Prynne, pp. 1146, 1198).

[109] See *infra* Appendix C, p. 177.

[110] C.85/90/15.

[111] Master William Lupus, who was signified by the archbishop of Canterbury, repented and was delivered in 1254 (*CCR, 1254-56*, p. 19).

[112] Master John de Appelby was signified by Archbishop Simon Sudbury on 17 May 1376 (C.85/10/27).

[113] Master John Macworth had been excommunicated by Master John Tylney, commissary of the bishop of Lincoln, who signified him for capture on 7 Feb. 1448 (C.85/112/38) and again on 5 Feb. 1449 (*ibid.*, no. 39). His absolution was signified on 3 July 1449 (*ibid.*, no. 41). On the controversial career of Macworth, see *Statutes of Lincoln Cathedral* (eds. H. Bradshaw and C. Wordsworth; Cambridge, 1892-79) 2. clxii-cxc.

[114] In 1281 (C.85/3/41), 1287 (C.85/100/67), and 1292 (C.85/35/35).

[115] In 1321 (C.85/120/4) and 1447 (C.85/138/1).

[116] In 1298 (C.85/88/21) and 1309 (C.85/7/37).

[117] Master Richard Elys, official of the Worcester consistory, imposed an excommunication on William Twyte, chaplain of the Calendaries, Bristol. The sentence was appealed to the court of the Arches, where the excommunication was judged unjust. Elys was ordered to pay the expenses which Twyte had incurred by reason of his appeal. Elys refused, was excommunicated, and, at length, was signified for capture in July 1432 (C.85/15/29).

[118] See *infra* Appendix E, p. 193.

[119] He appears six different times in the signification files. He was signified by Simon Sudbury, bishop of London, on 24 Oct. 1364 and was identified as "a priest staying in our diocese awhile" (C.85/121/4). Archbishop Whitlesey signified him as "a priest of our jurisdiction" on 28 May 1372 (C.85/11/14; London, Lambeth Palace Libr., Reg. Wytleseye, f. 53r). As archbishop of

The majority of *excommunicati capiendi* were lay persons. Among these would be found lords of the manor,[120] knights,[121] and squires;[122] local officials such as bailiffs[123] and reeves;[124] gentlemen, yeomen, and husbandmen;[125] citizens of cities such as London,[126] Wells,[127] York,[128] Carlisle,[129] and Hereford.[130] A list of excommunicates would include representatives of nearly every trade and craft; there would be skinner, tanner, currier,

Canterbury, Simon Sudbury requested his arrest on 9 Dec. 1376, describing him as "a priest recently of our diocese and of our province"; the writ was sent out of chancery to the sheriff of Essex (C.85/10/25 and dorse; *CPR, 1374-77*, p. 415). Sudbury on 21 Sept. 1377 again signified Ball, "a priest of Norwich diocese," who was excommunicated for disobeying mandates and warnings made to him by Sudbury, when he was bishop of London, and who remained under sentence for more than three years (C.85/10/28). Two years later William Courtenay, bishop of London, calling Ball a "capellanus," requested his capture (C.85/122/10). In 1381 Sudbury again took action. On 26 April he ordered his commissary to have Ball denounced as excommunicate (Wilkins 3. 152-53). Three days later he requested a writ for his arrest and the writ was duly sent to the sheriff of Kent (C.85/10/41 and dorse). The host of Kent released him on 11 June from the jail at Maidstone (this surely was the royal jail, but see Miss May McKisack, *The Fourteenth Century, 1307-1399* (Oxford, 1959), p. 408, who describes it as the archbishop's jail), and three days later Sudbury was beheaded at Tower Hill. Cf., *Fasciculi Zizaniorum* (ed. W. W. Shirley; R. S., 1858), p. 274.

[120] E.g., Reginald Malore, lord of Tachbrook, was signified by the bishop of Coventry and Lichfield on 24 Nov. 1314 and a writ for his arrest was issued to the sheriff of Warwicks. (C.85/56/24 and dorse).

[121] A sizeable number of significations concerning knights are extant for the late thirteenth and early fourteenth centuries. E.g., Reginald de Balum, kt., was signified by the bishop of Salisbury on 4 Jan., 22 Jan., and 1 April 1283 (C.85/145/75, 74, 77).

[122] E.g., William Caru, esq., of London diocese, was excommunicated for failing to pay his wife Rose two marks weekly alimony and was signified by Archbishop Arundel on 8 Aug. 1402 (C.85/12/30).

[123] E.g., Roger, bailiff of Cropedy, Oxon., was signified by the chancellor of Oxford on 29 March 1337 (C.85/208/2; Salter, pp. 29, 32).

[124] E.g., in 1287 Bishop Sutton of Lincoln requested the capture of Hugh, reeve of Milton (C.85/100/69).

[125] The fifteenth-century material from Coventry and Lichfield, mentioned below, shows men of these three ranks as subject to this procedure.

[126] E.g., William Balshale, citizen and tanner of the city of London, parishioner of St. Gregory-by-St. Paul's, was signified as excommunicate on 5 Feb. 1395 by Archbishop Courtenay (C.85/11/97). Balshale soon appealed to the apostolic see and on 20 Feb. 1395 at his request a writ superseding was sent to the sheriffs of London, requiring them likewise to cite the archbishop to appear in King's Bench on the quindene of Easter; the archbishop failed to appear and Balshale was acquitted (C. 47/111/22/ piece of that date, and dorse).

[127] William le Smith, citizen of Wells, was signified on 12 Feb. 1327 (*Reg. Drokensford, Bath and Wells*, p. 255).

[128] C.85/169/25.

[129] C.85/194/15.

[130] C.85/85/17.

saddler, glover, and shoemaker; weaver, draper, fuller, dyer, milliner, hatter, tailor, and mercer; brewer and vintner; scrivener, textwriter, book-binder, and stationer; smith, goldsmith, and locksmith; boatman, fisherman, and fishmonger; cooper, carpenter, mason, and slater; physician, surgeon, and apothecary; butcher and grocer; wire-drawer, armorer, and ironmonger; cartmaker and carter. Not even schoolmasters and scholars escaped. Some of the excommunicates were simply described as laborers or servants, although on occasion a cook or a groom was identified as such. Among the women who were signified for arrest were married women, widows, unmarried women, and concubines. Not all the persons signified were English and Welsh. In 1264 three French monks were signified by the bishop of Worcester,[131] and the surnames of six persons who were signified by the bishop of London in 1393 would invite the conclusion that they were aliens.[132]

The absence of any indication of occupation or status in most of the significations renders difficult any generalizations in this regard. Fortunately, the statute of 1 Henry V, c. 5, which required that certain kinds of writs should indicate the estate, degree, or mystery of the conversant,[133] was incorrectly interpreted by the chancery of the bishop of Coventry and Lichfield to pertain to the writ *de excommunicato capiendo*. As a consequence, the significations emanating from that chancery normally made mention of these details from the time of the statute until 1442.[134] During this period 75 persons (69 men and 6 women) were signified from this diocese. Of the 69 men only 8 were not identified in this way, yet 4 of these had occupational surnames (Smith, Milward, Webster, Ditcher), which with some assurance can be understood as designating their occupations.[135] An analysis of these 65 men shows that there were 25 husbandmen, 20 clerics (including 12 who had not paid the clerical subsidy and the Benedictine prior of Canwell), 5 yeomen, 2 gentlemen, 2 *literati*, 2 smiths, 2 millers, and one baker, ditcher, mason, slater, tailor, webster, and wire-drawer. Of the women 2 received no further identification; of the rest there were 2 servants, one widow, and a nun whom the mason had

---

[131] C.85/159/19.

[132] James Lumbard, Margaret van Briddey, William van Brussell, Ireton Gascoyn, Katherine Gascoyne, and William van Bergh (C.85/123/6).

[133] This applied to writs of actions personal, appeals, and indictments (*Statutes* 2. 171). Inclusion of the writ *de excommunicato capiendo* within the requirements of this statute was made by 5 Eliz. I, c. 23, no. 7 (*ibid.*, 4, 1, p. 453).

[134] From C.85/61/18 to C.85/62/40.

[135] Two men whose occupations are mentioned have surnames corresponding to their occupations: Richard Baxter, baxter (C.85/62/25), and Richard Milward, miller (*ibid.*, no. 30).

taken to wife. Impossible as it is to project these statistics onto a larger canvas, they nonetheless demonstrate in one diocese over a 28 year period the broad spectrum of society which was subject to capture as excommunicates.

IV. THE NUMBER OF EXCOMMUNICATES SIGNIFIED TO THE SECULAR ARM FOR ARREST[136]

It is not possible to plot with absolute accuracy the number of persons against whom the writ *de excommunicato capiendo* was sued, since the surviving signification files are admittedly incomplete. The accompanying graph and table propose to show in five-year totals from 1250 to 1534 the number of excommunicates in the *extant* significations.

Is it possible to gauge the relative completeness of these files? In an effort to gain some control over this question all external references to signification which have been encountered have been noted: sometimes significations were enregistered by the bishop's scribe or entered on the chancery rolls, sometimes cases were pursued further in either the ecclesiastical or secular courts. In all, 690 external references to cases in which the bishops had written to the king for the capture of excommunicates were found in these sources. A comparison of them against the extant files shows that with reference to these 690 significations the files are 75% complete; that is, in 516 cases some traces were found in the files. These 516 cases represent 6.8% of the total number of extant significations. Although a sampling of this size cannot provide the basis for general conclusions, it does provide the only possible reference for any attempted correlation.

One further *caveat*. It should be emphasized that a very large number — perhaps the majority — of cases of signification were *ad instantiam* cases. This meant that the litigation, excommunication, and signification depended on the initiative of a third party and not the church. The accompanying graph and table cannot, therefore, be used as a measure either of medieval *mores* or of ecclesiastical discipline; peak periods and low periods cannot with certainty be ascribed to determinable factors. Tempted as one may be to relate the peak of the late thirteenth century to the active

---

[136] It must be noted that the persons mentioned in this section are persons whose names appear on the signification files. This means, in effect, that writs were issued for their arrest. It is not suggested here that all of them were in fact arrested. On the number actually arrested see *infra* pp. 110-112. Procedures to thwart or, at least, to delay arrest were available; see *infra* chapters 4 and 5.

policies of Archbishop Pecham and the peak of the late fourteenth century to the efforts to collect the clerical subsidy, one must walk very warily indeed. The quantitative relationship between the extant files and the original files as well as the actual percentage of *ex officio* cases will perhaps never be known and in their absence firm conclusions are impossible.

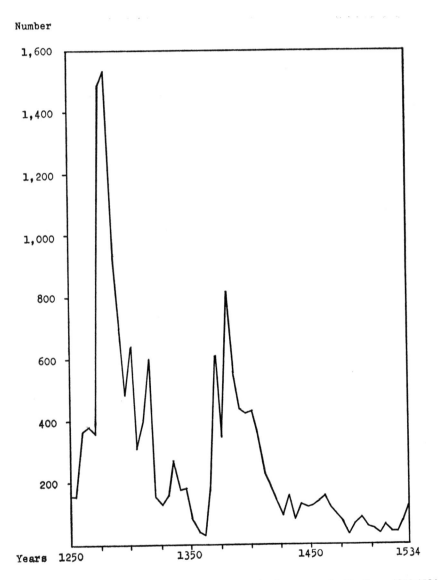

Fig. 1. — Graph of the number of excommunicates in the extant significations, 1250-1534.

Years	Number of excommunicates	Years	Number of excommunicates	Years	Number of excommunicates
1250-54	157	1350-54	79	1450-54	125
1255-59	152	1355-59	41	1455-59	146
1260-64	361	1360-64	29	1460-64	159
1265-69	380	1365-69	180	1465-69	124
1270-74	353	1370-74	613	1470-74	102
1275-79	1,443	1375-79	346	1475-79	68
1280-84	1,536	1380-84	812	1480-84	34
1285-89	935	1385-89	563	1485-89	70
1290-94	702	1390-94	441	1490-94	89
1295-99	485	1395-99	431	1495-99	61
1300-04	641	1400-04	435	1500-04	37
1305-09	302	1405-09	341	1505-09	39
1310-14	402	1410-14	235	1510-14	65
1315-19	594	1415-19	192	1515-19	47
1320-24	159	1420-24	147	1520-24	37
1325-29	131	1425-29	98	1525-29	61
1330-34	158	1430-34	160	1530-34	120
1335-39	273	1435-39	86	undated	373
1340-44	179	1440-44	133		
1345-49	183	1445-49	124	Grand total	16,869

Fig. 2. — Detailed tabulation of the number of excommunicates in the extant significations, 1250-1534.

V. Heretics and the Secular Arm

Several procedures were available to the English bishops in the late middle ages for invoking the secular arm against heretics and persons suspect of heresy. Only one of these was procedure by the writ *de excommunicato capiendo*. Just as this writ was used in cases concerning marriage, testaments, sacrilege, defamation, etc., so it could be and, in fact, was used in cases concerning "heretical pravity." The excommunication was imposed not for heresy but for contumacy, and it was *qua excommunicatus* that the heretic was subject to the constraint of the secular arm. Undue emphasis should not be given to heresy cases in the development of the procedure against excommunicates. Such cases were very few in number — one would look in vain to find more than 13 — and these were in no way formative.[137]

[137] For a listing of these cases found in the files of significations, and for an example of this type of signification see *infra* Appendix E, pp. 189-194. The provisions made by convocation for dealing with trials of persons suspect of heresy have been admirably set forth by Professor E. F. Jacob (*Reg. Chichele, Canterbury* 1. cxxix-cxxxviii).

Before 1382 no specific procedure existed in England for invoking the secular arm against heretics. Unless *ad hoc* arrangements were made — and this seems to have happened in the thirteenth century[138] — the bishop would have recourse to the machinery available against obdurate ex-communicates. This state of affairs could continue only as long as heresy cases were rare. The old methods were found inadequate to deal with the lollards and, as a result, the bishops of the Canterbury province in 1382 (and those of the York province two years later) requested the king for a specific procedure for dealing with heretics. By the new arrangement which resulted from their request the bishops were provided with commissions which allowed them to demand directly (i.e., without recourse to the royal chancery) the assistance of the sheriffs and other royal officials in handling heretics. At that, the penalty which the secular arm would impose extended only to imprisonment.[139] Confiscation of property was not added as a penalty until 1388.[140]

The principal change in the secular penalty came in 1401 with the statute *de heretico comburendo*. Heresy now became a secular offense; it was punishable by death by burning. When sentence of condemnation was made against a person who had refused to abjure or who had relapsed after abjuration, the sheriff or other local officer was to be present, if the bishop required it, to receive the heretic for public burning.[141] This statute did not establish a procedure by royal writ. In fact, there was no statutory basis for a writ *de heretico comburendo* until 1534 (25 Henry VIII, c. 14).[142] According to Sir Anthony Fitzherbert, the early sixteenth-century jurist, this was the reason why this writ was lacking in the registers of writs.[143]

---

[138] These early cases have been described by Stubbs *The Constitutional History of England* (Oxford, 1880) 3. 381, n. 1; and *Report of the Ecclesiastical Courts Commission, 1883 (Parliamentary Papers,* vol. 24, 1883, Historical Appendix no. 2, p. 52), Makower (*The Constitutional History and Constitution of the Church of England* (Eng. trans.; London, 1895), pp. 183-84), Maitland (Pollock and Maitland 2. 547-551), and H. G. Richardson ("Heresy and the Lay Power under Richard II," *EHR* 51 (1936) 1-4).

[139] A detailed account of these provisions is found in Richardson, especially pp. 7-8. A summary of the bishops' requests for legislation against lollards during the reign of Richard II is given by Richardson and G. O. Sayles, "Parliamentary Documents from Formularies," *BIHR* 11 (1933-34) 147-62.

[140] Wilkins 3. 204. More precise provisions for property confiscation were made by 2 Henry V (1414-15), c. 7 (*Statutes* 2. 181-84).

[141] *Ibid.* 2. 127-28; Wilkins 3. 254-56; London, Lambeth Palace Libr., Reg. Arundel 1. 56^(r-v). Its provisions are explained by Stubbs (*Const. Hist.* 3. 33-35, 386-87) and Makower (p. 187). Do we hear in the provision for the presence of the royal officer at the condemnation a distant echo of the Constitutions of Clarendon, c. 3 (*Select Charters*, pp. 164-65) ?

[142] *Statutes* 3. 454-55.

[143] Anthony Fitzherbert, *The New Natura Brevium* (London, 1730), pp. 601-02.

Yet his contention that the writ was not to be sued because the statute of 1401 did not provide for it was gainsaid by actual practice. In 1401 even before the enactment of the statute the writ was issued against William Sawtre, and it is in fact the form of this writ which is contained in Fitzherbert.[144] For the years 1467 to 1533 fifteen requests for this writ have been uncovered.[145] Likewise, in a fragmentary "register" of writs which can be dated *ca.* 1430 the form of the writ *de heretico comburendo* was included.[146] A few months before the enactment of the statute of 1534 Bishop Stokesley of London indicated to chancery that the mayor and one of the sheriffs of London were present when he uttered the sentence of condemnation against two heretics and that the heretics were "relinquished" to the secular officers. Stokesley's request led to the issuance of the writ *de heretico comburendo* on the following day.[147] The procedure in this case obviously combined the provisions of the statute of 1401 and the writ *de heretico comburendo*. The same procedure may have been followed in the other cases where this writ was sued before 1534.

The statutes of 1382 and 1401, it must be emphasized, did not abolish use of the writ *de excommunicato capiendo* in heresy cases; they merely added two further strings to the bishop's bow. Between 1382 and 1401 the bishop had two alternatives in seeking secular aid against heretics: the writ *de excommunicato capiendo* or the direct request to the local sheriff. At least three requests for this writ were made at this time (one each in 1387, 1391, and 1392). From 1401 to 1534 he apparently enjoyed three alternatives: he could treat the person as an excommunicate and request the usual writ; or he could treat him as a condemned heretic and, it would seem, either "relinquish" him directly to the sheriff for burning without the benefit of writ[148] or sue out of chancery the writ *de heretico comburendo*.

---

[144] *Ibid.* It is likewise in *Foedera* 8. 178; *Rot. Parl.* 3, 459. Maitland discusses the form of the punishment used against Sawtre and finds its justification in the canon law ("The Deacon and the Jewess," *Roman Canon Law in the Church of England* (London, 1898), pp. 176-77).

[145] For a list of these and for an example see *infra* Appendix E, pp. 191-94.

[146] London, BM, Add. MS. 35,205, mem. 6. This MS differs from the other registers of writs in that it is not a book but a roll and omits many of the more usual writs. The form of the writ found therein is that used against "W. de S. aliquando capellanum," undoubtedly William de Sawtre.

[147] For his request see *infra* Appendix E, pp. 194. Although there is no formal request in this document, the bishop relinquished them to the secular arm and to its punishment; it would be naive to assume that Stokesley did not know that his "certification" would lead to the issuance of the writ *de heretico comburendo*.

[148] I am grateful to Dr. John Fines for the information that in his research on heresy cases in the Coventry-Lichfield diocese in the fifteenth and early sixteenth centuries he has not encountered use of this direct method.

For this period the more lenient procedure was obviously the signification of excommunication; three such significations survive (one each for 1468, 1509, and 1529). Not enough details are known of these cases to allow certain conclusions, but it seems quite probable that these cases involved persons suspect of heresy who contracted contumacy by not coming to court when cited. It was the use of this writ in cases of suspicion of heresy that St. Thomas More defended on two occasions.[149] For the past twenty and thirty years, he maintained, such cases came only from the dioceses of Lincoln and London and their numbers were fewer than the number of judges sitting in either of the king's courts.[150]

---

[149] *The Apology,* chap. 46 and *The Debellacyon of Salem and Bizance,* chapt. 17 (English Works, London, 1557).

[150] *Debellacyon,* pp. 1005-06.

CHAPTER III

THE SIGNIFICATION PROCEDURE

PERSISTENCE in contumacy for more than forty days after excommunication rendered a person liable to signification. There was nothing further which the church could do; her severest penalty had been used without effect. For further action she could turn only to the secular arm for assistance in the hope that the capture of the excommunicate's body might spur his soul to repentance. By the thirteenth century there had been developed a definite procedure by which the force of the secular arm was brought to bear upon excommunicates. By the time that the excommunicate found himself lodged in a royal jail his case had been carried by a series of steps from the ecclesiastical court to the bishop, to the royal chancery, and finally to the sheriff and his agents. Throughout our entire period the signification procedure, reduced to its essential elements, meant that at the request of bishops the royal chancery issued writs to sheriffs for the arrest of excommunicates and for their detention until absolved.

I. Procedure in the Ecclesiastical Court

The canon law clearly intended that excommunication be used more to coerce the *contumax* to abandon his contumacy than to punish him for it. It is irrelevant that an individual judge may have acted vindictively and not medicinally when he imposed a particular sentence of excommunication, for the effects of the sentence were established by law in order to attain the purpose intended by law. The excommunication, it was hoped, would lead the offender to forsake his contumacy and hold himself in obedience to the authority of the church. Sometimes it succeeded, sometimes it did not. In the latter case, the church having used her ultimate weapon unsuccessfully could turn to the secular arm for further action.

Obviously some period was required between the imposing of the excommunication and the invoking of the secular arm in order to give the "medicine" an opportunity to have an effect. In the general law, as transmitted by Gratian's *Decretum*, after the lapse of a year an excommunicate was considered suspect of heresy and subject to the consequences thereof.[1] In England, however, the period of "more than forty days" was sufficient to establish obduracy: *quadraginta dies et amplius.* Lyndwood noted that the English procedure differed from the general procedure found in Gratian: "Et licet talis regulariter sit expectandus usque ad annum, 11 q. 3 *rursus*, tamen in hoc regno quoad invocationem brachii saecularis sufficit ut labantur 40 dies."[2] Mention of this forty-day period of time is first found in Pseudo-Edward, the early twelfth-century collection of laws.[3] Yet Archbishop Theobald decreed in the legatine council of 1151 that after the lapse of a full year an excommunicate could suffer disherison by the secular arm.[4]

In the absence of further material for the twelfth century it would be idle to speculate about actual practice. The fact remains, however, that when records emerge in the thirteenth century they reveal procedure on the basis of a period of forty days.[5] And so it remained through the rest of the middle ages.

---

[1] One encounters this in Gratian's *Decretum* (C.11 q.3 c.36, which is c.12 of the 5th Council of Carthage, A.D. 401), whence it soon became common teaching.

[2] 5.17. c. Auctoritate dei patris, v. *contemnentes* (ed., p. 348).

[3] "Et si eorum sententiam defugiendo uel superbe contempnendo paruipenderit, ad regem de eo clamor deferetur post dies XL" (*Die Gesetze der Angelsachsen* (ed. F. Liebermann; Halle, 1903-1916) 1. 631; for the full text see *supra* p. 21, n. 29).

[4] "Sanctorum patrum vestigia secuti precipimus ut hii qui anathematis sententia condemnantur, si per annum integrum in ea pertinaciter perseverent infames et detestabiles habeantur, ut neque in testimoniis neque in causis audiantur, et in principis sit potestate ipsos exheredare" (Avrom Saltman, *Theobald, Archbishop of Canterbury* (London, 1956), p. 548).

[5] This period is mentioned in the earliest extant signification (1216 × 1221); see *infra* Appendix B, p. 162. Likewise, the synodal statutes which Professor Cheney dates conjecturally 1225 × 1230 and which he attributes possibly to Hugh Foliot, bishop of Hereford, mention this period of time with reference to excommunications (*Councils* 2. 194). Specific mention too is found in a case in the *curia regis* in 1226 (*Curia Regis Rolls* 12. 426). In the following year when the king described the English procedure to his justiciar in Ireland, he said that the letters of the bishops requesting secular assistance testify that the excommunicates had remained under sentence "per xl dies et amplius" (see *infra* Appendix A, p. 161). Similarly, it was a period of forty days which was given to a felon in sanctuary to abjure the realm, and after that period, if he had not abjured, he could be seized (see R. F. Hunnisett, *The Medieval Coroner* (Cambridge, 1961), chap. 3). Forty-day periods are mentioned four times in Magna Carta in four different clauses (nos. 7, 14, 48, 61; *Select Charters*, pp. 294-95, 298, 301). On the continent this period was applied to excommunicates in certain places. For example, Simon de Montfort required money payments (*emenda*) of Albigensians after forty days (Auguste Molinier, ed., "Catalogue des actes de Simon et d'Amauri de Montfort," *Bibliothèque de l'école des chartes* 34 (1873) 453-54). The same period was used before the imposition of aggravated penalties by synods at Bordeaux in 1214 (*Foedera* 1. 1. 122) and Le Mans in 1247 (Mansi 23. 760). And the practice in the Duchy of Normandy of capturing excommunicates and seizing their property was based on a forty-day period according to a decretal

The lapse of forty days established the assumption that the excommunication had not secured its desired effect. It was not unusual during the thirteenth century for a contumacious person who remained unmoved by excommunication to be called "incorrigible." This meant simply that the church had been unable to effect his correction. The notion of incorrigibility appears to have contained two elements: first, the failure of the person to repent and, secondly, the inability of the church to use any more forceful means of correction. Incorrigibility constituted in canon law the general criterion for invoking the secular arm: "a principibus corrigantur quos ecclesia corrigere von valet."[6] It was applied to criminous clerics before they would be handed over to the secular jurisdiction.[7] It was applied, too, to obdurate excommunicates. "Cum ecclesia non habeat ultra quid faciat in hac parte" was the phrase consistently used in the significations.[8] Continued contumacy for more than forty days in the face of excommunication was sufficient to determine a person incorrigible and render him liable to signification.

The *terminus a quo* for this period was probably midnight after the excommunication, although it is possible that the period was reckoned *de momento ad momentum* from the time of the sentence.[9] The addition of the words "et amplius" in describing this period meant that forty complete days must elapse: on the fortieth day itself signification could not be made. The *terminus ad quem* was midnight at the end of the fortieth day. Hence, if a person was excommunicated on the last day of March, the earliest day on which a signification could be issued was the eleventh of May.

It has been assumed thus far in this discussion that the period was reckoned from the excommunication of the contumacious person. This,

---

letter of Innocent IV in 1254 (Potthast 15454; for the text see the long footnote in the Richter-Friedberg edition of the *Corpus Iuris Canonici* (Leipzig, 1879-1881) 2. 1096-1100). The origin of the forty-day period is a matter of speculation. Its appearance in early penitential books would suggest some connection with the forty days of Lent and, perhaps, ultimately with the forty days of Christ in the desert described in the synoptic gospels (see J. T. McNeill and H. M. Gamer, *Medieval Handbooks of Penance* (*Records of Civilization, Sources and Studies*, no. 29; New York, 1938), pp. 102-05, 108, 111, 113-115, *et alibi*).

[6] Gratian's capitulation to C.11 q.1 c.20.

[7] See R. Genestal, *Le privilegium fori en France du décret de Gratien à la fin du XIVe siècle* (Bibliothèque de l'École des hautes études, Sciences religieuses, vols. 35 and 39, 1921-24) 2. 10-12, 46-48, 89-92, 129-130); C. Duggan, "The Becket Dispute and the Criminous Clerks," *BIHR* 35 (1962) 1-28.

[8] Similarly, almost the identically same phrase appeared in *Cum non ab homine*, the decretal letter of Celestine III (1191-98) which dealt with the *traditio curiae saeculari* of criminous clerics (X 2.1.10; Jaffé 17639).

[9] See A. van Hove, *De consuetudine. De temporis supputatione* (Mechlin, 1933), pp. 239-244.

however, needs some modification. Although the overwhelming majority of significations stated that the person had remained under sentence of excommunication for more than forty days, many significations described the person as having remained under sentence of excommunication for more than forty days "post suam denunciacionem." Use of this expression varied widely. It was first used in significations by the archbishop of Canterbury in 1309[10] and was used occasionally by other bishops from the end of the fourteenth century, but not consistently; it does appear as common form in the dioceses of Canterbury, London, Norwich, and Winchester in the early sixteenth century. Yet in the significations from other dioceses (e.g., Ely, Coventry and Lichfield) the expression does not appear at all. Without doubt the *terminus a quo* in some cases and not just in cases of *ipso facto* excommunication was taken to be the denunciation of the person as an excommunicate.

Publicity of excommunication was directed to bringing knowledge of the sentence to the excommunicate himself, if he had been contumaciously absent from court when sentenced, and to his neighbours.[11] Such publicity was required in addition to sentence; it established the presumption that the excommunicate and the local Christian community were not ignorant of the sentence. A certain amount of publicity attended the actual giving of sentence, yet in addition it was usual for the excommunication to be announced on three successive Sundays at the parish church of the excommunicate, in the neighboring parishes, and perhaps, on occasion, in all the parishes of the deanery. Ioannes Andreae, writing *ca.* 1340, clearly distinguished between publication attendant upon sentencing and subsequent denunciation,[12] yet Lyndwood, almost a century later, in his gloss on Stratford's constitution *Saeculi principes* held that denunciation would take place if the actual sentence were given "coram multitudine."[13]

The obvious question arises: What was the *terminus a quo* in cases whose significations contain the *post suam denunciationem* clause? If one follows

---

[10] C.85/7/29.

[11] The necessity of bringing the excommunication to the attention of the excommunicate's neighbors is stated in the *Decretum* in a chapter to which Gratian gave the heading: "Excommunicatorum nomina uicinis omnibus palam et publice annuncientur" (C.11 q.3 c.20). Archbishop Stratford in his statutes for the court of the Arches in 1342 observed that excommunications were often given occultly, whereas their publication should be made in the open (Wilkins 2. 693).

[12] *Glos. ord.* on *Clem.* 3.7.1, v. *publice*.

[13] 3.28. c. Saeculi principes, v. *excommunicati* (ed., p. 254): "Ab homine vel a jure, et supple pro talibus denunciati, nam tunc excommunicatio est publica... Scias tamen, quod sufficit pro denunciatione, si veniat ad notitiam excommunicati, vel quod in judicio coram multitudine feratur sententia excommunicationis." Cf., *Glos. ord.* X 2.25.12, v. *publice* and 2.27.24, v. *ad probandum.*

Lyndwood, then theoretically it could have been either the actual sentencing, if the circumstances assured sufficient publicity, or the parochial denunciation. The actual practice is not easy to determine. In a number of cases in which the significations mentioned specifically that the excommunicate had been denounced in his parish church, parochial denunciation was clearly the *terminus a quo*;[14] in these cases the forty-day period would have been reckoned from the final of the three denunciations. In lack of further evidence it would be rash to suggest that parochial denunciation was used as the *terminus a quo* in all cases or even in the cases containing the denunciation clause. To be sure, Lyndwood in his gloss on Stratford's constitution *Saeculi principes* tells the reader to supply to the word "excommunicati" the words "et pro talibus denuntiati." Yet in that same gloss he allows that denunciation could take place in sentencing.[15] The emphasis throughout our period was on the fact that the excommunicate had remained under sentence for more than forty days. Perhaps it was to avoid the objection from an excommunicate that, although he had in fact remained under sentence for forty days, he had not remained so *knowingly*, since knowledge of the sentence came to him only some time later, that some bishops reckoned the time from the actual denunciation.

The significations of excommunication do not indicate the exact period which had elapsed. The expression *quadraginta dies et amplius* can conceal under the words *et amplius* periods of time extending from days into years. Significations were not sent by the bishops automatically at the end of forty days; the decision to signify was left in *ex officio* cases to the discretion of the judge and in *ad instantiam* cases to the initiative of the other party. The amount of time elapsing between the end of forty days and the issuance of the signification was subject to wide variation. In some cases longer periods were mentioned: sixty days,[16] almost eighty days,[17] twelve weeks,[18] three months,[19] four months,[20] six months,[21] one year,[22] one year and a half,[23]

---

[14] E.g., Richard Voyse was reported in a signification dated 8 April 1464 as having been denounced in the parish church of Studley, Bath and Wells diocese, of which he was a parishioner (C.85/81/13).

[15] See *supra* p. 75, n. 13.

[16] *Ely Diocesan Remembrancer*, no. 115 (Dec. 1894 - Jan. 1895), p. 347.

[17] "Per xl dies et fere tanto tempore duplicato" (C.85/44/2; cf., Salzman, p. 130).

[18] "Per duodecim ebdomodas et amplius" (C.85/188/27).

[19] C.85/82/10.

[20] C.85/23/2.

[21] C.85/10/9; C.85/76/19; C.85/90/27.

[22] C.85/11/82, 86; C.85/77/15, 27; C.85/82/11; C.85/86/13; C.85/90/14; C.85/93/12; C.85/124/41; C.85/126/24; C.85/144/1; C.85/153/31, 34; C.85/184/6; C.85/210/4.

[23] C.85/43/28; Salzman, p. 128.

almost two years,[24] two years,[25] three years,[26] four years,[27] eight years,[28] ten years,[29] and even twenty years.[30] In a few other cases it is possible to determine how much time passed. For example, John Towghton of Beckley, Sussex, was excommunicated by the archdeacon of Lewes in the church of Brightling on 23 June 1473 and his capture was requested by the bishop of Chichester on the following 13 August, i.e., 49 days later.[31] There was also the man from Worcester diocese who was excommunicated on 1 June 1475 and signified on 5 August after a lapse of 64 days.[32] In another case, the excommunication of Edmund de Hoo was signified in 1304 with mention of the period of "forty days and more,"[33] although he had been excommunicated as early as 1292.[34] Clearly the use of *quadraginta dies et amplius* indicated merely that the legal period allowed for the medicinal effect of excommunication had elapsed; the phrase in no way gives any indication of the period in excess of forty days — be it of days or of years — which had passed before the invoking of the secular arm.

The passing of forty days rendered an excommunicate "signifiable," but actual signification followed only after certain steps had been taken. In the first place, since signification was not automatic, it was necessary for someone to initiate the procedure. In criminal cases it was the judge who exercised discretion in this regard, and his action was probably motivated by the seriousness of the crime and the nuisance value of the criminal. In civil cases it was the instancer who would petition the court to invoke the secular arm. There is no way of determining the proportion of "signified" to "signifiable," but in view of the discretion allowed judge and instancer the proportion was probably quite variable.

If the judge or instancer wished the assistance of the secular power, nothing could be done until the court issued a decree that the secular arm was to be invoked. This could be done straightway upon verifying the lapse of forty days and the failure of the excommunicate to desist from his contumacy. Alternatively, the judge could cite peremptorily the excommuni-

---

[24] C.85/150/2.
[25] C.85/4/29; C.85/9/45; C.85/214/1.
[26] C.85/10/28; C.85/124/14.
[27] C.85/75/62.
[28] C.85/59/75.
[29] C.85/9/19; C.85/12/27; C.85/78/10.
[30] *Reg. Pecham, Canterbury*, pp. 100-01.
[31] See *infra* Appendix B, p. 166.
[32] C.85/165/31.
[33] C.85/6/76.
[34] C.85/4/53.

cate to appear before him on a certain day to show cause why the secular arm ought not to be invoked. If he failed to show adequate cause or if he absented himself contumaciously, the judge would then issue the decree. This term *causam quare non* gave the excommunicate an opportunity to disprove his contumacy. Further, the three or four weeks usually intervening between the citation and the juridical day on which the excommunicate was to appear allowed him, under virtual threat of capture, the occasion to desist from his contumacy and seek absolution. A less obvious reason for using this procedure was noted by Lyndwood, viz., it provided the ecclesiastical judge with a strong argument against the contumacious person in the event of a subsequent appeal.[35] Although the advantages of the use of the term *causam quare non* were many, it remained optional during our period. Lyndwood's gloss clearly assumed that the judge enjoyed the choice of citing to this term or not.[36] Examples of judges making use of this term survive for the thirteenth, fourteenth, and fifteenth centuries.[37] Lyndwood himself as official of the court of the Arches probably made frequent use of it, if one can judge from the entries in Chichele's register.[38] In most cases, however, there is no evidence that the term was used and in some cases positive evidence that it was not.[39] As in so many aspects of judicial procedure, the decision to cite to this term was left to the discretion of the ecclesiastical judge.

[35] "Et omissis argumentis in contrarium huic parti adhaereo, salvo judicio melius sentientis. Et haec opinio magis justificabitur ex hoc, si judex ecclesiasticus post lapsum 40 dierum citari fecerit excommunicatum ad proponendum causam rationabilem, quare non debeat scribi pro corporis sui captione, limitando sibi ad hoc terminum. In quo termino si comparens nullam causam proposuerit, vel per contumaciam abfuerit, imputet sibi ipsi quare tunc vel antea praetextu appellationis interpositae se non defendebat coram judice, a quo sententia hujusmodi fuit lata: ad cujus officium spectat dictam appellationem recipere, vel non recipere, ut notat Spec. ti. de appella. § nunc dicamus in principio" (Lyndwood 5.17. c. Praeterea contingit, v. *dari debet*; ed., pp. 351-52). The argument was simply that the appellant would be at the disadvantage of having to explain in the court of appeal why he had not appeared at this term in the lower court to prove that the excommunication was unjust.

[36] See preceding note. Yet, according to a formulary book of the court of the Arches probably of the late thirteenth century, "Debet excommunicatus citari antequam scribatur pro eius capcione" (London, Inner Temple, Petyt MS. 511.3, f. 39ᵛ). A form of the citation to the term *causam quare non* likewise appears in a York formulary book of the fifteenth century (Cambridge Univ. Libr., Add. MS. 3115, ff. 2ᵛ-3ʳ).

[37] *Reg. le Romeyn*, York 1. 54, n. 2; *Reg. Woodlock*, Winchester 1. 22-24, 80-81, 82-84, 241, 360, 489-490, 604-05, 655-56; *Reg. Sutton*, Lincoln 4. 41; *Reg. Baldock*, London. p. 40; *Reg. Sandale, Winchester*, pp. 73-74; *Reg. Wykeham*, Winchester 2. 138-140, 142; Reg. Courtney (London, Lambeth Pal. Libr.), ff. 11, 52ᵛ-53ʳ; *Reg. Chichele*, Canterbury 3, 392-93; 4. 152-53, 160-61, 201, 296.

[38] In addition to the Chichele references in the preceding note, see *ibid.*, 4. 284.

[39] E.g., the 49 days which elapsed between excommunication and signification in the case of John Towghton (see *supra* p. 77, and *infra* Appendix B, p. 166) would scarcely have allowed sufficient time after the fortieth day for citation.

Once continued contumacy was established whether by use of this term or not, the court decreed that the secular arm should be invoked. As a consequence of this decree a letter from the presiding judge was sent to the bishop in which he rehearsed at least the essential facts of the case and requested that the bishop signify the excommunicate.[40] If the bishop was himself acting as judge, a letter of this sort was obviously unnecessary; otherwise it was always used.

II. THE BISHOP'S REQUEST FOR SECULAR AID

The bishop normally assented to the request of the judge, and a signification issued from the episcopal chancery shortly thereafter. Usually the significations were drawn up within a week. For example, the official of the bishop of Bath and Wells requested the arrest of two excommunicates in a letter dated 28 September 1320, and the bishop sent to the royal chancery a signification under date of 30 September.[41] Some significations even bear the same date as the letter of request.[42] Delays were not unknown, and occasionally significations were not issued until more than a month later. For example, the keeper of the vacant see of Norwich was requested on 12 December 1415 to write for the capture of John Burton, dean of Lynn, but did not do so until the following 31 January.[43] Some delays were due to further efforts by the bishops to effect the reconciliation of the excommunicate as when Bishop Sutton of Lincoln ordered the dean of Preston to inform certain excommunicates that he was giving them a month in which to seek absolution before writing to the king.[44] A bishop

[40] After his trouble with Pecham and after the chancery decision on *auctoritas* (see *supra* pp. 37-39) Peter Quinel, bishop of Exeter, in a synodal statute of 1287 required that such letters coming to him should include the reason for the excommunication and the authority, whether ordinary or delegated, by which it was imposed (*Councils* 2. 1031). For an example of a request from an ecclesiastical judge see *infra* Appendix B, p. 175.

[41] The official's letter is found in *Reg. Drokensford, Bath and Wells*, pp. 180-81; the signification is C.85/37/10.

[42] E.g., Thomas Milling, bishop of Hereford, received a request dated 1 March 1480 from the archdeacon of Salop to invoke the secular arm against John Spencer (*Reg. Myllyng, Hereford*, p. 56) and issued a signification that same day (*ibid.*, pp. 56-57; C.85/93/13).

[43] *Reg. Chichele, Canterbury* 3. 392-94.

[44] The letter to the dean was sent on 19 Oct. 1293; they failed to seek absolution and were signified on 24 Nov. (*Reg. Sutton, Lincoln* 4. 122-23, 143; C.85/101/26). In a similar case, the bishop of Winchester on 19 Jan. 1308 informed the prior of Bermondsey that he had decided to write for his capture for non-payment of the subsidy due from the church of Camberwell, but that he would delay writing until after 2 Feb. in order to give him a further chance to pay (*Reg. Woodlock, Winchester* 1. 241). No record of his signification survives.

might on occasion have the excommunicate cited before him to show cause
why the signification should not be sent.[45] This happened, for example,
in 1306 when the archdeacon of London requested the bishop to signify
Raymond de Marsa, but the bishop "benignly" ordered him cited to a
term *causam quare non* before him.[46] Bishops obviously were not obliged to
act upon requests for significations, but in the face of a refusal a judge of an
inferior jurisdiction could appeal to the provincial court.[47] This happened,
for example, in 1316 when Roger Martival, bishop of Salisbury, having
received a request from the official of the prebendal jurisdiction of Bedwyn
for the capture of William Miller, refused to issue the signification "certis
ex causis quas sufficere reputamus," and the official thereupon made a
querela to the court of the Arches.[48] Delays and refusals, though not unknown
in the signification procedure, seem to have occurred by way of exception.

The signification which the bishop issued took the form of a letter patent,
under his seal, addressed to the king,[49] informing him that a certain person
or persons had remained obdurately excommunicate for more than forty
days and requesting that use be made of the secular arm.[50] At no time
could a writ be granted if the signification contained less information.
During the late thirteenth century the bishops became required to specify
that the excommunicate was "of our jurisdiction" or "of our diocese",
unless this was otherwise clear, and that the person had been excommunicated "by our ordinary authority."[51] Also, it became usual at about the
same time for the bishop to indicate that the excommunication had been
incurred because of contumacy. In 1304 Archbishop Corbridge of York
listed what he considered to be the essential elements: "per patentes

45 Whether the excommunicated person had already been cited by the judge to a *causam quare
non* is not clear in these cases.

46 *Reg. Baldock, London*, p. 40.

47 Lyndwode 5.17. c. Praeterea contingit, v. *praelatorum* ed., p. 350. See *supra* p. 25, n. 2.

48 The court directed the bishop to show cause within ten days to the official of Bedwyn
refusal or else have the excommunicate cited to appear in the Arches on the eighth juridical day
for his after a fortnight. Martival chose the latter course of action, and the records of the affair
end there. See Salisbury, Diocesan Registry, Reg. Martival 2. f. 274ᵛ and the printed *Reg. Martival, Salisbury* 2. 77-78.

49 Four examples have been noted of significations otherwise addressed: in 1346 one to the
chancellor (C.85/214/41) and one to the chancellor or his lieutenant (*ib.*, no. 40); in 1347 (C.85/
134/42) and in 1492 to the keeper of the realm (C.85/23/25).

50 For a selection of episcopal signification see *infra* Appendix B, pp. 162-67. On at least six
occasions the bishop merely forwarded the judge's request (*decretum*) to chancery (for a transcription of one of these see *infra* Appendix B, p. 175; the others are C.85/23/4; C.85/187/7;
C.85/188/5, 10, 11). On four other occasions notifications or certifications of excommunication
were sent instead of significations (C.85/13/32; C.85/62/33, 36; C.85/85/39).

51 See *supra* pp. 38-41.

litteras sigillo excommunicacionis signatas, qualiter et ob quam causam, saltem propter contumaciam et offensam, qua eciam auctoritate et quanto tempore excommunicati fuerint illi."[52] To obtain their effect significations during the rest of our period contained at least that much information which had become essential by the beginning of the fourteenth century. Examples of significations which chastely included the *essentialia* and little else can be found at almost any time.

Additional information is to be found in some significations of the thirteenth century and in the majority of significations in later centuries.[53] The amount of additional information which the bishops included varied considerably. The excommunicate might have been further identified by mention of his father,[54] his occupation or status,[55] the parish or place, sometimes, the county, where he lived.[56] The manner in which the ex-

---

[52] *Reg. Corbridge, York* 2. 84.

[53] The bishop probably included as much information in the signification as he had received in the letter of request from the ecclesiastical judge. A formulary book of the court of the Arches, possibly of the 1280's, contains two forms of request, one short and one long (London, Inner Temple, Petyt MS. 511.3, f. 39ᵛ): "*Litera officialis ad archiepiscopum pro capcione.* Venerabili in Christo patri ac domino domino I. dei gracia archiepiscopo suus humilis filius et deuotus officialis curie Cantuariensis salutem et tanto patri tam deuotam quam debitam in omnibus reuerenciam et honorem. Quia H. de T. rector seu porcionarius ecclesie de D. propter ipsius multiplicatas contumacias pariter et offensas manifestas in causis execucionis et diffamacionis in curia Cantuariensi motis et agitatis inter magistrum G. actorem ex parte una et dictum magistrum H. reum ex altera contractas sentencia maioris excommunicacionis eiusdem curie Cantuariensis auctoritate iam diu est, rite exstiterat, innodatus et per xl dies et amplius animo perseuerauit indurato et adhuc perseuerare non formidat sic ligatus claues ecclesie nequiter contempnendo, paternitatem uestram reuerendam humiliter duxi supplicandam quatinus ad ipsius excommunicati insolenciam reprimendam inuocare uelitis brachium seculare ut quem dei timor a malo non reuocat secularis potestatis seueritas saltim coherceat a peccato. Valeat et uigeat reuerenda paternitas uestra semper in domino. Datum etc. *Ecce alia forma:* Domine uestre, tenore presencium significo quod W. de N. est excommunicacionis maioris sentencia innodatus auctoritate curie Cantuariensis ob offensam et in eadem per xl dies et amplius pertinaciter perstitit animo indurato. Propter quod iuste poterit quando nobis placuerit et ab ea cuius interest fuerit requisiti inuocare contra ipsum brachium tanquam contra clauium ecclesie contemptorem. In cuius rei testimonium sigillum officialis curie Cantuariensis apposui presentibus uestre sanctitatis manibus porrigendis. Datum etc."

[54] E.g., the abbot of St. Albans in a signification dated 20 Oct. 1298 requested the capture of Richard son of Alexander de Langeley (C.85/212/22). There is even one example of identification by mention of the mother, apparently a widow: James and William sons of Sarah de Newbridge (C.85/43/20; Salzman, p. 128). Identifications by reference to the father of the excommunicate was by no means common.

[55] See *supra* pp. 62-66.

[56] The practice of designating the parish or place where the excommunicate had his domicile was frequent throughout the entire period, yet a very considerable number of excommunicates were described merely as "of our jurisdiction." The extent to which a person's surname actually

communicate had committed contumacy might be added: he failed to come when cited, or he refused to heed the warnings of the court, or he declined to accept the sentence, or to perform the penance. Some significations mentioned not only the type of case involved and the name of the instancer but also the names of the judge and even the lawyers. Frequently the metropolitan would state that a case concerning the subject of a suffragan devolved to his jurisdiction by way of appeal or *querela* or by virtue of his metropolitical visitation.[57]

That part of the text of the signification containing the petition remained substantially the same at all times. The bishop confessed the inability of the church to effect the reconciliation of the excommunicate and prayed the king's assistance according to the custom of the realm. At times the request was left as general as that; at other times the king was asked "to justice his body" or to seize and detain him; still at other times the bishop specifically requested that a writ for capture be sent to a certain sheriff.[58] A *donec* clause was usually added to indicate that the secular constraint should last until the excommunicate was absolved. However general the wording of the petition may have been, there was no doubt in anyone's mind that the bishop was requesting issuance of the writ *de excommunicato capiendo*. It was usual for the bishop to add the hope that the secular power would succeed where the fear of God had failed in turning the excommunicate from his sin.

The inclusion of the names of several excommunicates in a single signification was not unusual. When more than one person was excommunicated for contumacy in the same case and became subject to signification, it was standard practice to include all the names in one signification.[59] If the bishop's scribe had a large number of names, he could put them on a separate schedule, which would be sewn to the signification. As many as

referred to his place of residence is not verifiable in many instances. Some bishops were content to describe the excommunicate solely by his county. Examples of this can be seen in the files of the bishops of Worcester, Coventry and Lichfield, and Hereford. Some bishops (e.g., the bishop of Bath and Wells) seldom if ever identified excommunicates by county. The archbishop of Canterbury would frequently designate the suffragan diocese to which the excommunicate belonged.

[57] It was not necessary for the bishop to state in the signification the actual date of the excommunication, although this was required in certifications of excommunication presented in the king's courts to prove the exception of excommunication (*Year Book 20 Henry VI*, no. 12).

[58] This was frequently done by the abbots of Bury St. Edmunds and the bishops of Ely and Hereford.

[59] From this generalization must be excepted those significations concerning failure to pay the clerical subsidies, for in these cases the bishops often grouped in one signification the defaulters from one or more archdeaconry.

51 names have been found on a single signification.[60] What was unusual, and perhaps irregular, was the inclusion in one signification of the names of persons who were excommunicated in different and unrelated cases. For example, in 1338 the bishop of Norwich signified six persons who had been excommunicated in different cases before his official.[61] On one occasion in 1451 Archbishop Stafford included on one piece of parchment three entirely separate significations, each complete with its own protocol and text.[62] In another unusual variation Archbishop Pecham requested in a single signification not only the writ *de excommunciato capiendo* but also the writ *de vi laica amovenda*, both in connection with the same case of unjust possession of a benefice.[63] All of these were merely exceptions to the customary practice of including in one signification only the names of persons excommunicated in the same case.[64]

Authentication was given to the signification by apposition of the bishop's seal.[65] The seal was affixed to a tongue cut into the parchment from the right side below the text. Some fragments of seals can still be seen.[66] The bishop probably used the seal *ad causas*, which was the seal for normal business. Yet Archbishop Warham was in the practice of using the seal of his audience.[67] When a bishop did not have his own seal at hand, he

---

[60] C.85/3/13.

[61] "... prout per uarios processus coram dicto.. officiali nostro ex officio in hac parte habitos nobis liquet expresse..." (C.85/134/21). In the only other example of this the bishop of Coventry and Lichfield in 1389 signified one person excommunicated in an *ex officio* case and another excommunicated in an *ad instanciam* case (for transcription, see *infra* Appendix B, p. 170).

[62] The chancery clerk noted on the dorse that three separate writs were sent to the sheriff of Devon (C.85/19/26).

[63] This he first did on 7 Oct. 1280 and he subsequently repeated the request on 7 Nov. 1280 and on 7 and 12 May 1281 (C.85/3/14, 24, 32, 35).

[64] Several significations often emanated from the same bishop's chancery on the same day. E.g., the bishop of Bath and Wells sent four significations on 26 Sept. 1337 and four more on the following day (C.85/37/32, 33, 35, 36, 40-43). Two identical significations issued from the chancery of the archbishop of Canterbury on 22 May 1450, but this was quickly noticed by a clerk of the royal chancery, who marked one of them "dupplicatur" (C.85/19/12, 15).

[65] On the use of seals by bishops, see especially C. R. Cheney, *English Bishops' Chanceries 1100-1250* (Manchester, 1950), pp. 46-51; Miss Irene J. Churchill, *Canterbury Administration* (London, 1933) 1. 16-18; see, too, W. G. de Birch, *Cat. of Seals in the Dept. of MSS in the British Museum* 1 (1887) 157-421; R. C. Fowler, "Seals in the Public Record Office," *Archaeologia* 74 (1923-24) 103-116; W. H. St. John Hope, "The Seals of English Bishops," *Proceedings of the Society of Antiquaries* 11 (1885-87) 271-306; H. S. Kingsford, "The Epigraphy of Medieval English Seals," *Archaeologia* 79 (1929) 149-178; *idem*, *Seals* (SPCK, London, 1920); *Guide to Seals in the Public Record Office* (London, 1954), pp. 60-62.

[66] This is true of some of Archbishop Winchelsey's significations; see C.85/7/*passim*.

[67] "Et quia sigillum nostre audiencie ad manus non habemus, sigillum officialitatis curie nostre Cantuariensis presentibus apponi mandauimus et fecimus" (C.85/24/38, 39, 41, 42).

could use a seal belonging to someone else.˙ In this way, Bishop Sydenham of Chichester in 1433 used the seal of the sequestrator of the archdeaconry of Wells.[68] Again a vicar-general might use the seal of the absent bishop as Adam de Murimouth did in 1338 during the absence of Archbishop Stratford.[69] A signification without a seal would be returned to the sender; this the prior of Worcester learned in 1266 when, probably through inexperience with significations, he failed to affix his seal to a request which he sent to chancery during the vacancy of the see.[70]

The bishops must surely have kept some record of the significations sent to chancery; otherwise they could have been severely compromised in the event of a future action such as an appeal. The evidence concerning such records is far from extensive. It is true that most episcopal registers contain among the common letters some copies of significations,[71] but in no case are these anything more than a selection, and in some registers no significations appear at all.[72] Obviously the principal record of significations was not the episcopal register. But notations in Archbishop Pecham's register make it clear that it was the practice in his time to preserve in the archbishop's archives the letters (*decreta*) requesting him to invoke the secular arm.[73] At what time the archbishops began the practice of keeping a separate register of these *decreta* is not certain, but it seems quite certain that such a register, now unhappily lost, was kept at Lambeth from at least the beginning of Cardinal Kemp's pontificate (1452). Enregistered were the letters coming from whatever quarter — the Arches, the Audience, the courts at Canterbury — to the archbishop requesting him to seek the capture of an excommunicate or the release of an absolved person. This can be briefly demonstrated. A very large number of the extant significations beginning with Kemp's pontificate bear notarial endorsements which indicate that the signification agreed with a register: "concordat cum registro" or, less frequently, "concordat cum decreto."[74] The sign and

[68] C.85/47/12; Salzman, p. 138. In like manner, Archbishop Bainbridge of York used the seal of the dean of the Arches in 1511 (C.85/187/25) and Warham used the seal of the official of the court of the Arches (see preceding note).

[69] C.85/9/30.

[70] "Ista litera debet signari sigillo prioris Wygorniensis et reportari" (C.85/159/23 dorse).

[71] See, e.g., *Reg. Epp. Peckham* and *Reg. Chichele, Canterbury*.

[72] *Reg. Bourgchier, Canterbury*, although admittedly incomplete in its present state, contains not a single signification.

[73] *Reg. Pecham, Canterbury*, pp. 99, 100, 173-79. Concerning Pecham's archives, see Miss Irene Churchill, *Canterbury Administration* (London, 1933) 1. 7.

[74] During Chichele's pontificate two significations (one dated 1423 and the other 1426) bear the notarial endorsement "concordat cum decreto" and the signs and names of James Burbach and Duemyngyg(?) (C.85/15/1, 8). The reference to a register first appears on the dorse of a

name (or initials) of the archbishop's registrar or of another notary in the archbishop's chancery attest this concordance. The register could not have been the usual archiepiscopal register[75] or a court register,[76] and can only have been a separate register containing the *decreta*. When the letter of request was received at Lambeth, it was enregistered in this register.[77] The signification, when it came to be drawn up, took its information from this register. The notary attested to the agreement of the signification with the register. No doubt the date of the signification would have been noted in the register. The presence of similar endorsements — rare, to be sure — on the significations from the abbot of Westminster,[78] the bishops of Lincoln,[79] London, [80] Salisbury,[81] and from Wolsey as legate[82] would suggest that this procedure was not limited to the chancery of the archbishop of Canterbury.[83]

signification dated 12 July 1453 (C.85/19/33); it was notarized by William Saundir, who likewise notarized significations during the early years of Bourgchier's pontificate. Several notaries performed this task during Morton's time: John Belle, John Barrett, and H. M. (possibly Henry Mompeson). The signs and names of T. Grene and — Rolle appear on Dean's significations and Richard Spencer, J. Cooper, and John Heryng on those of Warham. Of the 263 significations of excommunication and certifications of absolution sent by the archbishops between the beginning of Kemp's pontificate (1452) and the end of Warham's (1532) 124 were notarized; 3 simply with "concordat," 26 with "concordat cum decreto," and 95 with "concordat cum registro." For a brief discussion of notaries and a generous selection of plates of notarial signs, see J. S. Purvis, *Notarial Signs from the York Archiepiscopal Records* (London, York, 1957).

[75] The archbishops, while occasionally enregistering significations and even *decreta* among their letters common, did not do so consistently and some perhaps not at all.

[76] The imagination balks at the thought of the archbishop's registrar going down river to Cheapside or, worse still, travelling to Canterbury, merely to determine the agreement of a signification with a court register. The Reverend Colin Morris has recently called attention to a roll of the consistory court of Lincoln for the years 1458-59 which contains the names of those suspended or excommunicated in that court ("A Consistory Court in the Middle Ages," *Journal of Ecclesiastical History* 14 (1963) 158). But Mr. Morris assures me that this is not a list of excommunicates whose capture was requested.

[77] Archbishop Warham on several occasions stated in significations that the information about the excommunicate had come from the *decreta*, which had been placed "in our register" (C.85/ 25/4, 5, 9; for transcription of no. 4, see *infra* Appendix B, p. 166). I am grateful to Dr. Michael Kelly, who has recently completed a study of Warham's pontificate, for the information that he is not aware of any *decreta* in the two massive volumes of Warham's register at Lambeth Palace.

[78] In 1472 (C.85/211/47), 1475 (*ibid.* nos. 51, 53), and 1476 (*ibid.* no. 55).

[79] In 1496 (C.85/115/1).

[80] In 1518 and 1520 (C.85/126/29, 30).

[81] In 1531 (C.85/150/3).

[82] From 1525 to 1529 (C.85/188/16-26, 29, 30, 33).

[83] The earliest extant registers of excommunications and absolutions, apart from the roll at Lincoln (note 76), date from the late sixteenth century: Southwell, 1573; Bath and Wells, 1588; Canterbury, 1597 (The Pilgrim Trust Survey of Ecclesiastical Archives (privately circulated; [London], 1952), *passim*).

Unfortunately the existing evidence does not throw much light on the manner in which the signification was taken to the king's chancery. In an instance case the adversary, at whose request the signification was issued, might have undertaken its delivery. This was done, for example, by Robert of West Torrington, who probably in 1297 brought the signification to chancery and who then took the writ to the sheriffs of London.[84]

Yet, in another instance case, the signification was sent by the archbishop of York to his official in 1301 with instructions not to execute it without first attempting a peaceful settlement of the case.[85] In 1399 two men were signified by the bishop of Worcester for failing to appear before the official of the peculiar jurisdiction of the rector of Withington in an office case, and the signification was apparently brought to chancery by the rector of Withington, who then stayed with the chancellor.[86] Presumably, too, the messengers used by the bishops for bringing other business of theirs to London and Westminster would have carried significations to chancery, and this may have been the normal procedure.

In view of the paucity of information available concerning delivery of significations it must suffice merely to indicate the means available for their delivery.

III. The Action of the Royal Chancery

A. *Writ* de cursu

Upon receipt of the bishop's signification chancery issued as a matter of course the writ *de excommunicato capiendo*. There is no evidence to suggest that it was ever anything but a writ *de cursu*; such it was in 1227[87] and such it remained through the rest of the middle ages. A writ *de cursu* was granted without special warrant, without investigation, without the summoning of the parties. In a word, the question of fees apart, it could be had for the asking, provided that it was requested in the proper form by the proper person.[88] So automatically were writs *de cursu* issued that they

---

[84] *Select Cases in the Court of King's Bench* 3 (ed. G. O. Sayles; Selden Soc., vol. 58, 1939) 60-61.

[85] *Reg. Corbridge, York* 1. 5.

[86] "Tradatur domino Iohanni Park rectori de Wythyndon commoranti cum cancellario Anglie" (C.75/164/48 dorse).

[87] This writ was contained in the earliest extant register of writs (London, BM, Cotton Ms. Julius C.II, f. 143ᵛ), which Henry III described as "formam breuium de cursu"; see Maitland, "The Register of Original Writs," *Collected Papers* 2. 130.

[88] The English practice was in contrast to the practice of France. Article 7 of the royal ordinance *Cupientes* (1228) regarding heretics of the *langue d'oc* gave the king explicit authority to

were left to junior clerks of chancery, the cursitors (or *clerici de cursu*), who copied them from their registers inserting the variables and who then passed them on to master clerks.[89] Significations, then, if in the proper form and sent by a prelate possessing the power to signify, were "practically warrants":[90] of themselves they sufficed for moving the great seal.

Difficulties did arise, but they were remarkably few. The clergy did feel constrained in the mid-thirteenth century to complain to the king that writs were not issuing upon their request. In 1258, a council of the clergy at Westminster and in 1261 a similar council at Lambeth complained *inter alia* in almost identical terms that royal letters often were not being granted for the capture of excommunicates when requested by bishops.[91] These councils consequently provided that bishops in such circumstances should warn the king and in the event of continued refusal should place under interdict all "civitates, castra, burgi, et ville" which he held in their diocese. A contemporary series of *gravamina* contains a like complaint ("excommunicati non capiuntur quandoque ad requisitionem prelatorum") and, in addition, the king's reply.[92] It was the king's position that he was not obliged to grant the writ, that he granted it when he saw fit, and that the bishops occasionally used this procedure in an

refuse the request of the bishops to have royal bailiffs seize the property of excommunicates after a year (*Recueil général des anciennes lois françaises* (eds. F. A. Isambert *et al.*; Paris, 1822-1833) 1. 230). As a result, excommunicates could oppose the bishop's request before a secular judge, who would decide whether the bishop had acted to an excess. If he had, then the secular arm would not be used. If he had not, both the property and the person of the excommunicate would be seized and held until he repented. See M. Morel, *L'Excommunication et le pouvoir civil en France du droit canonique classique au commencement du XVᵉ siècle* (Paris, 1926), pp. 109-110.

[89] See Pollock and Maitland 1. 150, 195-96; H. C. Maxwell-Lyte, *Historical Notes on the Use of the Great Seal of England* (London, 1926), p. 14; B. Wilkinson, *The Chancery under Edward III* (Manchester, 1929), p. 86; *idem, Studies in the Constitutional History of the Thirteenth and Fourteenth Centuries* (2nd ed.; Manchester, 1952), chap. 8; G. B. Flahiff, "The Writ of Prohibition to Court Christian in the Thirteenth Century," *Mediaeval Studies* 6 (1944) 264. For contemporary descriptions of the cursitor's office, see *Fleta* vol. 2 (eds. H. G. Richardson and G. O. Sayles; Selden Soc., vol. 72, 1953), pp. 125-26, and the *Ordinaciones Cancellarie* edited by Wilkinson, *Chancery*, pp. 217-223).

[90] Maxwell-Lyte, p. 216.

[91] The 1258 council may have met initially at Merton in Surrey (*Councils* 2. 568-570). Its statute relating to the capture of excommunicates (*ibid.*, pp. 576-77) was closely followed in the phrasing of the statute of 1261 (*ibid.*, p. 676). Lyndwood has written a valuable commentary on this latter statute (5.17. c. Praeterea contingit; ed., pp. 349-352).

[92] *Councils* 2. 689. In his response to the immediately preceding *gravamen*, which concerned another aspect of the signification procedure, the king asserted that he granted the writ only "de gratia speciali cum sibi placuit" (*ibid.*). Cheney dates this series of *gravamina ca.* 1261, soon after the council of that year (*ibid.*, pp. 666-667), whereas Flahiff assigns them to the years 1258 × 1261 (G. B. Flahiff, *art. cit.*, pp. 299-300).

attempt to usurp the *ius proprium* of the king. Exactly what right of the king the bishops were allegedly usurping is not clear.

Despite such royal protestations the writ was and remained a writ *de cursu*. In fact, so much a matter of course had the issuance of writs *de excommunicato capiendo* become that they were issued in opposition to writs of prohibition already issued by chancery.[93] What happened was this. A. had B. cited to appear in a case before an ecclesiastical judge and B., claiming that the matter involved was not within the competence of the church's jurisdiction, sued out of chancery writs of prohibition, by which A. and the ecclesiastical judge were forbidden to take any further action. Nonetheless, A. with the leave of the ecclesiastical judge continued to prosecute his case in the ecclesiastical court. Quite naturally B. refused to appear before this court, since he denied its competence. His absence led to contumacy and from contumacy to excommunication. After waiting forty days A. requested that B. be captured and, accordingly, the bishop sent the signification to chancery. Thereupon chancery issued the writ *de excommunicato capiendo* against A., although it had already issued writs prohibiting further action and these very writs were being contravened by the bishop's signification. An example in point is the case between Thomas de Remigny and Richard chaplain of Liddeford in an ecclesiastical court in 1231: although Thomas secured writs of prohibition, Richard continued prosecution of the case in the ecclesiastical court and obtained Thomas' excommunication, signification, and, indeed, imprisonment.[94] This kind of practice was known to Bracton and, no doubt, to the clerks of the king's chancery.[95] It is quite possible that the refusal at times by chancery to grant the writ for capture in the years immediately preceding 1258 was an attempt to halt the practice of attempted circumventions of writs of prohibition and that these refusals gave rise to the clerical com-

---

[93] For a detailed analysis of prohibitions, see Flahiff, *art. cit.*, *Mediaeval Studies* 6 (1944) 261-313; 7 (1945) 229-290; *idem*, "The Use of Prohibitions by Clerics against Ecclesiastical Courts in England," *Mediaeval Studies* 3 (1941) 101-116; Miss Norma Adams, "The Writ of Prohibition to Court Christian," *Minnesota Law Review* 20 (1935-36) 289-290.

[94] *Bracton's Note Book* (ed. F. W. Maitland; London, 1887) 2. 424. Flahiff has given examples of other cases in which capture was used to contravene prohibitions ("The Writ of Prohibition...," *Mediaeval Studies* 7 (1945) 244, n. 87).

[95] Bracton, *De legibus* 4. 270-71. An interesting case appears on the *Curia Regis Rolls* (13. 480) for the years 1228-29. A certain sheriff was summoned to appear before the king's court because he had failed to execute two different writs in the same case: (i) a writ to summon the bishop of Norwich to appear in the king's court for holding a plea against a prohibition in a case between Hamo Ruffus and a certain chaplain Jocelin; and (ii) a writ for the capture of Hamo Ruffus, who had been excommunicated after the prohibition. The poor sheriff was caught in the cross fire.

plaints to which reference has already been made.[96] In any event, the years that followed saw many other examples of ecclesiastical authorities successfully suing writs of capture despite contrary writs of prohibition.[97] Remedies against such actions by the ecclesiastical authorities were mentioned as early as Bracton and found their way into registers of writs before the end of the thirteenth century: the person whose arrest was so ordered could sue out of chancery a writ superseding the writ for capture.[98] Whatever lay behind the clerical complaints of 1258-1261 concerning the failure of chancery to issue the writs for capture upon request, the fact remains that in the numerous series of clerical complaints which were made subsequently, many of which contained complaints concerning the capture of excommunicates, the clergy never again complained of the failure of chancery to issue the writ when so requested.

Further complaint was indeed made — not by the clergy but by the Commons. In 1351, moved perhaps by the same currents of anti-clericalism that gave rise to the Statutes of Provisors (1351) and Praemunire (1353), the Commons petitioned that the writ should not be granted upon a bishop's signification unless first there was issued a *scire facias* against the party in order to determine if the case pertained to the secular or the ecclesiastical forum.[99] What this meant in practice was that chancery should not issue the writ merely upon receipt of the bishop's signification in its proper form; rather the excommunicate was first to be called before the king's court so that he would have the opportunity to show that the case belonged to the secular courts; only if he failed would the writ be issued. This amounted to allowing a judicial review of each signification. So well established had the writ of capture become as a writ *de cursu* that the response labeled the petition as contrary to the law of the land as well as the law of the church.[100] At the same time, the Commons likewise re-

---

[96] Flahiff has pointed to the preoccupation with the question of prohibitions during the 1250's (*art. cit., Mediaeval Studies* 6 (1944) 293-98).

[97] See, e.g., the cases preserved by Prynne, pp. 115ᵛ, 117, 120, 120ᵛ, 475-77, 580, 614-15, 643-44, 778-79, 1024.

[98] Bracton, *De legibus* 4. 270. It appears in the second stage of the excommunication cluster in the registers of writs (see *infra* Appendix J, pp. 212-13). A later rubric indicates that, if the writ superseding was requested before the return of the writ of prohibition, it was to be sued out of chancery, but, if the day for the plea had already arrived, then the writ superseding was to be issued by the justice in the court of common pleas, if they were still sitting (*Reg. omn. brev.*, f. 67ᵛ).

[99] "Item prie la dite Commune que Brief Ad capiendum excommunicatum ne soit graunte par signification de Evesque, avant ceo que Scire facias soit suy devers la partie, q'il puisse avoir son Respons si la cause soit de lay-fee ou de lay-contract, ou de espirituelte" (*Rot. Parl.* 2. 230).

[100] "Pur ceo que ceste Petition est si bien encontre la Ley de la terre come de Sainte Eglise, il semble au Conseil q'ele ne doit estre ottroie" (*ibid.*).

quested that, when a writ was issued for the capture of an excommunicate,
the latter should have a *response* to determine if the case pertained to the
church's courts; king and council rejected this petition out of hand as
unreasonable.[101] Thus, significations were to be honored without question.[102]

On occasion chancery may have rejected significations because the form
was deficient, as, for example, when a signification was sent back to the
bishop of Hereford in 1305 because he neglected to address the king as *his*
lord[103] or when an unsealed signification was returned to the prior and
chapter of Worcester[104] or when the archbishop of Canterbury failed to
identify the excommunicate as of his jurisdiction.[105] Yet instances of
rejected significations were extremely rare, and their rejections were due
merely to deficiencies in form.

When Lyndwood was writing *ca.* 1430 concerning the *de cursu* nature of
the writ *de excommunicato capiendo*, he was summing up what had been,
save for the problems of the 1250's, the uninterrupted practice for the
previous two hundred years: the writ was to be granted as often as and
whenever it was requested, and the prelate was not held to prove it.[106]
He went even further to say that the secular authorities, even if they knew

---

[101] "Item quant Lettre d'Escomyngement est mys countre partie de lui faire nient responsable,
que la partie eit son Respons si la cause soit per Ley-contract ou de espirituelte." *Responsio*
"Pur ce que ceste Petition est noun resonable, il semble au Roi et a son Conseil q'ele n'est mie a
granter" (*ibid.*). This petition differs from the previous one in that the previous petition sought
to give the excommunicate an opportunity to stop the issuance of the writ, whereas this petition,
apparently proposed as an alternative in the event of the rejection of the first petition, sought to
give the excommunicate a remedy *after* the issuance of the writ.

[102] In 1342 Archbishop Stratford had reiterated the automatic nature of the issuance of this
writ (Wilkins 2. 708-09), in a constitution on which Lyndwood has written a useful commentary
(3.28. c. Saeculi principes; ed., pp. 264-67).

[103] In a signification dated 21 May 1305 the salutation reads "excellentissimo principi ac domino
reuerendo domino Edwardo," thus omitting "suo" before "reuerendo" (C.85/89/18). A chancery
clerk wrote on the dorse: "Ista litera remittitur quia non scripsit domino regi tanquam domino
suo." The signification was subsequently resubmitted to chancery with the word "suo" added
interlinearly. The next surviving signification from the bishop of Hereford is dated 29 Oct. 1305
and bears the same interlinear addition (*ibid.*, no. 17). The word "suo" appears in 1306 in the text
(*ibid.*, no. 19) but is omitted in 5 out of the next 10 significations covering the years 1308 to 1314
(*ibid.*, nos. 20-29), before it finally became fixed as part of the form.

[104] See *supra* p. 84.

[105] See *supra* p. 38.

[106] "Hoc fieri debet quoties et quando praelatus ecclesiasticus habens ad hoc potestatem sive
auctoritatem scribit domino regi pro excommunicato capiendo; nec tenetur praelatus facere
fidem de processu suo. Sed judex secularis debet ei credere" (5.17.3 c. Praeterea contingit, v.
dari debet; ed., p. 351; cf., 3.28. c. Saeculi principes, v. *adhibetur*; ed., p. 266).

that the ecclesiastical sentence was unjust, must still issue the writ, for only the *executio* and not the *cognitio* pertained to them, and, hence, the king should not inquire about the justice of the ecclesiastical sentence. Lyndwood found no reason to doubt the *de cursu* nature of the writ. Like so many other points affecting the ecclesiastical courts it had been settled in the thirteenth century, and, by a curious *volte-face*, when it was attacked in the fourteenth, it was the king and his councilors who defended it.

B. *Issuance of the writ*

Where it is possible to determine the date of the writ and to compare it with the date of the signification, one sees that the writ was usually issued without delay. Dating clauses on instruments from the English chancery must always be approached with some caution. The date of the writ *de excommunicato capiendo* probably does not represent the date of the engrossment of the writ or the date on which the great seal was affixed; it would seem to represent rather the date when the decision was made in chancery that the writ should be issued.[107] Since this writ was a writ *de cursu*, there is no reason to think that the decision in chancery was long delayed after receipt of the signification. Extant writs bear this out. In only 36 cases is it possible to compare the dates of *Significavits* with their corresponding significations. Twenty-four of these writs bear dates no later than eight days after their significations. Three, in fact, have the same date as their significations and, strangely enough, two others antedate the requests by one day.[108] Among the remaining twelve, the interval between the date of the signification and the date of the writ extends in nine cases beyond a month, even to six months in one instance. In one case the writ was dated 68 days after one request for it and one day before another request for it. These longer intervals may, indeed, represent delayed delivery of the signification to chancery, or it is quite possible in some of these instances that the writ which survives resulted from a fresh signification now, unhappily, not extant. In addition to these 36 cases dates can occasionally be found in the bottom margin of a signification or on its dorse. For

---

[107] "There is reason to believe that Letters Patent and Letters Close founded upon petitions, bills, and the like were made to bear the date of the actual receipt of the King's instructions, or, more probably, that of the settlement in Chancery of any questions arising therefrom" (Maxwell-Lyte, *The Great Seal*, p. 250). As this same author demonstrates in detail, the meaning of dates on instruments receiving the great seal is not always clear, nor did the chancery always act consistently (*ibid.*, pp. 241-265). For further comments, see J. F. Willard, "The Dating and Delivery of Letters Patent and Writs in the Fourteenth Century," *BIHR* 10 (1932) 1-11.

[108] For other examples of antedating in the royal chancery, see Maxwell-Lyte, pp. 253-58.

example, it was noted on the dorse of a signification from the bishop of Lincoln dated 31 October 1324 that a chancery clerk had delivered it to the keeper of the rolls on 2 November.[109] More often such dates found on significations stand alone and unexplained. Of this kind ten have been found and the added date was within a fortnight of the date of the signification except in one case when it was 25 days later. These dates refer, it would appear, either to the date of the delivery of the signification to chancery or to the date given to the writ. In either case, if they are taken with the cases previously cited, they serve to reveal a process which moved through chancery without delay and with the haste befitting its purpose.

The existing records disclose precious little about the route of the writ through chancery.[110] Presumably, when the bearer presented the signification in chancery, he indicated the sheriff or other royal officer (e.g., the constable of Dover Castle) to whom the writ should be sent. Occasionally a bishop might include this information in the text of the signification as the bishops of Hereford did consistently for the years 1281 to 1283.[111] But such a practice was quite exceptional. It is true, of course, that excommunicates were frequently identified as belonging to a certain parish, village, county, or, more commonly, diocese; yet identification solely by diocese would have been insufficient for this purpose because most dioceses comprised many counties in whole or in part and, in any case, identification of the excommunicate by place of his domicile was no assurance that he was at home. It was clearly necessary for the bearer of the signification to indicate the actual *whereabouts* of the excommunicate so that the writ could be directed to the sheriff of that place. He may well have transmitted this information by word of mouth at the chancery; at least it can be said that there is no surviving trace of any such written transmission.

<hr/>

[109] "Ista certificacio liberata fuit Ricardo de Ayremyme custodi rotulorum cancellarie regis in hospicio eiusdem Ricardi in uico de Bredstret, London, per manus magistri Iohannis de Hildesleye clerici regis dicte cancellarie secundo die Nouembris anno etc. xviii^{mo}" (C.85/104/12 dorse). Unfortunately, the date of the writ cannot be determined.

[110] The two standard works on chancery are H. C. Maxwell-Lyte, *Historical Notes on the Use of the Great Seal* (London, 1926) and B. Wilkinson, *The Chancery under Edward III* (Manchester, 1929). On particular aspects see F. M. Powicke, "The Chancery during the Minority of Henry III," *EHR* 23 (1908) 220-235; Miss L. B. Dibben, "Chancellor and Keeper of the Seal under Henry III," *EHR* 27 (1912) 39-51; T. F. Tout, "The Household of Chancery and its Disintegration," *Essays in History Presented to R. L. Poole* (ed. H. W. C. Davis; Oxford, 1927), pp. 46-85; A. E. Stamp, "Some Notes on the Court and Chancery of Henry III," *Historical Essays in Honour of James Tait* (eds. J. G. Edwards *et al.*; Manchester, 1933), pp. 305-311; B. Wilkinson, "The Chancery," *The English Government at Work, 1327-1336* (eds. J. F. Willard *et al.*; Cambridge, Mass, 1940-1950) 1. 162-205.

[111] C.85/86.

It was probably the chancery clerk receiving the signification and authorizing the writ who noted on the dorse of the signification the sheriff to whom the writ was to be addressed. Such dorsal notations appear only rarely in the thirteenth century — the earliest, however, is on a signification of 1244[112] — but became more frequent in the course of the fourteenth century and were standard procedure by the 1430's. There can be no doubt that these notations were made in chancery. They were written in a hand different in every instance from the hand of the signification and, although these notations are normally terse (e.g., "Deuonie" or, perhaps, "uicecomiti Deuonie"), fuller endorsements where they occur show that they are instructions given within chancery itself (e.g., "fiat breue uicecomiti Deuonie").[113] From these dorsal notations much can be gleaned.

It is learned, in the first place, that writs were usually directed to the local sheriff. If the excommunicate was from the diocese of Canterbury, then usually the writ went to the sheriff of Kent. During the 1440's the bishop of Exeter sent 19 significations to chancery and of these all but one had dorsal notations, and 16 of these 18 indicate that the writs were sent to either the sheriff of Cornwall or the sheriff of Devon, the remaining two being sent to the sheriff of Middlesex.[114] As was the case with these latter two, writs occasionally went to distant places. One finds, for example, a writ sent to the sheriff of York for the arrest of a London man in 1464,[115] or a writ to Wiltshire in 1408 for the arrest of a rector and a woman from the diocese of Carlisle.[116] In each of these cases some fairly precise knowledge of the whereabouts of the excommunicate was probably had, since only one writ issued forth as a result of each signification.

Writs were often issued to the sheriffs of London in pursuance of excommunicates from the provinces. Examples can be found of writs having been sent to London against excommunicates from remote dioceses such as Exeter,[117] Llandaff,[118] St. Davids,[119] Hereford,[120] York,[121] Salisbury,[122] Coventry and Lichfield,[123] and Bath and Wells,[124] and from nearer dioceses

[112] C.85/97/5.
[113] C.85/75/41 dorse.
[114] C.85/79-80.
[115] C.85/21/2 dorse.
[116] C.85/196/17 dorse.
[117] C.85/73/42; C.85/75/9 dorse; C.85/76/11, 13, 27 dorses.
[118] C.85/167/36 dorse.
[119] C.85/167/8, 24 dorse, 28, 31, 34 dorse, 35 dorse.
[120] C.85/91/38 dorse.
[121] C.85/180/25 dorse; C.85/182/11 dorse; C.85/186/27 dorse.
[122] C.85/146/50 dorse; C.85/147/30, 34 dorse; C.85/148/9 dorse; C.85/149/16, 33 dorses.
[123] C.85/57/16, 28 dorse; C.85/58/7 dorse; C.85/60/7; C.85/62/9 dorse; C.85/63/26, 28 dorses.
[124] C.85/40/14, 17, 18 dorses; C.85/41/21 dorse.

such as Canterbury,[125] Winchester,[126] Lincoln,[127] and Ely.[128] London, then
as now, had attractions for persons wishing to lose themselves; given the
emigration to London which did exist, the newcomer would hope to find
anonymity not only in a large city but in a large city which was continually
receiving newcomers.[129]

Frequently, however, more than one writ emanated from chancery in
response to a single signification. This was only to be expected when
several excommunicated persons from different counties were mentioned
in the same signification. For example, when Archbishop le Romeyn of
York requested in a signification of 1289 the capture of fifteen persons, a
writ was sent to the sheriff of Lancaster for seven and a writ to the sheriff
of Westmoreland for the other eight.[130] Nonetheless, the usual reason for
multiple issuance of writs upon a single signification was simply the uncertainty concerning the whereabouts of the excommunicate. In 1282
writs for the capture of Roger de Bilda were sent to the sheriffs of Nottingham and York because, as the chancery notation confessed, it was not known
in which county he could be found.[131] Likewise, the bishop of Coventry
and Lichfield in requesting the capture of Richard Crue in 1518 asked that
writs be directed not only to the county of Chester but to other places
as well, since Crue had no fixed address.[132] It was not unusual for a single
excommunicate to be pursued by two or more writs. Thus, against the
widow Christina Messenger of Salisbury diocese writs were issued in 1436
to the sheriffs of Berkshire, London, and Middlesex.[133] This practice of

[125] C.85/8/19 dorse; C.85/16/29 dorse; C.85/17/14 dorse; C.85/18/9.

[126] C.85/153/31 dorse; C.85/155/5 dorse; C.85/156/1, 11 dorses, 13, 29 dorse; C.85/157/16 dorse, 17, 18 dorse, 41 dorse.

[127] C.85/103/35 dorse; C.85/104/12 dorse; C.85/106/36 dorse; C.85/109/37 dorse; C.85/110/9, 38 dorses; C.85/111/14, 34 dorses; C.85/112/7, 38, 39 dorses; C.85/113/1, 14 dorses; C.85/114/5, 6, 14 dorses; C.85/115/3, 8, 18 dorses.

[128] In 1352 Bishop de Lisle signified Robert Beauchamp of Duxford, Cambs., "qui ad ciuitatem Londonie se transtulit" (C.85/68/14).

[129] The migration to London has been the subject of a detailed monograph by Eilert Ekwall (*Studies on the Population of Medieval London* (Stockholm, 1956), see esp. pp. xxxi-lxviii), which Josiah C. Russell has commented on in his article, "Mediaeval Midland and Northern Migration to London, 1100-1365," *Speculum* 34 (1959) 641-45.

[130] C.85/174/59 dorse. For other obvious examples of this, see the dorses of C.85/2/3; C.85/19/24; C.85/71/19; C.85/81/9; C.85/108/23; C.85/137/20.

[131] "... quia ignoratur utrum possit inueniri in uno comitatu uel in alio" (C.85/173/18).

[132] "Obsecramus ut uicecomiti Cestrie ac aliis officiariis uestris regiis infra regnum Anglie pro eo quod idem Ricardus Crue nullum certum domicilium habet literas uestras pro corporis sui capcione ut moris est in hac parte dirigere dignemini" (C.85/64/6). On the procedure in such franchises as Chester see *infra* pp. 112-15.

[133] C.85/149/16 dorse.

multiple writs must have reached its apex in 1531 when ten writs were issued for the arrest of William Coo of Norwich diocese: to the sheriffs of Norfolk, Suffolk, Cambridgeshire, Hertfordshire, Essex, London, Middlesex, Kent, Huntingdonshire, and Lincolnshire.[134] Whether he was caught in this web of writs, alas, is not known.

One thing is quite certain from the London writs and from the practice of multiple writs in general: many excommunicates fled their localities in hope of avoiding arrest. Some came to London; others went to neighboring counties; a few traveled the length of the country. Not all were successful as a man from Durham realized when he found himself being confined to Newgate by the sheriff of London.[135]

Once it was determined to whom the writ was to be sent, it could then be engrossed by one of the twenty-four cursitors who were responsible for writs *de cursu*.[136] Whether in this period individual cursitors wrote writs for specific regions of the country, as indeed happened later, is not clearly revealed in the records, although the presence of similar chancery notations on significations from York in the late thirteenth century and on no other significations is suggestive of some division of labor.[137] The engrossed writ went from the cursitor to a chancery clerk,[138] probably of the first grade, who took responsibility for it and who presumably presented it to the chancellor or master of the rolls for apposition of the great seal.[139]

---

[134] C.85/25/30 dorse. The signification was sent in the name of Archbishop Warham. It should be noted that in the case of conjoint counties (e.g., Norfolk and Suffolk, London and Middlesex) separate writs seemed to have been sent to the sheriff under each of his titles.

[135] C.202/C.63/9.

[136] See Maxwell-Lyte, p. 14; Wilkinson, *Chancery under Edward III*, pp. 74, 86.

[137] C.85/170/68 dorse; C.85/171/41; C.85/173/68, 75 dorse; C.85/174/43. The office of cursitor for Yorkshire existed in the time of Elizabeth I (C.I.A. Ritchie, *The Ecclesiastical Courts of York* (Arbroath, 1956), pp. 109-110) and was said in the time of James I to have been bought for as much as £1,300 (Maxwell-Lyte, p. 15).

[138] The names of such chancery clerks appear occasionally on the dorses of significations: "Tradatur M. Iohanni Bowland" (C.85/147/39: dated 1380; for him see Wilkinson, pp. 177, 205); "Tradatur Skarle uel Melton" (C.85/59/63: dated 1382; for Skarle see Wilkinson, p. 66, n. 9, and Maxwell-Lyte, p. 11; for Melton see Wilkinson, p. 67, n.); "Tradatur domino Thome de Midelton clerico cancellarie regis" (C.85/59/64: dated 1382; for him see Wilkinson, pp. 67, n.; 83, n. 4); "Roderham" (C.85/123/24: dated 1400; for him see *CPR, 1399-1401*, pp. 35, 203, 262, 273, 445); "Wynbusshe" (C.85/62/18: dated 1426; for him see *CPR, 1422-29*, p. 340). The "Skarle uel Melton" notation would argue against a single clerk of the first grade having responsibility for this writ. In view of the large number of writs *de cursu* issued — as many as a hundred and often two or three hundred in a single day in the early fourteenth century (Maxwell-Lyte, p. 296) — it would not be unexpected if responsibility for writs *de cursu* was shared by several senior clerks.

[139] The endorsement on a signification dated 31 Oct. 1324 shows a chancery clerk delivering

The writ was addressed in the king's name to his chief officer in the shire, borough, or franchise.[140] It stated that the bishop of a certain diocese had signified ("significauit") to the king that a particular person had remained in excommunication for more than forty days and that, since the church could do nothing further to effect his correction, the sheriff should capture and detain him in prison until absolved. The actual amount of information which the writ contained concerning the circumstances of the excommunication no doubt depended on the amount of information contained in the bishop's signification. As a rule, it can be said that the writ in its *relatio* merely restated what was in the signification, *mutatis mutandis*. From at least the late thirteenth century the form of the writ in the registers of writs identified the excommunicate as belonging to the jurisdiction of the bishop, unless this was otherwise evident, and specified the authority by which he had been excommunicated.[141] Verbal variations can be found in the mandate enjoined by the king on his officer, but the meaning was clearly the same in every instance: he was to seize the excommunicate and detain him until such time as he was absolved from his excommunication.

Precious few copies of writs *de excommunicato capiendo* survive, for several good reasons. In the first place, the writ was not a returnable writ — the sheriff was not required to reply to chancery or elsewhere regarding what action he took upon the writ.[142] Furthermore, one would search in vain for records of this writ surviving in the shires, for the regrettable fact is that there is extant only one shrieval roll of writs received (Bedfordshire-Buckinghamshire, 1333-1334) and, incomplete as it is, it contains no copies of the writ *de excommunicato capiendo*.[143] Likewise, as was true of so many other chancery writs, it was not enrolled on the chancery rolls.[144] This does not mean that chancery failed to keep records of this writ. On the

the actual signification to the keeper of the rolls; see *supra* p. 92. Perhaps the keeper wished to check the signification against the writ.

[140] For examples of actual writs see *infra* Appendix F, pp. 195-97.

[141] See *supra* pp. 40-41.

[142] Describing the previous nature of the writ as "not returnable into anye Courte that might have the Judgement of the well executing and serving of the said Writt, according to the Contentes thereof, but hitherto have been lefte only to the discretion of the Sherifes and their Deputies," a statute of 5 Eliz. I (c. 23, no. 1) provided that thereafter the writ was to be returned into the King's Bench in the term following (*Statutes* 4. 1. 451).

[143] See *Rolls from the Office of the Sheriff of Beds. and Bucks., 1332-1334* (ed. G. H. Fowler; *Quarto Memoirs of the Beds. Historical Record Soc.*, vol. 3, 1929). See too C. H. Jenkinson and M. M. Mills, "Rolls from a Sheriff's Office of the Fourteenth Century," *EHR* 43 (1928) 24-27.

[144] "It is absolutely certain that a considerable number of the instruments issued under the Great Seal in the middle ages were never enrolled" (Maxwell-Lyte, p. 363). "Not all chancery letters were recorded on the chancery rolls" (Wilkinson, p. 54).

contrary, chancery preserved the bishops' significations and used them as their record of the procedure, and it is these which form the present chancery class among the public records.[145] To be sure, this was an imperfect record, since it included mention neither of the date of the receipt of the signification nor, as a rule, of the date of the writ; yet it did provide a complete file of the significations which had moved the great seal. This appears to have satisfied the practical needs of the clerks in chancery.

C. *Chancery fees*

A word must be said about fees. Writs, in general, were subject to a fine, which varied according to the writ, and a sealing fee, standard at 6d. for original writs from the fourteenth century.[146] As a result of a petition in 1334 Edward III provided that writs *de cursu* would be subject only to a sealing fee and not to a fine.[147] In some cases the king would remit even the sealing fee as he did in 1362 in favor of certain receivers of charters of pardon.[148] The scraps of evidence which survive for the writ *de excommunicato capiendo* do little to illuminate this dark subject; they do show that at least for part of the middle ages some charge was made for this writ. An entry in the pipe roll for Michaelmas 1205 describes Honorius the archdeacon of Richmond as owing one palfrey "pro capiendis quibusdam excommunicatis," yet it does not state that the payment was due in connection with a procedure by royal writ nor, even if it is assumed that the procedure was by royal writ, does the entry preclude the possibility that the palfrey was due for several writs.[149] It seems quite certain that in 1296 a

---

[145] The printed register of writs (f. 68ᵛ) refers to these files. The rubric containing this reference begins to appear in MS. registers of the fourteenth century (e.g., London, BM, Harl. MS. 1118, f. 85ʳ; BM, Add. MS. 22162, f. 47ʳ; BM, Royal MS. 11.A.IX, f. 42ᵛ). There was exemplified on the patent rolls under date of 12 May 1350 a signification from the bishop of Lincoln, "remaining on the files of the chancery" for the arrest of the abbot of Brunne (*CPR, 1348-1350*, p. 506). A chancery clerk wrote across the bottom of a signification dated 1439 the note, "Originale istius copie remanet de recordo in cancellaria regis" (C.85/92/31c). The significations kept now in chancery class C.85 are not on their original files.

[146] On the subject of chancery charges see Pollock and Maitland 1. 195; Maxwell-Lyte, pp. 327-359; Wilkinson, pp. 59-61; *idem*, "The Seals of the Two Benches under Edward II," *EHR* 42 (1927) 397-401.

[147] *Rot. Parl.* 2. 376.

[148] *Ibid.*, p. 272. Maxwell-Lyte (p. 331) calls attention to the exemptions prevailing in the eighteenth century.

[149] *The Great Roll of the Pipe for the Seventh Year of the Reign of King John, Michaelmas 1205* (ed. Sidney Smith; Pipe Roll Soc., n.s., vol. 19, 1941), p. 58. In that same Michaelmas roll palfreys were commonly entered as payments made or due. Its value was probably contingent on its condition. Mention was made of a palfrey of 15 marks (p. 115) and of a "good palfrey" which was owed for a lamprey (p. 33).

fine was being charged for this writ, for in that year a chancery clerk was directed to write a writ *gratis* in favor of the marshal of the sheriff of York.[150] If such a fine was still being made in 1334, it was swept away, at least temporarily, with the fines for all writs *de cursu*. The depositing of a writ with the clerk of the hanaper in 1424 may suggest that some payment was to be made to that clerk, who was the treasurer of the chancery.[151]

Charges were likewise made in the ecclesiastical courts, but here the only evidence is from the sixteenth century. The Supplication against the Ordinaries made by the Commons in 1532 complained, *inter alia*, of the excessive fees charged in the Court of the Arches; the cost of a signification, it alleged, was twelve shillings. Archbishop Warham rejoined that the Commons were surely aware that he had already initiated reforms which had reduced some of the fees by half, some by two-thirds, and had done away with some others entirely. Yet he did not deny that the schedule of fees once had force in the Arches.[152] The ecclesiastical court may have paid the chancery fees out of the fees which it received for the signification; otherwise the total cost (the fee of the ecclesiastical court plus the fee of chancery) would have been very considerable. Later in the sixteenth century complaint was made of the high cost of the writ and a contemporary fee-list shows a correspondingly high fee in the ecclesiastical courts.[153]

---

[150] "Domine R. de Sutton, scribatis istud breue gratis pro marescallo uicecomitis Eboraci" (C.85/176/9 dorse). Roger de Sutton was described as a king's clerk in 1299 (*CPR, 1292-1301*, p. 438). Two other endorsements of significations of the thirteenth century (1265 and 1266) appear to indicate a payment, but because of their faded condition no firm conclusion is possible (C.85/159/22 dorse; C.85/169/49 dorse).

[151] "Tradatur Magistro Henrico Kays clerico de Hampir" (C.85/137/35 dorse). On the dorse of a certification of absolution in 1450 a similar note is found: "Domino Roberto Kyrkham clerico de Hannaperio" (C.85/19/14). It must be remembered that the hanaper was probably the department of chancery where sealed writs were dispatched and claimed (see Wilkinson, p. 55) and, in this event, the depositing of these two writs in that department may have been unconnected with payments for them. Mention should be made here that an endorsement of a signification of 1476 refers to the clerk of another chancery department: "To Maistre Broun clerk of the pety Baigge" (C.85/22/21).

[152] These complaints exist in several redactions, which are calendared in *Letters and Papers Foreign and Domestic of the Reign of Henry VIII*, vol. 5 (1880) no. 1016. The originals are S.P.2/L/198, 203-04; S.P.6/1/88; S.P.6/7/108ᵛ-109ʳ: "Item a *significauit* in to the chancery for to have the kyngys writ *de excommunicato capiendo*, xii s." See *Documents Illustrative of English Church History* (eds. H. Gee and W. J. Hardy; London, 1896), p. 148. The role of the Supplication in the subsequent submission has been studied by Dr. Michael J. Kelly in his Alexander Prize Essay on "The Submission of the Clergy," *TRHS*, 5th ser., 15 (1965) 97-119. Warham's response is in Gee and Hardy, p. 166.

[153] Thomas Cartwright urged in "A Second Admonition to the Parliament" (1572) that "some sharp punishment would be provided by the civil magistrate for him that contemneth excommuni-

IV. Delivery of the Writ

For delivery of the sealed writ from chancery to the sheriff several means were employed. As in the case of other chancery and exchequer writs addressed to the sheriffs, the writ *de excommunicato capiendo* was probably delivered by the king's messengers.[154] Examples are not wanting, however, of cases where the writ was delivered by the excommunicate's adversary or by an officer of the ecclesiastical court. For example, Robert of West Torrington, a litigant in a case concerning the church of Rand probably in 1297, not only brought to chancery the signification by the archbishop of Canterbury against his adversary, but also delivered the writ to the sheriffs of London and joined their serjeant in searching from place to place for the excommunicate, who at length was seized and confined at Newgate.[155] Similarly, in 1426 the writ which resulted from an excommunication in an *ex officio* case in the Lichfield consistory was handed over by chancery to a canon of Lichfield cathedral for delivery.[156] The exact place where the excommunicate was staying was seldom indicated in the text of the writ, and no doubt one of the duties of the bearer of the writ — whether king's messenger or an interested party — was to transmit this information to the sheriff, probably *viva voce*, if it was available.

Some delay in delivery of the writ was inevitable in most cases, for there was not a rider waiting outside Westminster Palace to take each newly sealed writ. Writs are known to have accumulated; delivery was made when a sufficient number of writs made the journey of a messenger feasible, and in the meantime weeks could have passed. It would have been in-

---

cation, but with lesse charge then a significavit" (*Puritan Manifestos* (eds. W. H. Frere and C. E. Douglas; Church History Soc., vol. 72, 1907), pp. 121-22). A list of fees for the York courts in 1547 indicates that a litigant would pay to the ecclesiastical judge and to the scribe 16d. each for the decree of the court which was sent to the bishop requesting signification and, in addition, 5s. to each of them for the signification (C. I. A. Ritchie, *The Ecclesiastical Courts of York* (Arbroath, 1956), pp. 228-29). Mr. R. A. Marchant, in his study, *The Puritans and the Church Courts in the Diocese of York, 1570-1642* (London, 1960), p. 9, states that the signification procedure was so expensive that it was "generally confined to civil actions where the cost could be recovered from the offending party."

[154] In general, concerning delivery of writs see J. F. Willard, "The Dating and Delivery of Letters Patent and Writs in the Fourteenth Century," *BIHR* 10 (1932) 1-11; Mary C. Hill, *The King's Messengers, 1199-1377* (London, 1961), pp. 90-92.

[155] *Select Cases in the Court of King's Bench* 3 (ed. G. O. Sayles; Seldon Soc., vol. 58, 1939) 60-61. The case is reported in the Hilary term of 1298.

[156] "Tradatur magistro Willelmo Admoneston ad deliberandum" (C.85/62/15 dorse). For a similar example see *supra* p. 86, n. 86.

conceivable for chancery to dispatch a messenger to the sheriff of Cumberland with only one *Significavit* in his pouch.[157] Only in three cases is it possible to ascertain the exact time intervening between the date of the writ and its receipt by the sheriff, and they demonstrate the inconsistency in this matter. At one extreme, it was almost the end of 1292 before the sheriff of Westmoreland received a writ which had been dated the previous April 2nd;[158] at the other extreme, the sheriff of Sussex received a writ in 1430 on the very day on which it was dated.[159] Possibly more representative, however, was the third case, which happily can be traced in its three stages. The archbishop of Canterbury in a signification dated 16 January 1309 requested the capture of the knight John de Wyggeton, who had been excommunicated in the court of the Arches at the instance of his wife.[160] The ensuing chancery writ was dated only six days later, 22 January, and reached the sheriff of Rutland on 6 February, exactly three weeks after the signification.[161] In this general connection the date of the capture of the excommunicate, if known, can be useful, since imprisonment naturally presupposes receipt of the writ. For example, chancery issued under date of 22 September 1348 a writ for the arrest of Roger le Theselere, and on 19 October, twenty-seven days later, Roger was confined to Newgate prison by the sheriffs of London.[162] Or, again, two rectors of Winchester diocese were captured by the bailiff of the sheriff of Southampton on the feast of Epiphany, 1432, by virtue of a writ dated the previous 24 November, an interval of forty-three days between writ and capture.[163] If one may judge from such cases as remain, there is no reason to doubt that delivery normally took place within a matter of weeks. Yet in an individual case a bishop could succeed in getting the wheels to turn faster as, for example, in 1406 when a writ was ordered sent to the bishop of Exeter "with all haste."[161]

---

[157] J. F. Willard has presented two interesting tables which indicate the interval between the date of chancery instruments and their receipt by the bishop of Rochester, 1323-1331, and by the bishop of Worcester, 1302-07. He concludes that "the majority of royal missives were without doubt received by the men to whom they were sent two or more weeks after the indication of time on the writs themselves" (*art. cit.*, pp. 9-11).

[158] "Istud breue michi liberatum fuit die dominica proxima ante natale domini proximo preteritum" (C.202/C.5/97 dorse).

[159] C.47/132/5 undated memorandum. For a transcription of this, see *infra* Appendix G, pp. 198-200.

[160] C.85/7/24.

[161] Wyggeton did not come into his bailiwick, the sheriff contended, and he was unable to take any action (C.202/C.10/42 dorse).

[162] C.202/C.46/10, 11.

[163] See *infra* p. 106, n. 196.

[164] "Fiat inde breue et mittatur cum omni festinacione domino episcopo Exoniensi" (C.85/

Some writs fell victim to the vagaries of a medieval delivery system and were never delivered.[165] On seven recorded occasions in the fourteenth and fifteenth centuries chancery sent a writ superseding the writ for capture only to get the reply from the sheriff that he had not received the first writ. For example, the bishop of Bath and Wells in a signification dated 21 September 1395 requested the arrest of Robert and Alice Curteys,[166] yet the sheriff of Somerset in an undated return to a superseding writ of 28 October 1395 stated that he had not received the *Significavit*.[167] A scribal error in chancery could easily send a writ astray as seems to have happened in 1447 when a chancery clerk directed that a writ sued against an excommunicate "staying in the city of London" be sent to the city of Lincoln.[168] But such undelivered and misdirected writs were probably never very numerous.

It was not unknown for bishops to bypass the king's chancery and signify excommunicates directly to the sheriffs. The provost and chapter of Beverley Minster by terms of their charter of liberties of 1202, confirmed by every succeeding king up to and including Henry VI, could signify excommunicates to the sheriff of Yorkshire directly.[169] Bishop Grosseteste in a celebrated case signified an incontinent cleric to the sheriff of Rutland in 1250; in the conflict resulting from the sheriff's inaction Grosseteste's use of direct signification was not challenged.[170] In 1267 Henry III granted Walter Giffard, archbishop of York, the special power to signify excommunicates directly to any sheriff,[171] and within a matter of weeks the archbishop is seen using the procedure of direct signification.[172] When an excommunicate was staying in a part of the realm where the king's writ did not run, direct signification was the rule.[173] When it came to requesting

78/7 dorse). That the writ was to be *sent* to the bishop is puzzling. Presumably he was in London and would bring the writ back to Devon with him.

[165] This was a difficulty not peculiar to the writ *de excommunicato capiendo*; see Miss Hill, *The King's Messengers*, p. 104; J. F. Willard, *art. cit.*

[166] C.85/39/7.

[167] Separate superseding writs receiving the same reply were sent to the sheriff (C.47/129/6/ dorse of piece dated 28 Oct. 1395; C.202/C.100/8 dorse). For similar returns, see C.47/104/8/dorse of piece dated 16 June 1414; C.202/C.63/8 dorse; C.202/C.78/21-23 dorse.

[168] C.85/112/32 and dorse.

[169] See *infra* Appendix C, p. 176.

[170] Matt. Paris, *Chronica Majora* (ed. H. R. Luard; R. S., 1872-1883) 5. 109-110. The cause of the ensuing controversy was simply the fact that Grosseteste had excommunicated the sheriff of Rutland, a minister of the king.

[171] *Reg. Giffard, York*, p. 103. The grant is dated 18 Sept. 1267.

[172] On 9 Nov. 1267 Giffard signified John Marchaunt of Wombleton to the sheriff of Yorkshire: "cum ... nobis a domino rege concessum sit quod hujusmodi excommunicatos ad nostrum cohercere debeatis mandatum" (*ibid.*, p. 109).

[173] See *infra*, p. 113.

the release of excommunicates who had been absolved, the bishops frequently sent their requests directly to the sheriff.[174] In the procedure developed against heretics in 1382 and 1401 the bishops were permitted to seek the assistance of the sheriffs directly.[175] As a procedure against excommunicates, however, direct signification to a *sheriff*, apart from special cases by royal privilege such as Beverley, was probably never widespread after the mid-thirteenth century and did not survive that century. Its roots undoubtedly are to be found in the text of the Conqueror which allowed bishops to seek the aid of the king *or sheriff* against contumacious excommunicates. The long, dark tunnel of the twelfth century may well conceal a general practice of direct signification by the bishop to the sheriff.

V. Execution by the Sheriff

Since the execution of the writ pertained to the sheriff, his position in this entire procedure was most crucial. The previous steps were predictable once the bishop had decided to invoke the secular arm: a signification would be sent to chancery and a writ would be issued from chancery to the sheriff. Subsequent events in the county were not so predictable. Not all sheriffs were equally efficient nor were all immune from intimidation or corruption. In order to insure the cooperation of the sheriffs, canonical censures were repeatedly threatened against them for failure to execute the writ. At the Council of Oxford in 1222 the bishops excommunicated all those who for sake of gain, spite, or some other reason maliciously refused to execute this writ.[176] This sentence of excommunication, like the other excommunications of 1222, became part of the standard English list of excommunications throughout the rest of the middle ages; it was repeated in synods provincial and diocesan[177] and was announced to the

---

[174] See *infra*, p. 145.

[175] See *supra*, p. 69.

[176] "Excommunicamus etiam omnes illos qui gratia lucri, vel odii, vel alias malitiose contempnunt exequi domini regis mandatum contra excommunicatos editum claves ecclesie contempnentes" (*Councils* 2. 107).

[177] Such synods as those at Lincoln (1239 ?; *Councils* 2. 276), Salisbury II (1238 × 1244; *ibid.*, p. 387), Ely (1239 × 1256; *ibid.*, p. 521), Norwich (1240 × 1243; *ibid.*, p. 357), Chichester (1245 × 1252; *ibid.*, p. 466), Winchester (1262 × 1265; *ibid.*, p. 723), and Exeter II (1287; *ibid.*, p. 1058) repeated almost verbatim the Oxford excommunication. In the York statutes (1241 × 1255; *ibid.*, p. 496) a somewhat different form was given to the excommunication: "Eadem sententia innodamus omnes illos qui mandata regia pro cohercendis excommunicatis a quibuslibet impetrata, gratia vel odio alicuius persone seu lucri causa, exequi malitiose different vel omittunt." This kind of form was also used at Durham III (1276; *ibid.*, p. 820) and Chichester II (1289; *ibid.*, p. 1089).

faithful several times each year in the Great Curse.[178]

The bishops supplemented the use of penalties by repeated complaints to the king about the failure of sheriffs to act upon the royal writ. Grosseteste in articles of grievance stated that sheriffs frequently failed to do so.[179] The *gravamina* of the Council of London in 1257 included the complaint that sheriffs did not always execute the writ.[180] The councils which met in 1258 at Merton and Westminster and in 1261 at Lambeth declared in almost identical language that excommunicates were often not captured.[181] The council of the southern province which met at Reading in the summer of 1279 repeated the excommunication — as old as 1222 — against those refusing to execute the writ for capture,[182] yet within a matter of months Archbishop Pecham was constrained to appear at the Michaelmas parliament to explain that this excommunication did not apply to royal ministers.[183] How strange this would have sounded to the ears of Grosseteste! The 1279 excommunication was repeated two years later at the council of Lambeth[184] and in similar form was retained in the Great Curse, but such were really meaningless in view of the fact that the execution of the writ pertained solely to royal ministers, who were excluded by Pecham from this excommunication. The king's intentions can perhaps

[178] "Also they [are accursed] that recyveth the Kynges writtes or maundementes to take such as beth accursed, and for mede or favour or any other wilful cause doth not execucion therof, and they that lette suche execucion or procure wrongful delyveraunce of suche as beth accursed" *Reg. Chichele, Canterbury* 3. 257). This is the version enjoined on the southern province by Chichele in 1434. Cf., the text in Wilkins 3. 524, and that printed with Lyndwood's *Provinciale* in the Oxford edition of 1679, p. 73 of the third pagination.

[179] "Item, cum ad invocationem episcoporum dominus rex scribit vicecomitibus pro excommunicatis capiendis, ipsi vicecomites pluries explere huiusmodi mandatum dissimulant, in gravem lesionem regiminis ecclesiastici" (*Councils* 2. 472). The date of these *gravamina* is not certain. Professor Cheney suggests conjecturally 1253 (*ibid.*, pp. 467-68).

[180] "Item, vicecomites tales excommunicatos ad mandatum domini regis non capiunt" (*ibid.*, p. 541).

[181] *Ibid.*, pp. 576, 676.

[182] "Item,... excommunicantur omnes illi qui malitiose contempnunt exequi mandatum regis de excommunicatis capiendis, vel eorum impediunt captionem seu procurant iniustam eorum liberationem contra decretum ecclesiastice discipline" (*ibid.*, p. 849).

[183] "Memorandum quod venerabilis pater I. Cantuariensis archiepiscopus ... confitebatur et concessit... secundo, quod non excommunicentur ministri regis, licet ipsi non pareant mandato regis in non capiendo excommunicatos" (*ibid.*, pp. 856-57). Lest there be any doubt about the nature of these concessions, the chancery scribe described them in a marginal heading as "Revocationes provisionum concilii Rading'."

[184] *Ibid.*, p. 907. The article by Miss Hilda Johnstone ("Archbishop Pecham and the Council of Lambeth of 1281," *Essays in Mediaeval History Presented to T. F. Tout* (eds. A. G. Little and F. M. Powicke; Manchester, 1925), pp. 171-188) should be read in the light of the subsequent remarks by Cheney ("Legislation of the Medieval English Church," *EHR* 50 (1935) 407-08) and Powicke (*The Thirteenth Century, 1216-1307* (2nd ed.; Oxford, 1962), p. 479, n. 3).

be more clearly seen in his reply in 1280 to the complaint of the clergy that
sheriffs sometimes neglected the execution of the writ for the capture of
excommunicates.[185]   Answering in a markedly conciliatory tone, he
assured the bishops that the sheriffs had not singled them out for special
harassment, for he too experienced similar difficulties at the hands of
slothful and careless sheriffs; he, furthermore, promised to correct and
punish such negligence.[186] The point seems to have been that the king
wished to reserve the punishment of sheriffs to himself and to keep them
free from ecclesiastical censure as had been provided for by the Constitutions of Clarendon. He apparently succeeded in silencing clerical
complaint in this regard, for the bishops did not complain once
again — despite complaints about other aspects of the signification procedure during the next fifty years — about the failure of sheriffs to execute
this writ.[187] This is particularly significant of the *gravamina* of 1309 and
1316, which proposed to repeat the articles of 1280 which were still out-
standing.[188]

[185] "Item, vicecomites aliquando negligunt capere excommunicatos prece vel pretio, favore
vel amore corrupti; et sic per negligentiam ipsorum leditur nervus ecclesiastice discipline" (*Councils* 2. 883).

[186] The replies to these *gravamina* exist in two redactions: the first in the *memoriale* drawn up by
the clergy from the oral reply made "in the kings presence, presumably by the chancellor" (E. B.
Graves, "Circumspecte agatis," *EHR* 43 (1928) 13-14; see, too, H. G. Richardson and G. O.
Sayles, "The Clergy in the Easter Parliament, 1285," *EHR* 52 (1937) 230-31), and the second
in the more formal reply found in Wickwane's register (*Historical Papers and Letters from the Northern
Registers* (ed. J. Raine; R. S., 1873), pp. 70-78). Professor Cheney has published both in *Councils*
2. 873-886. The response in the *memoriale* simply stated, "Quando negligunt capere excommunicatos seu captos presumunt dimittere sine mandato ecclesie vel regis vel ad mandatum ecclesie
non dimittunt, sunt proculdubio puniendi" (*ibid.*, p. 884). The reply found in Wickwane's
register is much fuller: "Vicecomites, non solum in hoc sed etiam in multis et fere in omnibus,
etiam in preceptis regis specialiter iniunctis sibi, nedum pigre sed temere exequuntur quod man-
datur. Unde nuper accidit quod mandabatur vicecomiti cuidam quod decem et octo homines
venire faceret coram rege, personaliter nominatos, pro quodam flagitio manifesto, ac ipse mutatis
personis retento tamen numero personarum duos tantum inter ceteros iuxta mandatum nominatos
venire fecit, quod non intendit rex relinquere inpunitum. Unde non mirentur prelati de factis
vel negligentiis vicecomitum. Et rex, cum querelas huiusmodi audierit prelatorum, comperta
veritate proponit vicecomites corripere et ut tenetur castigare" (*ibid.*).

[187] An excellent introduction to the three series of articles of 1285 and their replies is provided
by Richardson and Sayles, *art. cit.* (see preceding note), pp. 220-234. Belonging possibly to 1295
are a series of undated clerical articles (*Councils* 2. 1138-1147) Complaints were also proposed
both in 1300 and 1301 (*ibid.*, pp. 1206-1218). In 1309 some of the complaints of 1280 and all of
those presented in the parliaments of 1300 and 1301 were repeated (*ibid.*, pp. 1269-1274). Another
such cumulative series was presented in 1316 and led to the *Articuli cleri* of that year (*Statutes* 1.
171-74). Further articles were presented in 1327 (*Rotuli Parliamentorum Anglie hactenus inediti* (eds.
H. G. Richardson and G. O. Sayles; Camden 3rd ser., vol. 51, 1935), pp. 106-110).

[188] It is true that Archbishop Winchelsey in an undated letter (1294 × 1303) to Boniface VIII
indicated some of the difficulties under which the church in England was laboring and repeated

When the writ reached the shrieval house, it no doubt passed to the chancery side where it fell to the responsibilities of the returner of writs. He and his staff would record its receipt probably in a register-book or roll kept for writs from the king's chancery.[189] The roll of writs received which was kept by the sheriff of the conjoint counties of Bedfordshire and Buckinghamshire for the years 1333-34, a unique find, reveals a careful system of recording the contents of writs received and the action taken upon them.[190] This roll, although containing about 2,400 writs, is incomplete and contains no record of writs *de excommunicato capiendo*. Yet in a case in King's Bench in 1285 a clerk of the sheriff of Cumberland said that royal writs *de excommunicato capiendo* were kept by the sheriff on a file.[191] Presumably other sheriffs kept similar records, for they were often required to supply copies of the *Significavit* to the king's courts. For example, the sheriffs of London responded to a writ *scire facias* dated 19 July 1346 by sending to chancery a copy of a *Significavit* dated the previous 18 October, eight months earlier.[192] If a sheriff kept no register in which he recorded the receipt of *Significavit* writs or if he did not at least keep them on files, he obviously could not respond to such demands for copies.

The sheriff depended on his bailiffs for the execution of this writ. The Bedfordshire-Buckinghamshire sheriff's roll for 1333-34 indicates clearly that the usual mode of executing a royal writ was by issuance of a shrieval writ to the bailiff of one of the hundreds or to a bailiff itinerant. The writ *de excommunicato capiendo* was executed in like manner. As early as 1246 the under-sheriff of Bedfordshire is found writing to a bailiff for the arrest of an excommunicated deacon.[193] Fortunately, a detailed description of

---

verbatim the complaints of 1280 that sheriffs were neglecting the capture of excommunicates (*Reg. Pontissara, Winchester*, p. 205).

[189] Miss Mabel H. Mills has described the division of responsibility in the sheriff's central administrative office in her article, "The Medieval Shire House (*Domus Vicecomitis*)," *Studies Presented to Sir Hilary Jenkinson* (ed. J. Conway Davies; London, 1957), pp. 254-271).

[190] See *supra* p. 96, n. 143.

[191] "in ligula ipius uicecomitis" (*Select Cases in the Court of King's Bench* I (ed. G. O. Sayles; Seldon Soc., vol. 55, 1936) 146-47).

[192] C.47/109/5.

[193] Robert de Ekindon was signified by Bishop Grosseteste on 6 Aug. 1246 (C.85/97/8; *Rotuli Roberti Grosseteste, episcopi Lincolniensis, A.D. 1235-1253* (ed. F. N. Davis; Lincoln Record Soc., vol. 11, 1914), p. 505), and a writ was issued to the sheriff of Beds. for his arrest. In turn, a writ was sent by Richard de Pertenhall, the under-sheriff, to his bailiff Robert Druval, in which he repeated the royal writ (but without the dating clause) and added: "et ideo tibi mando quatinus visis literis istis predictum Robertum capere facias et iniicere in Gaolam Bedeford" (*A Digest of the Charters Preserved in the Cartulary of the Priory of Dunstable* (ed. G. H. Fowler; Publications of the Beds. Historical Record Soc., vol. 10, 1926), pp. 175-76).

the procedure in the county survives in one fifteenth-century case, and it demonstrates the role of the bailiff and the ultimate accountability of the sheriff.[194] On 14 June 1430 a writ for the arrest of Vincent Fynche, an excommunicate of Chichester diocese, was issued at the request of Archbishop Chichele, and it reached William Uvedale, sheriff of Sussex that same day.[195] Uvedale thereupon issued a written command to eight bailiffs itinerant to capture Fynche and bring him to the castle at Guildford. On 8 August of that year six of these bailiffs arrested Fynche at Netherfield, the village where he lived, about three miles from Battle. For fear that he might be rescued from them by force they took him straightway to Battle and there they pressed into service seven local men to assist them in conducting Fynche to Guildford Castle. The party of the six bailiffs, the seven men from Battle, and the prisoner set out from Battle without delay and reached Turner's Hill that night, having stopped en route for rest at Hoadley and for rest and nourishment at Nutley. Next day they traveled via Reigate to Guildford, arriving at the castle in the afternoon. Over modern roads the same journey would be about 75 miles. That it was accomplished in 1430 in less than two days suggests that this party of fourteen, obviously on horseback, traveled at a considerable pace. Other factors in this case, now unknown, could have necessitated the measure of speed and security used by the bailiffs. Perhaps there was fear that powerful friends might try to free Fynche as was to happen a year later in the neighboring county of Southampton when in a similar case a group of men attacked the bailiff and fled with his prisoner.[196] At any rate, Fynche was

---

[194] For a transcription of the memorandum containing this description, see *infra* Appendix G, pp. 198-200. A writ *certiorari* dated at Battle 9 Sept. 1431 was sent by Duke Humphrey in the name of Henry VI to the sheriff of Sussex, requesting from him information concerning the manner in which the writ for the arrest of Vincent Fynche had been executed. The sheriff responded by sending (i) the original *significavit*, (ii) the *certiorari*, and (iii) a memorandum describing the capture and subsequent events (C.47/132/5).

[195] Chichele's signification is probably that of 30 May 1430, on which the name of an excommunicate of Chichester diocese has been torn off (C.85/15/22). Although the sheriff twice in the memorandum gave 13 June as the date of the writ, the *significavit* is clearly dated 14 June.

[196] John Belyn, rector of Mottistone, Isle of Wight, and John, rector of Crux Easton, both of Winchester diocese, were signified as excommunicates on 16 Nov. 1431 (C.85/156/23) and a writ dated 24 Nov. was issued for their arrest. Walter Veer, sheriff of Southampton, related the subsequent events: "Virtute istius breuis corpus Iohannis rectoris ecclesie parochialis de Crokeston infranominati captum fuit apud Est Wodhay [i.e., East Woodhay] in comitatu infrascripto in festo epiphanie domini ultimo preterito per Iohannem Yonge balliuum domini regis et meum uirtute cuiusdam precepti huius breuis prius prefato balliuo directi. Venit quidam Iohannes Stegraue de Est Wodhay in comite Southampton gentilman et Willelmus Webbe de eadem in comitatu predicto husbondman simul cum aliis ignotis et in rectorem a custodia predicti balliui ui et armis ceperunt et abduxerunt et eidem balliuo insultum fecerunt et ipsum uerberauerunt, uulnerauerunt, et

committed to jail at Guildford on 9 October, less than two months after the issuance of the writ.[197]

The existing evidence would suggest that, when capture took place, it followed fairly quickly after issuance of the writ. For example, it is possible to establish in ten cases between 1385 and 1397 the approximate period intervening between the issuance of the writ and the imprisonment of the excommunicate. Only in five of these cases did a month or more intervene: 30 days,[198] 37 days,[199] 47 days,[200] 61 days,[201] and 80 days.[202] In the other five cases arrest was effected with remarkable speed. On 6 October 1393 a writ was issued to the sheriff of London for the arrest of Thomas Henley, and within four days he was in prison.[203] Nicholas the rector of Penallt, Llandaff diocese, was captured and imprisoned by the sheriffs of London within nine days of the writ's issuance.[204] Although the London sheriffs seem to have been able to act with unusual swiftness and effective-

---

maletractauerunt contra pacem domini regis. Per quod Iohannes Belyn rector de Motteston infranominatus et predictus Iohannes rector ecclesie de Crokeston a balliua mea plene recesserunt nec umquam in eadem inueniri possunt" (C.47/100/9 dorse of piece dated 24 Nov. 1431).

[197] Subsequently, according to the memorandum, Fynche took gravely ill in jail and "requested" to return to Battle to perform the penance imposed on him by the archbishop. This he did on 21 Sept. 1430, but his condition would not allow his return to Guildford and he went instead to his own house at Netherfield, where he expired on 27 Sept. He may have been the same Vincent Fynche who, together with William Cheyne, the king's justice, William Fynch, sheriff of Sussex from 5 Nov. 1430 to 26 Nov. 1431, and others, acquired seisin of property in June 1430 (CCR, 1429-1435, pp. 45, 69).

[198] The chaplain Robert Shropham was signified by the bishop of London on 11 April 1390 (C.85/122/42). By virtue of a writ bearing the date 10 April (C.202/C.92/152) Shropham was imprisoned by the sheriffs of London in Newgate by 10 May (C.47/111/20/ dorse of piece bearing that date).

[199] Writs were issued to the sheriff of Bristol on 26 Oct. 1392 and 3 Feb. 1393 for the arrest of Frater Philip Russell of St. Mark's hospital, Billeswick. On 8 Feb. 1393 he was declared an outlaw and his imprisonment was ordered. By 12 March he was in prison at Bristol (C.47/99/4/ pieces bearing these dates). For more on Russell, see VCH Gloucs. 2. 116.

[200] William Clerk of Dartmouth, signified by the archbishop of Canterbury on 6 May 1390 (C.85/11/56), was the subject of a writ dated 12 Oct. 1390, by reason of which he was imprisoned by the sheriff of Devon before 28 Nov. (C.47/96/4/pieces bearing these dates).

[201] A writ dated 28 Jan. 1395 was sent to the sheriffs of London for the capture of William Menusse, chaplain, of London diocese. By 30 March he was lodged in Newgate (C.47/111/22/ pieces bearing these dates).

[202] On 17 April 1385 when Thomas atte Pond of Kirtling sued a scire facias out of chancery he was being held in the castle at Cambridge on a significavit dated 26 Jan. (C.47/92/4/pieces bearing these dates). One may justifiably assume that atte Pond had not been detained very long in jail before suing the scire facias.

[203] C.47/11/22/pieces dated 6 and 10 Oct. 1393.

[204] C.202/C.99/27, 28.

ness, other sheriffs could likewise be quick to act. For example, the sheriff of Cambridgeshire in October 1386 had John Petyt, chaplain of Fulbourn, Ely diocese, confined in the castle at Cambridge within ten days after the date of the writ;[205] likewise, the sheriff of Wiltshire imprisoned the chaplain William Wynselaw before 14 June 1397 by virtue of a writ issued on 4 June.[206] In one case in the middle of the previous century the sheriff of Warwickshire was apparently so quick to capture a canon of St. Margaret's Church, Warwick, that it was charged, but not proved, that he had acted before receipt of the king's writ.[207]

The place of detention for the excommunicate whom the sheriff had apprehended was the king's prison in his shire.[208] Presumably, if there were two or more royal prisons, he would be sent to the nearest. In some conjoint counties one prison served both as in the case above of Vincent Fynche, who was capturd in Sussex and imprisoned in Surrey, or of the man from Tollesbury in Essex who was imprisoned at Hertford.[209] Prisoners in medieval jails provided for their own food and paid a fee for lodging; those unable to do so lived as paupers, subject to the charity of the community. The procedure of gaol delivery did not affect imprisoned excommunicates. They were not like other prisoners; the bishop still retained a form of jurisdiction over them in that the expected mode of delivery was by a writ sued by the bishop after their absolution. In the course of time other means of obtaining writs of delivery were made available by chancery — these are discussed in detail in the next two chapters — but even these new writs were writs peculiar to the excommunicate. They were not writs used for other classes of persons and merely applied to excommunicates, *mutatis mutandis*; rather they had to do with appeal and the requirements for absolution. If an imprisoned excommunicate was unwilling or, more likely, unable because of the expense or because of inexperience to initiate such further legal action, he would languish in prison until absolved.

[205] C.47/92/4/pieces dated 16 and 26 Oct. 1386.

[206] C.47/134/4/41, 42.

[207] *Select Cases of Procedure Without Writ under Henry III* (eds. H. G. Richardson and G. O. Sayles; Selden Soc., vol. 60, 1941), pp. 112-113.

[208] For medieval English prisons see R. B. Pugh, "The King's Prisons before 1250," *TRHS*, 5th ser., 5 (1955) 1-22; Miss Margery Bassett, "Newgate Prison in the Middle Ages," *Speculum* 18 (1943) 233-246; *eadem*, "The Fleet Prison in the Middle Ages," *University of Toronto Law Journal* 5 (1943-44) 383-402. Some useful information is found in W. A. Morris, *The Medieval English Sheriff to 1300* (Manchester, 1927), pp. 115-116, 230-232; *idem*, "The Sheriff," *The English Government at Work*, 1327-1336 (eds. W. A. Morris *et al.*; Cambridge, Mass., 1940-1950) 2. 61-63.

[209] Robert Waterman and Maud Ace were both mentioned in the *significavit* of 4 Oct. 1414 to the sheriff of Essex, but only Waterman was captured (C.47/98/7/pieces bearing that date, and dorse).

It was not the general practice in England throughout our period for the sheriffs to distrain the goods of signified excommunicates, unlike the practice prevailing in parts of France whereby seizure of goods took place after a year's excommunication;[210] nonetheless, distraint was used in England to some extent during the thirteenth century. In 1223 the sheriff of Buckinghamshire seized the land and rents of Lawrence Peyur, an excommunicate who had fled the county, and in that same year the sheriff of Essex seized the land but apparently not the body of the excommunicate Robert Hakum.[211] In December of 1254 a royal writ ordered the sheriffs of Gloucestershire and Herefordshire not to capture the body of Anna de Hauhisia nor to seize her property as commanded by an earlier writ, since she was subsequently absolved.[212] Again, in the following month similar mandates were sent to the sheriffs of Yorkshire and Nottinghamshire in connection with the case of John de Eyvill.[213] Only once thereafter, in 1281, is there evidence that a sheriff seized the goods of a signified excommunicate.[214] Apart from these five cases there is no evidence of distraint of the property of excommunicates. Nothing regarding it appears in the surviving significations and *Significavit* writs. It was a thirteenth-century occurrence, perhaps never widespread and certainly not without common law analogues.

---

[210] See the provisions of the royal ordinance *Cupientes* (1228) in *Recueil général des anciennes lois rançaises* (eds. F. A. Isambert *et al.*; Paris, 1822-1833) 1. 230, and the comments of Maurice Morel, *L'Excommunication et le pouvoir civil en France du droit canonique classique au commencement du XVe siècle* (Paris, 1926), p. 70. Pope Innocent IV in a decretal letter of 1254 stated that it was the custom of Normandy for sheriffs to seize the person and property of recalcitrant excommunicates (see *supra*, p. 20, n. 26).

[211] *Rotuli litterarum clausarum in turri Londinensi asservati* (ed. T. D. Hardy; London, 1833-1844) 1. 540, 562-64.

[212] "... supplicantes quatinus id quod in hac parte ad regiam pertinet magestatem circa liberacionem persone et terrarum ipsius secundum deum et iusticiam facere dignemini..." (C.85/167/7. "Mandatum est vicecomiti Glouc' quod mandata regis ei directa de ipsa Hawysia tanquam excommunicata capienda et de seisina facienda predicto Henrico de terris et possessionibus ipsius Hawisie non exequantur" (*CCR, 1254-56*, p. 14).

[213] The mandate is dated 19 Jan. 1255 (*ibid.*, p. 27).

[214] John Rammesdene had been excommunicated and, at length, signified on 13 May 1281 at the instance of his wife (C.85/212/11). He was subsequently absolved and the bishop's request for his delivery dated 4 Sept. 1281 indicated that the sheriff of Sussex and Surrey had custody of his goods (*ibid.*, no. 12).

VI. Effectiveness of the Signification Procedure

How effective was this system of signification? How frequently did the request of the bishop lead to the capture of the excommunicate? These questions are quite distinct from the question of the success of this system, for the measure of its ultimate success, judged solely on the basis of its stated purpose, was the repentance and absolution of the excommunicates. In some sense the answers to the questions here raised must be unsatisfactory. There is no file of returned writs indicating the action taken in each case; there is nothing surviving of shrieval records which could afford the basis of a statistical analysis.

When a sheriff failed to capture an excommunicate, frequently chancery issued another writ against the same excommunicate. Some of these repeated writs formed merely a species of the multiple writ, because the second writ was sent to another sheriff.[215] But the second writs were often sent to the same sheriff and, in this case, constituted a stimulus to the sheriff to act. The original *Significavit* was valid until executed; the new writ gave the sheriff no further warrant for action. It merely served the purpose of calling to his attention the continued freedom of the excommunicate. For example, the archbishop of Canterbury signified Edmund de Hoo, rector of Risby, on 2 August 1290 and repeated the signification five times: 16 September 1292, 18 April 1300, 25 February 1302, 26 November 1303, and 1 May 1304.[216] Similarly, the Cistercian abbot of Rewley was signified on 14 October 1391 and again the following year on 15 December.[217] Archbishop Giffard of York took the unusual step in 1269, after already having sued two writs to the sheriff of Yorkshire for the arrest of John Stanegrave without effect, of writing directly to the sheriff to warn him to take action before he found it necessary to write to the king again.[218] The greatest weakness in the signification procedure was the non-returnable nature of the writ; the repeated writ in some measure supplied for this defect.[219]

---

[215] E.g., significations were sent to chancery in 1467 on 4 June and 4 Sept. against Stephen Milward and John Brown respectively, and writs issued for their arrest to the sheriff of Gloucs. (C.85/21/37, 35); on 2 Dec. following a single writ was requested and it was sent to the sheriff of Bristol (*ibid.*, no. 32).

[216] C.85/4/49, 53; C.85/5/36; C.85/6/30, 59, 76. It is always possible, of course, that some of these later significations resulted from fresh sentences of excommunication.

[217] C.85/11/68, 82.

[218] The significations in question had been sent to the king on 3 Nov. 1268 and 18 March 1269 (C.85/170/14, 16). The archbishop's letter to the sheriff is dated 8 June 1269 (*Reg. Giffard, York*, pp. 142-43).

[219] From the fourteenth century registers of writs contain a *pluries* form of the writ *de excommuni-*

The delay of the sheriff in executing a writ need not be attributed to inaction on his part, for not every writ issued for the capture of an excommunicate could be executed. In the case of writs issued to several sheriffs against a single excommunicate only the sheriff of the place where the excommunicate was staying could execute the writ. Even when the writ for the capture of an excommunicate was sent to only one sheriff, there was no assurance that the excommunicate would not flee the shire or go into hiding. For example, in 1300 when the sheriff of Kent was ordered to capture seventeen rectors and vicars, he succeeded in capturing only twelve and the remainder he did not find in his bailiwick.[220] Perhaps a sheriff could not execute the writ because the excommunicate was indeed staying within his bailiwick but in a liberty which had return of writs and in which the sheriff's officers could not act unless they had a royal instrument bearing a *non omittas* clause. Thus, in 1344 the sheriff of Surrey reported that, since the excommunicate was in the liberty of the archbishop of Canterbury at Croydon, he could only give the writ to the bailiff of the liberty and that the bailiff gave no response and took no action.[221] In another case the sheriff was unable to execute the writ because the excommunicate had died before he received the writ,[222] and in another the excommunicate was already in jail for another reason.[223]

---

cato capiendo, according to which the sheriff was ordered to capture the excommunicate or be present in King's Bench on a specific day to show why he had not done so. The registers add the *regula* that attachment could be made just as in replevin *mutatis mutandis*. See, e.g., London, BM, Harl. MS. 118, f. 81ᵛ, and the printed edition, f. 65ᵛ. Despite its presence in the registers only one example of the use of this writ has come to light; it is dated 3 Oct. 1329 (K.B. 29/1/m.71).

[220] See Prynne, p. 906, where he prints C.202/C.7/181.

[221] The excommunicate was Agnes late servant of Walter Pistor (C.202/C.41/82, 83). An endorsement on the signification, dated 13 Feb. 1281, for the arrest of William de Wreklesham indicated that the writ should bear such a clause: "fiat mencio quod non obstante libertate ecclesie Wintoniensis" (C.85/3/59). In 1226 the king ordered the abbot of Bury St. Edmunds to capture the excommunicate Matthew de Malinges, who was staying in his liberty, and to hand him over to the sheriff of Norfolk (*Rotuli litterarum clausarum in turri Londinensi asservati* 2. 117).

[222] Walter Foke of Exeter was the subject of a writ dated 12 Oct. 1390, but the sheriff of Devon reported that he had died "diu ante recepcionem huius breuis" (C.47/96/4/dorse of piece bearing that date).

[223] This is the interesting case of the Trinitarian priest Richard Richardson, member of the Hounslow house, but resident in the appropriated chapel at Werland, Devon. In a case between the minister of Hounslow, on the one hand, and two vicars-choral of Exeter cathedral and other people, on the other, he became excommunicated and his capture was requested by Bishop Oldham of Exeter on 11 Oct. 1510 (C.85/82/2). A writ dated 12 Oct. issued from chancery to the sheriff of Devon, who sent on 20 Oct. under his seal a warrant to Henry Copleston, keeper of the king's jail at Exeter, concerning his capture. The keeper replied that he had imprisoned Richardson on 5 Oct. as ordered by John Rowe, the king's justice of the peace in Devon. The keeper was instructed to keep Richardson in custody until he made satisfaction (K.B. 29/142/m.33ᵛ). Ri-

Some measure of the efficiency of the signification system can be had through a study of the records of subsequent action taken by excommunicates, since these records occasionally reveal the fact of an excommunicate's imprisonment. To be sure, the records of such actions refer only to a small minority of excommunicates and frequently these records supersede the writ for capture without stating whether the excommunicate had been captured. Chancery did not always know. The writ superseding often told the sheriff to deliver the excommunicate "if he is in prison." Despite these factors it is possible to discover in these records the names of 428 excommunicates of whom it can be said with certainty that they suffered imprisonment by virtue of the writ *de excommunicato capiendo*. They can be found from as early as 1225 and as late as 1529, and among them would be numbered clerics and lay people of almost every degree and status. They form a representative cross-section of those who were signified.

The simple fact that the signification procedure continued to be used testifies to its effectiveness. If it could not accomplish what it proposed to do, the system would undoubtedly have fallen into desuetude. Yet it did not. Litigants were still applying for the writ in the sixteenth century. Furthermore, many persons fled in the face of this writ to other counties and even to faraway cities to escape its effect. If the writ was predictably ineffectual, one need scarcely have fled from Wales to London to avoid capture. In sum, the writ *de excommunicato capiendo* was probably as effective as any royal writ for capture.

VII. Note on Wales and the Counties Palatine

Over vast areas of the realm the writs of the king did not run. The Marches of Wales lay beyond the usual administrative machinery of the kingdom.[224] The same is true of the quasi-regal counties palatine, whose administration duplicated the king's. Such were Chester and Durham from at least the twelfth century and possibly even from before the advent

---

chardson soon appealed his case to the Arches, where he was absolved *ad cautelam* "in persona procuratoris sui." Archbishop Warham requested on 30 Nov. 1510 a writ for his delivery (C.85/24/16), and the writ was issued under date of 1 Dec. The writ was not allowed until Richardson appeared before the king's justices on the Monday after the next Easter (K.B. 29/142/m.33ᵛ). At length, he submitted to Oldham on 23 Feb. 1512 (Exeter, Devon County Record Office, Reg. Oldham, f. 172ᵛ).

[224] In general, see W. H. Waters, *The Edwardian Settlement of North Wales and its Administrative and Legal Aspects (1284-1343)* (Cardiff, 1935). Professor Glanmor Williams' recent study of the church in medieval Wales (*The Welsh Church from Conquest to Reformation*, Cardiff, 1962) replaces all previous treatments of the same topic.

of the Normans, and Lancaster, a county palatine from 1351 and a duchy from 1399.[225] The procedure which prevailed elsewhere by which the bishop would sue out of the royal chancery a writ to the sheriff did not apply in these areas, for the king had no sheriffs there. The stewards of the Welsh lords and the sheriffs of the palatinates were not royal officials.

Two different circumstances could have presented themselves when it came to invoking the secular arm. First, there was the situation whereby the person excommunicated by a bishop from one of these areas had fled beyond the dominial or palatine jurisdiction into a county where the king's writ did run. The procedure in such circumstances was the same as that already described: the bishop would write to the king's chancery and a writ would be issued to the sheriff of the county where the excommunicate was staying. For example, the bishop of Durham requested the king in 1286 to issue a writ for the arrest of a priest "now at Oxford."[226] Similarly, the bishop of Llandaff in 1300 signified a monk of Cardiff "now in London."[227] Once in a royal shire an excommunicate was wholly subject to the force of the king's writ.

The second situation which presented itself was that in which a bishop wished to signify an excommunicate who was staying in a jurisdiction beyond the king's writ. In such a case the bishop would normally contact the secular authority directly and the matter would then be handled internally. This is true not only of the bishops whose dioceses lay wholly or partly within these jurisdictions but of other bishops as well. The county palatine of Durham was unusual in that the bishop of Durham was secular and spiritual lord in that county. If it was desired that the secular arm be used against a person who had been excommunicated by the authority of the bishop of Durham, the procedure followed three steps. First, the official of the ecclesiastical court sent a letter to the bishop in which he requested secular assistance. The bishop, in turn, ordered his chancellor to issue the writ to the sheriff of the county. Finally, the writ was issued

[225] See G. T. Lapsley, *The County Palatine of Durham* (New York, 1900); Robert Somerville *History of the Duchy of Lancaster*, vol. 1, *1265-1603* (London, 1953); idem, "The Preparation and Issue of Instruments under Seal in the Duchy of Lancaster," *Studies Presented to Sir Hilary Jenkinson* (ed. J. Conway Davies; London, 1957), pp. 372-389; J. F. Baldwin, "The Chancery of the Duchy of Lancaster," *BIHR* 4 (1926-27) 129-143; G. Barraclough, "The Earldom and County Palatine of Chester," *Transactions of the Historic Society of Lancashire and Cheshire* 103 (1951) 23-57. The National Library of Wales possesses significations of excommunication for Flint from Henry VIII to Elizabeth I and for Pembroke for George II; the significations from the county palatine of Chester for the years 1378-1396, 1551, 1663-68 are kept in the Public Record Office, London (*Guide to the Contents of the Public Record Office* (London, 1963) 1. 171, 176).
[226] C.85/198/17.
[227] C.85/167/19.

in the bishop's name. All the stages can be followed in the case of Hughtred Wrowe. His capture was requested in a letter of 1 March 1312 from the official to the bishop; on the twentieth day of the same month the bishop's mandate was sent to chancery and the writ was issued on the same day.[228] When other bishops desired the capture of persons whom they had excommunicated and who were staying in county Durham, they wrote directly to the bishop of Durham. In 1415, for example, Archbishop Bowet of York wrote to Bishop Langley of Durham as secular lord for the capture of two chaplains who had been excommunicated in the courts of York.[229]

With regard to Wales one must immediately distinguish the counties of Anglesey, Cardigan, Caernarvon, Carmarthen, and Merioneth, which belonged to the king and formed his principality, from the remainder of Wales which formed the Welsh Marches. In the former counties procedure was similar to the procedure followed in the counties of England: royal writs were sent to royal officers in these counties.[230] It is with respect to the Welsh Marches that a different procedure was followed. When an excommunicate was staying there, the bishops could and did write directly to the chancellors or stewards of the lordships. An examination of the registers of the bishops of Hereford show this as standard practice.[231] Thus, a scribe noted in the register of Archbishop Courtenay in 1387 that because of the exemption of certain Welsh lordships significations were to be sent not to the king but directly to the stewards of the lordships;[232] and the archbishop wrote at that time directly to the steward of the lordship of Ceri[233] just as his predecessor Archbishop Sudbury had done in

---

[228] *Registrum Palatinum Dunelmense* (ed. T. D. Hardy; R. S., 1873-78) 1. 165-66.

[229] *Reg. Langley, Durham* 2. 59-60.

[230] Shortly after the conquest Edward I in 1284 gave to his officers in Wales the mandate, enduring for three years, to obey requests from the bishop of Bangor for the capture of excommunicates (*Cal. Chanc. Rolls*, p. 293), yet in 1298-99 the bishop of Bangor was impelled to complain to the king that he was aggrieved "de excommunicatis capiendis, viz., quod excommunicati capientur de caetero, sicut capi consueverint temporibus principum maxime Wallensium" (Prynne, p. 811, who renders the last word "Wallenses"). Concerning direct royal authority it should be added that Marcher lordships did occasionally fall into the hands of the king, and in such cases the signification procedure was by royal writ. Thus in 1509, royal writs were sent to the lordships of Bromfield, Yale, and Chirk (C.85/24/15 dorse) and in 1517 to the lordship of Usk (*ibid.*, no. 34 dorse), all of which were by then in the king's hands.

[231] *Reg. Poltone, Hereford*, pp. 4-5; *Reg. Spofford, Hereford*, pp. 131-32, 141; *Reg. Myllyng, Hereford* pp. 73, 97-98, 103; *Reg. C. Bothe, Hereford*, p. 197.

[232] "Memorandum quod sunt in Wallia quedam dominia ab exaccionibus regiis et retornis, breuium exempta quorum senescallibus pro capcione excommunicatorum scribitur et non regi sub forma superius annotata" (London, Lambeth Palace Library, Reg. Courteney, f. 72ᵛ).

[233] *Ibid.* For a transcription of this, as typical of these direct significations to Wales, see *infra* Appendix B, p. 172.

1375 with regard to the lordship of Glamorgan.[234] This is as one would expect. Yet one would not expect to find the archbishop of Canterbury signifying to the king persons from the exempt lordships or, indeed, to find chancery issuing writs for their capture. Strangely enough, this is the case. For example, Richard II in 1386, having been apprised by the archbishop of Canterbury of the continued excommunication of a very large number of ecclesiastics of Llandaff diocese for failure to pay the clerical subsidy, ordered the exchequer to issue writs for their arrest to the marcher lords in that diocese.[235] Somewhat different are the later examples in which the writs were sent not to the marcher lords but rather to one of their officers. Thus, in 1450 at the request of John Kemp, archbishop of Canterbury, the royal chancery issued to the steward of the lordships of Usk and Caerleon a writ for the arrest of three persons from Wales.[236] Similarly, in 1520 a royal writ *Significavit* was sent to the chancellor or steward of the lordship of Ewyas Lacy.[237] These royal writs must have appeared to the local officials as external warrants and, as such, could set in motion the local machinery against excommunicates.[238]

[234] London, Lambeth Palace Library, Reg. Sudbury, f. 111ᵛ.

[235] *CCR, 1305-89*, pp. 149-150.

[236] "Emanauit litera super ista materia penultimo die Maii anno etc. xxviii Henrico Griffits senescallo Ricardi ducis Eboraci in dominiis de Vske et Carsleon in marchiis Wallie ad iusticiandas personas de quibus infra fit mencio secundum consuetudinem patrie" (C.85/19/12 dorse).

[237] "Cancellario siue senescallo Georgii Neuille militis domini de Bargauenny dominii sui de Ewyas Lacy in partibus de Southewall seu eorum aut eorum alterius deputato ibidem" (C.85/24/44 dorse).

[238] Perhaps falling into this same group would be the request of the bishop of Hereford in 1281 that the king write to the lord of Abergavenny for the capture of an excommunicate (C.85/86/13). Not wholly dissimilar in this respect was the action of the bishop of Coventry and Lichfield, who in 1518 asked the king to write to the sheriff of Chester (C.85/64/6).

CHAPTER IV

THE EFFECT OF APPEAL

L EGAL systems in civilized societies contain within themselves provisions for reducing to a minimum the possibility of human error
and malice in the devising and administering of their laws. The need
for such provisions is met in part by allowance for equity procedure and for
customs contrary to and beyond the law, but nowhere is the recognition
of the possibility of error and malice more evident than in the provisions
made for appeals. Indeed, without an appellate procedure the administration of justice could never be more than primitive. Medieval canon
law devoted considerable attention to appeals, basing itself on Roman law
but departing from it freely in matters of detail.[1] The canonical teaching
on appeal was not without effect on the legal position of the excommunicate
and, in fact, provided the English excommunicate with an opportunity
to evade or, at least, to postpone secular action against him. By the mid-
thirteenth century this opportunity was seized, and there developed by
the end of that century types of action which were used throughout the
rest of the period here under study. This chapter describes these actions
against the background of the canon law on appeals.

I. CANONICAL PROVISIONS FOR APPEAL

The system of judicial appeals which operated in the ecclesiastical courts
of the middle ages took its form within the hierarchichal structure of the
church.[2] This structure made the distinction between inferior and superior
courts quite clear and with it the route of appeal. For practical purposes,
it can be said that in England the court of the archdeacon was the lowest
court hearing cases of all types. Superior to it was the court of the bishop,
often called his consistory. These were both courts of first instance, but,

---

[1] The title *De appellationibus* in the Decretals of Gregory IX contains 73 chapters (X 2.28).

[2] For a survey of certain aspects of the canonical teaching on appeals see A. Amanien, "Appel,"
Dictionnaire de droit canonique 1. 764-807. For England, Brian Woodcock has reconstructed the
practice from the records of the ecclesiastical courts of the diocese of Canterbury (*Medieval Ecclesiastical Courts in the Diocese of Canterbury* (London, 1952), chap. 5).

in addition, the bishop's court was court of appeal from the court of the archdeacon. The metropolitan of each province maintained a provincial court, which heard cases appealed from the courts of his suffragans: in the province of Canterbury the court of the Arches, which was wont to sit at the church of St. Mary-le-Bow in London, and in the northern province the court of chancery, which sat at York. At the top of this structure was the court of the apostolic see, from which there was no appeal. A person could appeal either from a grievance (*a gravamine*) inflicted on him by the judge or his adversary or from a sentence interlocutory or definitive; from a sentence an appeal had to be made within ten days, to be counted from the day on which the person first gained knowledge of the sentence. But whatever the type of appeal, it followed either one of two courses. The appellant could appeal to the next superior court and could continue *a gradu ad gradum* until he reached the apostolic see. Alternatively, he could appeal at any time directly to the apostolic see and this, according to the canonists, because the pope was universal ordinary (*ordinarius cunctorum*). Tuitorial appeals were a type of appeal to the apostolic see whose use was peculiar to the British Isles. In fact, a tuitorial appeal was two appeals; the person appealed his sentence or grievance to the apostolic see and at the same time appealed to the court of the metropolitan for protection (*tuitio*) for a year so that he could prosecute his appeal at Rome without suffering any injury during the interval.[3]

The principal effect of an appeal was to suspend the matter under appeal and to allow nothing further to be done by the lower court. Hence, the lower court could not execute its sentence until the court of appeal dismissed the appeal and remitted the case. Yet the suspensive effect of appeal did not apply in the case of excommunication; even after an excommunicate appealed, he was still under sentence of excommunication and could be denounced as such.[4] The reason given by Innocent III in his decretal *Pastoralis* (1204) was simply that in the case of excommunication sentence and execution of sentence were not separable.[5] Raymond

---

[3] The system of tuitorial appeals still awaits the specialized investigation which it merits. Outlines of its operation are provided by Woodcock (*ibid.*, pp. 64-67) and Miss Irene Churchill (*Canterbury Administration* (London, 1933) 1. 427, 460-65). The suffragans of the Canterbury province raised several objections to the system in 1282. The obvious point was that this system allowed a person to appeal from the court of the archdeacon to the court of the Arches for protection, thus effectively bypassing the court of the bishop. This dispute is fully reconstructed by Miss Decima L. Douie, *Archbishop Pecham* (Oxford, 1952), pp. 208-211.

[4] Eugène Vernay has described the status of an excommunicate who appeals his sentence in his introduction to *Le "Liber de Excommunicatione" du Cardinal Bérenger-Frédol* (Paris, 1912), pp. lviii-lxiv.

[5] X 2.28.53 (Potthast 2350).

of Pennafort and others after him added two further reasons: (i) excommunication is a spiritual penalty confirmed by Christ, from whom there is no appeal; and (ii) no one is excommunicated except for contumacy, and a *contumax* cannot appeal.[6]

A further difficulty presented itself to the excommunicate in that he could not be a plaintiff in an ecclesiastical court: "excommunicatus non habet personam standi in iudicio." Alexander III was conscious of this difficulty and distinguished whether the excommunication was imposed before or after the appeal. In the former case he ought to be absolved by the archbishop or, if the archbishop would allow it, by the bishop from whom he appealed, and the absolution should precede the hearing of the appeal; in the latter case there was no need for absolution since the excommunication clearly did not hold.[7] Innocent III, however, in 1203 made a more basic distinction: was the excommunication appealed as unjust or as null?[8] If it was appealed as unjust, then the validity of the excommunication was not in doubt and absolution was required before the appeal could be heard. If it was appealed as null either because the sentence had been imposed after an appeal or because the sentence expressed an intolerable error, the validity of the sentence was in question; in which cases it was the practice of the apostolic see to absolve the excommunicate *ad cautelam* before proceeding to hear the appeal. The lines of future development were now clear. It remained for the practice of the papal court to be extended to the western church and for the reasons for nullity to be expanded. A decree of the first Council of Lyons (1245) provided that absolution *ad cautelam* could be denied to an appellant only if his adversary or the judge *a quo* proved within eight days that the excommunication was for manifest offense, and Innocent IV in commenting on this decree held that it applied only in cases where the excommunicate claimed that excommunication had been imposed after appeal.[9] To the two cases in which this applied as set forth by Innocent III others were soon added. Raymond of Pennafort gave a third: that the excommunicating judge lacked jurisdictional competence.[10] Hostiensis listed

---

[6] *Summa sancti Raymundi de Peniafort* 3.33.55 (Rome, 1603, p. 433).

[7] *PL* 200, 1263; 1 Comp. 1.23.2.

[8] X 5.39.40 (Potthast 1830). Although Innocent did not explicitly use the terms "just" and "null," it is quite clear that this is the distinction which he is making. See Bernard of Parma in *Glos. ord.* X 5.39.40, v. *in Sardicem* and Ioannes Andreae in *Glos. ord.* on *Sext.* 5.11.2, v. *solet* and in *Novella in Sextum* 5.11.2 (Venice, 1499; reprinted Graz, 1963, pp. 290-95).

[9] The decree is found in *Con. Oec. Decr.*, pp. 267-68, and in *Sext.* 5.11.2; Innocent's remarks appear in *In V libros decretalium commentaria* X 5.39.61.10.

[10] *Summa sancti Raymundi de Peniafort* 3.33.33 (p. 413).

eight cases where nullity could be alleged and the appellant absolved *ad cautelam*.[11] Innocent IV said that the excommunication had been imposed merely to prevent him from taking legal action.[12] Bérenger Frédol, who at the very beginning of the fourteenth century wrote a specialized treatise on absolution *ad cautelam*, said that in his day this type of absolution was to be given to anyone requesting it.[13]

Absolution *ad cautelam*, then, was granted only in cases where the appellant alleged that the sentence was null. If he alleged that the sentence was not just, then he would have to seek simple absolution (i.e., absolution in its normal form). By absolution *ad cautelam* the excommunicate was truly absolved; he reverted to his status *ante sententiam*. No longer could exceptions of excommunication be raised against him by his adversaries. Those with whom he came in contact were not bound by the severe provision concerning social intercourse with excommunicates. At the same time, this procedure allowed the appellant, if he were a priest, to celebrate the divine offices without fear of incurring irregularities. Although he was absolved and enjoyed the effects of absolution, the excommunicate who was absolved *ad cautelam* was not considered to have confessed the validity of his excommunication; the sentence was held to have been in doubt, and he was absolved purely as a precaution to take account of the possibility that the sentence might have been valid. If there was no doubt, there was no need of absolution. Yet the status of the excommunicate who was thus absolved differed from the status of an excommunicate who was absolved by simple absolution after repentence: although absolved, he still stood liable to re-excommunication if he failed to sustain his appeal or if he failed to prosecute it within a year. Before the judge would absolve him, he had at least to swear that he would obey the court's decision. The suffragan bishops of the Canterbury province wished to underline this difference when they complained to Pecham in 1282 that such absolutions

---

[11] *Summa Hostiensis* 5. de clerico excommunicato deposito vel interdicto ministrante. 4. These eight cases are reducible to the basic three enumerated by Raymond of Pennafort. Ioannes Andreae added four other cases for a total of twelve (*Glos. ord.* in *Scxt.* 5.11.10, v. *ad cautelam*).

[12] *In V libros decretalium commentaria* X 5.39.40 (Venice, 1578, f. 228ᵛ).

[13] "Hodie autem videtur cuilibet petenti debere dari absolucio ad cautelam" (p. 4). He further stated it as his considered opinion that "ubicumque probabiliter dubitatur an aliquis sit excommunicatus vel non ut quia dicitur sentencia nulla et de hoc alique presumpciones apparent, non tamen constat, vel quia fama est quod aliquis est excommunicatus, non tamen aliter constat et talis vult anime sue vel fame consulere vel actum aliquem exercere a quo repelleretur excommunicatus, talis potest et debet ad cautelam absolvi" (p. 7). His treatise was entitled *De absolucione ad cautelam* and has been edited by Eugène Vernay together with Frédol's list of *ipso facto* excommunications (see *supra* p. 117, n. 4). On Frédol see Paul Viollet, "Bérenger Frédol, Canoniste," *Histoire littéraire de la France* 34. 62-178.

were being published by the provincial court without specific mention that the absolution had been granted *ad cautelam*.[14] Yet it should be emphasized that absolution *ad cautelam* was not conditional but absolute; as such, it was to influence substantially the practice of secular constraint against excommunicates.

II. The Use of Appeal to Avoid Capture

It was altogether natural for the canonical provisions for judicial appeals to enter into the procedure for signifying excommunicates. Excommunications, like other *gravamina* and sentences, were often the subject of appeal from one court to another. Since the judge *ad quem* could not proceed without first absolving the excommunicated appellant, he absolved him *ad cautelam* at the beginning of proceedings (*ante omnia*). Once absolved, the appellant was no longer subject to coercion by the secular arm as an excommunicate since he was not now an excommunicate; writs would not be issued for his capture and writs which had been issued before absolution were rescindable. Such cases appear throughout our entire period. In 1239, for example, four men who had been excommunicated by the archbishop of Canterbury and for whose arrest a writ had been issued to the sheriff of Staffordshire, appealed to the papal legate, who absolved them; the king thereupon sent another writ to the sheriff ordering him not to molest these men and, if they had been captured, to release them.[15] Four years later Henry III wrote from France to his regent and two other officials not to issue writs *de excommunicato capiendo* if the excommunicate had appealed his excommunication.[16] By this time, there can scarcely be any doubt, the king's chancery recognized that an appeal would lead to a change in the status of an excommunicate and that after an appeal "nichil innouetur." Two methods of proceeding in cases of excommunicates who appealed their excommunications were to develop and to exist simultaneously: one in which the ecclesiastical judge — and, radically, the bishop — controlled the procedure; another in which they were bypassed and the royal chancery in effect judged the legitimacy of such appeals.

The first of these procedures, used from the mid-thirteenth century, may have been the usual procedure at that time but by the beginning of

---

[14] *Reg. Epp. Peckham* 1. 330; cf., *ibid.*, pp. 333, 336, 339. See Miss Douie, *Archbishop Pecham*, p. 208.

[15] *CCR, 1237-1242*, p. 154.

[16] *CCR, 1242-47*, pp. 66-67.

the fourteenth century it was exceptional and so it remained. In this procedure the excommunicate who appealed and was absolved was treated in the same way as an excommunicate who repented and was absolved. The bishop by whose authority the absolution was granted wrote to chancery, informing the king of the absolution and requesting supersedence of the writ for capture and, if the excommunicate had been captured, his release. In the case of an appeal the absolution was granted by the judge *ad quem* and, hence, the letter to chancery was normally written by the bishop by whose commission the judge *ad quem* acted. Thus in 1282 when Richard Braynford and his son appealed their excommunications from the court of a suffragan bishop to the court of the metropolitan where they were absolved, it was Archbishop Pecham who wrote to chancery requesting supersedence of the writ sued by his suffragan.[17] In an unusual case in 1389 the excommunicate appealed from the special commissary of the archbishop of Canterbury to the archbishop's audience; after his absolution the archbishop requested a writ to supersede the writ for capture which he had sued against him.[18] In the event, however, of a direct appeal to the apostolic see, the request was sent to chancery by the bishop from whose jurisdiction the appeal had been made. The reason is clear: just as the pope could not request the capture of an excommunicate, so too he could not request supersedence. For example, in 1273 when seven men who had been excommunicated and signified by Richard Gravesend, bishop of Lincoln, appealed to Rome, it was Gravesend who requested that the superseding writ be sent.[19] When the appeal to the pope was made from the archbishop's court, the same procedure was followed.[20] In the early sixteenth century when chancery honored significations from papal judges-delegate, the cases which gave rise to the excommunications were presumably cases which devolved to the pope by way of appeal.[21]

[17] C.85/3/73. In another case, Thomas Redeland in 1454 appealed his excommunication from the Norwich consistory to the court of the Arches where he was absolved; the archbishop thereupon requested a writ for his deliverance (C.85/19/35). In a somewhat similar case, it was the official of the Arches, Master Humphrey Hawardyn, and not the archbishop, who wrote on 6 Feb. 1503 to chancery for the issuance of a superseding writ in favor of Robert Boys, an excommunicate whom he had absolved on 15 Oct. 1502 (C.85/23/55).

[18] C.85/11/51.

[19] C.85/99/7.

[20] E.g., on 1 Feb. 1322 Archbishop Reynolds wrote to chancery for a writ of supersedence for John de Derset, who had appealed to the apostolic see (C.85/8/51). For transcription see *infra* Appendix H, p. 201.

[21] E.g., in one case in 1512 the signification was sent by Master Richard Tollet, canon of Exeter, who together with the dean of Exeter and two canons of Lichfield was hearing the appeal (C.85/207/3). He complained that despite the absolution *ad cautelam* of Nicholas Ferby, who had appealed

To the general rule (viz., in this mode of procedure the request for supersedence was to be made by the bishop *ad quem* save in the case of appeals to the apostolic see when it was to be made by the bishop *a quo*) one case stands out as a clear exception. Although Anna Hauhisia appealed her excommunication from the bishop of Llandaff to the court of Canterbury in 1254, the subsequent request for supersedence was not sent by the archbishop of Canterbury but by the bishop of Llandaff.[22] No other example of such action by the bishop *a quo* has come to light; this case may have been conditioned by peculiar circumstances or may be attributable to some uncertainty at that time concerning the correct way of proceeding.

This first type of procedure in cases of appeal accounted for only a very small number of cases, if one may judge from extant evidence. Clearly this procedure, although eminently consistent with canon law and other features of the signification procedure, was used in cases of appeal only by way of exception from at least the beginning of the fourteenth century. By that time another procedure had become well established and remained in the ascendancy for over two centuries and must be considered the principal procedure in cases of appeal.

This second and principal procedure consisted essentially in the appellant giving proof in chancery that he had appealed his excommunication to a higher ecclesiastical court and in his requesting supersedence of the writ for his capture. It was not the bishop, either *a quo* or *ad quem*, who took the initiative; he was bypassed, although modifications and refinements were made in the course of time to give some protection to his rights in the matter. Exactly when this practice began cannot be determined from the available evidence, but it had become so developed by 1285 that it was the subject of an article in the clerical *gravamina* of that year. The bishops complained that, when an excommunicate asserted before the king's court that he had appealed to the apostolic see, he should not be upheld by the secular arm, since the secular court had no competence in matters of appeal and since absolution to such a one would not be granted at Rome until cognizance was taken of the appeal. In the ensuing exchange between king and clergy concerning this article the royal side gave the assurance that this practice was not employed indiscriminately

---

from Warham's audience, the archbishop had secured his imprisonment as a result of a signification dated 27 April 1512 (C.85/24/27). A similar example, reflecting probably an early practice which existed before the rule became fixed, is seen in a case in 1239. The papal legate and his delegate judges wrote to the king requesting the release of four men who had appealed from the archbishop of Canterbury and whom the archbishop's judge, the archdeacon of Stafford, had refused to absolve (*CCR, 1237-1242*, p. 154).

[22] *CCR, 1254-56*, p. 14; C.85/167/7.

but only in cases of notable persons who were actively (*cum effectu*) prosecuting appeals which could be presumed legitimate.[23] It is clear, then,
that by 1285 chancery was superseding writs *de excommunicato capiendo*
in certain cases of appeal to Rome and that appeal and its active prosecution rather than absolution were used as the criteria for supersedence.[24]

Records of such cases begin to appear during the 1290's, become more
common in the early fourteenth century, and continue throughout the
rest of the medieval period; a total of 328 cases has been found.[25] These
reveal a smoothly functioning procedure of appeal followed by supersedence in favor of petitioners without apparent distinction of rank. By
1317 the practice was no longer restricted to appeals to the apostolic see
but had been extended to include appeals of every kind. The procedure
was fully formed by that time. Essentially, the appellant would prove in
chancery the fact of his appeal and chancery would give his opponents a
day in King's Bench and, pending that day, allowed the appellant his
freedom in mainprise. How it worked in practice remains to be discussed.

In the first place, the excommunicate or his proctor — for the excommunicate might already have been lodged in a royal prison — came to
chancery to establish two facts: (i) that an appeal had been made and (ii)
that it was being actively prosecuted. The first was proven by an authentic
instrument. The best proof of appeal was a letter from the judge *ad quem*
which indicated that he had taken cognizance of the appeal. This could
be a testimonial letter to that effect or a copy of the inhibition sent to the
judge *a quo*. Chancery often acknowledged, for example, that knowledge
of the excommunicate's appeal was gained "per quasdam literas sigillo
officialis curie Cantuariensis signatas in cancellaria nostra exhibitas."[26]

[23] The relevant texts are in *Councils* 2. 957-58, 960, 963. The clerical position was to be argued
at length by Lyndwood in the fifteenth century, yet his discussion was not provoked by any known
contemporary dispute (see *infra* pp. 134-136).

[24] That the refusal of bishops to request supersedence might have accounted for this second
method seems unlikely. There is evidence of only one instance of this: the case of Master Robert
de Appelby, parson of Scawby, Lincoln diocese, in 32 Edward I (1303-04). His proctor secured
the annulment of the excommunication imposed on him in the court of the Arches. Because the
archbishop of Canterbury refused to write for his release, he made the request himself (Prynne,
p. 1041). Not entirely dissimilar was the case in 1239 in which the judge refused absolution (see
supra p. 121, n. 21).

[25] It is possible to determine in 304 cases the courts to which the appeals were made: 220 to the
apostolic see (of which 101 were tuitorial appeals to the court of Canterbury and 6 were tuitorial
appeals to the court of York); 73 to the court of Canterbury; 8 to the audience of the archbishop
of Canterbury; one each to the legatine audience of Cardinal Wolsey, the Norwich consistory, and
the conservators of the order of Sempringham.

[26] See, e.g., C.202/C.19/177.

Since a large number of the appeals were made to the apostolic see, the letter from the judge *ad quem* was often a papal bull.[27] At first, this was duly acknowledged in the writ which the appellant sued out of chancery,[28] but during the course of the fourteenth century a rubric was inserted in the registers of writs which reminded the chancery clerks that it sufficed to say that the fact of the appeal was established by public instruments without mentioning papal letters specifically.[29] General references of this kind in cases appealed to the apostolic see appear by 1326 and seem to have become standard by the early years of Edward III.[30]

An alternative method for establishing in chancery the fact of an appeal was to exhibit an instrument of appeal. This document was usually drawn up in the name of the excommunicate's proctor, was witnessed by several men, and was notarized by a notary public; it stated that the excommunicate was appealing his excommunication from one specific court to another.[31] Although an instrument of appeal as such did not prove that the appeal had been sent to the superior court or that it had been accepted by that court or *a fortiori* that the excommunicate had been absolved, it was nonetheless accepted in chancery as proof of appeal; the question of absolution was not considered.[32] This anomaly was not lost on the bishops as is evident from their complaint of 1285. The rejoinder to the bishops indicated what was to be the practical solution: the excommunicate would have to establish his active prosecution of the appeal. If the appellant was able and willing, he could produce witnesses in chancery who would testify to his active prosecution of the appeal; it sufficed, however, for him to swear to it himself.[33] For example, in 33 Edward I (1303-04) two signi-

---

[27] Letters from papal judges-delegate were also admitted in proof of appeal. E.g., in 1310 three men of Norwich diocese were excommunicated in the court of Canterbury and signified for capture by the archbishop on 18 May (C.85/7/41). They subsequently appealed to the apostolic see, and judges-delegate revoked the sentence. The men in order to prove their appeal in chancery exhibited letters from the judges-delegate (C.202/C.10/141).

[28] See, e.g., C.202/C.16/226 (dated 1320): "sicut per literas papales bullatas super hoc confectas et in cancellaria nostra exhibitas plenius apparet."

[29] See, e.g., London, *BM*, Harl. MSS 961, f. 33r and 1118, f. 85r; the rubric is printed in *Reg. omn. brev.*, f. 68v.

[30] For the earliest example of this, see the writ dated 20 July 1326 (C.202/C.22/273).

[31] A number of these instruments of appeal can still be found among the chancery miscellany; see especially C.47/18/6 *passim* and C.47/20/4-6 *passim*.

[32] William Durandus in his *Speculum iuris* stated that the appealed party was not held to believe the assertion of his adversary that he had appealed unless he were shown an instrument of appeal (2.1. de citatione. 4.3).

[33] "Et debet probare diligentiam suam in prosecutione appellationis per testes, vel jurare: sed oportet quod hoc fiat infra annum a tempore appellationis etc." (*Reg. omn. brev.*, f. 68v; this rubric appears in the same MSS cited *supra*, n. 29).

fications from the archbishop of Canterbury and one from the bishop of Salisbury were thwarted by excommunicates who came to chancery with instruments of appeal to the apostolic see, which they were said to be prosecuting.[34] In 1348 an excommunicate was described as prosecuting his tuitorial appeal "in quantum potest."[35] And four years later an excommunicated woman from Kingston-upon-Hull was said by chancery to be "prepared" to prosecute her appeal.[36] In many cases the appeal was drawn up just prior to its presentation in chancery and obviously the appellant had little opportunity to have begun actual prosecution. Future prosecution was clearly the question before chancery in such cases, and the oath of the appellant with regard to prosecution must have been *ad futurum*. There is no evidence that chancery wrote to the court of appeal to ascertain the truth of the assertions of the excommunicate.[37] Hence, it was with relative ease that an excommunicate could counteract the writ *de excommunicato capiendo*: he could merely present an instrument of appeal and swear to its active prosecution.[38]

The time elapsing between the sentence of excommunication and the appeal to the higher ecclesiastical court was obviously more than forty days, since the appeal was not made by the excommunicate until he had been signified by the bishop. An obvious question presents itself: how could an excommunicate appeal his sentence after the lapse of more than forty days, since appeals from sentence had to be made within ten days? The answer appears to be that the excommunicate was not appealing his excommunication as a sentence but rather as a *gravamen*. His appeal would

---

[34] Prynne, p. 1041.

[35] C.202/C.46/10.

[36] She was Alice wife of William Lytelwylle of Kingston-upon-Hull (C.202/C.50/19; cf., C.47/136/11/piece dated 18 Feb. 1353).

[37] One might possibly see such a consultation in the unusual case of William Clerk of Dartmouth in 1390 and 1393. See *infra* Appendix H, p. 203 for the details. In the case of John Stowe (or Stowte) in 1414 chancery consulted with the dean of the Arches, but here the consultation concerned whether he had prosecuted an appeal (C.47/18/6/32). Since his signification was dated 19 Sept. 1411 (C.85/124/8), it seems safe to assume that he had gained supersedence pending an appeal at that time and that in 1414, more than the year allowed for prosecution of his appeal having elapsed, his adversary sought his recapture. At any rate, the dean of the Arches found no record in the register of his court concerning an appeal by John Stowe (C.47/18/6/33).

[38] There is a single instance of a third way of proceeding. In 22 Edward I (1293-94) the archbishop of York excommunicated and signified the prior and subprior of Holy Trinity, York. They claimed exemption from the archbishop's jurisdiction and appealed to the apostolic see. They gained remedy from the king by exhibiting not their appeal or a letter from the court *ad quem* but their charters which proved their exemption; see Prynne, p. 610. For a later stage in this controversy see C. 85/176/32 and *Cal. Chanc. Warr.*, pp. 95-96.

deny his contumacy on the grounds, perhaps, that he was cited to an unsafe place or at too short notice: to him his excommunication and subsequent signification constituted grievances with continuing effects. As long as a *gravamen* perdured, an excommunicate could appeal from it, even if a month or more had elapsed from its inception.[39] The bishops never raised this question of the time elapsing between sentence and appeal, although they attacked the appeal procedure on other grounds.

The reason why a signified excommunicate claimed in chancery that he had appealed his excommunication was to gain supersedence of the writ for capture.[40] In the earliest extant examples chancery issued a writ to the local sheriff ordering him to supersede the writ which had already been sent to him; if he had secured the capture of the excommunicate, he was to deliver him. The sheriff was to take this action "donec de consilio nostro aliud duxerimus ordinandum." There is no evidence to suggest that at this time any security was required before supersedence. Thus, Master William de Caldewell, vicar of Stoke by Nayland, Norwich diocese, probably in 1289 (certainly before 1290), claimed in chancery that he had appealed from the bishop of Norwich to the apostolic see, and thereupon a writ was issued to the sheriff of Norfolk for his deliverance with the *donec* clause added.[41] In such cases the adversaries of the excommunicate could come to chancery and oppose supersedence, but they had to gain knowledge of the excommunicate's action by their own devices, since chancery did not inform them. In Caldewell's case his adversary, William Barry, asserted in chancery that Caldewell had not in fact appealed, and chancery ordered his recapture. By 1304 chancery was responding to objections made by adversaries to such appeals by giving the excommunicate a day in which to reply in the presence of his adversaries, if they wished to attend.[42]

This general way of proceeding continued at least until the first decade of the fourteenth century, but two major developments were then to take place: supersedence was not to be granted until the adversaries were given

---

[39] Durandus considers this matter: "Ubi per interlocutoriam laeditur quis, et continue grauatur, non transit in rem iudicatam post decem dies... Per quae potest colligi quod... quandiu durat grauamen, tandiu potest etiam post decem dies appellari. Quandiu enim non reuocat, tandiu grauat, et ideo semper appellatur" (*Speculum iuris* 2.2. de appellationis. 5.5-6).

[40] In a few cases the writ for capture had not yet been issued and the excommunicate succeeded in stopping its issuance. This is clearly what happened in three cases in 33 Edward I (1303-04) (Prynne, p. 1041), in 1376 (C.85/184/1 and dorse) and another in 1408 (C.85/13/21 and dorse).

[41] C.202/C.4/111, which is printed in Prynne, pp. 426-27.

[42] See the case of Edmund de Hoo (Prynne, p. 1040). The objections were made before supersedence was given, yet chancery ordered the sheriff of Suffolk to release Hoo, who was to appear before the king and council on the quindene of Michaelmas.

a day to oppose, and the excommunicate was to be released in the interim only in mainprise.

The older chancery practice of superseding capture but reserving the right of recapture is last heard of in 1305.[43] In the following year three excommunicated appellants were released only on condition that they could find mainpernors who would guarantee their presence in chancery in the event that the court of appeal failed to revoke their excommunications.[44] This was but a transitional type of procedure, yet it may have introduced the requirement of mainprise before supersedence. In the meantime, chancery by 1310 made use of the practice of not granting supersedence without first giving the excommunicate's adversaries a day to oppose.[45] But it is not clear whether at that time temporary supersedence until the day in court was granted in mainprise, nor is the picture any clearer in the light of a similar case in 1316.[46] The earliest case in which it can be said with certitude that the two procedures were used together is the case of John Malmesbury, who appealed to the court of Canterbury from the bishop of Llandaff in 1318.[47] From that time it was the accepted practice of chancery in such cases, and so it remained through the rest of the middle ages.

During the next two hundred years and more the chancery procedure in cases of ecclesiastical appeals remained almost unchanged. Once appeal and prosecution of appeal were established by the excommunicate chancery issued two writs: an *interim supersedeas* to the sheriff to whom the

---

[43] See Prynne, p. 1109; for a similar case two years earlier see *ibid.*, pp. 985-86, which was entered on the Close Rolls (*CCR, 1302-07*, p. 99).

[44] This is the case of the abbot and two monks of Sawley who were signified as excommunicates by the archbishop of York on 25 July 1306 (C.85/178/3) and were soon imprisoned. They appealed to the apostolic see and their case was delegated to three canons of Lincoln. The abbot and his two monks requested supersedence by virtue of their appeal, but chancery required that they obtain mainpernors who would insure their presence in chancery within three weeks after any summons which might prove necessary if the judges-delegate did not revoke their sentences; if the judges did revoke their sentences, the mainpernors were acquitted of their obligation. See Prynne, pp. 1146, 1198.

[45] A writ dated 16 July 1310 ordered the sheriff of Norfolk to summon the parson of Hedenham to appear in King's Bench on the morrow of the Assumption to show cause why the writ for the capture of three excommunicates of Norwich diocese should not be superseded pending their appeal to the pope (C.202/C.10/141).

[46] C.202/C.13/23.

[47] C.202/C.14/193. There really was no need for chancery to inform the sheriffs in the writs of 1310 and 1316 (*supra* nn. 45-46) that supersedence was in mainprise. In each instance the sheriff was told to supersede the writ for capture in the interim before the adversary's day in court. In these cases the excommunicates could have found mainpernors in chancery. Hence, interim supersedence in mainprise could have been the practice from as early as 1310, or even 1306.

writ of capture had been sent and a *scire facias* to the sheriff of the excommunicate's adversary.

The interim supersedence which chancery ordered, it must be emphasized, had effect only until the day when the parties appeared in court to determine if a supersedence should be given pending the appeal. This initial supersedence was dependent upon the excommunicate obtaining sufficient mainprise to secure his appearance in court.[48] Frequently the excommunicate would find his mainpernors in chancery. When he did not, the writ sent to the sheriff would direct him to supersede only if the excommunicate should find mainpernors in the county. In such cases the excommunicate usually found mainpernors and the sheriff would effect supersedence.[49] Yet it was not unknown for the excommunicate to be unable to obtain mainpernors before the sheriff, and as a consequence in these cases the writ for capture was not superseded by the sheriff.[50] But by about the end of the fourteenth century excommunicates were able to produce sufficient mainpernors in chancery, and it was no longer necessary for the sheriffs to be concerned about them.[51]

The obligation which the mainpernors undertook was to have the excommunicate present in King's Bench on the day assigned, and this obligation they assumed under a specific penalty. Originally the mainpernors agreed to their own imprisonment in case of default — "corpus pro corpore," as it was described in the writ. The number of mainpernors varied from case to case and could be as many as five or six but was more usually between two and four.[52] In the 1370's, however, imprisonment was replaced by money payments. A writ dated 20 February 1372 ordered

[48] On mainprise see Elsa de Haas, "Concepts of the Nature of Bail in English and American Criminal Law," *University of Toronto Law Journal* 6 (1945-46) 385-400; Pollock and Maitland 2. 584-590.

[49] Sheriffs could normally allow most criminals to be released in mainprise, but captured excommunicates were explicitly excluded in 1275 by the first Statute of Westminster, c. 15 (*Statutes* 1. 30) and, in response to a Commons' Petition, by statute of 1446 (*Rot. Parl.* 5. 110). Cf., the case in the 1250's where the sheriff released an excommunicate when the prisoner paid him 40s. (*Select Cases of Procedure Without Writ Under Henry III* (eds. H. G. Richardson and G. O. Sayles; Selden Soc., vol. 60, 1941), pp. 112-113).

[50] E.g., in response to the writ dated 4 Oct. 1336 the sheriff of Lincs. informed chancery that William Costard did not succeed in finding mainpernors (C.202/C.32/116). Similar examples can be found in 1341 (C.47/96/2/piece date 28 Aug. 1341), 1353 (C.202/C.51/71), 1360 (C.202/C.58/46), 1361 (C.202/C.59/9), and 1369 (C.202/C.67/78).

[51] The latest case which has been noted in which chancery instructed the sheriff to deliver the excommunicate if he presents the sheriff with sufficient mainprise was in 1390 (C.202/C.92/105).

[52] The abbot of Sawley in 1306 had twelve mainpernors (Prynne, p. 1198; *CCR, 1302-07*, pp. 521-22).

the sheriffs of London to effect the interim release of Robert Poyntell, vicar of Ticehurst, Sussex, because he had three mainpernors from whose lands and chattels would be levied £40. each in the event of his non-appearance in court.[53] Money penalties immediately became very common, and the penalty of imprisonment virtually disappeared by 1378.[54] Not only did the numbers of mainpernors continue to vary as before, but the amount of the money penalties varied from case to case for no apparent reason. In 1397 an excommunicated woman obtained the interim supersedence of her capture with only two mainpernors pledged for the sums of 10 marks each.[55] At the other extreme, Bartholomew Wilmyngton, farmer of the manor of Moor Hall in Sussex, gained interim supersedence in 1389 only after four mainpernors pledged £100. each and, in a very unusual move, he himself pledged a further £100.[56] Four mainpernors at £20. each was not unusual nor was two at the same amount. A wide variation prevailed at all times, and this suggests that these matters were arranged with respect to each case individually.

The mainpernors usually agreed to nothing more than the appearance of the excommunicate in King's Bench on the specified day, and the justices exonerated them of their pledge upon his appearance. If the case was continued to another day, new pledges had to be found,[57] unless the original mainpernors had pledged in the beginning not only to his initial appearance but also to his appearance *a die ad diem*.[58] In a certain number

---

[53] C.202/C.70/30. Poyntell had been signified by the bishop of Chichester on 12 Feb. 1372 (C.85/45/21; Salzman, p. 133). He was signified again on 11 November that same year (C.85/45/23; Salzman, p. 134). An undated rescript to a direct appeal to the court of the Arches by Poyntell exists in a formulary book (Cambridge, Gonv. & Caius MS. 588, f. 90r), but this was probably not the appeal which he pleaded in chancery, since the former was a direct appeal and the latter a tuitorial appeal.

[54] The only later case of *corpus pro corpore* mainprise which has come to light was in 2 Henry IV (1400-01) (C.202/C.106/68).

[55] C.202/C.101/81. For transcription see *infra* Appendix H, pp. 201-02.

[56] C.202/C.89/40. For another example of four mainpernors at £100. each see the case of William Menusse of London diocese (C.47/111/22/piece dated 30 March 1395). Only one other instance has been found of excommunicates pledging to their own appearance: in 1445 Nicholas Tuke and John Ive of Norwich diocese found four mainpernors at £20. each and, in addition, pledged themselves £40. each for their own appearance (C.202/C.160/2).

[57] See C.47/90/3/dorse of piece dated 18 Jan. 1386; C.47/98/6/dorse of piece dated 9 July 1387; C.47/120/3/piece dated 15 July 1387. Cf., the case of Thomas Symond of Aylesbury (see next note).

[58] E.g., in 1324 the mainpernors of John Banyard, vicar of Wheatacre, Norwich diocese, pledged in this manner (C.202/C.19/177). It may have been some uncertainty about the nature of the original mainprise that caused difficulty for Thomas Symond of Aylesbury later in that century. He had been excommunicated and, in turn, signified by the bishop of Lincoln on 4 July 1384 (C.85/108/1). By virtue of his appeal to the court of Canterbury a writ was issued for his interim

of cases mainpernors agreed, in addition to the excommunicate's appearance, that he would prosecute his appeal;[59] occasionally the justice in
King's Bench required mainprise of this kind before acquitting an excommunicate.[60] In at least two cases in which the excommunicates failed
to prosecute their appeals the mainpernors were summoned into King's
Bench to show cause why they should not forfeit their pledges.[61] But in
the usual form which mainprise took the danger was very remote that the
excommunicate would absent himself from court, for it was clearly to his
advantage to appear.[62]

The purpose of the hearing in King's Bench was to determine whether
the capture of the excommunicated person should be superseded pending
his appeal. It gave his opponents an opportunity to oppose supersedence
before the king's justices. Thus, at the same time as the *interim supersedeas*

supersedence in mainprise on 7 Oct. 1384 (C.47/91/4/piece with that date). When the parties
appeared by their attorneys on the octave of Martinmas, the case was continued until the quindene of Easter; on that day Symond's mainpernors did not have him there and the recapture of
Symond was ordered (C.47/91/3/piece dated 28 April 1385). Symond soon found three entirely
new mainpernors, and the writ for his recapture was superseded on 20 May 1385 (*ibid.*, piece with
that date). Interestingly enough, his capture was ordered by a subsequent writ dated 15 Oct. 1385
(C.202/C.85/105), but by claiming appeal he again gained an interim supersedence on 28 Nov.
(*ibid.*, no. 106; see *CCR, 1385-89*, p. 101, where it is dated 24 Nov.). The case was then continued
from the quindene of Easter to the octave of John the Baptist, to the octave of Michaelmas, and
to the octave of Hilary in the following year (C.202/C.85/106 dorse).

[59] E.g., according to the writ dated 10 Oct. 1393 concerning the release of the excommunicate
Thomas Henley four mainpernors pledged at £40. each "quod ipse appellacionem suam predictam cum omni diligencia qua decet prosequetur et quod ipse erit paratus coram nobis in cancellaria predicta ad diem predictum ad faciendum et recipiendum quod curia nostra considerauerit" (C.47/111/22/piece with that date).

[60] See, e.g., C.47/120/3/piece dated 3 Jan. 1386; C.47/110/16/piece dated 29 Sept. 1386;
C.47/106/3/piece dated 6 March 1387; C.47/111/19/piece dated 17 Feb. 1389.

[61] The sheriff of Notts. was ordered by a writ dated 6 Feb. 1402 to summon the mainpernors of
William Darley of Nottingham to appear on the quindene of Easter to show separately why £40.
should not be levied from their lands and chattels because Darley had failed to prosecute his
appeal (C.202/C.107/113). On 13 May 1480 a similar writ was sent to the sheriff of Norfolk with
respect to Christina Baker *alias* Clerk of Intwood, who, although she had gained temporary supersedence of her capture on 25 June 1477, had not in the meantime prosecuted her appeal (*CCR,
1476-1485*, pp. 173-74, 208).

[62] Those who undertook mainprise were in most cases men from the excommunicate's locality.
E.g., in 1358 Richard Hawe of Buckland, Dorset, obtained as his mainpernors two men from
Dorset (C.202/C.56/37). Yet in some cases the mainpernors were London merchants or, occa-
sionally, chancery clerks. William Seftford, parson of Norton Bavant, Wilts., in 1379 found four
London merchants (baker, tailor, skinner, and draper) who pledged his appearance at £20. each
(C.202/C.77/74). It would be unrealistic to suppose that men undertook the obligations of main-
prise out of pure altruism or Christian charity; surely the excommunicate recompensed his mainpernors in some way.

was issued, chancery issued a writ *scire facias* requiring the local sheriff to cite the opponent to appear in court; the two writs were combined in a single writ if the same sheriff was involved in each. At first the person so cited was the one at whose instance the excommunication had been imposed in the ecclesiastical court: in instance cases the excommunicate's adversary and in office cases the bishop himself. From 1332 it became increasingly common to cite in instance cases not only the instancer but the bishop as well.[63] Only six cases appear after 1332 in which the instancer alone was cited.[64] In another case in 1344 the instancers were first cited and, when they failed to appear, the archbishop of Canterbury was then cited.[65] During the reign of Richard II instancers were cited less and less and bishops more and more, so that after 1391 the practice of citing instancers had virtually ceased; in the fifteenth century it was only the bishop who was called to oppose supersedence.[66]

The parties could appear in King's Bench either personally or by attorneys, the former being more common for excommunicates and the latter for bishops.[67] In fact, whenever the bishop wished to be present, it was always by attorneys,[68] except in one unusual case when he actually appeared in person before the royal justice.[69] But generally the bishop did

[63] The earliest case in which both instancer and bishop are seen being called to appear is the case of William Noyl of London, who had been excommunicated at the instance of Adam de Holand and signified by the archbishop of Canterbury, both of whom the sheriffs of London were ordered by a writ dated 6 April 1332 to cite for appearance (C.202/C.28/240).

[64] In 1333 (C.202/C.29/74), 1339 (C.202/C.36/11), 1344 (C.202/C.41/80), 1362 (C.202/C.60/ unnumbered piece), 1365 (C.202/C.63/8), and 1374 (C.202/C.72/84).

[65] C.202/C.41/84. Four *scire facias* writs of 1382 and 1383 cited the bishop and the instancer to appear "coniunctim uel separatim" (C.202/C.80/34, 35; C.202/C.81/26, 29). Indeed, in many cases the hearing in King's Bench proceeded with only the instancer appearing to oppose (see, e.g., the case of the excommunicate Petronilla Hodere of Romney: C.47/92/4/pieced date 28 April 1385).

[66] Several such *scire facias* writs are found in 1391, the last being dated 5 Nov. 1391 (C.202/ C.95/5). Subsequently only two similar writs are to be found: one dated 20 Feb. 1395 (C.47/ 111/22/piece with that date) and the other from the second year of Henry IV (1400-01) (C.202/ C.106/68). These examples, however, are clearly exceptions to the practice illustrated by the large number of contemporary *scire facias* writs.

[67] Typical of this is the case of John Farbon of Lincoln, who appeared personally in King's Bench on the quidene of Easter, 1385, while the bishop of Lincoln appeared by his attorney John of Lincoln, clerk (C.202/C.84/63 dorse).

[68] E.g., on the octave of Trinity, 1405, Thomas Arundel, archbishop of Canterbury, was represented by Thomas Smyth, his attorney (C.47/102/2/dorse of piece dated 10 May 1405). Likewise, when the dean and chapter of York were exercising the power of signification *sede vacante* in 1353, they appeared in court by attorney in response to a *scire facias* (C.47/136/11/piece dated 18 Feb. 1353).

[69] Thomas Arundel, bishop of Ely, who was, it should be noted, also chancellor of the realm,

not appear either in person or by attorney, and the same can be said, but to a lesser extent, of the instancer. Only very rarely did the excommunicate fail to appear.[70]

The disposition of the matter before King's Bench was fairly predictable. The excommunicate was almost always dismissed as acquitted *sine die* by the royal justice. In most cases this came as a consequence of the failure of the opponents to appear. Even when the instancer or the bishops' attorney appeared, he might have succeeded in obtaining one or more continuance,[71] but hardly ever did he succeed in stopping supersedence.[72] Of the more than three hundred cases of appeal which have come to light only one has been found in which supersedence was denied in King's Bench.[73] Plainly, an excommunicate who undertook an appeal of his ex-

appeared in person on the quindene of Martinmas, 1386, in the case of John Petyt of Fulbourn, Cambs., not to oppose the latter's appeal but to testify to his absolution: "ad quem diem ... prefatus episcopus ad tunc ibidem personaliter existens testificatus fuit quod idem Iohannes Petyt sancte ecclesie in hac parte, prout attinet, plenarie satisfecit" (C.47/92/4/dorse of piece dated 26 Oct. 1386).

[70] Only in one case has it been discovered that an excommunicate absented himself. On the quindene of Hilary, 1391, the bishop of Lincoln appeared by his attorney John Rothewell, but William atte Kyrk of Sidbrooke, Lincs., the excommunicate, did not come (C.202/C.93/114 dorse) What action was taken as a consequence does not apear, but in view of the unusual fact that the writ sent to the sheriff on 10 Dec. 1390 instead of instructing him to supersede until the hearing instructed him rather to supersede pending the appeal ("tu prefate uicecomes capcioni corporis ipsius Willelmi atte Kyrke uirtute mandati nostri predicti faciende pendente dicte appellacionis negocio supersedeas per manucapcionem supradictam") — the very purpose for which he and the bishop were to appear — atte Kyrke perhaps saw no practical reason for appearing (C.202/C.93/114).

[71] E.g., the abbot and convent of Cirencester, instancers to the excommunication of the layman John de Beckote of Salisbury diocese (signified by Courtney, 4 Nov. 1385 — C.85/11/12), appeared in King's Bench on the octave of the Purification, 1386, by their attorney, and the case was continued until the third week after Easter (C.47/90/3/dorse of piece dated 18 Jan. 1396). In another case, the justices granted three continuances before acquitting the excommunicate and on no occasion did anyone appear to oppose supersedence. This case involved the powerful king's clerk Richard Medford in the single surviving example of his use of the power of signification as prebend of Thurrock. He signified John Northfolk and his wife Joan and, although as a consequence of their appeal to the court of the Arches he was cited to appear in King's Bench on the octave of Hilary, he failed to appear, and the case was continued to the quindene of Easter, to the octave of Trinity, to the quindene of Michaelmas, when the Northfolks were at last acquitted (C.47/98/6/dorse of piece dated 16 Oct. 1387).

[72] The usual comment was that he knew nothing to say in opposition to the excommunicate's supersedence. E.g., Hugh Bavent appeared in King's Bench as attorney for John Trefnant, bishop of Hereford, on the quindene of Michaelmas, 1393, "et nichil sciuit dicere in effectu quare infrascriptus Thomas [More] recederet quietus de curia" (C.47/101/3/dorse of piece dated 26 Aug. 1393).

[73] William Cleve, rector of Nursley, Bucks., was signified for arrest by the bishop of Lincoln on 26 March 1412 (C.85/111/23). After appealing to the apostolic see he sought the usual remedy

communication could confidently expect not to be arrested during the year which was the *tempus utile* for prosecuting his appeal.

After the year had expired, his opponents could complain in chancery that the excommunicate had failed to prosecute his appeal and should be recaptured. For example, in 1320 Joan la Chambre, who had instanced the excommunication of Henry Ernesfast in the previous year but whose efforts to gain his capture were blocked by his appeal, secured from chancery a writ for the appearance of Ernesfast in King's Bench to show why he should not be captured for failure to prosecute his appeal within due time.[74] Similarly, in 1418 the abbot of Westminster obtained a *significavit* against William atte Wood, who had failed to prosecute his appeal to the apostolic see.[75] An excommunicate who decided to use the means of appeal to avoid capture and who had no intention of pursuing his appeal exposed himself to the danger of recapture after a year, but he must surely have realized that the initiative for his recapture lay with his opponents and not the court. Within a year anything could happen: one's opponent might die, a peaceful settlement might be arrived at, etc. It is not surprising that many excommunicates, faced with the prospect of capture now or of possible capture in a year's time, ran the risk of the latter to avoid the former.

III. THE ARGUMENT AGAINST THE ACTION OF CHANCERY

This second and principal method of proceeding in cases of appeal, which has just been described, was open to serious objections on the part of the church. Excommunicates were having their capture superseded by

---

in chancery, and a writ *scire facias et interim supersedeas* under date of 14 Aug. 1412 was dispatched to the sheriff of Bucks. (*CCR, 1409-1413*, p. 333). When Cleve appeared in court on the quindene of Michaelmas, it was found that his appeal had no force and he was committed to the Fleet (*ibid.*). Subsequently he claimed appeal in chancery on at least three occasions, and on each occasion similar writs were issued to the same sheriff: 3 Nov. 1412 (*ibid.*, p. 408), 1 Feb. 1413 (*ibid.*), 12 May 1413 (*CCR, 1413-19*, pp. 78-79). According to an undated entry in the register of Philip Repingdon, bishop of Lincoln (1405-19), a commission was issued to John Southern, official of Lincoln, to absolve Cleve (*Reg. Repingdon, Lincoln* 2. 298).

[74] C.202/C.16/237.

[75] For a transcription of the abbot's signification see Appendix C, pp. 183-85. For other cases in which significations were sent to chancery after failure of excommunicates to prosecute their appeals and in which writs were issued for capture without a further hearing in King's Bench, see the cases of Agnes Nowers of Knossington, Leics., in 1373 (C.85/107/15), and William Darley of Nottingham in 1404 (C.85/185/22). In 1402 Archbishop Arundel requested the capture of Nicholas Cherwode and Robert Knyght of London diocese for not prosecuting their appeal to the apostolic see, but chancery refused to admit the form of his request and did not issue the writ (London, Lambeth Palace Library, Reg. Arundel 1. 418r).

virtue of appeal rather than by virtue of absolution; this objection was raised only once, in 1285,[76] and apparently the clergy were satisfied to base their case on the question of jurisdiction. To the church it appeared as if the secular jurisdiction was judging the legitimacy of appeals from one ecclesiastical court to another. The church's position during the course of the exchange between the clergy and the king in 1285 over this question of jurisdiction can be summarily stated: lay courts have no competence over ecclesiastical appeals and, hence, cannot rule on the legitimacy of such appeals, since cognizance of ecclesiastical appeals pertains solely to the ecclesiastical forum.[77] When the bishops complained about this same question in 1309, they argued that chancery should give greater credence to a signification from a bishop than to an assertion by an excommunicate.[78]

In the first part of the fifteenth century Lyndwood, who as official of the court of the Arches was personally familiar with the question in practice, took up and developed these clerical arguments in his *Provinciale*.[79] He did not believe that an excommunicate who had been signified for arrest should be able to evade arrest by showing an instrument of appeal to a secular judge. A judicial investigation is necessary to determine whether an appeal is valid or invalid, whether it should be held or not, and whether it is legitimate or not. Such an investigation does not pertain to the secular judge and, hence, no legal determination can be made by him on these questions. It is possible for an appeal to be drawn up according to the correct legal form but still to be manifestly frivolous and frustratory; as such, it is not deferred to by ecclesiastical judges and the effects of appeal do not take place. Yet it is only in the ecclesiastical forum that the frivolous and frustratory nature of an appeal can be determined. If the

---

[76] See *supra* p. 122.

[77] *Ibid.*

[78] "Item, quando inferiores subditi excommunicati suggerunt se appellasse ab ordinariis suis predictis, et super hoc proferunt quandoque instrumenta notariorum super huiusmodi suis appellationibus, petitur ut plus credatur litteris ordinariorum quam ipsorum assertioni predictae" (*Councils* 2. 1272). A similar complaint appears in an undated series of *gravamina* in the register of John de Halton, bishop of Carlisle, following a document of the year 1302: "Item ubi excommunicati per ordinarios domini regis se suggerunt appellasse, unde eorum assercioni reditur, et breve pro eorum capcione ordinariis denegatur et, si capti fuerint, consimili assercioni liberantur" (*Reg. Halton, Carlisle* 1. 172).

[79] 5.17. c. Praeterea contingit, v. *dari debet*; ed., pp. 351-52. This gloss on a constitution of Boniface of Savoy (1261) is one of the longest glosses to the *Provinciale* (1430). There is no evidence to suggest that this question had given rise to any controversy in Lyndwood's time. Lyndwood's concern may be traceable to frustrations which he experienced in the Arches, when he found sentences of his thwarted by such appeals.

secular judge could supersede the capture of an excommunicate merely upon the presentation of an instrument of appeal, it would be quite possible for a legitimate sentence to be superseded by an illegitimate appeal. The secular judge is neither the judge *a quo* nor the judge *ad quem* of the appeal and, consequently, enjoys no competence over it. Besides, the forum of the secular judge, particularly in England, does not take cognizance of ecclesiastical matters, and such a judge is at fault if he in any way intrudes himself into the question of ecclesiastical appeals. Likewise, when an excommunicate appeals his sentence as null, he is nonetheless to be considered as excommunicate until he proves his appeal; the proof is admitted and determined by the ecclesiastical judge *ad quem* and not by the secular judge. The allegation that such an appeal is an exception used by the excommunicate to delay or impede his capture cannot be accepted because what a person excepts he must prove, and such proof cannot be received before a secular judge even by presentation of an instrument of appeal, of whose force he is ignorant or presumed ignorant. Because the secular judge is certain of the excommunication and doubtful of the appeal, he should adhere to what is certain rather than to what is doubtful.

The canonist's arguments seem watertight, but practice gainsaid them. The secular authorities, in fact, acted as arbiters over ecclesiastical appeals. To the objections raised by the clergy in 1285 the king replied that he was not deferring to the appeals of malicious appellants but only to those of appellants who were actively prosecuting their appeals. When pressed further, he replied that the appeals to which he deferred were presumed legitimate because they were made by "persone notabiles."[80] If a brief had been drawn up in rebuttal to Lyndwood's arguments, it would surely have argued that the secular authorities were not taking the place of the ecclesiastical judge. The bishops by signifying an excommunicate brought the matter within the purview of the secular court and, hence, the secular court had to interest itself in further developments in the case. Besides, Lyndwood implied that the legitimacy of an ecclesiastical appeal was being acknowledged by the secular judge solely on the basis of an instrument of appeal presented by the excommunicate. Not so; in many cases letters from the ecclesiastical judge *ad quem* testifying to the legitimacy of the appeal were produced in evidence and, where instruments of appeal were presented, the excommunicate had to establish by witnesses or by oath that he was actively prosecuting his appeal. Moreover, the opponents of the excommunicate were given ample opportunity to appear in King's

[80] See *supra* p. 123.

Bench to oppose supersedence; pending that hearing, the excommunicate's capture could be superseded only temporarily and in mainprise.

The assurance of the secular authorities could not refute the radical
jurisdictional argument of Lyndwood, for clearly the legitimacy of appeals
from one ecclesiastical court to another ecclesiastical court was determinable
only in the ecclesiastical forum. Yet the church made no official protest
after 1285 and acceded in practice to a *modus vivendi* whereby the secular
judges concerned themselves with the legitimacy of ecclesiastical appeals.

CHAPTER V

ABSOLUTION AND RECONCILIATION

THE secular coercion of an obdurate excommunicate was directed primarily towards his correction and return to the church. His contumacy had given rise to the penalty of excommunication, and his continued contumacy to the use of the secular arm. The bishop invoked the aid of the king for the same reason that he had already used excommunication: to cure the person of his contumacy. It was common form for the bishop to express in his signification the hope that the secular power would succeed, where the fear of God had failed, in turning the excommunicate away from evil.[1] The king, in turn, ordered the sheriff to detain the excommunicate until he was absolved from the sentence of excommunication. It was this absolution which effected the reconciliation of the excommunicate to the church. Once he was absolved, there was no further reason for his continued imprisonment — the procedure had had its intended effect — and the bishop requested his release. Hence, the mere capture of a signified excommunicate did not make the procedure a success, since the excommunicate for want of repentance could remain indefinitely in prison; success, rather, must be measured in terms of the excommunicate abandoning his contumacy and returning *ad gremium ecclesiae*.

I. THE NATURE AND PROCEDURE OF ABSOLUTION

When an excommunicated person against whom the secular arm was used sought absolution, he stood before the law as any other excommunicate: absolution meant the same for him, the same conditions prevailed before it could be granted, and the same method was used to effect it. Absolution from excommunication meant simply the lifting of the sentence.[2]

---

[1] Typical of the expressions used in the significations were these two: "ut quem timor dei a malo non reuocat saltem coherceat regie maiestatis"; and "ut quem dei timor non reuocat secularis saltem cohercio cohibeat a peccato."

[2] The remarks which follow concerning the nature of absolutions and its requirements apply to the teaching of the canonists from the thirteenth century to the end of our period. The examples

From the twelfth century it came to be distinguished from absolution from sin. The full reconciliation of an excommunicate required absolution from excommunication in the external forum as an act of jurisdiction, which could be performed even by a layman, and absolution from sin in the forum of the sacrament of penance as an act of order and jurisdiction, which could be performed only by a priest. The two absolutions became joined on the rare occasion when the solemn form of absolution was used; conceivably a priest who was absolving a person from the sentence in the external forum might have absolved him from the sin publicly at the same time. Even so, the two absolutions were formally distinct, having different objects and being performed by virtue of different authorities.[3] The absolution which is here treated is absolution from excommunication, which effected the reconciliation of the excommunicate *quoad ecclesiam militantem*.[4]

The general rule applying to absolution from excommunication stated that he who excommunicated a person should absolve him, but like most general rules it is in need of some refinement.[5] An excommunication *ab homine* could be lifted only by the person who imposed it, his successor, his superior, or his delegate. Thus, if the official of the bishop of Hereford excommunicated a person in the consistory court of Hereford because of contumacies committed in not obeying the court's citation, for the purposes of absolution the person who imposed this excommunication *ab homine* was the bishop of Hereford, since it was by his authority that his official acted. Hence, this excommunicate could receive absolution from the bishop of Hereford or, if he had died or had been translated, from the bishop who succeeded him. Likewise, he could be absolved by anyone

given are drawn from those found in the signification records for the same period. For a convenient summary of the classical canonical teaching on absolution from excommunication see the treatment by Eugène Vernay in his introduction to Le *"Liber de Excommunicacione" du Cardinal Bérenger Frédol* (Paris, 1912), pp. lxiv-lxxiii; cf., T. Ortolan, "Censures ecclésiastiques," *Dictionnaire de théologie catholique* 2. 2. 2131-36.

[3] For perhaps the clearest statement of this distinction see the discussion by William of Rennes in his mid-thirteenth-century gloss on the *Summa* of Raymond of Pennafort, in which he cited the authority of Huguccio (*Summa sancti Raymundi de Peniafort* (Rome, 1603, p. 448) 3.34.14, v. *nam sacerdotibus*).

[4] E. Vacandard and A. Vacant have described the teaching on absolution from sin for the patristic and medieval periods in sections of the long article on "Absolution des péchés." *Dictionnaire de théologie catholique*, 1. 1. 145-191. Cf., Henry C. Lea, *A History of Auricular Confession and Indulgences in the Latin Church* (Philadelphia, 1896); Oscar D. Watkins, *A History of Penance* (London, 1920).

[5] For typical expressions of this teaching see Hostiensis in the thirteenth century (*Summa* 5. de sententia excommunicationis. 12) and St. Antoninus of Florence in the fifteenth century (*Tractatus utilis et necessarius de excommunicatione* in *Tract. univ. iur.* 14 (Venice, 1584) f. 384ᵛ).

delegated to do so by the bishop of Hereford; in practice, this usually meant his official, who may or may not have been the same person who had imposed the penalty in court. If the excommunicate approached the archbishop of Canterbury or his delegate (e.g., the official of the court of the Arches or the dean of the Arches), he could not receive absolution unless the matter had come to the archbishop's jurisdiction by reason of an appeal or a metropolitan visitation, since a metropolitan was not ordinary of the subject of his suffragans.[6] The pope as universal ordinary could absolve anyone.

When a person incurred excommunication *latae sententiae*, the excommunicator was actually the legislator. For example, if a layman struck a cleric, he was *ipso facto* excommunicated, because the general law of the church imposed this penalty for such a crime; he was, then, excommunicated by the pope. Absolution from excommunications *latae sententiae* which were incurred by violation of the general law should have been reserved, according to the general rule, to the pope. In fact, however, the pope reserved absolution of only some of these excommunications to himself; others he reserved to local ordinaries. In the absence of an explicit reservation to the pope or the local ordinary, absolution could be given by simple priests. Even explicit reservations would not apply in circumstances in which they might cause harm to souls.[7] In danger of death any priest could absolve from any excommunication whether *ab homine* or *latae sententiae*.[8]

In all but a few cases the excommunicates against whom the weight of the secular power was invoked had been excommunicated *ab homine*. Unless they appealed to a higher jurisdiction, their absolution pertained to the jurisdiction of the bishop by whose authority they had been excommunicated. Generally, in practice the excommunicate would present himself before the court which had excommunicated him and from a judge of that court receive absolution from the censure.[9] This meant that the

---

[6] This matter received its precision in the decretal *Venerabilibus* of Innocent IV, 1254 (Potthast. 15454; *Sext.* 5.11.7).

[7] In 1190 Clement III made certain exceptions in favor of women, the aged, infirm, and destitute (Jaffé 16623; X 5.39.13). Innocent III extended these in 1199 to include all persons impeded by any just cause (Potthast 700; X 5.39.29).

[8] In 1298 Boniface VIII gave decretal authority to the common teaching of the canonists (*Sext.* 5.11.22).

[9] There is no evidence to suggest that the solemn form of reconciliation at the doors of the church by the bishop and twelve priests was used in any of these cases. For examples of this solemn form see *De antiquis ecclesiae ritibus libri*, Lib. 3, cap. 5 (ed. Edmund Martène; Antwerp, 1736-38; vol. 2, cols. 912-917). By the thirteenth century the solemn form had become rare and by the end of that century it had all but disappeared. Durandus noted "iudices non sequuntur

man excommunicated in the consistory court of Hereford would come before that same court for absolution. Personal presence by the excommunicate was not insisted upon;[10] if he was already in prison, it would have been usual for him to be represented at the absolution by his proctor. For example, Thomas de Brompton, rector of Eyton, was absolved in 1324 in the court of the bishop of Coventry and Lichfield in the person of Master Stephen de Bromele, his proctor.[11] In at least one case, however, the bishop ordered the sheriff to release the excommunicate so that he could appear in court to be absolved in person.[12] Similarly, in 1518 chancery issued a writ for the release in mainprise of an excommunicate so that he could try personally to gain absolution.[13] Again, for a just reason, but probably only in criminal cases, the bishop could commission a member of the local clergy to absolve the excommunicate.[14]

The excommunicate either *per se* or *per alium* stood before the judge not just as a person who had incurred a penalty, but as a person who had been guilty of protracted contumacy and who now professed his willingness to obey. In order to confirm the sincerity of this profession the judge required the excommunicate to take an oath of future obedience. In most cases he swore in a general way to obey the mandates of the church ("parere mandatis ecclesie") or to stand to the law of the church ("stare iuri ecclesie"). Yet in place of this general oath or in addition to it the judge might require a specific oath of obedience to his own mandates ("parere mandatis iudicis").[15] The use of the oath of obedience was insisted upon by ca-

hodie hanc formam" (*Speculum Iuris* 2.3. de sententia. 6. 35). The simple form of absolution (see *infra* p. 143) was given usually by the judge in court or in his own rooms; for an example of the latter see Brian L. Woodcock, *Medieval Ecclesiastical Courts in the Diocese of Canterbury* (London, 1952), p. 112, n. 2.

[10] The excommunicate had to be present in person only for solemn absolution ("nunquam absolutio excommunicationis danda est per procuratorem"). For a just reason non-solemn absolution could be given with the excommunicate *in absentia* and represented by his proctor (Innocent IV, *In quinque libros decretalium commentaria* X 5.39.15).

[11] C.85/57/1. For other examples of this see the cases of John Trevelian of Exeter diocese in 1449 (C.85/80/13) and John Roggers of Winchester diocese in 1515 (C.85/24/30).

[12] Bishop Beckington in 1453 so requested the release of John Kyng, formerly rector of Fiddington, for this purpose (*Reg. Bekynton, Bath and Wells* 1. 199).

[13] See *infra* Appendix B, pp. 173-74.

[14] See the commission from the bishop of Lincoln to the dean of Lincoln in 1293 to receive caution from the excommunicate Thomas Bruning (*Reg. Sutton, Lincoln* 3. 116) and the commission from the archbishop of York to the dean of Retford, Notts., in 1287 to absolve the brothers Thomas and Gilbert de Blida (*Reg. le Romeyn, York* 1. 259).

[15] Hostiensis required the oath "de stando mandatis excommunicatoris" in cases in which it was clear that the excommunicate had been justly sentenced for contempt. To him the two oaths differed in this way: "quando iurat stare mandatis iudicis, non includitur successor; quando vero mandatis ecclesie, tunc includitur" (*Summa* 5. de sententia excommunicationis. 14).

nonists from the late twelfth century,[16] yet it did not pertain to the substance of absolution, and absolutions granted without an oath were still valid.[17] In the canonical parlance of the times the oath was referred to as "cautio iuratoria." This was demanded whether the excommunication had been incurred because of mere contumacy or because of offense. If it had been incurred because of manifest offense, the judge demanded in addition that satisfaction be made or, at least, guaranteed before absolution.[18] In *ex officio* cases satisfaction could be due to the court, which had suffered expenses due to the drafting and serving of documents. It would pertain to the judge to determine the amount of restitution due. In *ad instantiam* cases these court costs had been borne by the excommunicate's adversary, who may have suffered other losses as well due to the contumacy of the excommunicate. In these cases the judge would call the adversary to determine the extent of the loss and the nature of the recompense. Satisfaction could be made immediately by recompensing the court or the adverse party for losses suffered, yet the canonists did not insist on actual satisfaction before absolution. As the minimal requirement they insisted that persons excommunicated for manifest offense must first promise future satisfaction and bind themselves to it by pledge or fidejussors before they could be absolved. They called this "caucio sufficiens" or "caucio idonea."[19] The pledge was a *res mobilis* given to the injured party as a

[16] E.g., Bernard of Pavia taught that "sine iuramento non sit absolvendus" (*Summa decretalium* 5.34.8; Regensburg, 1860, p. 275).

[17] Clement III in the decretal *Cum desideres* (1187 × 1191) stated that the oath of obedience had come into use in these cases by custom and was not absolutely necessary (Jaffé 16555; X 5.39.15). This was the common teaching of the canonists (see, e.g., *Glos. ord.* X 5.39.15, v. *ad cautelam* and v. *nisi forma ecclesiae*) except for Hostiensis, who explicitly dissented (*Summa* 5. de sententia excommunicationis. 14).

[18] Innocent III made these distinctions between mere contumacy and offense and between manifest and doubtful offense in the decretal *Ex parte* (1205): "Credimus distinguendum, utrum in aliquem interdicti vel excommunicationis sententia sit prolata pro contumacia tantum, quia scilicet citatus stare noluit iuri; vel etiam pro offensa, quia videlicet iussus noluit maleficium emendare. In primo casu credimus congrue satisfieri, ut huiusmodi sententia relaxetur, si prius sufficiens standi iuri cautio tribuatur; in secundo vero casu, si offensa est manifesta, non credimus sufficiens praestetur emenda. Si vero dubia est offensa, sufficere credimus ad relaxandam eandem, si parendi mandato ecclesiae competens satisfactio praebeatur" (Potthast 2467; X 5.40.23). In the decretal *Cum olim* (1207) he defined offense: "quae vel per confessionem, vel probationem legitime nota fuerit, aut evidentia rei, quae nulla possit tergiversatione celari" (Potthast 3110; X 5.40.24). See *supra* p. 46.

[19] The identification of sufficient (or suitable) caution with satisfaction by pledge or fidejussors enjoyed currency throughout our period. In at least six places Bernard of Parma made this identification in his gloss on the Decretals. Typical was this comment of his: "Nomine cautionis, nuda promissio intelligitur ...: sed cum additur, idonea vel sufficiens, pignoratitia vel fideiussoria intelligatur" (*Glos. ord.* X 3.21.8, v. *cautionem idoneam*; see also *ibid.* 2.6.5, v. *cautione*; 2.13.8, v. *sufficienti cautione*; 2.17.1, v. *sufficientem*; 2.24.7, v. *sufficienti cautione*; 5.40.23, v. *sufficiens*).

guarantee of future satisfaction; the fidejussors, on the other hand, were a group of men who promised to make satisfaction if the excommunicate failed to do so. It was the judge who determined sufficient caution: the nature of the pledge, the number and quality of the fidejussors, and the time permitted for actual satisfaction.[20] Sufficient caution had to be made before the judge would absolve them. If the judge absolved persons excommunicated for manifest offense without exacting sufficient caution that they would satisfy, the absolution was still valid but the judge became bound to make the satisfaction himself in case of default.[21] What constituted sufficient caution in cases in which only court costs were due was determined by the judge alone.[22] In cases in which the adversary was injured the judge would consult with him about the sufficiency of caution,[23] yet in the final analysis even in such cases the decision concerning caution belonged to the judge.

The failure of an absolved person to make the cautioned satisfaction led not only to the loss of the caution but also to his excommunication. Although he was said to have fallen back into his excommunication, he actually incurred a new excommunication. When, for example, in 1282

[20] If the judge's decision was unjust, the aggrieved party could appeal (Ioannes Andreae, *In quinque decretalium libros novella commentaria* X 5.40.23). The period which was allowed for satisfaction, as one would expect, was subject to variation, yet in some cases the period was rather short. E.g., in 1312 the bishop of Worcester received caution from four fidejussors that Richard de Stonhouse, an imprisoned excommunicate, would make satisfaction within eight days (*Reg. Reynolds, Worc.*, pp. 42-43), and the two Blida brothers (see *supra* p. 140, n. 14), who were absolved in March 1287, gave caution, unspecified, to pay 28 marks to certain merchants of Lucca by Lady Day (*Reg. le Romeyn, York* 1. 259).

[21] *Summa Hostiensis* 5. de sententia excommunicationis. 14, on which Lyndwood's remarks are principally based (3.28 c. Saeculi principes, v. *nec possunt*; ed., p. 265).

[22] See Woodcock, *Medieval Ecclesiastical Courts*, p. 97.

[23] See the *Ordo iudiciarius* of Aegidius de Fuscarariis (written 1260 × 1262), in which he declared that the adversary should appear in order to give the judge an estimate of the offense (Wahrmund 3. 1. 175). The same opinion was given by Durandus: "Nam ubi petitur, uocandi sunt omnes, qui laederentur, si fieret, quod petitur ... et adversarius eius laederetur, si absolueretur, cum teneatur sibi soluere expensas excommunicatus .... Item, restitutio non est, nisi partibus praesentibus, danda" (*Speculum iuris* 2.1. de contumacia. 4.11). Lyndwood held this same view in his gloss on the provincial constitutions "... cum tamen tales ad instantiam alicujus excommunicati, absolvi non debeant nisi parte vocata et praesente, vel saltem per contumaciam absente" (3.28.5, v. *non habita mentione*; ed., p. 265). A synod of the province of Cashel went even further in 1453 by stating that consent of the parties and satisfaction pertained to the substance of absolution "Statuit et declarat concilium, quod ordinarii non absolvant excommunicatos absque consensu partium, et sine sufficiente cautione, et si contrarium fecerint, non tenet absolutio" (Wilkins 3. 570). It is to the consultation with the adversary concerning satisfaction and caution before absolution that reference is made when the excommunicate is said to have been absolved "de consensu partis aduerse"; for an example see *infra* Appendix I, p. 207.

Gilbert Bokeler and his wife Roysa of London did not satisfy as they had promised, Archbishop Pecham excommunicated them again and signified their names for a second time to chancery for arrest.[24]

When caution, both simple and sufficient, had been offered, the judge proceeded to absolve the excommunicate. No solemnity attended the absolution. The judge simply stated that he was absolving the excommunicate; he used a form probably similar to the form given by Durandus: "Ego absoluo te auctoritate Dei omnipotentis et sanctorum Petri et Pauli apostolorum et auctoritate mihi commissa a tali excommunicatione." Still, it sufficed for the judge to say merely, "Te noueris absolutus."[25] Notifications of the absolution were sent to those who had been notified of the excommunication, and just as the person's excommunication had been publicly announced, so now his absolution.[26]

There remained for the judge to give the absolved person a *mandatum* to perform a specific penance for his offense.[27] The mandates, according to Hostiensis, were to be "iusta et rationabilia."[28] The penance could take the form of pious acts such as giving alms or going on a pilgrimage. In 1307 the knight William Sampson collected these and more. He had committed incest with two of his daughters and adultery with two other women. The judge ordered him to stand before the high altar during Mass at Southwell Minster, clothed only in a tunic, unshod and ungirded, carrying a three-pound candle, and to repeat the action in two other churches on the following two Sundays; in addition, he was to feed three poor men for a week and, finally, was to undertake a pilgrimage to Canterbury on the Monday after Michaelmas.[29] Pecuniary penances were imposed in other cases; also, penances by pious acts were on occasion commuted to money payments. Innocent IV in 1254 sanctioned the regional custom of exacting pecuniary penances,[30] but the canonists continued to

---

[24] They were originally signified on 8 Feb. 1282 and the signification after failure to make the promised satisfaction was issued on the following 19 Nov. (*Reg. Pecham, Canterbury*, p. 178; *Reg. Epp. Peckham* 3. 1028).

[25] *Speculum Iuris* 2.3. de sententia. 6.35.

[26] See X 5.39.39.

[27] For a discussion of the practice in the courts at Canterbury see Woodwock, pp. 97-99.

[28] *Summa* 5. de sententia excommunicationis. 14.

[29] *Reg. Greenfield, York* 4. 13. He had been signified by the dean and chapter of York *sede vacante* in 1305 (C.85/177/66) and subsequently imprisoned (*Reg. Greenfield, York* 4. 9-10). On 16 Aug. 1307, after Sampson had appeared twice in Southwell Minster, the archbishop suspended the appearances in the two other churches provided that he would give the alms and go on the pilgrimage (*ibid.*, p. 14).

[30] In the Decretal *Venerabilibus* addressed to the bishops of the province of Rouen (Potthast 15454; *Sext.* 5.39.7).

point out that the canons did not permit such penances.[31] Even when permitted by custom, their use may have been restricted to *ex officio* cases. At any rate, pecuniary penalties were inflicted in certain cases by ecclesiastical judges in England.[32] In the *Articuli cleri* of 1316, however, the king enacted that persons who were given pecuniary penances could effectively oppose them by requesting writs of prohibition, whereas those who agreed to the commutation of corporal penances to pecuniary penances could not use prohibitions.[33] Nonetheless, in two different cases at Rochester in 1321 money payments were required: in one case £5. to be given to the bishop and in the other £20., later suspended, to pious uses;[34] apparently these penalties were not opposed by writs of prohibition. In the following century Lyndwood in discussing what disposition an archdeacon should make of money obtained in this way held that it should be turned to pious uses unless the archdeacon required it for his own subsistence.[35]

Pecuniary penances, like other forms of penance, were imposed after the excommunicate had been absolved and were not pre-conditions for absolution. Failure to pay the pecuniary penance within due time, like the failure to carry out other forms of penance, left the person liable to re-excommunication. Before absolution the excommunicate was not required to make any money payment, since satisfaction could be merely promised by sufficient caution and since, according to the common canonical teaching, no fee could be charged for absolution.[36]

[31] See, e.g., William Durandus, *Speculum Iuris* 2.3. de sententia. 1.7, and Ioannes Andreae, *Novella in Sextum* 5.39.7.

[32] Archbishop Stratford acknowledged this in the provincial constitution *Accidit novitate perversa* of 1342 (Wilkins 2. 707-08). Woodcock describes cases of commutation to money payments in the evidence from the courts at Canterbury (pp. 98-99). In his gloss on this constitution Lyndwood provides a useful summary of canonical opinion on the question whether the use of pecuniary penance was to be limited to *ex officio* cases (3.28 c. Accidit novitate, v. *licet*; ed., p. 261).

[33] Statutes 1. 171.

[34] *Reg. Hethe, Rochester* 1. 214-216.

[35] *Provinciale* 1.10. c. Eisdem etiam, v. *poena canonica* (ed., p. 52) and 1.10 c. Archidiaconi, v. *sub poena* (ed., p. 53); cf., 3.28. c. Accidit novitate, v. *pecuniarias* (ed., p. 261).

[36] William of Pagula, the English canonist, in his *Summa summarum* (1319 × 1322) posed the question whether money should be given for absolution, and his answer was typical of canonical teaching on this point: "Indignum est et ecclesiastice racioni contrarium ut absolucionis beneficium redimatur" (London, BM, Royal MS. 10.D.X, f. 297vb).

II. Delivery of the Excommunicate from Prison

An imprisoned excommunicate desirous of absolution would undergo the procedure just described. Once absolved, he was no longer an excommunicate; the secular constraint had accomplished its purpose and, accordingly, steps were taken to remove this force from him. The procedure involved in doing this closely paralleled, *mutatis mutandis*, the procedure involved in securing his capture: at the request of the absolving judge the bishop sent to chancery a certification of absolution and chancery sent a writ to the sheriff superseding his capture. There is no reason to think that this procedure by royal writ does not date from the same time as the parallel procedure by royal writ for capture. Earlier, the bishop probably notified the sheriff directly, bypassing the royal chancery, and there is evidence to show that this practice continued long after royal writs of delivery came into use.[37] The royal writ for delivery was in use at least by 1223.[38] Although the earliest extant register of writs (1227) does not contain it, Bracton included a brief discussion of it in his treatise,[39] and examples of this writ can be found throughout the rest of the medieval period.

The ecclesiastical judge initiated the procedure very soon after the excommunicate's absolution by sending a letter to the bishop, in which he requested the bishop to secure supersedence of the person's capture. For example, on 26 June 1428 Lyndwood sent a letter to Archbishop Chichele, in which he asked the archbishop to request the release from the Fleet of Nicholas Baker.[40] Obviously in cases in which the bishop himself had absolved the excommunicate, such letters would not be necessary. Once the bishop was informed of the absolution, there remained for him to send a certification of absolution to chancery.

The certification of absolution was a letter patent from a bishop which recounted with varying degrees of detail the fact that a certain person

---

[37] See *infra* pp. 147-48.

[38] For the release of Robert Hakum, whose absolution Eustace of Fauconberg, bishop of London, had certified to chancery see *Rotuli litterarum clausarum in turri Londinensi asservati* (ed. T. D. Hardy; London, 1833-1844) 1. 564.

[39] *De legibus* 4. 327-28.

[40] *Reg. Chichele, Canterbury* 4. 290-91. As early as 1424 Nicholas Baker of North Crawley, Bucks., had been involved in a tithes dispute with his rector Master Thomas Seman and for contumacies in the court of the Arches was excommunicated and soon signified (C.85/15/5). Later in the same dispute Lyndwood on 8 March 1428 requested the archbishop to sue Baker's capture (*Reg. Chichele* 4. 285-86), and the archbishop complied (C.85/15/16). The absolution soon followed.

who had been excommunicated by the bishop's authority and signified
for arrest has now been absolved and his capture should be superseded.[41]
The actual request in some cases was merely a general request that the
king do what pertained to him; in other cases, the king was asked to supersede the writ for the excommunicate's capture; in others, he was asked
not to pursue his capture and, if he was already in prison, to release him;
in still other cases, the bishop knew that the person was in prison and
asked for his release. The meaning in all cases was quite clear: whatever
effect the writ *de excommunicato capiendo* had should cease. On several
occasions what was sent to chancery was not a letter patent from the bishop
to the king but a public notification of the person's absolution; these
succeeded in gaining the required chancery writ.[42]

In the case of Nicholas Baker, already referred to, Chichele acted
promptly and sent the certification of absolution to chancery under date
of 29 June.[43] The same promptness characterized the response of other
bishops to similar requests from their judges.[44] The bishop who sent the
certification was not necessarily the same bishop who had signified the
person's excommunication; he could be his successor or, if the case had
been appealed, his metropolitan; or, indeed, he could be a vicar acting in
the bishop's absence or the keeper of the spiritualities *sede vacante*.[45] In
any case, the certification of absolution came from the same jurisdiction,

---

[41] The certifications of absolution in the Public Record Office are kept in chancery class *Significations of Excommunication, etc.*, mixed in with the significations. The earliest dates from the
years 1254 × 1258 (C.85/97/65).

[42] Some of these notifications were addressed to the clergy of the diocese or province and
contain a clause ordering publication of the person's absolution on three Sundays or feast days.
E.g., such a notification from Archbishop Chichele under date of 27 April 1426 was presented in
chancery in favor of William Warter of London diocese (C.85/15/8). Others of these notifications
were addressed to all and singular to whose attention they might come. E.g., in 1283 a notification
of this sort from the archbishop of York ("Vniuersis pateat per presentes...") was presented in
favor of three men who had been excommunicated in the court of York (C.85/173/46). The bishop
of Coventry and Lichfield used still another type of notification when the notification which he
sent under date of 23 March 1430 was addressed to all spiritual and temporal judges and notified
them of the absolution of Isabel Drewe (C.85/62/33). The presentation of notifications instead
of letters patent was truly exceptional; they account for a scant 2.5% of the total number of
instruments presented at chancery in this connection.

[43] *Reg. Chichele, Canterbury* 4. 291.

[44] E.g., John Persyvale was absolved on 23 Feb. 1390, and on 26 Feb. the abbot of Westminster
requested his release (C.85/210/19); he had been signified for capture on 20 Jan. 1390 (*ibid.*,
no. 17). The bishop of Norwich on 4 July 1518 requested supersedence of the capture of a man
who had been absolved on 1 July (C.85/140/23). Philip Tyndalle was absolved on 16 Feb. 1531
and his release was requested by the bishop of Lincoln on the following day (C.85/115/20).

[45] For examples of certifications of absolution see *infra* Appendix I, pp. 205-210.

if not from the same person, as the signification of excommunication or from a superior jurisdiction.

Chancery responded to the bishop's request by issuing as a matter of course a writ superseding the writ for capture. Like the signification of excommunication, the certification of absolution was, as it were, a warrant for a royal writ to be issued under the great seal. No review of the case was made by the chancery clerks; no questions were asked. The chancery writ, as a writ *de cursu*, was issued automatically to the sheriff, subject only to the routine delays endemic to any chancery.[46] Exactly what the writ ordered the sheriff to do depended on what action chancery knew that the sheriff had taken, and the chief source of this knowledge was no doubt the bishop's certification. The writ took one of three forms: it directed the sheriff (i) to desist from capturing the excommunicate or (ii) to deliver him or (iii) to supersede his capture and, if he was in prison, to deliver him. Of course, if the writ for capture had not yet been issued, chancery acting internally would not permit it to be issued.

If writs *de excommunicato capiendo* had been issued to several sheriffs against a single excommunicate, superseding writs were issued to as many sheriffs. This applied even in cases in which the excommunicate was in prison, for it was of limited value to be released by one sheriff only to be arrested by another. Richard Aubin, dean of Heacham and rector of Tatterford, Norfolk, discovered this when in 1278 after being released from prison in Norwich he arrived in London and was straightway placed in Newgate by the mayor and bailiffs of London, who had received a writ for his arrest which chancery never superseded.[47] Typical of what no doubt was the usual practice in instances of multiple signification was the case of John de Burmyngham of Lincoln; after his absolution he secured the issuance of writs of supersedence to the sheriffs of Staffordshire, Warwickshire, and Leicestershire, to whom writs for his capture had been sent.[48]

Bishops not uncommonly bypassed chancery and sent their requests for supersedence directly to the sheriffs. The actual terms of the writ *de*

---

[46] Some registers of writs have a form of this writ addressed to the keeper of the Fleet (f. 66ʳ of the printed edition), but no actual writs of this kind have come to light.

[47] Aubin had been signified as early as 1275 (C.85/4/13), but the signification which led to writs being issued to Norfolk and London was dated 10 Dec. 1277 (C.85/2/43). On 22 April 1278 a royal writ was directed to the archbishop of Canterbury, ordering him to investigate the facts of Aubin's alleged capture at London. On 6 May the archbishop reported that the dean of the Arches had conducted an investigation and found that Aubin had indeed been captured at London by reason of a writ issued in response to the same mandate which had led to his arrest at Norfolk (Prynne, pp. 197-98).

[48] C.85/105/24 and dorse.

excommunicato capiendo did not require the sheriff to detain the body of the
excommunicate until he received a writ for his delivery; the sheriff was
only required to detain him in prison until he made satisfaction or, 'n an
alternative form, until he received absolution. In the thirteenth, fourteenth, and fifteenth centuries many instances of this direct procedure can
be found. For example; Archbishop Pecham wrote directly to the sheriff
of Warwickshire in 1282 for the release of a rector from Warwick prison.[49]
It would appear that the archbishops of York used this direct procedure
almost exclusively from 1245 to 1313.[50] It was used by bishops from the
dioceses of Bath and Wells,[51]   Hereford,[52] Salisbury,[53] Winchester,[54]
and Worcester.[55] Clearly some bishops were using both procedures at the
same time, but the basis for the distinction is not apparent. Although
after the first quarter of the fourteenth century instances of direct requests
to sheriffs still appear, their frequency is not so great. Perhaps other
bishops encountered the same opposition as Bishop Trefnant of Hereford
was to encounter in 1398, when his direct request to the sheriff was not
honored because the sheriff refused to deliver excommunicates save by
royal writ.[56] In all events, this direct procedure had the clear advantage
for bishops of dioceses distant from the king's chancery that it effected the
person's release without enduring the delays entailed in having a certification sent to chancery and then a writ sent from chancery to the sheriff.

Without the sanction of either episcopal request or royal writ some
sheriffs acted independently and released excommunicates from prison.
The practice existed before the middle years of the thirteenth century,
but appears to have ceased in the early part of the next century. In 1234
the bishop of Norwich complained to the king that the sheriff of Norfolk
and Suffolk was acting in this way.[57] Other cases appear during the
1250's as when the sheriff of Warwickshire took forty shillings from an

---

[49] *Reg. Epp. Peckham* 1. 285. Richard de Ablyntone, rector of Halford, Worcester diocese,
had been signified for capture by Pecham on 19 Dec. 1281 (C.85/3/48). The letter to the sheriff
is dated 1 Feb. 1283.

[50] The signification files for York for these years appear quite full, yet only a single request for
supersedence is to be found, in 1283 (C.85/173/46). During the same period the registers of
Archbishops le Romeyn, Newark, Corbridge, and Greenfield contain examples of direct requests
to sheriffs. In fact, le Romeyn's register contains a form letter of a direct request to the sheriff
of Notts. (*Reg. le Romeyn, York* 1. 242).

[51] In the case of John Kyng (*supra* p. 140, n. 12).

[52] C.85/91/24. For a transcription see *infra* Appendix I, pp. 209-10.

[53] *Reg. Martival, Salisbury* 2. 348.

[54] *Reg. Woodlock, Winchester* 1. 157.

[55] *Reg. Cobham, Worcester*, p. 19.

[56] See *supra* n. 52.

[57] See *CCR, 1234-37*, p. 13; Prynne, p. 80.

excommunicate and released him.[58] It was no doubt cases such as this that caused the bishops in 1257 to complain to the king of the independent action of the sheriffs.[59] In the constitution formulated by the English clergy at Merton in 1258 and promulgated with some changes in 1261 the bishops decreed that sheriffs and bailiffs who acted in this fashion should be publicly and solemnly excommunicated.[60] In 1279 there was added to the Great Curse the excommunication of all those who procured the unjust release of imprisoned excommunicates, but no specific mention was made of sheriffs.[61] In three series of *gravamina* dating from the early years of the fourteenth century the bishops were quite specific. They complained that the sheriffs often allowed captured excommunicates to roam the county and to be released without episcopal consent.[62] After that, however, nothing further is heard of sheriffs acting independently of episcopal consent and royal writ.

---

[58] The exact date is uncertain. William Maunsel, sheriff of Warks., freed John, canon of St. Margaret's Church, Warwick (*Select Cases of Procedure Without Writ Under Henry III* (eds. H. G. Richardson and G. O. Sayles; Selden Soc., vol. 60, 1941), pp. 112-113). In a similar case the keepers of the king's prison at York in 1252 released Christina de Pokelington on Easter Sunday so that she could receive Communion, and later, although she refused absolution and made no satisfaction, they released her completely (C.85/169/7). It is indeed puzzling that this excommunicated woman expected to be admitted to the Eucharist.

[59] "Item, vicecomites tales excommunicatos ad mandatum domini regis non capiunt; et si capiant, liberant sine mandato regio et satisfactione" (Councils 2. 541).

[60] The 1258 version: "Praeterea cum excommunicati et de mandato prelatorum, secundum regni consuetudinem, capti et carceri mancipati aliquando per regem et quandoque per vice-comites aliosque ballivos sine consensu prelatorum et satisfactione congrua liberentur... Vice-comites autem et alii ballivi qui eos liberaverint, non prestita satisfactione Ecclesiae vel emenda, publice excommunicentur anathemate, et excommunicati solempniter denuntientur. Si tamen de mandato regio ad hoc processerint, mitius cum eis arbitrio ordinariorum agatur" (*Councils* 2. 576-77). The 1261 version: "Preterea contingit interdum quod excommunicati de mandato prelatorum, secundum regni consuetudinem, capti et carceri mancipati, aliquando per regem et quandoque per viecomites aliosque ballivos, sine consensu prelatorum ad quorum mandatum sic captorum debet liberatio fieri, nulla satisfactione prestita, liberantur... Vicecomites autem et alii ballivi qui eos liberaverint, non prestita satisfactione ecclesiae vel emenda, innodentur sententia simili et tales pupplice nuntientur. Si tamen de mandato regio ad hoc processerint, mitius cum eis arbitrio ordinariorum agatur" (*ibid.*, p. 676). See Lyndwood's gloss on this constitution (5.17. c. Praeterea contingit; ed., pp. 349-352).

[61] "Excommunicantur omnes illi qui ... procurant injustam eorum liberationem contra decretum ecclesiasticae disciplinae" (*Councils* 2. 849). Although Pecham in the Michaelmas parliament of that year declared that the king's ministers were not included in this excommunication (*ibid.*, pp. 856-57), he reaffirmed the excommunication without any exceptions in 1281 (*ibid.*, p. 907), and it became part of the list of excommunications which was repeated several times in every parish church each year; see *supra* p. 102.

[62] In the clerical articles, belonging perhaps to 1295, they complained: "Item quod vicecomes vel alii ad quos pertinet excommunicatos ad mandatum regium capere et incarcere si id deferant,

III. The Writ de cautione admittenda

Early in the history of the signification procedure there developed a counter-procedure by which a captured excommunicate could be delivered from prison without the consent of the bishop; it centered about the writ *de cautione admittenda*. This writ is first seen in use as early as 1223, having all the appearance of a well-established procedure. Essentially, by this procedure excommunicates who had offered caution and requested absolution only to be refused could sue writs out of chancery requiring the bishop to accept the caution and request their release.

As the procedure first appears, it consists of two stages. The purpose of the first stage was to warn the bishop. This was carried out usually by two writs, one to the bishop, warning him to admit the caution or otherwise the king would act, and another to the sheriff, directing him to go to the bishop with the same warning and to report to chancery if the bishop refused. If the bishop did refuse, the procedure moved to its second stage: again two writs were issued, one to the bishop and the other to the sheriff. They contained an ultimatum: if the bishop refused in the presence of the sheriff to admit suitable caution, the sheriff was to effect the release of the excommunicate.[63]

---

vel taliter captos sine ordinariorum ad quorum insanttiam sic capiebantur assensu a carcere liberent gravitor puniantur, quia in maioris excommunicationis sententiam incidunt ipso facto tanquam violatores ecclesiastice libertatis" (*Councils* 2. 1139). In the undated series in the register of John de Halton, bishop of Carlisle, belonging possibly to the years 1301 × 1302, they further complained: "Item licet vicecomites plerumque permittunt excommunicatos et incarceratos, discurrere per totum comitatum, quos graciose sic captos assignant pro carceracione durante excommunicacione, ante communem deliberacionem debito modo capti in contemptum ecclesiastice liberantur discipline, propter quod sibi pene hiis diebus timetur" (*Reg. Halton, Carlisle* 1. 172, see *Councils* 2. 1271 n. 2) in a series of complaints dated 1309 which are described as "gravamina prius non proposita," but which are clearly related to the series in Halton's register, the bishops in similar language stated, "Item, vicecomites plerumque permittunt excommunicatos per invocationem brachii secularis captos et incarceratos discurrere per totum comitatum ante omnem liberationem debito modo factam in contemptum regis et ecclesiastice discipline, propter quod petitur remedium adhiberi" (*Councils* 2. 1272).

[63] The case of Simon de Seis illustrates this two-stage procedure (*Rotuli litterarum clausarum in turri Londinensi asservati* 1. 541, 563). A writ dated 8 April 1223 was sent to the bishop of Lincoln, bidding him to accept Simon's security and to effect his release or otherwise "sustinere nullatenus poterimus quin ipsum delberari faciamus"; no writ to the sheriff appears for the first stage. The writs of the second stage are dated 12 Sept. 1223. The bishop was ordered to accept the caution and to direct the sheriff of Lincoln to release him; "alioquin mandauimus eidem uicecomiti ut ipsum a prisona nostra liberare non differat"; the sheriff was sent a mandate that in face of the bishop's refusal he should release Simon under bail of six men. It should be noted that the writs of the second stage in this case in their original form ordered the sheriff to take the excommunicate's

By the 1250's the preliminary stage of monition may not have been very much in use, and the procedure probably began with the second stage.[64] Bracton does not mention the monition, and a register of writs which belongs to about 1254 does not contain it.[65] When the procedure was described in reply to clerical complaints of about 1260, no reference was made to this preliminary stage, but the detail was added that the sheriff took the excommunicate with him when he approached the bishop.[66] Before long other refinements were made. By 1284 the bishop was given an opportunity to get redress by suing out of chancery a writ for the recapture of excommunicates who had been unjustly freed by the sheriff.[67] Probably by about the same time inaction by the bishop could have led to the matter being taken into King's Bench.[68]

These refinements which were introduced underline rather than obscure the point at issue: has the excommunicate offered sufficient caution for his offense? If the excommunicate had been guilty only of contumacy (*contumacia tantum*), little difficulty would arise, for he had only to swear

---

caution before releasing him but this clause was deleted. On this same point, Bracton's sample writ includes a directive to the sheriff to seize the excommunicate's security (*De legibus* 4. 271-72).

[64] Only a single case with a preliminary stage appears after this time. On 22 Nov. 1307 a writ was issued to the sheriff of Norfolk ordering him to report to chancery if the vicar-general of Norwich diocese refused to heed the warning to absolve Alan de Suthwerk (C.47/122/2/piece of that date). Nothing further was required because, as the sheriff noted on the dorse, the vicar-general complied.

[65] It contains a single writ of ultimatum addressed to the sheriff (London, BM, Add. Ms. 35179, f. 82r-v). See *infra* Appendix J, p. 212.

[66] "Ad requisitionem episcoporum consuevit rex aliquando de gratia speciali cum sibi placuit excommunicatos facere capi et detineri, quousque ab ipsis cautio vel emenda prestita fuisset, nec eos liberavit nisi per episcopos ultra cautionem idoneam seu emendam ab ipsis excommunicatis oblatam malitiose detinerentur. In quo casu scribere solet rex ministris suis per quos excommunicatos ipsos capi fecerit ut personaliter una cum dictis incarceratis ad prelatos ipsos accederent, et si prelati predicti in presentia ministrorum ipsorum cautionem idoneam seu emendam ab ipsis excommunicatis accipere recusarent, tunc quasi malitiose detentos ipsi ministri eos liberarent Aliter autem per regem non liberantur" (*Councils* 2. 689).

[67] The earliest extant writ for recapture which appears is dated 6 July 1284; it directed the sheriffs of London to arrest Richard de la Knolle and Robert de Montibus unless they had been delivered from Newgate for a legitimate reason (Prynne, p. 322). This writ, however, was probably entered into registers of writs only at a later date (see *infra* Appendix J, p. 214).

[68] The bishops had complained in 1280 that royal writs were requiring them to absolve excommunicates by a certain day or to appear in court (*Councils* 2. 879). The complaint was repeated by Archbishop Winchelsey to Boniface VIII in an undated letter (*Reg. Pontissara, Winchester* 1. 204) and by the English clergy to the king in a series of *gravamina ca.* 1295 (*Councils* 2. 1139) and in 1316 (*Statutes* 1. 172). No examples of this practice survive, and a form of the writ has not appeared in the registers of writs which have been examined. In 1280 and again in 1316 the king replied that such writs would not be issued thereafter, but in the delayed reply in 1280 he denied that such writs had issued from chancery (see *infra* p. 152, nn. 76-77).

obedience. If he was even guilty of offense but made actual satisfaction, again little difficulty would arise provided the satisfaction was agreeable to the injured party. The cases which were involved in these actions in chancery were cases in which the excommunicate was guilty of offense and did not make actual satisfaction. Since the ecclesiastical judge was the sole arbiter of the suitability of the pledge of forgiveness which such an excommunicate would offer in lieu of actual satisfaction, his judgment was open to challenge. In fact, the excommunicate in sueing the writ *de cautione admittenda* was alleging in chancery that he had requested absolution from the judge and offered suitable caution but that the caution was refused *propter malitiam*.[69] In some cases the excommunicate's gambit was successful: the bishop in face of the royal writ might accept his caution, absolve him, and bid his release.[70] Generally however, the bishop replied to chancery that he would accept sufficient caution were it offered but the excommunicate had not offered it. For example, in 1302 Humphrey atte Grenehelde of East Farleigh, Kent, secured writs *de cautione admittenda* to the archbishop of Canterbury and the sheriff of Kent, and the latter returned that indeed Humphrey had found two fidejussors who would pledge themselves for his obedience to the law but they refused to pledge themselves for his satisfaction.[71] In such cases the caution was not canonically sufficient and the ecclesiastical judge was forbidden by law to accept it; actually, he became bound himself to satisfaction if he accepted insufficient caution.

The bishops insistently pointed out their inability to accept insufficient caution, and this writ consequently became a frequent subject of clerical grievance. As early as 1257 the clergy complained that royal writs were being used for the release of excommunicates without the consent of the signifying prelate and without any satisfaction.[72] In the provisions of the synods of 1258 and 1261 the bishops legislated against sheriffs executing such writs but did not excommunicate them if they acted by royal mandate and not of their own accord.[73] So incensed were the bishops that they even legislated against clerks who wrote such writs. In the *gravamina* dating from about the same time the clergy complained that such a practice of releasing imprisoned excommunicates violated the rights of those pre-

---

[69] According to the admission of the bishops themselves in the first series of *gravamina* in 1285 the king could rightly order the release of excommunicates maliciously detained (*Councils* 2. 957).

[70] For an example see *supra* p. 151, n. 64.

[71] Prynne, p.. 929. Two years later two men were similarly willing to give caution on behalf of the abbot and certain monks of Furness Abbey regarding only their future obedience but not their satisfaction; the caution was refused (*ibid.*, pp. 1085-86).

[72] *Councils* 2. 541.

[73] For texts of both 1258 and 1261 see *supra* p. 149, n. 60.

lates to whom alone delivery of excommunicates pertained, but the royal
reply said that the writ of release was issued only in cases of malicious
detention.[74] In 1280 they complained that writs were requiring ordinaries
to absolve excommunicates within a certain time or to appear in court.[75]
According to Pecham's *memoriale* the response was that such writs would
be issued in the future only in cases where excommunication could lead to
lèse-majesté,[76] but the more official response denied that the writ was used
at all and challenged the bishops to exhibit a copy.[77] A similar complaint
five years later (May-June 1285) received the reply that the writ was
issued only in cases of malice and in cases in which the bishop was an
opponent of the imprisoned person.[78] The bishops, in turn, thought it
unreasonable for chancery to show more credence to liars than to bishops,
even if the bishops were parties to the case.[79] The king conceded that the
general supposition was that delivery would be by episcopal request.[80]
Winchelsey in his undated complaint to Boniface VIII merely repeated
the clerical complaint of 1280.[81] When the English bishops again objected
to this practice, probably in 1295, they argued that excommunicates
would never be corrected if the practice was allowed.[82] In 1300 the bishops
again insisted that provisions for satisfaction must be made before delivery.[83]
When the complaints of the English church were sent to the Council of
Vienne (1311-1312), the bishops restated this same position.[84] In the

[74] For the text of the royal reply see *supra* p. 151, n. 66.

[75] *Councils* 2. 879.

[76] "Rex discernit: quod talis litera nunquam exire imposterum permittatur nisi in casu quo posset evenire ledi per excommunicationem regiam libertatem" (*ibid.*).

[77] "Tale breve non manavit a curia quod sciatur, nec debet exire; si tamen aliquis tale acceperit, ostendatur" (*ibid.*).

[78] "Non deliberentur capti per captionem; conceditur nisi diutius detineantur per episcoporum malitiam postquam optulerint cautionem, et nisi episcopi sint partes versus ipsos captos" (*ibid.*, p. 957).

[79] "...Irrationabile videtur contra episcopum credere mentienti, etiamsi episcopi sint partes, nisi episcopus pupplice requisitus per vicecomitem iustitiam facere denegaret; et iccirco frequenter liberantur mentientes episcopis inconsultis" (*ibid.*, p. 960).

[80] "...Supponebatur in eodem tractatu satis consessum fuisse quod non liberetur sinedebita requisitione episcoporum" (*ibid.*, p. 962).

[81] *Reg. Pontissara, Winchester* 1. 204.

[82] *Councils* 2. 1139.

[83] *Councils* 2. 1213.

[84] "Ecclesia Anglicana dicit quod si aliqui excommunicati per ordinarios steterint in excommunicatione per xl dies et ecclesia invocet brachium seculare ad capeindum excommunicatos huiusmodi, tam de iure quam de conseutudine regni Anglie approbata, licet per banna regis fuerint et incarcerati, ante tamen prestitam satisfactionem vel cautionem ydoneam per ministros regios a carceribus liberantur contra ius et antiquam consuetudinem supradictam" (*Councils* 2. 1356).

Articuli cleri of 1316 Edward II attempted to settle the accumulated clerical grievances, but on the question of the writ *de cautione admittenda* he was content to repeat the reply of 1280.[85] The matter was clearly not settled, for the clergy raised the familiar complaint again in 1327[86] and in 1342[87], but by then the practice had seen its day. A few cases survive after that time, but they are very few; another procedure was replacing it in popularity.

An alternative method of procedure had been developed in chancery, one which excommunicates could use with equal facility and more beneficial results than the writ *de cautione admittenda*. The alternative was the supersedence procedure available to appellants, which has been described in the preceding chapter. By both procedures the excommunicate could succeed in being released from prison and in quashing the writ *de excommunicato capiendo*, but, if he followed the procedure based on alleged inadmission of caution, he still remained excommunicated, even though he would have escaped secular coercion. But by following the procedure based on appeal he was absolved *ad cautelam* from his excommunication by the judge of the court of appeal *ante omnia* and, hence, was free from both secular and spiritual coercion. If the volume of extant cases can provide a criterion, the procedure by alleged inadmission of caution was withering while the procedure by appeal reached full flower in the second half of the fourteenth century.

IV. The Number of Imprisoned Excommunicates Absolved

Although the ultimate purpose of the signification procedure was stated to be the reconciliation of excommunicates to the church, it comes as a regrettable but ineluctable fact that the historian will never know the number of imprisoned excommunicates who repented and were absolved. Chancery records are incomplete in themselves and, even if they were complete, they would indicate only those whose release was ordered by royal writ and would show nothing of the possibly large number whose release was requested by the bishops directly to the sheriffs.

---

[85] *Statutes* 1. 172. It is not without interest that the reply repeats verbatim the reply of 1280 as found in the *memoriale* of Archbishop Pecham, in which the king promised to use this writ only in cases where excommunication could lead to *lèse-majesté*. See *supra* p. 153, n. 76.

[86] The royal reply at this time offered to strike a bargain with the bishops. If they were to state in their significations the reasons why they had excommunicated the person and were to give the assurance that the sentence was imposed in this connection and not for another matter, then the writ *de cautione admittenda* would not be used (*Rotuli Parliamentorum Anglie hactenus inediti 1279-1373* (eds. H. G. Richardson and G. O. Sayles; Camden Third Ser., vol. 51, 1935), p. 108).

[87] Wilkins 2. 708-09.

The extant chancery records do bear witness, however, to continuing practice of delivery by royal writ. The table which follows gives in ten-year totals the number of extant certifications of absolution.

The fact that the total of certifications of absolution is only 5.6% of the total of significations of excommunication offers no basis for conclusion, given the incompleteness of both types of records.

1250-59	2	1310-19	50	1370-79	45	1430-39	7	1490-99	6
1260-69	5	1320-29	24	1380-89	18	1440-49	21	1500-09	9
1270-79	20	1330-39	24	1390-99	18	1450-59	22	1510-19	8
1280-89	26	1340-49	11	1400-09	15	1460-69	19	1520-29	4
1290-99	14	1350-59	0	1410-19	10	1470-79	12	1530-34	3
1300-09	17	1360-69	4	1420-29	11	1480-89	1	Grand Total	426

FIG. 3. — Detailed tabulation of the number of extant certifications of absolution, 1250-1534

In 248 of these cases it is possible to compare the date of signification of excommunication with the date of certification of absolution and, thus, to determine the intervals. The fact emerges that in more than half of these cases the person's release was requested within three months of his signification and that in over 80 % release was requested within nine months.[88] Some of the intervals are exceedingly short. For example, the bishop of Ely on 30 April 1293 signified four men for capture and on the following 10 May certified their absolution.[89] Or, even more quickly, two rectors whose excommunications were signified by the bishop of London on 10 July 1374 were certified as absolved five days later.[90] In some cases, on the contrary, the intervening period extended into years. Over seven years elapsed in the case of Thomas Pampylyon.[91] It is always possible that in such cases later significations, now lost, were made. In all events, when absolution took place, it usually followed fairly quickly upon the invoking of the secular arm.

---

[88] The following statistics illustrate this. The first number in each column is the number of months after signification within which absolution was certified; the second number is the number of certifications of absolution in each period.

1 — 40	7 — 11	13 — 7	19 — 1	30 — 1
2 — 53	8 — 8	14 — 1	20 — 2	34 — 1
3 — 34	9 — 6	15 — 2	21 — 2	51 — 2
4 — 28	10 — 4	16 — 1	23 — 1	54 — 2
5 — 14	11 — 8	17 — 3	26 — 1	70 — 1
6 — 8	12 — 3	18 — 1	28 — 1	85 — 1

[89] C.85/67/9, 11.

[90] C.85/121/41, 42.

[91] His signification was dated 14 Feb. 1427 (C.85/15/15; cf., *Reg. Chichele, Canterbury* 4. 284) and his certification of absolution 11 March 1434 (C.85/16/2).

EPILOGUE

THIS study ends with the period of the reforming statutes of Henry VIII; it would be stretching the word "medieval" in the title very far indeed to continue beyond the mid-1530's. Yet the procedure which this study describes did not end at that time but continued in use into the next century and forms part of the ecclesiastical and legal history of those years. The reforming legislation forbade appeals to Rome, it is true, but the legislation actually had little effect on the internal machinery of the ecclesiastical courts. They continued to function by pre-Reformation procedure. Parties continued to be cited in the same way; contumacies continued to be contracted for the same reasons; excommunication was still used to punish the contumacious; and the secular arm stood ready to punish obdurate excommunicates. Papal judges-delegate were replaced by judges commissioned in individual cases by the king and council to form a high court of delegates, and they signified in the same manner as had the papal judges-delegate. But apart from that change the signification procedure was not noticeably affected by the Reformation.

The sixteenth century did witness some legislation touching upon this procedure, but nothing substantial. A statute of 2 Edward VI (1548-49) simply allowed ecclesiastical judges to signify persons whom they had excommunicated for withdrawal of tithes.[1] More important, however, was the statute of 5 Elizabeth I (1562-63), which made provisions for the more efficient execution of the writ *de excommunicato capiendo*: thereafter sheriffs were to return the writ to chancery by the next term with an indication of what action they had taken, and their failure to do so was punishable by fine.[2] Despite this legislation the writ *de excommunicato capiendo* was bound to be affected by anti-excommunication sentiments, and its demise was fairly predictable.[3] The chancery files contain noticeably fewer and fewer significations during the closing two decades of the sixteenth century. By the 1590's they have begun to peter out: the last from Exeter in 1595, from York and Lincoln in 1597, and from Canterbury in 1598. After 1600

---

[1] C. 13, no. 13 (*Statutes* 4. 1, p. 57).

[2] C. 23 (*ibid.*, pp. 451-53).

[3] For the effect on ecclesiastical discipline of the infrequent use of this writ see the remarks of F. Douglas Price ("The Abuse of Excommunication and the Decline of Ecclesiastical Discipline under Queen Elizabeth," *EHR* 57 (1942) 106-115).

significations are found only from Hereford, the last in 1611, and from Chester, the last in 1690.[4] It is quite clear that by the end of the sixteenth century this procedure had ceased to be significant.

In the early nineteenth century a statute was enacted which forbade the use of excommunication against contumacious persons unless their contumacy was incurred by disobedience to a definitive or interlocutory sentence; against such excommunicates the secular arm would act only to the extent of imprisonment for six months, and against the other contumacious persons it provided a new writ, *de contumace capiendo*.[5] The gradual diminution of the jurisdiction of ecclesiastical courts made these provisions but faint echoes of the distant time when a Norman invader established courts having competence over every matter "quae ad regimen animarum pertinet" with excommunication as their own ultimate weapon and, beyond, the power of the secular arm to coerce obdurate excommunicates to repentance.

---

[4] See *Guide to the Contents of the Public Record Office* (London, 1963) 1. 42, 176.

[5] 53 George III, c. 127, as quoted by Felix Makower, *The Constitutional History and Constitution of the Church of England* (Eng. trans.; London, 1895), p. 456, nn. 36-37.

APPENDICES

APPENDIX A

AN EARLY DESCRIPTION OF THE SIGNIFICATION
PROCEDURE

An entry on the close rolls of a letter of 18 Jan. 1227 from Henry III to the Justiciar of Ireland, in which the king extended to Ireland the procedure used in England against obdurate excommunicates (C.54/36/m.21; printed in record type in Rotuli litterarum clausarum in turri Londinensi *(ed. T. D. Hardy; London, 1833-34) 2. 166, and calendared in* Calendar of Documents relating to Ireland, 1171-1251 *(London, 1875), no 1481).*

Rex G. de Marisco iusticiario Hibernie salutem. Significauit nobis uenerabilis pater L. Armakanensis archiepiscopus quod, cum quidam canonici sui de Luuethe et alii de archiepiscopatu suo propter manifestam contumaciam suam et suos enormes excessus excommunicati sint, per censuram ecclesiasticam nolentes iusticiari et in contumacia sua perdurantes per xl dies, incorrigibiles existunt. Cum autem consuetudo regni nostri Anglie sit quod, postquam litteras archiepiscoporum et episcoporum nostrorum Anglie receperimus patentes et testificantes quoscumque excommunicatos perdurasse per xl dies et amplius, manus regias ad ipsos extendamus uidelicet de ipsis per corpora eorum iusticiandis secundum consuetudinem Anglie donec sancte ecclesie tam de iniuria ei illata quam de contemptu ab eis fuisset satisfactum, uobis mandamus quod, cum predictus archiepiscopus et ceteri archiepiscopi et episcopi nostri Hibernie nobis significauerint per litteras suas patentes de huiusmodi excommunicatis in contumacia sua per xl dies perdurantibus, ipsos per corpora eorum iusticietis donec sancte ecclesie tam de iniuria ei illata quam de contemptu ab eis sit satisfactum. Teste ut supra [i.e., Westminster, 18 Jan. 1227].

APPENDIX B

SELECTED SIGNIFICATIONS OF EXCOMMUNICATIONS

1. *One of the earliest extant significations, 1216 × 1221 (C.85/117/1; printed in* H. C. Maxwell-Lyte, *Historical Notes on the Use of the Great Seal of England* (London, *1926*), p. 216).[1]

Reuerendo domino suo Henrico dei gracia illustri regi Anglie, domino Hibernie, duci Normannie, Aquitanie, et comiti Andegauie W. eadem gracia Londoniensis episcopus salutem et debitam domino reuerenciam et honorem.

Cum Phillipus Lohout clericus pro sua inobediencia multiplici et contemptu sentenciarum domini pape et domini legati per quadraginta dies et amplius excommunicacionis sentencia extiterit innodatus et adhuc in sua contumacia perseuerans beneficium absolucionis non meruerit, hoc uestre excellencie intimamus ut ad eius maliciam reprimandam et ne eius pertinacia malignandi certis transeat in exemplum manum uelitis apponere regie potestatis. Valeat excellencia uestra in domino.

2. *Examples of significations from bishops.*

a) *Signification of John de Wyngate by Boniface of Savoy, archbishop of Canterbury, 16 Sept. 1266.*

(C.85/1/38)

Excellentissimo domino suo H. dei gracia regi Anglie, domino Hibernie, duci Aquitanie B. eiusdem miseracione Cantuariensis archiepiscopus, tocius Anglie primas, salutem et tocius felicitatis augmentum.

Cum Iohannes de Wyngate pro sua multiplici contumacia et manifesta offensa per quadraginta dies et amplius excommunicatus fuerit et in eadem sentencia adhuc pertinaciter perseuerit claues ecclesie contempnendo ac ecclesia non habeat ultra quid faciat contra eum, serenitatem regiam requirimus et rogamus regalis ad hoc potencie brachium inuocantes quatinus secundum regni uestri consuetudinem exequamini quod uestrum est in hac parte. Valeat dominacio uestra bene et diu in domino Iesu Christo.

Datum apud Wyngtham die Iouis post festum exaltacionis sancte crucis anno domini M°CC°lx°sexto.

---

[1] Two other significations date from the same time. One concerns the same excommunicate Philip Lohout (C.85/117/3) and the other concerns a certain William de Goldham (*ibid.*, no. 2).

b) *Two significations from Archbishop Stratford.*

1) *Signification of Lambert de Walcote of Lincoln diocese for his contumacies in a marriage case before the Court of the Arches, 24 July 1341.*

(C.85/9/44)

Excellentissimo principi domino suo domino Edwardo dei gracia Anglie et Francie regi illustri Iohannes permissione diuina Cantuariensis archiepiscopus, tocius Anglie primas, et apostolice sedis legatus salutem in eo qui regibus dat regnare.

Excellencie uestre regie intimamus quod Lambertus de Walcote iuxta Folkyngham Lincolniensis diocesis propter suas manifestas contumaciam pariter et offensam pro eo quod in quadam causa matrimoniali ac spoliacionis possessionis copule coniungalis que uertitur inter Iohannem Beseiule de Hardyngthorn actricem ex parte una et prefatum Lambertum reum ex altera per appellacionem ipsius Lamberti ad nostram Cantuariensem curiam legitime deuoluta et in eadem indecisa pendente sumptus litis et alimonie in quibus eidem mulieri legitime extitit condempnatus, iussus, et monitus canonice soluere recusauit eidem in maioris excommunicacionis sentencia per presidentem curie nostre predicte in ipsum rite prolata per quadraginta dies et amplius iam perseuerauit et adhuc perseuerat animo indurato claues ecclesie nequiter contempnendo. Cum igitur sancta mater ecclesia non habeat ultra quid faciat in hac parte, uestre placeat regie maiestati contra eum exercere quod secundum regni uestri Anglie consuetudinem fuerit faciendum ut quem dei timor non reuocat saltem coherceat animaduersio regie potestatis. Quam ab hostium incursibus protegat Iesus Christus.

Scriptum apud Maghfeld xxiiii die mensis Iulii anno domini millesimo trecentesimo quadragesimo primo et nostre translacionis octauo.

2) *Signification of four men of the London diocese at the instance of the abbot and convent of the monastery of St. John, Colchester, 28 July 1345.*

(C.85/9/71)

Excellentissimo principi domino suo domino Edwardo dei gracia regi Anglie et Francie et duci Hibernie Iohannes permissione diuina Cantuariensis archiepiscopus, tocius Anglie primas, et apostolice sedis legatus salutem in eo qui regibus dat regnare.

Significamus excellencie uestre regie quod Iohannes de Witham, Iohannes atte Loste, Iohannes Taillour, et Willelmus Payn Londoniensis diocesis nostreque Cantuariensis prouincie propter suas manifestas contumacias seu pocius offensas in non parendo mandatis et monicionibus canonicis auctoritate nostre Cantuariensis curie ad instanciam religiosorum uirorum .. abbatis et conuentus monasterii sancti Iohannis Colecestre sibi factis maioris excommunicacionis sentencia legitime innodati in eadem per quadraginta dies et amplius animo indurato perseuerarunt et adhuc contemptis ecclesie clauibus perseuerant in animarum suarum periculum manifestum. Cum igitur sancta ecclesia ultra non habeat quid faciat in hac parte, dignitati supplicamus regie quatinus contra eosdem Iohannem, Iohannem, Iohannem, et Willelmum exercere dignemini quod secundum regni uestri Anglie consuetudinem conuenit regie maiestati ut quos dei timor a malo non reuocat saltem a peccato cohibeat animaduersio regie potestatis. Quam conseruet altissimus et de hostibus det triumphum.

Datum aput Lambeth u^{to} kalendas Augusti anno domini millesimo CCC^{mo} quadragesimo quinto et nostre translacionis duodecimo.

c) *Signification from Robert Braybrooke, bishop of London, 9 Oct. 1389.*

(*C.*85/122/39)

Excellentissimo principi et domino suo domino Ricardo dei gracia regi Anglie et Francie illustri et domino Hibernie Robertus permissione diuina Londoniensis episcopus salutem in eo per quem reges regnant et principes dominantur.

Excellencie uestre regie tenore presencium intimamus quod nuper presidens consistorii nostri Londoniensis legitime procedens dominos Ricardum Stapilford et Iohannem Brystowe capellanos de monasterio fratrum cruciatorum Londonie, Iohannem Prentys, Ricardum Barbour, et Iohannam Chirchegate mulierem coram eo super certis articulis statum et iurisdiccionem dicti consistorii suarumque animarum correccionem tangentibus responsuros legitime citatos pluries precognizatos et sufficienter expectatos nullo modo comparentes pronunciauit prout erant merito contumaces et pro suis huiusmodi contumaciis excommunicauit et sic excommunicatos mandauit et fecit auctoritate nostra publice nunciari. In qua quidem excommunicacionis sentencia per quadraginta dies et amplius contemptis ecclesie clauibus perseuerauerunt et adhuc perseuerunt animis eorum induratis. Cum igitur ecclesia non habeat ultra quid facere debeat in hac parte, excellencie uestre regie supplicamus ut contra ipsos dominos Ricardum et Iohannem capellanos necnon Iohannem, Ricardum, et Iohannam predictos sic excommunicatos exercere dignemini quod secundum regni uestri consuetudinem regie conuenit maiestati ut quos dei timor a malo non reuocat saltem coherceat animaduersio regie potestatis.

Datum in manerio nostro de Hadham die nona mensis Octobris anno domini millesimo CCC^{mo}lxxxx^{mo} et nostre consecracionis anno octauo.

d) *Signification of the layman Richard Lyttelyngton by Archbishop Walden at the instance of Master Robert Hallum, rector of Northfleet (later bishop of Salisbury), 10 Feb. 1399.*

(*C*.85/12/9)

Excellentissimo in Christo principi ac domino domino Ricardo dei gracia regi Anglie et Francie et domino Hibernie Rogerus eadem permissione archiepiscopus Cantuariensis, tocius Anglie primas, et apostolice sedis legatus salutem in eo qui regibus dat regnare.

Vestre excellencie regie tenore presencium intimamus quod Ricardus Lyttelyngton laicus nostre prouincie Cantuariensis ac iurisdiccionis ordinarie et immediate in hac parte notorie subditus et subiectus in quibusdam causis uiolacionis libertatis et immunitatis ecclesiastice ac dampnabilis perturbacionis et manifesti impedimenti diuini officii in ecclesia parochiali de Northflet decanatus de Shoreham nostre iurisdiccionis prefate per ipsum Ricardum iniuste factarum et contra sancciones canonicas temere attemptatarum super quibus in prefata nostra iurisdiccione ad promocionis instanciam dilecti filii magistri Roberti Hallum rectoris eiusdem ecclesie de Northflet alias rite et legitime ac iudicialiter coniuctus extitit et confessus propter ipsius Ricardi manifestam contumaciam pariter et offensam in comparendo coram certo nostro commissario ad hoc legitime deputato certis die et loco competentibus ad quos rite, legitime, ac peremptorie extiterat euocatus condignam et canonicam penitenciam ad ipsius Ricardi anime meram correccionem pro suis demeritis in ea parte infligendam sicut prius se astringebat corporali iuramento in forma iuris debita recepturus contractus fuit et est maioris excommunicacionis sentencia auctoritate nostra ordinaria rite et canonice innodatus et pro sic excommunicato publice et solempniter denunciatus. In qua quidem sentencia per quadraginta dies et amplius perseuerauit et adhuc perseuerat animo pertinaciter indurato claues sancte matris ecclesie nequiter contempnendo. Cum igitur ecclesia ultra non habeat quid facere debeat in hac parte, celsitudini regie supplicamus quatinus pro capcione corporis prefati Ricardi sicut premittitur excommunicati secundum laudabilem regni uestri consuetudinem in talibus hactenus usitatam scribere dignemini ut quem dei timor a malo non reuocat saltem coherceat animaduersio regie potestatis. Quam ad ecclesie et regni felix regimen et tutamen in prosperis et uotiuis diu conseruet et dirigat clemencia redemptoris.

Datum in manerio nostro de Oteford decimo die mensis Februarii anno domini millesimo CCC^{mo} nonogesimo octauo et nostre consecracionis anno secundo.

e) *Signification dated 13 Aug. 1473 from the bishop of Chichester for the capture of John Towghton of Beckley, Sussex, who was excommunicated before the official of the archdeacon of Lewes on 23 June 1473.*

(C.85/48/7; cf. Salzman, p. 139)

Excellentissimo principi et domino domino nostro Edwardo dei gracia illustrissimo regi Anglie et Francie quarto Iohannes permissione diuina Cicestrensis episcopus salutem in domino nostro saluatore Iesu Christo.

Ad uestre excellencie noticiam deducimus ac per presentes significamus quod quidam Iohannes Towghton de Bekkele nostre Cicestrensis diocesis propter ipsius manifestam contumaciam in quadam causa detencionis et subtraccionis bonorum spiritualium ecclesie de Bekkele predicta uicesimo tercio die mensis Iunii iam ultimo preterito coram officiali domini archidiaconi Lewensis nostre predicte diocesis in ecclesia de Bryghtlyng ordine ac processu legitimo in ea parte de iure requisitis in omnibus obseruatis excommunicatus fuit sentencia maioris excommunicacionisque pro eadem auctoritate nostra palam ac publice effluxis hiis iam diebus extiterat denunciatus. In qua quidem sentencia maioris excommunicacionis animo indurato perseuerat in presenti. In cuius rei testimonium sigillum nostrum presentibus apposuimus.

Datum in manerio nostro de Amberle terciodecimo die mensis Augusti anno domini millesimo CCCCmo septuagesimo tercio et nostre consecracionis anno quartodecimo.

Dorse: Sussexie.

f) *Signification (4 Nov. 1525) by Archbishop Warham of John Smith of Lincoln diocese, who had been excommunicated for failing to appear in the Court of the Arches in a tithes case with the vicar of Langford.*

(C.85/25/4)

Excellentissimo et inuictissimo in Christo principi et domino nostro Henrico dei gracia Anglie et Francie regi, fidei defensori, et domino Hybernie Willelmus permissione diuina Cantuariensis archiepiscopus, tocius Anglie primas, et apostolice sedis legatus utriusque uite prosperitatem in eo per quem reges regnant et principes dominantur.

Vestre regie maiestati tenore presencium significamus quod quidem Iohannes Smythe Lincolniensis diocesis, nostre Cantuariensis prouincie, notorie subditus et subiectus fuit et est propter ipsius manifestam contumaciam pariter et offensam in non comparendo coram dilecto filio magistro Petro Lygham decretorum doctore officiali curie Cantuariensis certis die et loco competentibus ad quos legitime et peremptorie extiterat citatus cuidam domino Rolando Clerke uicario perpetuo ecclesie parochialis de Langford dicte diocesis et prouincie in quadam causa subtraccionis decimarum de iusticia responsurus auctoritate dicte curie nostre Cantuariensis maioris excommunicacionis sentencia canonice innodatus et pro sic excommunicato publice et solemniter denunciatus. In qua quidem excommunicacionis sentencia per xl dies et amplius post huiusmodi denunciacionem computando stetit et perseuerauit et adhuc stat et perseuerat nimis pertinaciter animoque indurato claues sancte matris ecclesie nequiter contempnendo in anime sue graue periculum et aliorum Christifidelium perniciosum exemplum prout per literas autenticas dicti nostri officialis sigillo officii sui et dicte curie munitas et penes registrum nostrum dimissas euidenter liquet et apparet.

Cum igitur sancta mater ecclesia ulterius non habeat quod faciat in hac parte, celsitudini uestre regie supplicamus quatinus ad ipsius Iohannis excommunicati obstinanciam reprimendam brachium uelitis secularis extendere et pro corporis sui capcione scribere secundum regni uestri Anglie consuetudinem in talibus hactenus usitatam dignemini ut quem dei timor a malo non reuocat saltem coherceat animaduersio uestre regie maiestatis. Quam ad populi sui regimen et munimen diu conseruet in prosperis clemencia saluatoris.

Datum in manerio nostro de Lambith quarto die mensis Nouembris anno domini millesimo quinquagesimo xxu^{to} et nostre translacionis anno xii^{do}.

Dorse: Concordat cum registro — J. Heryng.
Herts. Breue de excommunicato capiendo super has literas factum directum fuit uicecomiti comitatus predicti.

3) *Significations from persons acting in the place of the bishop.*

a) *Signification by an official of the archbishop of Canterbury, 7 January 1248.*
(C.85/1/6)

Excellentissimo domino suo H. dei gracia regi Anglie, domino Hybernie, duci Normannie, Aquitannie, et comiti Andeganie seruus eius humilis et deuotus H. de Mortuomari officialis domini Cantuariensis salutem in eo qui dat salutem regibus.

Cum Robertus Crestien in excommunicacione steterit continua per quadraginta dies et amplius et adhuc in preiudicium salutis anime sue et aliorum communicancium cum eodem claues ecclesie pertinaciter contempnendo perseuerat in eadem et ecclesia dei quid faciat ultra non habeat, hoc nostre excellencie duxi significandum supplicans humiliter quatinus iuxta regni nostri consuetudinem de eo fieri precipiatis iusticie complementum ut quem dei timor non reuocat secularis saltem cohercio cohibeat a peccato.

Datum apud Orpinton in crastino epiphanie anno domini mccxl octauo.

b) *Signification by a vicar-general of the archbishop of Canterbury, 12 June 1263.*

(C.85/1/35)

Excellentissimo domino suo H. dei gracia illustri regi Anglie, domino Hibernie, et duci Aquitannie magister P. de Auxon reuerendi patris B. eadem gracia Cantuariensis archiepiscopi, tocius Anglie primatis, officialis et ipsius in transmarinis partibus agentis uicarius salutis gaudium et felicitatis augmentum.

Cum dominus Willelmus de Swynesford miles, Walterus Gurum clericus, Thomas frater eius, Willelmus Cras, Galfridus Tinctor de Berchamsted, et Iohannes Carrectarius in excommunicacione iam steterint per quadraginta dies et amplius et adhuc in dispendium anime sue salutis et aliorum cum eis communicancium claues ecclesie contempnendo pertinaciter perseuerent in eadem, excellencie uestre supplicamus quatinus, cum ecclesia dei quid faciat ultra non habeat, iuxta regni uestri consuetudinem de ipsis fieri percipiatis iusticie complementum ut quos dei timor a malo non reuocat saltem secularis cohercio cohibeat a peccato. Valeat celsitudo regia per tempora longa.

Datum apud Bermundes in crastino sancti Barnabe apostoli anno domini m°cc°lx° tercio.

c) *Signification by the keeper of the spirituality of Bath and Wells, sede vacante, 29 Sept. 1495.*

(C.85/23/46)

Exellentissimo in Christo principi et domino nostro domino Henrico dei gracia regi Anglie et Francie illustri et domino Hibernie Thomas Gilbert decretorum doctor reuerendissimi in Christo patris et domini domini Iohannis miseracione diuina tituli sancte Anastacie sacrosancte Romane ecclesie presbiteri cardinalis, Cantuariensis archiepiscopi, tocius Anglie primatis, et apostolice sedis legati ad quem omnis et omnimoda iurisdiccio spiritualis et ecclesiastica que ad episcopum Bathonensem et Wellensem sede plena ipsa sede iam uacante notorie dinoscitur pertinere per totam diocesim Bathonensem et Wellensem custos spiritualitatis ac uicarius in spiritualibus generalis salutem in eo per quem principes regnant et reges dominantur.

Excellencie uestre regie innotescimus per presentes quod Willelmus Walshman de parochia Sancti Cutberti de Wellia dicte Bathonensis et Wellensis diocesis propter suam multiplicatam et iniquam offensam in polluendo cimiterium ecclesie cathedralis Wellensis uiolenter ac temere et maledicte fuit et est per nos excommunicatus et pro excommunicato per ciuitatem et diocesim Bathonensem et Wellensem antedictam publice denunciatus. In qua quidem excommunicacionis sentencia per xl^{ta} dies et amplius perseuerauit et adhuc perseuerat animo pertinaciter indurato claues sancte matris ecclesie nequiter contempnendo.

Cum igitur sancta mater ecclesia ultra non habeat quid faciat in hac parte, celsitudini uestre regie tenore presencium humiliter supplicamus quatinus pro ipsius Willelmi Walshman excommunicati corporis capcione secundum uestri regni consuetudinem scribere dignemini ut quem timor dei a malo non reuocat saltem coherceat animaduersio regie potestatis. Quem ad ecclesie sue regimen et munimen conseruet in prosperis clemencia conditoris.

Datum Wellia sub sigillo quo utimur in huiusmodi uicarii officio penultimo die mensis Septembris anno domini millesimo CCCC^{mo} nonagesimo quinto.

Dorse: Somersete.

4) *Significations of special interest.*

a) *Signification in the case of an* ipso facto *excommunication, 24 May 1311.*
(C.85/7/46)

Excellentissimo principi domino suo domino Edwardo dei gracia regi Anglie illustri, domino Hibernie, et duci Aquitannie Robertus permissione diuina Cantuariensis archiepiscopus, tocius Anglie primas, salutem in eo per quem reges regnant et principes dominantur.

Excellencie uestre tenore presencium intimamus quod Willelmus filius Iohannis dicti le Cok de Maydestane, Walterus frater eius, et Iohannes de Beggebury nostre diocesis quos auctoritate nostra ordinaria in maioris excommunicacionis sentenciam a canone latam canonice nunciauimus incidisse et per alios fecimus solempniter nunciari. In ipsa per quadraginta dies et amplius post denunciacionem predictam animo indurato pertinaciter perdurarunt et adhuc contemptis ecclesie clauibus perseuerant.

Cum igitur ecclesia ultra non habeat quid faciat in hac parte, regie celsitudini supplicamus quatinus ad ipsorum excommunicatorum rebellionem salubrius reprimendam exercere dignemini contra ipsos auxilium brachii secularis ut quod ecclesiastice nocioni in hac parte deesse dinoscitur maiestatis regie per ecclesiam implorato presidio suppleatur. Valeat et crescat in Christo cum gaudio regia celsitudo.

Datum apud Lamheth ix kalendas Iunii anno domini millesimo CCC^{mo} undecimo, consecracionis nostre xuii^o.

b) *A single signification from the bishop of Coventry and Lichfield containing the names of two persons excommunicated in different cases, 10 Oct. 1389.*

(C.85/60/8)

Excellentissimo principi et domino domino Ricardo dei gracia regi Anglie et Francie illustri Ricardus permissione diuina Couentrensis et Lichfeldensis episcopus salutem in eo per quem reges regnant et principes dominantur.

Dominacionis uestre celsitudini patefacimus per presentes quod Iohannes Russchale capellanus de comitatu Warruico nostre diocesis propter suas contumacias in non ueniendo coram officiali nostro ex officio nostro contractas et Robertus Lecmufeld dicti comitatus et diocesis propter suas eciam contumacias pariter et offensas in non ueniendo coram eodem officiali nostro ad instanciam Iohannis Newehay uicarii ecclesie de Austeleye contractas sunt maioris excommunicacionis sentencia auctoritate nostra ordinaria innodati et pro talibus publice habiti et reputati. In qua quidem excommunicacione per quadraginta dies et amplius persteterunt et adhuc persistunt animo indurato claues ecclesie contempnendo.

Quocirca excellencie uestre regie attencius supplicamus quatinus ad malicias dictorum Iohannis Russchale et Roberti conuincendam extendere dignemini uestre regie dexteram maiestatis iuxta consuetudinem regni laudabilem in eodem hactenus usitatam. Valeat uestra regia excellencia in domino Iesu Christo per tempora longiora.

Scriptum in manerio nostro de Heywode x die Octobris anno domini millesimo CCC^{mo} octuagesimo nono.

c) *Signification by Archbishop Stafford of a person excommunicated under his predecessor, Archbishop Chichele, 28 Nov. 1443.*

(C.85/17/5)

Excellentissimo in Christo principi et domino domino Henrico dei gracia regi Anglie et Francie et domino Hibernie Iohannes permissione diuina Cantuariensis archiepiscopus, tocius Anglie primas, et apostolice sedis legatus salutem in eo per quem reges regnant et principes dominantur.

Cum magister Willelmus Byconyll legum doctor nuper audiencie recolende memorie domini Henrici Cantuariensis archiepiscopi ultimi et immediati predecessoris nostri causarum et negociorum auditor in quadam causa diffamacionis que per uiam querele coram eo in dicta audiencia inter Robertum Greyndore armigerum Cantuariensis prouincie partem querelantem et actricem ex parte una et Iohannem Ioce Herefordensis diocesis partem querelatam et ream ex altera aliquamdiu uertebatur legitime procedens sentenciam pro parte dicti Roberti Greyndore contra partem dicti Iohannis Ioce tulerit et promulgauerit diffinitiuam. Per quam quidem sentenciam diffinitiuam pronunciauit et declarauit auctoritate ordinaria dicti predecessoris nostri prefatum Iohannem Ioce in maioris excommunicacionis sentenciam in constitucione prouinciali que sic incipit "Ex auctoritate dei patris omnipotentis"[2] in hac parte edita et debite promulgata proinde latam temere incurrisse eaque ligatum et inuolutum ac excommunicatum fuisse et pro tali publice denunciari eadem auctoritate mandauit et fecit dictusque Iohannes Ioce in huiusmodi excommunicacionis sentencia per quadraginta dies et amplius perseuerauit et adhuc perseuerat animo pertinaciter indurato claues sancte matris ecclesie nequiter contempnendo.

Et quia sancta mater ecclesia ulterius non habet quod faciat in hac parte, celsitudini uestre regie humiliter supplicamus quatinus ad ipsius Iohannis obstinanciam reprimendam uelitis auxilium porrigere brachii secularis et pro ipsius corporis capcione scribere secundum regni uestri Anglie consuetudinem in talibus hactenus usitatam ut quem dei timor a malo non reuocat saltem coherceat animaduersio regie maiestatis. Quam ad ecclesie et regni munimen diu conseruet in prosperis clemencia saluatoris.

Datum in manerio nostro de Lamehith uicesimo octauo die mensis Nouembris anno domini millesimo CCCC^{mo} xliii^o et nostre translacionis anno primo.

Dorse: Gloucestrie.

d) *Signification conjointly from Cardinal Wolsey and Archbishop Warham by reason of their joint probate jurisdiction, 19 Oct. 1527.*

(C.85/207/6)

Excellentissimo in Christo principi et domino domino Henrico dei gracia Anglie et Francie regi fidei defensori et domino Hibernie illustratissimo Thomas miseracione diuina tituli sancte Cecilie sacrosancte ecclesie presbiter cardinalis, Eboracensis archiepiscopus, Anglie primas et cancellarius, apostoliceque sedis eciam de latere legatus, ac Willelmus permissione diuina Cantuariensis archiepiscopus, tocius Anglie primas, et apostolice sedis legatus salutem in eo per quem reges regnant et principes dominantur.

Celsitudini uestre regie tenore presencium intimamus quod quidem Iohannes Betson ciuis Londonie administrator pretensus bonorum, iurium, et creditorum Willelmi Dorone nuper ciuitatis Londonie defuncti fuit et est propter suas manifestas contumacias pariter et offensas contractas excommunicaconis sentencia auctoritate nostra ordinaria canonice

---

[2] This refers to the list of excommunications promulgated by the Council of Oxford, 1222 (*Councils* 2. 106).

innodatus. In qua quidem excommunicacionis sentencia postquam fuit pro sic excommunicato publice et solemniter denunciatus per quadraginta dies et amplius perseuerauit et adhuc perseuerat animo pertinaciter indurato claues sancte matris ecclesie contempnendo in anime sue eciam periculum et aliorum quam plurimorum exemplum perniciosum.

Cum igitur sancta mater ecclesia ulterius non habeat quid facere debeat in hac parte, maiestati uestre regie humiliter supplicamus quatinus pro ipsius Iohannis Betson excommunicati corporis capcione scribere dignemini secundum regni uestri Anglie consuetudinem in talibus hactinus usitatam et obseruatam ut quem timor dei a malo non reuocat saltem coherceat animaduersio regie maiestatis. Quam ad felix regni sui regimen et munimen regat et dirigat qui regnat in eterno solio mansionis.

Datum Londonie sub sigillis nostris quoad sigillatum presencium xix° die mensis Octobris anno domini millesimo quingentesimo xxuii°.

Notarial sign : T(?). Engall.

e) *Signification sent by Archbishop Courtenay to the steward of the earl of the Welsh March of Ceri, 24 Aug. 1387.*

(London, Lambeth Palace Library, Reg. Courteney, f. 72ᵛ)

Willelmus etc. dilecto in Christo filio .. senescallo dominii domini .. comitis marchie de Kerry in Wallia Meneuensis diocesis nostreque prouincie Cantuariensis salutem, graciam, et benediccionem.

Vobis tenore presencium intimamus quod Griffinus ap Dauid Meneuensis diocesis capellanum se pretendens in quodam collacionis siue prouisionis negocio coram dilecto filio magistro Iohannes Mawreward legum bacallario uirtute commissionis nostre sibi in ea parte facte inter dominum Griffinum Castell capellanum partem actricem ex parte una et prefatum dominum Griffinum ap Dauid partem querelatam ex altera de et super uicaria ecclesie parochialis sancti Michaelis in Kerry predicto eiusdem diocesis et eius occasione pendente fuit et est ad instanciam dicti domini Griffini Castell nostra auctoritate ordinaria maioris excommunicacionis sentencia canonice innodatus sicque excommunicatus publice denunciatus. In qua quidem excommunicacione per quadraginta dies et amplius perseuerauit et adhuc perseuerat animo pertinaciter indurato claues ecclesie nequiter contempnendo.

Cum igitur ecclesia ultra non habeat quid facere debeat in hac parte, uobis supplicamus quatinus contra prefatum dominum Griffinum ap Dauid sic excommunicatum exercere dignemini quod secundum regni Anglie consuetudinem in talibus hactenus fieri consueuit ut quem dei timor a malo non reuocat saltem coherceat animaduersio brachii secularis.

Datum apud Tonbrigg die, mense, et anno domini supradictis.

f) *Signification (1 Oct. 1518) requesting the capture of Nicholas Hunte of Hindolveston, Norfolk, who, although previously signified and imprisoned, was released in mainprise in order to gain absolution but failed to do so because he was unwilling to submit to the court's injunctions and to offer caution.*

(C.85/140/24)

Excellentissimo ac inuictissimo in Christo principi et domino nostro supremo domino Henrico dei gracia regi Anglie et Francie ac domino Hibernie illustrissimo uester humilis et deuotus Ricardus permissione diuina Norwicensis episcopus salutem in eo per quem reges regnant et principes dominantur cum omni subieccione.

Celsitudini uestre regie tenore presencium certificamus quod die mercurii uidelicet quarto die mensis Aprilis anno domini millesimo quingentesimo xuiii° in manerio nostro de Hoxne comparuit coram nobis quidam Nicholaus Hunte de Hyldolueton nostre Norwicensis diocesis ac copiam cuiusdam breuis uestri regii, ut asseruit, ueram nobis exhibuit, tradidit, et liberauit. Cuius tenor sequitur et est talis:

Rex uicecomiti Norfolkie salutem. Licet nuper ad requisicionem uenerabilis patris Ricardi episcopi Norwicensis per literas suas patentes nobis significantis Nicholaum Hunte de Hyldolueston sue diocesis propter suam manifestam contumaciam auctoritate ipsius episcopi ordinaria excommunicatum esse nec se uelle per censuram ecclesiasticam iusticiari tibi per breue nostrum precepimus quod ipsum Nicholaum per corpus suum secundum consuetudinem Anglie iusticiares donec sancte ecclesie tam de contemptu quam de iniuria ei illata ab eo esset satisfactum, quia tamen Robertus Drewe de parochia sancti Edmundi in Lumberdestrete London cordyn, Willelmus Hogons de parochia sancti Olaui in Southwarke in comitatu Surreye yoman, Ricardus Feey de ciuitate Norwicensi draper, et Willelmus Corbet de ciuitate Norwicensi gent coram nobis in cancellaria nostra personaliter constituti manuceperunt uidelicet quilibet eorum sub pena uiginta librarum pro prefato Nicholao quod ipse citra quindenam sancti Iohannis Baptiste proximi futuri seipsum prefato episcopo personaliter presentabit uel procuratorem suum mittet ad prestandam eidem episcopo caucionem idoneam de stando iuri et parendo mandatis sancte ecclesie et ad petendum in hac parte beneficium absolucionis a sentencia excommunicacionis predicte in forma iuris obtinendum et quod idem episcopus per literas suas patentes super huiusmodi absolucione sua nos in cancellaria nostra predicta citra eandem quindenam debite certificabit aut seipsum idem Nicholaus si premissa in forma predicta minime obseruata fuerint, extunc infra octo dies post quindenam predictam prisone in qua ad presens in custodia tua existit reddet ac restituet, ibidem moraturus donec sancte ecclesie tam de contemptu quam de iniuria predictis ab eo fuerit satisfactum, tibi precipimus quod execucioni dicti breuis nostri ulterius faciende interim supersedeas ac ipsum Nicholaum a prisona predicta qua sic detinetur si ea occasione et non alia detineatur in eadem sine dilacione interim deliberari facias per manucapcionem predictam. Teste meipso apud Westmonasterium xuii° die mensis Marcii anno regni nostri nono.

Unde nos Ricardus episcopus antedictus, quia idem Nicholaus alias erat per sentenciam diffinitiuam excommunicatus per dilectum nobis in Christo magistrum Thomam Hare legum doctorem officialem principalem curie consistorii nostri Norwicensis in quadam causa subtraccionis decimarum que coram eo in dicto consistorio inter dominum Robertum Newman rectorem ecclesie parochialis de Ryburgh Magna dicte nostre diocesis partem actricem et querelantem ex una et prefatum Nicholaum Hunte partem ream et querelatam partibus ex altera aliquandiu uertebatur et pendebat, remissimus eundem Nicholaum Hunte prefato officiali nostro principali ab huiusmodi excommunicacionis sentencia iuxta tenorem breuis uestri huiusmodi absoluendum quodque idem Nicholaus Hunt prout debite est nobis in hac parte certificatum coram eodem magistro Thoma Hare officiali nostro principali personaliter constitutus seipsum iuxta iuris exigenciam iniunccionibus canonicis submittere aut caucionem idoneam iuxta tenorem breuis huiusmodi prestare uel exponere non curauit, ymo expresse renuit et recusauit, neque prisone postea ex hoc se reddidit aut restituit uel de contemptu aut iniuria ullo modo satisfecit iuxta formam et effectum breuis uestri prelibati set in contemptum clauium sancte matris ecclesie mandati uestri regii ac omnium Christifidelium exemplum perniciosum adhuc animo obstinaci et indurato in huiusmodi sua pertinacia rebellione et excommunicacione impune perseuerat.

Cum igitur sancta mater ecclesia non habeat ulterius quid in hac parte facere debeat, auxilium brachii uestri secularis, christianissime princeps, ad tantam maliciam refrendam duximus inuocandum et attente inuocamus enixe supplicantes quatinus quod uestre ulterius in hac parte incumbit regie maiestatis officio peragere, exequi, et demandare dignetur ipsa uestra regia sublimitas prelibata. Quam ad populi sui et regni uobis commissi felix regimen et munimen dirigat in prosperis filius Marie uirginis gloriose per tempora diutina duratura. In cuius rei testimonium sigillum nostrum fecimus hiis apponi.

Datum in manerio nostro Hoxne primo die mensis Octobris anno domini M° quingentesimo xuiii° et nostre consecracionis anno xuiii°.

Dorse: Norfolkie.

g) *Request from the dean of the Arches to Archbishop Morton to signify to chancery the excommunication of John Cryne, late of Thorpland, Norwich diocese, 23 March 1489. Morton instead of sending a signification sent the dean's request, which chancery honored by issuing a writ to the sheriffs of London.*

(C.85/23/5)

Reuerendissimo in Christo patri et domino domino Iohanni permissione diuina Cantuariensi archiepiscopo, tocius Anglie primati, et apostolice sedis legato uester humilis et deuotus Humfridus Hawardyn legum doctor decanus ecclesie beate Marie de Arcubus Londonie ac officialitate curie uestre Cantuariensis uacante commissarius uester generalis et eiusdem curie presidens obedienciam et reuerenciam tanto reuerendissimo patri debitam cum honore.

Cum quidam Iohannes Cryne nuper de Thorplond Norwicensis diocesis uestreque prouincie Cantuariensis propter eius contumaciam manifestam in non comparendo coram nobis certis die et loco competentibus ad quos fuit legitime euocatus cuidam Willelmo Sparke ciuitatis Londonie in quodam querele negocio quod idem Willelmus Sparke contra dictum Iohannem Cryne monere et prosequi intendit de iusticia responsurum nuper fuerit et sit auctoritate eiusdem uestre curie Cantuariensis maioris excommunicacionis sentencia innodatus et pro sic excommunicato publice denunciatus. In qua quidem maioris excommunicacionis sentencia per quadraginta dies et amplius perseuerauerit et adhuc perseuerat animo pertinaciter indurato claues sancte matris ecclesie nequiter contempnendo in anime sue graue periculum aliorumque exemplum perniciosum plurimorum.

Vestre igitur paternitati reuerendissime supplicamus humiliter et deuote quatinus ad excommunicati huiusmodi obstinaciam reprimendam regie maiestati pro ipsius excommunicati corporis capcione secundum regni Anglie consuetudinem in hac parte hactenus usitatam et obseruatam scribere dignemini cum fauore ut quem timor dei non reuocat saltem coherceat animaduersio regie potestatis. Ad ecclesie uestre regimen et munimen necnon gregis dominici uobis commissi conseruacionem et paternitatem uestram reuerendissimam conseruet altissimus per tempora longiora.

Datum Londonie x° kalendas Aprilis anno domini milessimo CCCC^mo lxxx^mo octauo.

Dorse: Concordat cum registro — J. Belle.
        Londonie.

APPENDIX C

SIGNIFICATION OF EXCOMMUNICATION FROM NON-EPISCOPAL JURISDICTIONS

1) *List of inferior prelates who could signify.*

Listed here are the prelates below the rank of bishop who possessed the power to signify the capture of excommunicates, the years for which their significations are extant, and the dates and terms of surviving grants of this privilege. If not otherwise specified, the grant was made to the prelate without term and presumably was held at the king's pleasure during tenure of office.

Prelate	Significations	Grants
Beverley Minster, Provost & Chapt.[1]	1203[2] 1318[3] 1319[4] 1346[5]	8 Oct. 1206[6] 20 April 1242[7] 1 Jan. 1262[8] 26 June 1297[9] 7 Sept. 1310[10] 30 Nov. 1330[11] 10 Feb. 1378[12] 28 Aug. 1380[13] 26 April 1382[14] 1 March 1401[15] 25 Nov. 1413[16] 13 March 1428[17]
Bury St. Edmunds, Abbot	1248 1260 1264 1268 1280 1282 1283 1286 1287[18] 1305[19] 1306 1308 1314-1319 1338 1435[20]	17 Nov. 1321[21] 3 June 1338 for lifetime[22] 20 June 1353 for lifetime[23]

Notes: see pp. 179-182.

Prelate	Significations	Grants
Cambridge University, Chancellor[24]	1384 1530[25]	8 April 1383 for 5 years[26]
Colchester, archdeacon		6 Nov. 1402[27]
Ely, archdeacon	1391[28]	27 Jan. 1391[29]
Evesham, abbot	1298 1372 1381 1458[30]	26 Jan. 1332 to abbot & successors[31] 22 June 1377 × 2 Nov. 1381 confirmed[32]
Lincoln, archdeacon	1383 1384[33]	26 Dec. 1383[34]
London, St. Martin-le-Grand, royal free chapel, dean	1263 1313 1315 1345-1346 1444[35]	19 Dec. 1443 for 20 years[36]
London, St. Paul's Cathedral, dean	1386[37]	17 March 1386[38]
Norfolk, archdeacon	1384[39] 1389[40] 1403[41]	7 March 1384[42] 13 June 1389[43] 29 Dec. 1402 for 3 years[44]
Oxford University, chancellor[45]	1337-1339 1342 1357 1364-1366 1373 1376-1377 1380-1388 1391-1397 1401-1409 1411 1414 1445 1532[46]	8 June 1335 for 3 years[47] 28 July 1338 for 3 years[48] 3 Feb. 1340 for 2 years[49] 10 Nov. 1347 for 5 years[50] 6 Feb. 1352 for 5 years[51] 1 June 1357 for 5 years[52] 1 May 1359 for 5 years[53] 7 May 1364 for 5 years[54] 6 June 1369 for 5 years[55] 4 Nov. 1372 for 5 years[56] 25 June 1379 for 5 years[57] 16 June 1393 for 5 years[58] 4 Nov. 1399 for 20 years[59]
Penkridge, royal free chapel, dean[60]	1280-1281 1283-1284 1288 1442[61]	
Richmond, archdeacon[62]	1203[63] 1205[64] 1316-1317 1338 1340 1345 1384 1387 1511 1531[65]	25 Nov. 1351 for tenure[66] 7 Aug. 1375[67] 20 May 1383[68] 19 Feb. 1385[69]

12

Prelate	Significations	Grants
St. Albans, abbot	1259 1268 1277-1281 1285 1288 1292-1295 1300 1303 1314 1324 1329-1330 1334-1335 1337-1338 1344 1346-1347 1405 1435 1446 1449 1453 1468 1470 1472 1516[70]	23 Jan. 1331 to abbot & successors[71]
Shrewsbury, royal free chapel, dean	1285 1346[72]	
Stafford, royal free chapel, dean	1247 × 1259 1260 1262-1263 1347[73]	
Taunton, archdeacon	1244 × 1263[74]	
Tettenhall, royal free chapel, dean	1268[75]	
Thurrock, preb. in royal free chapel, Hastings	1387[76]	23 May 1387 for tenure[77]
Waltham, abbot	1281 1287[78]	
Westminster, abbot	1272 1278 1292 1388-1398 1401-1408 1410-1411 1415-1419 1423 1444	9 May 1365 for 3 years[83] 29 June 1379 for 3 years[84] 16 Aug. 1388 for 3 years[85] 26 May 1392 for 5 years[86] 7 Nov. 1397 for 4 years[87] 12 May 1401 for 5 years[88] 22 Nov. 1406 for 5 years[89] 15 July 1413 for 12 years[90] 3 May 1429 for 10 years[91]

Prelate	Significations	Grants
	1448	14 June 1482[92]
	1472	
	1474-1476	
	1481[79]	
	1502	
	1503[80]	
	1504[81]	
	1511[82]	

[1] Unlike the others in this list, who followed the normal practice of procedure by royal writ, the provost and chapter of Beverley Minster according to a charter of its liberties could signify directly to the sheriff of Yorks., without need of recourse to the royal chancery, the names of those excommunicated for detention of thraves or for some other crime. Secular aid for the collection of these thraves was provided for by Henry I (*ca.* 1125-1135) in a writ to the archbishop of York and the justices, sheriff, reeves, and royal ministers of York: "Si quis super hoc aliquid detinuerit, vos faciatis ei inde habere plenariam justitiam, ne super hoc amplius inde clamorem audiam pro peniuria pleni recti" (*Early Yorks. Charters*, vol. 1 (ed. W. Farrer; Yorks. Archaeological Soc., 1914), no. 97; William Dugdale, *Monasticon Anglicanum* (London, 1817-1830) 6. 1308); this was confirmed by Henry II (1155-1162) (*EYC* 1, no. 108). The explicit provisions made in the charter confirmed in 1202 were often published *in pleno comitatu* (*Beverley Chapter Act Book* (ed. A. F. Leach; Surtees Soc., 1898-1903) 1. 358-59), and in 1318 the king wrote to the sheriff of Yorks. to remind him of this privilege (*ibid.* 1. 366-67). In an early fourteenth-century form found in the act book the provost and chapter were directed to write directly to the sheriff without mentioning themselves by name (*ibid.* 1. 287). Despite this unique privilege of bypassing the royal chancery, this was not always done as examples from the years 1203 and 1346 clearly demonstrate.

[2] Prynne, p. 8.

[3] *Beverley Chapter Act Book*, 1. 358-59.

[4] *Ibid.*, 1, 368.

[5] C.85/214/41. For transcription see *infra* pp. 185-86.

[6] "Volumus etiam et firmiter precipimus quod omnes detentores trauarum sancti Iohannis collatarum ab antecessoribus nostris in liberam elemosinam vel ab aliis in usus prepositi vel clericorum Beverlaci, qui a predicto preposito et capitulo fuerint excommunicati propter ipsarum travarum detentionem vel propter alium excessum ad mandatum predicti prepositi et capituli, etiam non expectato alio mandato secundum consuetudinem regni nostri, a vicecomite Eboracensi et ballivis de Eborachyra capiantur et teneantur, donec id predicte ecclesie et preposito plenarie emendetur" (*Cal. Chart. Rolls* 3. 141-42).

[7] *Cal. Chart Rolls* 1. 269.

[8] *Ibid.*, 2. 39.

[9] *Ibid.*, 2. 468.

[10] *Ibid.*, 3. 141-42.

[11] *Ibid.*, 4. 195.

[12] *CPR*, *1377-81*, p. 120.

[13] *Ibid.*, p. 542.

[14] *Ibid.*, *1381-85*, p. 118.

[15] *Ibid.*, *1199-1401*, pp. 456-57.

[16] *Cal. Chart. Rolls* 5. 457-58.

[17] *CPR, 1422-29*, pp. 490-91.

[18] For these years from 1248 to 1287, see C.85/213/1-10.

[19] Prynne, p. 1147.

[20] For these years from 1306 to 1435, see C85/213/12-24.

[21] *Cal. Chanc. Warr., 1244-1326*, p. 526.

[22] *CPR, 1338-40*, p. 89.

[23] *Ibid., 1350-54*, p. 470.

[24] When not possessing the power of signification, the chancellor secured the capture of excommunicates through the bishop of Ely as in the caes of Thomas atte Pond in 1382 (*Ely Diocesan Remembrancer* (1895), p. 192).

[25] For these two years, see C.85/209/39-40.

[26] *CPR, 1381-85*, pp. 241-42.

[27] *CPR, 1401-05*, p. 175.

[28] C.85/214/56.

[29] *CPR, 1388-92*, p. 375.

[30] For these years, see C.85/213/28, 30-31; C.85/214/60.

[31] *CPR, 1330-34*, p. 249.

[32] In a signification of this date the abbot stated, "Cum ita sit quod per cartam illustri principis domini Edwardi nuper regis, aui uestri, per uos confirmata graciose sit concessum quod nos et successores nostri de personis nostre iurisdiccionis auctoritate nostra excommunicatis per ministros uestros capiendis curie uestre regie per literas nostras patentes significare possimus..." (C.85/213/31).

[33] C.85/214/47, 51. The first of these was dated 24 Sept. 1383, two months before the date of the letters patent.

[34] *CPR, 1381-85*, p. 219. This grant was revoked by the general revocation of 28 April 1391 (see *infra* pp. 182-83).

[35] C.85/214/25-27, 37, 42, 58.

[36] *CPR, 1441-46*, p. 238.

[37] C.85/214/53.

[38] *CPR, 1385-89*, p. 127. This grant was revoked by the general revocation of 28 April 1391 (see *infra* pp. 182-83).

[39] C.85/214/50 and 52. There were two significations sent by John de Freton in this year, the first of which, dated 14 Jan. 1384, was sent before the date of the letter patent.

[40] C.85/214/55. This signification from Richard Medford dated 10 Jan. 1389 predates the letter patent, although he claimed to be acting "iuxta privilegium ab ipsa regia magestate michi graciose indultum."

[41] C.85/214/57. In this signification Thomas Langley requested the capture of eight excommunicates "iuxta tenorem literarum uestrarum regiarum michi ex gracia celsitudinis uestre regie concessarum."

[42] *CPR, 1381-85*, p. 396.

[43] *Ibid., 1388-92*, p. 48. Richard Medford had also been granted the same privilege as prebendary of Thurrock (*infra*). This grant of 1389 was revoked by the general revocation of 28 April 1391 (see *infra* pp. 182-83).

[44] *Ibid., 1401-05*, p. 187.

[45] When the university did not possess the power of signification, the writ would have been secured through the bishop of Lincoln as was done in 1292 when the chancellor sent to Oliver Sutton, bishop of Lincoln, ten names of persons whom he had excommunicated (*Reg. Sutton, Lincoln* 4. 1-2).

[46] These significations have been calendared and introduced by H. E. Salter, *Snappe's Formulary,*

pp. 22-29. For the year 1414 see C.202/C.130/106. In addition, on 4 Nov. 1516 Peter Ligham, commissary in the university, signified to Archbishop Warham, chancellor of the university, the contumacy of an excommunicate (*Letters and Papers, Domestic and Foreign* 2. 1. no. 2509).

[47] *CPR, 1334-38*, p. 119. An attempt to gain this privilege in 1320 was unsuccessful: "quod fiat sicut antiquitus fieri consueuit" (*Rot. Parl.* 1. 371; reprinted in *Collectanea, Third Series* (ed. Montagu Burrows; Oxford Historical Soc., vol. 32, 1896), p. 120). Three successful petitions in the files of ancient petitions (printed in *ibid.*, pp. 96, 121-22, 137-38) cannot be precisely dated.

[48] *CPR, 1338-1340*, p. 118.

[49] *Ibid.*, p. 412; printed in *Mediaeval Archives of the University of Oxford* (ed. H. E. Salter; Oxford Historical Soc., vols. 70, 73, 1920-21) 1. 138-39. The two years were to begin at the expiration of the previous grant (i.e., from 28 July 1341).

[50] *CPR, 1345-48*, p. 428.

[51] *Ibid., 1350-54*, p. 226; printed in Salter, *Mediaeval Archives* 1. 147.

[52] *CPR, 1354-58*, p. 566.

[53] *Ibid., 1358-61*, p. 193.

[54] *CPR, 1361-64*, p. 493.

[55] *Ibid., 1367-70*, p. 255; printed in Salter, *Mediaeval Archives* 1. 192.

[56] *CPR, 1370-74*, p. 209.

[57] *Ibid., 1377-81*, p. 369; printed in Salter, *Mediaeval Archives* 1. 205.

[58] *CPR, 1391-96*, p. 288; printed in Salter, *Mediaeval Archives* 1. 224.

[59] *CPR, 1399-1401*, p. 94.

[60] The archbishop of Dublin, provided he was not Irish, would normally be dean of Penkridge.

[61] C.85/198/20; C.85/214/15-20, 59.

[62] When the archdeacon did not possess the power to signify excommunicates, the archbishop of York would signify at his request: in 1369 (C.85/183/36), 1481 (C.85/187/8), 1519 (C.85/188/5), and 1522 (C.85/188/9-11).

[63] *Curia Regis Rolls* 2. 298.

[64] *The Great Roll of the Pipe for the Seventh Year of the Reign of King John, Michaelmas 1205* (ed. Sidney Smith; Pipe Roll Soc., n.s., vol. 19, 1941), p. 58.

[65] For the years 1316 to 1531 see C.85/214/29-30, 33-35, 38-39, 49, 54; C.85/215/1-2.

[66] *CPR, 1350-54*, p. 182.

[67] C.81/30592-94.

[68] *CPR, 1381-85*, p. 274.

[69] *Ibid.*, p. *536*. This grant was revoked by the general revocation of 28 April 1391 (see *infra* pp. 182-83).

[70] For these dates, see C.85/212; for 1338 see the misplaced signification C.85/210/9; for 1314, see also *Cal. Chanc. Warr.*, p. 395.

[71] *CPR, 1330-34*, p. 46; see also Thomas Walsingham, *Gesta abbatum* (R.S., London, 1867-69) 2. 283-284. Count Weiss suggests that this grant gained through the good offices of Richard de Bury may be related to a gift of books made by the abbot to Bury at about this time. (Roberto Weiss, "The Private Collector and the Revival of Greek Learning," *The English Library before 1700* (edited by Francis Wormald and C. E. Wright; London, 1958), p. 113).

[72] C.85/214/2-7, 11-13, 43.

[73] C.85/214/10.

[74] C.85/214/9.

[75] C.47/98/6/piece dated 16 Oct. 1387.

[76] *CPR, 1385-89*, p. 309. This was a personal grant to Richard Medford, king's clerk. See *supra* under Norfolk.

[77] C.85/213/26-27.

[78] C.85/210-211.

79 C.47/118/79/piece dated 22 Dec. 1481.
80 For 1502 and 1503, see C.85/211/56-57.
81 C.47/118/84/ piece dated 5 July 1504.
82 C.85/211/58.
83 *CPR, 1364-67*, p. 112.
84 *Ibid.*, *1377-81*, p. 370.
85 *Ibid.*, *1385-89*, p. 499.
86 *Ibid.*, *1391-96*, p. 55.
87 *Ibid.*, *1396-99*, p. 251.
88 *Ibid.*, *1399-1401*, p. 481.
89 *Ibid.*, *1405-08*, p. 273.
90 *Ibid.*, *1413-16*, p. 64.
91 *Ibid.*, *1422-29*, p. 533.
92 *Ibid.*, *1476-85*, p. 298.

2) *Revocation by Richard II of his grants to those lower than the rank of bishop of the privilege of signifying excommunicates, excepting the abbot of Westminster and the chancellor of the University of Oxford, 28 April 1391 (entered on the patent rolls: C.66/332/mem. 12 ; the privy seal letter is C.81/524/7179 ; the revocation is calendared in* CPR, 1388-92, *p. 415).*

De reuocacione [*margin*].

Rex omnibus ad quos etc. salutem.

Supplicarunt nobis uenerabiles patres archiepiscopi Cantuariensis et Eboracensis et omnes episcopi prouinciarum suarum ut cum per leges sancte ecclesie ac eciam per consuetudinem regni nostri et per cursum cancellarie nostre a tempore cuius memoria non habetur usitatos et obseruatos solum pertinuisset et adhuc pertineat ad prefatos archiepiscopos, episcopos, et predecessores suos temporibus suis et ad custodes spiritualium dictorum archiepiscopatuum et episcopatuum tempore uacacionis et ad nullum alium in auxilium et supportacionem legum et libertatum sancte ecclesie ad petendum et inuocandum auxilium brachii secularis ad iusticiandos et obedire faciendos mandatis sancte ecclesie illos qui tam per contumaciam quam alio modo infra iurisdicciones suas sunt excommunicati et se nolunt mandatis predictis obedire et super hoc ad certificacionem ipsorum archiepiscoporum et episcoporum in cancellariam nostram predictam de nominibus huiusmodi excommunicatorum et inobediencium separatim missam breue nostrum de Significauit directum fuisset uicecomiti comitatus ubi tales excommunicati et inobedientes fuerint conuersantes ad eos iusticiandos et obedire faciendos dictis mandatis sancte ecclesie ac nuper aliqui archidiaconorum suorum ac alii iurisdiccionem ecclesiasticam exercentes propter proficuum archidiaconatuum et iurisdiccionum suorum attrahendum ac propter iura et iurisdicciones predictorum archiepiscoporum et episcoporum diminuenda nobis prosecuti fuissent ad concedendum eisdem archidiaconis et aliis predictis quod ad nudas certificaciones suas in cancellariam nostram predictam de gentibus per eos excommunicatis mittendas breue nostrum de Significauit concedatur ad huiusmodi gentes per eos excommunicatas capiendas et in prisona detinendas consimili modo quo fieri consueuit ad certificaciones predictorum archiepiscoporum et episcoporum ac dictorum predecessorum suorum et sic usurpare et attrahere uoluissent penes ipsos iurisdiccionem predictorum archiepiscoporum et episcoporum contra dictas leges et libertates sancte ecclesie ac consuetudinem regni nostri predicti et cursum cancellarie nostre antedicte in ipsorum archiepiscoporum et episcoporum et successorum suorum graue preiudicium ac ecclesiarum et iurisdiccionum suarum lesionem non modicam et populi nostri dampnum et importabilem oppressionem uelimus premissa in saluacionem legum et libertatum sancte ecclesie predictarum ac usuum et consuetudinum regni et cancellarie nostrorum predictorum toto tempore per nobiles progenitores nostros ut predictum est usitatorum et consuetorum benigne considerare et ulterius concedere quod omnes patentes et litere in tali casu et materiis de nobis per predictos archidiaconos et alios tempore nostro impetrate reuocentur et penitus adnullentur.

Nos supplicacioni ipsorum archiepiscoporum et episcoporum in hac parte annuentes de gracia nostra speciali et de assensu magni consilii nostri omnes huiusmodi literas patentes predictis archidiaconis et aliis tempore nostro in hoc casu ut premittitur factas tenore presencium duximus reuocandas et adnullandas ex causa supradicta, literis patentibus dilectis nobis in Christo abbati et conuentui Westmonasterii ac dilectis nobis cancellario et uniuersitati Oxoniensi in casu predicto per nos concessis dumtaxat exceptis. Et hoc omnibus quorum interest innotescimus per presentes. In cuius rei etc. Teste rege apud Westmonasterium xxuiii die Aprilis [1391].

per breue de priuato sigillo

3) *Signification (22 March 1418) from the abbot of Westminster for the capture of William atte Wood, who after having appealed his sentence and being released in mainprise has failed to prosecute his appeal (C.85/211/33). Atte Wood was soon captured by virtue of a writ dated 9 May 1418 (C.202/C.124/87), but gained another hearing by complaining in chancery that he was in fact prosecuting his appeal and that the abbot was acting contrary to an apostolic inhibition (C. 47/111/32/piece dated 2 June 1418; draft copy is in unsorted file C.202/F.2).*

Excellentissimo in Christo principi et domino domino Henrico dei gracia regi Anglie et Francie ac domino Hibernie illustri Willelmus eadem gracia abbas monasterii Westmonasterii reuerencias et honores in eo per quem reges regnant et principes dominantur.

Quia uestra regia celsitudo nobis de gracia speciali per uestras literas patentes de dato quintodecimo die Iulii anno regni uestri primo concessit et licenciam dedit quod per duodecem annos proximos futuros cancellario uestro pro tempore existenti per literas nostras patentes significare uel certificare possimus de nominibus omnium illorum de iurisdiccione nostra qui auctoritate nostra propria sunt uel erunt excommunicati et in huiusmodi excommunicacione per quadraginta dies moram traxerint et quod dictus cancellarius pro tempore existens breuia in cancellaria uestra sub magno sigillo uestro fieri et consignari faciet ad dictos excommunicatos ad certificacionem uel significacionem nostram capiendos prout per certificacionem uel significacionem episcoporum regni uestri Anglie pro eis qui auctoritate sua ordinaria excommunicati existunt in saluacionem iurisdiccionis sancte ecclesie fieri consueuit ac cum eadem uestra regia celsitudo ad significacionem, requisicionem, et supplicacionem nostras per literas nostras patentes eidem uestre celsitudini nuper factas Willelmum atte Wode nostre iurisdiccionis propter ipsius multiplices contumacias pariter et offensas coram archidiacono nostro monasterii predicti contractas auctoritate nostra ordinaria excommunicatum et pro sic excommunicato palam, publice, ac solempniter denunciatum per corpus suum per breue uestrum de excommunicato capiendo secundum consuetudinem regni uestri Anglie arestari siue iusticiari preceperit et realiter incarceratum per uicecomites Londonie habuerit donec sancte ecclesie tam de contemptu quam de iniuria ei illata ab eo foret satisfactum ac cum ipse Willelmus pretextu cuiusdam appellacionis pretense sub dato mensis Iulii die septima anno domini millesimo quadringentesimo xu^{to} a dicta sentencia excommunicacionis ad sedem apostolicam licet friuole interposite per instrumentum publicum confectum et in cancellaria uestra exhibite per manucapcionem Willelmi Jeys de London cotilere, Willelmi Capwode de Barnet in comitatu Middylsex maltman, Iohannis Herbere de London baker, et Simonis Fyssher de London hornere pro dicto Willelmo de prosequendo huiusmodi appellacionem suam sub certa pena in cancellaria predicta factam a prisona qua occasione predicta detinebatur liberatus fuisset, idem tamen Willelmus atte Wode predictam appellacionem suam infra tempus de iure ad hoc limitatum prout debuit et a parte iuris et aliorum premissorum fuit et est astrictus citra liberacionem suam predictam ea occasione factam prosequi non curauit ipsaque appellacio notorie diserta extitit et existit prout per idem instrumentum publicum predictum supradicta appellacione confectum et in cancellaria uestra predicta exhibitum ut prefertur dilucidius poterit apparere adeo quod idem Willelmus in sentencia excommunicacionis predicte toto et omni tempore predicto perseuerauit et adhuc perseuerat animo pertinaciter indurato claues sancte matris ecclesie nequiter contempnendo in ipsius anime graue periculum et aliorum perniciosum exemplum plurimorum. Vestram igitur regiam magestatem rogamus et humiliter supplicamus eidem quatinus ad dicti Willelmi excommunicati obstinanciam reprimendam uelitis ut prius brachium extendere uestri auxilii secularis contra eundem excommunicatum exercendo quod secundum regni uestri consuetudinem in talibus regie conuenit maiestati ut quem timor dei et seueritas ecclesiastice discipline a malo non reuocant saltem coherceat animaduersio regie potestatis et quod ecclesiastice cohercioni deesse dinoscitur in hoc casu uestre regie magestatis potencia suppleatur. Magnificenciam uestram regiam diu regat altissimus et conseruet ad ecclesie sancte sue et regni uestri regimen et munimen.

Datum in monasterio nostro predicto xxii° die mensis Marcii anno domini millesimo quadringentesimo xuii^{mo}.

Dorse: Londonie.

4) *Signification to the royal chancery by the provost and chapter of Beverley Minster, 18 May 1346.*

(C.85/214/41)

Excellentissimo in Christo principi et domini domini nostri domini regis Anglie et Francie illustri .. cancellario .. prepositus et .. capitulum ecclesie collegiate beati Iohannis Beuerlaci quicquid poterint cum omni reuerencia et honore.

Vestre dominacioni uenerande denunciamus et significamus quod Theobaldus de Troy procurator ecclesie de Cottyngham, Iohannes Takell de eadem, Nicholaus Faber de eadem, Walterus Gylling de Cottyngham, Adam Cocus de eadem, et Andreas Carter de eadem propter suam contumaciam multiplicatam pariter et offensam ad instanciam dilecti confratris et concanonici nostri domini Willelmi de Kildesby prebendarii prebende altaris sancti Andree in ecclesia nostra predicta contractas eo quod ipsi sepius et legitime moniti et requisiti trauas sancti Iohannis Beuerlaci de autumpno ultimo preterito ab ipsis pro carucis suis quibus in campis parochie de Cottyngham terras suas coluerunt dicto dilecto confratri nostro et prebende sue predicte notorie debitas et ad ostia grangiarum suarum solui consuetas eidem uel eius procuratori soluere non curarunt, set huiusmodi nostris monicionibus spretis et contemptis huiusmodi trauas eidem soluere recusarunt maioris excommunicacionis sua auctoritate nostra ordinaria seruatis iuris ordine et processu qui in hoc casu requiruntur sunt inuoluti. In qua quidem excommunicacionis maioris sentencia iidem Theobaldus, Nicholaus, Walterus, Adam, et Andreas per quadraginta dies et amplius animis pertinaciter induratis claues sancte matris ecclesie contempnendo perseuerarunt et perseuerant in presenti.

Cum igitur sancta mater ecclesia quid ulterius contra eosdem faciat non habeat, uestram dominacionem uenerandam humiliter requirimus et rogamus quatinus ad insolenciam predictorum Theobaldi, Nicholai, Walteri, Ade, et Andree salubriter reprimendam pro capcione corporum eorundem uicecomiti Eboraci et eius ministris secundum formam cuiusdam breuis regii quod quondam pro capcione corporum huiusmodi excommunicatorum optinuimus cuius tenor inferius continetur uel sub alia forma que uobis placuerit scribere et demandare uelitis. Tenor enim dicti breuis talis est:

Rex uicecomitibus Eboraci salutem. Cum inter ceteras libertates dilectis nobis in Christo .. preposito et .. capitulo ecclesie sancti Iohannis Beuerlaci per cartas progenitorum nostrorum quondam regum Anglie et confirmacionem nostram quas inspeximus concessas contineatur quod omnes detentores trauarum sancti Iohannis collatarum ab antecessoribus nostris in liberam elemosinam uel ab aliis in usus .. prepositi uel clericorum Beuerlaci qui a predicto .. preposito et capitulo fuerint excommunicati propter ipsarum trauarum detencionem uel propter aliquem alium excessum ad mandatum predicti .. prepositi et .. capituli eciam non expectato alio mandato secundum consuetudinem regni nostri a uicecomitibus Eboraci et balliuis nostris de Eboracsira capiantur et teneantur donec id predicte ecclesie et .. prepositi plenarie emendetur. Tibi precipimus quod omnes a prefatis .. preposito et .. capitulo occasione huiusmodi detencionis aut alterius excessus illati excommunicatos ad mandatum ipsorum .. prepositi et .. capituli quociens per ipsos fueris requisitus non expectato alio mandato secundum consuetudinem regni nostri usitato capi et in prisona nostra detineri faciatis quousque super huiusmodi detencione aut excessu modo debito et iuxta tenorem cartarum et confirmacionis nostre predictarum eis fuerit satisfactum. Texte meipso apud Eboracum iiiito die Decembris anno regni nostri duodecimo.

Ad honoris incrementa uestram dominacionem reuerendam conseruet altissimus per tempora feliciter duratura.

Datum Beuerlaci xuiii die Maii anno domini millesimo CCCmo quadragesimo sexto.

Dorse : Excellentissimo principis et domini domini nostri regis Anglie et Francie illustri cancellario.

Per capitulum et prepositum ecclesie beati Iohannis Beuerlaci.

APPENDIX D

THE SECULAR ARM AND THE COLLECTION OF CLERICAL SUBSIDIES

1) *Royal letter of 11 July 1374 to the sheriffs of shires in the diocese of Lincoln by which they are instructed to act upon direct requests from the bishop for the use of the secular arm against persons excommunicated for not paying the clerical subsidy* (entered on the Close Rolls: C.54/212/m. 18; see CCR, 1374-77, p. 37).

De rebellis in solucione subsidii capiendis.

Rex uicecomiti Lincolniensi salutem. Quia datum est nobis intelligi quod quamplures religiosi ac alii beneficiati et stipendiarii exempti et non exempti Lincolniensis diocesis infra comitum predictum commorantes censuras episcopi Lincolniensis non uerentes set claues ecclesie dampnabiliter contempnentes porciones subsidii quinquaginta milium librarum nobis per prelatos et clerum regni nostri Anglie in auxilium expensarum quas pro saluacione dicti regni nostri nos facere oportebit nuper concessi ad quas racionabiliter sunt assessi soluere manifeste recusarunt et recusant in presenti, per quod dictum subsidium absque iuuamine brachii secularis leuari non ualeat ullo modo, uolentes manus nostras ad hoc apponere adiutrices, nos aduertentes rebellionem predictam non solum in libertatis ecclesie lesionem uerum eciam in contemptum regie maiestatis cedere manifestum et uolentes eo pretextu remedium apponere oportunum, tibi precipimus firmiter iniungentes quod non obstantibus quibuscumque libertatibus seu priuilegiis ecclesiasticis omnes et singulos tam religiosos quam beneficiatos et stipendiarios exemptos et non exemptos quoscumque infra diocesim ipsius episcopi et comitatum tuum commorantes qui porciones ipsos de subsidio predicto contingentes soluere recusauerunt et prefato episcopo aut eius ministris et deputatis rebelles fuerunt in hac parte de quorum nominibus per ipsum episcopum tibi denunciatum fuerit absque more et diffugio capias et arestes et eos ad porciones ad quas tibi per certificacionem dicti episcopi constiterit ipsos assessos esse per districciones et incarceracionem corporum suorum et alios uias et modos quibus melius fore uideris soluendum cum omni celeritate compellas et prefato episcopo et eius ministris et deputatis in leuacione subsidii predicti auxilians sis et intendens quociens et quando per ipsos seu eorum aliquem super hoc ex parte nostra fueris requisitus. Et hoc sub periculo quo intendit nullatenus omittas. Teste rege apud Westmonasterium xi die Iulii.

Consimilia breui diriguntur uicecomitibus subscriptis sub eadem data

uidelicet: uicecomiti Leycestrie, uicecomiti Rotelandie, uicecomiti North-
amptonie, uicecomiti Oxononie, uicecomiti Bukinghanie et Bedfordie,
uicecomiti Huntundone, uicecomiti Hertfordie.

2) *Signification of six ecclesiastics by Bishop Dispenser of Norwich for their
failure to pay the clerical subsidy, 24 April 1376.*

(C.85/135/12)

Excellentissimo principi et domino suo domino Edwardo dei gracia
illustri Anglie et Francie regi et domino Hibernie Henricus permissione
diuina Norwicensis episcopus salutem in eo per quem reges regnant et
principes dominantur.

Excellencie uestre tenore presencium intimamus quod Willelmus persona ecclesie de Belagh, Adam uicarius ecclesie de Stanford, Thomas
persona ecclesie de Tatersete sancti Andree, Willelmus persona medietatis
ecclesie de Wetherden, Henricus uicarius de Ressynglond, et Iohannes
persona ecclesie de Aysch in decanatu de Loose propter suas contumacias
manifestas, rebelliones pariter et offensas occasione non solucionis decimarum triennalium uidelicet et annalium uestre celsitudini per clerum
uestrum Anglie ultimo concessarum suis terminis legitime per nos prefixis
eisdem et assignatis tam in non ueniendo quam iuri non parendo et hucus-
que in dictarum decimarum solucione quatenus eos concernit contemptibiliter cessando coram nobis ex officio nostro in hac parte procedentibus
commissas et contractas maiorum excommunicacionum sentenciis auctoritate nostra ordinaria innodati, iusticia suadente, et pro excommunicatis
palam, pupplice, et in specie denunciati, in eisdem sentenciis per quadraginta dies et amplius dampnabiliter perstiterunt claues contempnentes
ecclesiastice discipline et adhuc in ipsis perseuerant cordibus induratis in
animarum suarum graue periculum et aliorum exemplum perniciosum et
uestri iuris regii dispendium et iacturam.

Cum igitur sancta mater ecclesia non habeat quid ultra faciat in hac
parte, magestati uestre regie supplicamus quatenus ad ipsorum excommunicatorum rebelliones reprimendas exercere dignemini contra ipsos
auxilium brachii secularis ut quos dei timor a malo non reuocat secularis
potestas coherceat a peccato. Ad regimen populi uestri uniuersalis et munimen uestram celsitudinem custodiat trinitas increata.

Datum Norwico xxiiii[to] die Aprilis anno domini millesimo trescentesimo
septuagesimo sexto et consecracionis nostre [septimo].

APPENDIX E

THE USE OF THE SECULAR ARM AGAINST HERETICS

1) *List of heretics and those suspect of heresy who appear in the signification files.*

The following list contains the names of persons encountered in the preparation of this study against whom the secular arm was invoked because of heresy or suspicion of heresy. The names of these persons are here listed according to whether the writ *de excommunicato capiendo* or the writ *de heretico comburendo* was sued against them. Also encountered were cases which concerned matters touching heresy, although no explicit reference to heresy was made in the significations; these too are here included and are prefixed by a dagger. The date is the date of the reguest for the writ.

De excommunicato capiendo

5 Nov. 1316
> Adam Knyght of Magna Derset in Warwicks. and his sister Alice, both vehemently suspect of heresy, were signified as excommunicates by the bishop of Coventry and Lichfield (C.85/56/31).

19 March 1370
> Nicholas Drayton of London diocese was judged heretical, excommunicated, and signified by the bishop of London (C.85/121/13). The writ issued from chancery on 20 March (*Foedera* 6. 651).

16 Jan. 1387
> Master Nicholas Hereford, the Wyclifite, was signified by Archbishop Courtenay (for transcription see *infra* p. 193). On 17 Jan. commissions were issued by the king to prominent laymen in Notts., Leics., and Derbs. to secure his arrest (*CPR, 1385-89*, p. 316).

† 15 July 1387
> Thomas Durham was signified by the chancellor of the University of Oxford for disobeying warnings "super quibusdam artis magice et maliciose diffamacionis articulis" (C.85/208/55; Salter, p. 35).

10 Sept. 1391
> Nicholas Ipswich (Yepeswych), layman, of the city of London was excommunicated for not appearing before the dean of the Arches "to answer to certain heretical and erroneous articles which he has held, preached, and dogmatized in the city of London and elsewhere in the province" and was signified by the archbishop (C.85/11/74).

3 Feb. 1392

> Margaret Layborn and Joan daughter of David Smyth of Shrews-
> bury were excommunicated in a case of heretical pravity heard by
> the bishop of Hereford, who signified them (C.85/91/2). The signi-
> fication was repeated on 3 July 1392 and 1 Dec. 1393 (C.85/91/5, 9).

† 9 Nov. 1394

> Thomas Whelwryght, John Whelwryght, Richard Bullock, chap-
> lains, Simon Colyn, and Thomas Patteshull, lollards of Northampton,
> were signified by the bishop of Lincoln (C.85/109/38).

† 12 March 1397

> John *alias* William Grenlefe, *sortilegus*, of Melton Ross, Lincs., was
> signified by the bishop of Lincoln (C.85/109/49).

† 12 May 1441

> Hugh Knyght, husbandman, of Devon was excommunicated for
> disrespect to the image of the Virgin in the chapel of St. John the
> Baptist at Newport in the parish of Bishop's Tawton and subse-
> quently was signified by the bishop of Exeter (C.85/79/25).

† 13 July 1447

> John Rox was excommunicated for not performing the penance
> imposed on him for use of the art of necromancy, incantation, and
> sortilege, and was subsequently signified by the bishop of Lincoln
> (C.85/112/34).

26 Jan. 1468

> Edmund Byrst of Bobbingworth, Essex, suspect of the crime of
> heresy, was excommunicated and subsequently signified by the
> bishop of London (C.85/125/28).

20 Oct. 1509

> Thomas Cudworth of Silkstone, West Riding, was excommunicated
> for failing to purge himself of suspicion of heresy and was signified
> by the vicar-general of the archbishop of York (C.85/187/22). The
> signification was repeated on 12 March 1510, when the vicar-general
> stated that Cudworth had been unjustly delivered from York Castle
> where he had been imprisoned (C.85/187/23), and again on 8 Feb.
> 1511 (*ibid.*, no. 25).

29 May 1529

> John Tyndall *alias* Hochyn of the city of London in a heresy case
> was declared excommunicate by Bishops Tunstall of London, Long-
> land of Lincoln, and Clerk of Bath and Wells, and was signified by
> Cardinal Wolsey in his capacity as legate (C.85/188/28).

De heretico comburendo

10 July 1467

    William Barow of Walden, a relapsed heretic, was signified by the bishop of London (C.85/125/25).

2 July 1477

    John Hoddesdon of the parish of Amwell, Herts., William Browne of the parish of Ware, Herts., and Peter Boore late of Ware now of the parish of Amwell, having relapsed after abjuration, were signified by the bishop of London (C.85/125/34).

12 May 1503

    William Stone, relapsed heretic, was signified by the bishop of London (S.C.1/44/79 or 82).

2 May 1511

    Robert Harysay of the city of Canterbury, son of iniquity, "propter suos uarios dampnatos et manifestos errores et hereses necnon opiniones dampnabiles contra fidem catholicam et sanctam matrem ecclesiam per ipsum Iohannem nonnullis modis et mediis doctos et predicatos per nos legitime et canonice conuictus et hereticus iudicatus," was signified by the archbishop of Canterbury (C.85/24/22).

2 May 1511

    William Carder of Tenterden, Canterbury diocese, described as in the preceding case, was signified by the archbishop of Canterbury (for transcription see *infra*, pp. 193-94).

2 May 1511

    Agnes Grevell, Canterbury diocese, described as in the two preceding cases, was signified by the archbishop of Canterbury (C. 85/24/25).

19 May 1511

    John Brown of Ashford, Kent, Canterbury diocese, described as in the three precedings cases, was signified by the archbishop of Canterbury (C.85/24/20). According to Foxe he was burned on 30 May 1517 (John Foxe, *The Acts and Monuments* (London, 1843-49) 4. 181-82); perhaps this should read 1511.

18 Aug. 1511

    Robert Cosyn of Little Missenden, William Tillesworth, William Scryvyner, Nicholas Colyns, and Thomas May of Amersham, Bucks., relapsed heretics, were signified by the bishop of Lincoln and left to the secular arm "ad omnem iuris effectum qui exinde sequi poterit aut debet" (C.85/115/10). Tillesworth was burned at Amersham and Cosyn probably at Buckingham, but Foxe supplies no dates (Foxe 4. 123-24, 214).

24 Sept. 1511

William Swetyng of the parish of Chelsea and James Brewster late of Colchester, relapsed heretics, were signified by the bishop of London (C.85/126/19). They were burned together at Smithfield on 18 Oct. 1511 (Foxe 4. 180-81, 216).

3 Oct. 1511

Edward Walter of Maidstone, described as were the others from Canterbury diocese in May of the same year, was signified by the archbishop of Canterbury (C.85/24/21).

16 Dec. 1514

Richard Hunne of the parish of St. Margaret, Bridge Street, London, a heretic, although dead, was signified by the bishop of London with the request that whatever remains to be done the secular arm should do (C.85/126/26; for a transcription, see E. Jeffries Davis, "The Authorities for the Case of Richard Hunne (1514-15)," *EHR* 30 (1913) 487-88).

1 March 1518

Thomas Man, although he had abjured before Master Thomas Hedde, leg. dr., vicar-general in spirituals of the London diocese, relapsed and was signified by the bishop (C.85/126/28). He was burned at Smithfield 29 March 1518 (Foxe 4. 213).

28 Jan. 1522

Thomas Barnard, James Murden of Amersham, Robert Rave of Boveney, and John Scryvyner, probably all of Bucks., were declared relapsed heretics by definitive sentence and were signified by the bishop of Lincoln, who insisted that "per premissa nec mortem nec corporis diminucionem neque membrorum mutilacionem intendimus ipsis aut ipsorum alicui" (C.85/115/13; see Foxe 4. 245).

22 Dec. 1531

Thomas Benett of the parish of St. George in the city of Exeter was tried by Master Thomas Berwode, decr. dr., vicar-general in spirituals, in Exeter cathedral on 20 Dec. 1531 on charges of holding, preaching, saying, and dogmatizing opinions iniquitous, heretical, erroneous, and contrary to the determination of the church; he was declared a manifest heretic. The bishop of Exeter signified his name to chancery, and the writ was issued on 31 Dec. (C.85/82/13 and dorse).

3 July 1533

John Fryth and Andrew Huett were condemned as heretics by the bishop of London in the presence of the mayor and one of the sheriffs of the city of London, to whom they were forthwith handed over. This signification informs chancery of this, and on 4 July the writ was issued (for transcription, see *infra* p. 194).

2) *Signification of Master Nicholas Hereford for contumacies in a heresy case,* *16 January 1387.*

(C.85/11/25)

Excellentissimo principi et domino suo domino Ricardo dei gracia regi Anglie et Francie illustri Willelmus permissione diuina archiepiscopus Cantuariensis, tocius Anglie primas, et apostolice sedis legatus salutem in eo per quem reges regnant et principes dominantur.

Vestre regie celsitudini tenore presencium intimamus quod Magister Nicholaus Hereford doctor in theologia propter suam manifestam contumaciam pariter et offensam in non comparendo coram nobis certis competentibus die et loco ad quos legitime extitit euocatus super certis articulis hereticis et erroneis per ipsum in diuersis locis nostre Cantuariensis prouincie et iurisdiccionum nostrarum immediatarum communiter et generaliter ac publice predictis et doctis personaliter responsurus nuper contractas sentencia maioris excommunicacionis auctoritate nostra ordinaria publice et legitime innodatus existit et in eadem sentencia per quadraginta dies et amplius perseuerauit et adhuc indurato animo perseuerat claues ecclesie nequiter contempnendo in anime sue grande periculum et plurimorum perniciosum exemplum.

Cum igitur sancta mater ecclesia non habeat ulterius quid facere debeat in hac parte, maiestati uestre regie humiliter supplicamus quatinus pro ipsius excommunicati capcione scribere dignemini secundum regni Anglie consuetudinem in talibus hactenus usitatam ut quos dei timor a malo non reuocat secularis brachii disciplina cohibeat a peccato. Vestram conseruet dominus excellenciam ad populi sui regimen per tempora diuturna.

Datum in manerio nostro de Lamhith xui die mensis Ianuarii anno domini millesimo CCC^{mo} lxxxui^{to} et nostre translacionis sexto.

3) *"Relinquishing" of William Carder of Tenterden, convicted heretic, to the* *secular arm (i.e., to death by burning), 2 May 1511, by Archbishop Warham.*

(C.85/24/24)

Excellentissimo principi et domino domino Henrico dei gracia regi Anglie et Francie ac domino Hibernie illustrissimo Willelmus permissione diuina Cantuariensis archiepiscopus, tocius Anglie primas, et apostolice sedis legatus salutem in eo per quem reges regnant et principes dominantur.

Vestre regie celsitudini tenore presencium significamus quod quidem iniquitatis filius Willelmus Carder de Tenderden nostre Cantuariensis

13

diocesis propter suos uarios dampnatos et manifestos errores et hereses necnon opiniones dampnabiles contra fidem catholicam et sanctam matrem ecclesiam per ipsum Willelmum nonnullis modis et mediis doctos et predicatos per nos legitime et canonice conuictus est et hereticus iudicatus.

Cum igitur sancta mater ecclesia non habeat quod ulterius facere debeat in hac parte, uestre regie celsitudini[1] et brachio uestro seculari dictum hereticum relinquimus.

Datum in manerio nostro de Knoll secundo die mensis Maii anno domini millesimo quinquagentesimo undecimo et nostre translacionis anno octauo.

Dorse: uicecomiti Kancie ad exequendum.

4) *Request for the writ* de heretico comburendo. *Bishop Stokesley of London on 3 July 1533 informs the king that he had condemned John Fryth and Andrew Huett as heretics in the presence of the mayor and one of the sheriffs of London, to whom they were handed over; the following day chancery issued a writ for the burning of the heretics.*

(C.85/126/39)

Excellentissimo in Christo principi et domino nostro domino Henrico octauo dei gracia Anglie et Francie regi, fidei defensori, et domino Hibernie illustri Iohannes permissione diuina Londoniensis episcopus omnimodas reuerencias cum omni subieccionis honore.

Cum nos alias in quodam inquisicionis heretice prauitatis negocio contra quosdam Iohannem Fryth et Andream Huett nostrarum diocesis et iurisdiccionis rite et legitime procedentes eosdem Iohannem Fryth et Andream Huett hereticos et eorum utrumque hereticum obstinatum, impenitentem, et incorrigibilem iudicauerimus ac sentencialiter et diffinitiue condempnauerimus necnon dictos Iohannem et Andream honorando uiro domino Stephano Peters maiori ciuitatis uestre Londonie et Iohanni Marten uni ex uicecomitibus eiusdem ciuitatis adtunc nobiscum in iudicio personaliter presentibus iuxta iuris exigenciam reliquerimus et tradiderimus, idcirco omnia et singula premissa sic per nos gesta uestre regie celsitudini innotescimus et certificamus per presentes sigillo nostro sigillatas.

Datum tercio die mensis Iulii anno domini millesimo quingentesimo tricesimo tercio et nostre consecracionis anno tercio.

Dorse: Memorandum quod iiii[to] die Iulii anno infrascripto emanauit breue de heretico comburendo ex mandato domini cancellarii Anglie.

[1] *Ms.*: celsitudine.

APPENDIX F

SELECTED WRITS **DE EXCOMMUNICATO CAPIENDO**

1) *Writ to the mayor and sheriffs of London at the request of the bishop of Worcester for the arrest of the cleric Ralph de Brakeleg, 7 July 1264.*

(C.202/C.1/8)

Henricus dei gracia rex Anglie, dominus Hybernie, et dux Aquittannie maiori et uicecomitibus Londonie salutem.

Significauit nobis uenerabilis pater W. Wigorniensis episcopus per litteras suas patentes quod Radulfus de Brakeleg clericus propter suam manifestam contumaciam excommunicatus est nec se uult per censuram ecclesiasticam iusticiari. Quia uero postestas regia sacrosancte ecclesie in querelis suis deesse non debet, uobis precipimus quod predictum Radulfum per corpus suum secundum consuetudinem Anglie iusticiares donec sancte ecclesie tam de contemptu quam de iniuria ei illata[1] ab eo fuerit satisfactum. Et quia dictus R. in ciuitate Londonie frequenter conuersatur, supplicauit nobis idem uenerabilis pater quod uobis pro dicto negocio exequendo ipsas litteras mitteremus.

Teste me ipso apud Sanctum Paulum Londonie uii die Iulii anno regni nostri xluiii.

2) *Writ to the sheriff of Rutland at the request of the archbishop of Canterbury for the capture of the knight John de Wygeton, 22 Jan. 1309.*

(C.202/C.10/42 and dorse)

Edwardus dei gracia rex Anglie, dominus Hibernie, et dux Aquitannie uicecomiti Rotelandie salutem.

Significauit nobis uenerabilis pater Robertus archiepiscopus Cantuariensis per litteras suas patentes quod Iohannes de Wygeton miles Lincolniensis diocesis in quadam causa ad curiam suam Cantuariensem legitime deuoluta propter manifestam contumaciam suam auctoritate ipsius archiepiscopi ordinaria excommunicatus est nec se uult per censuram ecclesiasticam iusticiari. Quia uero potestas regia sacrosancte ecclesie in suis querelis deesse non debet, tibi precipimus sicut alias precepimus quod predictum Iohannem per corpus suum secundum consuetudinem Anglie iusticies

---

[1] *Ms.*: illatam.

donec sancte ecclesie tam de contemptu quam de iniuria ei illata ab eo
fuerit satisfactum uel causam nobis significes quare mandatum nostrum
alias tibi inde directum exequi noluisti uel non potuisti.

Teste me ipso Langeleye xxii die Ianuarii anno regni nostri secundo.

Cotesbr' [chancery clerk]

Dorse: Litera patens est in filaco.

Istud breue michi liberatum fuit die Iovis proximo post purifi-
cacionem beate Marie et primum breue. Et nullum aliud breue
prius inde ad me uenit, et Iohannes de Wygeton non uenit in
balliua mea postquam istud breue ad me uenit et ideo dictum
Iohannem iusticiare non possum.

3) *Writ to the sheriff of Kent at the request of the abbot of Westminster for the
capture of Richard Baker, vicar of Aylesford, Kent, and Robert Wadyngham,
lately parson of Dengie, East Essex, 29 June 1391.*

(C.202/C.95/2)

Ricardus dei gracia rex Anglie et Francie et dominus Hibernie uicecomiti Kancie salutem.

Cum sextodecimo die Augusti anno regni nostri duodecimo concesseri-
mus dilecto nobis in Christo abbati Westmonasterii quod ipse per trien-
nium extunc proximum sequentem continue numerandum per literas suas
patentes cancellario nostro Anglie pro tempore existenti significare possit
et certificare de nominibus singulorum de iurisdiccione ipsius abbatis qui
maioris excommunicacionis uinculo fuerint innodati et quod dictus cancellarius noster pro tempore existens breuia nostra in cancellaria nostra
fieri et sub magno sigillo consignari faciat pro capcione illorum de iurisdiccione predicta qui sic per dictum abbatem fuerint excommunicati et
per quadraginta dies perseuerauerint in eadem ad significacionem siue
certificacionem ipsius abbatis supradictam, prout ad significacionem et
certificacionem episcoporum Anglie prefato cancellario Anglie faciendam
de excommunicatis auctoritate ipsorum episcoporum huiusmodi capiendis
fit et fieri consueuit, ac idem abbas per literas suas patentes nobis signifi-
cauerit quod Ricardus Bakere uicarius ecclesie de Aylesford et Robertus
Wadyngham nuper persona ecclesie de Dengey sue iurisdiccionis auctoritate ipsius abbatis ordinaria excommunicati sunt nec se uolunt per censuram ecclesiasticam iusticiari. Quia uero potestas regia sacrosancte
ecclesie in querelis suis deesse non debet, tibi precipimus quod predictos
Ricardum et Robertum per corpora sua secundum consuetudinem Anglie
iusticies donec sacrosancte ecclesie tam de contemptu quam de iniuria ei
illata ab eis fuerit satisfactum.

Teste me ipso apud Westmonasterium xxix die Iunii anno regni nostri quintodecimo.

Clid [chancery clerk]

Dorse: Execucioni istius breuis faciende uirtute alterius breuis domini regis de supersedendo michi directi et huic breui conficte omnino supersedi.

Per Ricardum de Berham uicecomitem.

APPENDIX G

DESCRIPTION BY THE SHERIFF OF SUSSEX OF THE CAPTURE OF THE EXCOMMUNICATE VINCENT FYNCHE, 1430

(C.47/132/5/undated memorandum)

Memorandum quod quartodecimo die Iunii anno regni Henrici sexti octauo ego Willelmus Vuedale tunc uicecomes Sussex recepi quoddam breue domini regis michi directum in hec uerba:

> Henricus dei gracia etc. uicecomiti Sussex salutem.
>
> Significauit nobis uenerabilis pater Henricus archiepiscopus Cantuariensis ac custos spiritualitatis episcopatus Cicestrensis sede uacante per literas suas patentes quod Vincencius Fynche Cicestrensis diocesis propter suas manifestas contumacias auctoritate ipsius archiepiscopi ordinaria excommunicatus est nec se uult per censuras ecclesiasticas iusticiari. Quia uero potestas regia sacrosancte ecclesie in querelis suis deesse non debet, tibi precipimus quod ipsum Vincencium per corpus suum secundum consuetudinem Anglie iusticies donec sancte ecclesie tam de contemptu quam de iniuria ei illata ab eo fuerit satisfactum.
>
> Teste Humphrido duce Gloucestrie custode Anglie apud Westmonasterium xiii° die Iunii anno regni nostri octauo.

Virtute cuius breuis ego prefatus Willelmus quoddam preceptum fieri feci in hec uerba:

> Willelmus Vuedale uicecomes Sussex Nicholao atte Hope, Thome Yonge, Stephano Dogery, Iohanni Tiler, Willelmo Gateman, Willelmo Alman, Iohanni London, et Iohanni a Bery balliuis suis itinerantibus hac uice salutem. Mandatum domini regis in hec uerba recepi:
>
> > Henricus dei gracia etc. uicecomiti Sussex salutem. Significauit nobis uenerabilis pater Henricus Cantuariensis archiepiscopus ac custos spiritualitatis episcopatus Cicestrensis sede uacante per literas suas patentes quod Vicencius Fynche Cicestrensis diocesis propter suas manifestas contumacias auctoritate ipsius archiepiscopi ordinaria excommunicatus est nec se uult per censuras ecclesiasticas iusticiari. Quia uero potestas regia sacrosancte ecclesie in querelis suis deesse non debet, tibi precipimus quod ipsum Vincencium per corpus suum secundum consuetu-

dinem Anglie iusticies donec sancte ecclesie tam de contemptu
quam de iniuria ei illata ab eo fuerit satisfactum. Teste Hum-
phrido duce Gloucestrie custode Anglie apud Westmonasterium xiii° die Iunii anno regni nostri octauo.

Virtute cuius breuis uobis et cuilibet uestrum mando quod non
omittatis etc. quin capiatis seu unus uestrum capiat predictum
Vincencium ita quod eum habeatis coram me apud castrum de
Gildeford indilate ibidem commoraturum donec sancte ecclesie
tam de contemptu quam de iniuria predicta ei illata ab eo fuerit
satisfactum etc.

Cuius quidem precepti auctoritate et uigore prefati Thomas, Stephanus,
Iohannes, Willelmus Gateman, Willelmus Alman, et Iohannes London
octauo die Augusti tunc proximo sequenti predictum Vincencium apud
Nedersfeld in parochia de Bello ceperunt. Et quia metuebant sibi de
rescussu eiusdem Vincencii eis manu forti faciendo ipsum Vincencium
usque uillam de Bello duxerunt et ibidem, ut executores mandati domini
regis, Willelmum Arnold, Robertum Langregg, Ricardum Courteys,
Willelmum Stapelegh, Willelmum Gyles, Ricardum James, et Nicholaum
Wedde uirtute precepti predicti requirebant ad eos auxiliandum et forti-
ficandum in conduccione eiusdem Vincencii usque castrum predictum
iuxta tenorem precepti predicti. Subsequenterque prefati Thomas,
Stephanus, Iohannes, Willemus Gateman, Willelmus Alman, Iohannes
London, Willelmus Arnold, Robertus, Ricardus Courteys, Willelmus
Stepelegh, Willelmus Gyles, Ricardus, et Nicholaus prefatum Vincencium
eodem die a dicta uilla de Bello usque Hadlegh et ibidem respirantes,
abinde usque Nottelee, et abinde post respiracionem et recreacionem ibidem
captas usque Turnoreshull ibidemque pernoctantes, in crastino tunc
proximo sequenti usque Reygate, ac ipso Vincencio ibidem quiescente et
manducante, post prandium usque castrum predictum uirtute precepti et
requisicionis predictorum saluo et secure cum omni mansuetudine et
quiete possibili legitime perduxerunt et ipsum michi ibidem deliberauerunt.
Quem tunc gaole domini regis ibidem uirtute breuis predicti commisi
ibidem commoraturum donec sancte ecclesie in forma predicta ab eo foret
satisfactum. Qui quidem Vincencius ibidem sic sub custodia mea degens
cepit grauiter infirmari et tandem ad excitacionem et procuracionem quorumdam amicorum et benevolorum suorum in se reuersus et sacrosancte
ecclesie in hac parte satisfacere uolens penitenciam sibi apud predictam
uillam de Bello faciendam per prefatum archiepiscopum iniunctam pro-
misit se facturum petens ut usque eandem uillam ad penitenciam illam
perimplendam duceretur. Qui ex hac causa usque predictam uillam de
Bello uicesimo primo die Septembris tunc proximo sequenti per me cum

omni qua potui quietitudine ductus, penitenciam predictam in quibusdam literis ipsius archiepiscopi contentam et per decanum siue curatum ecclesie parochialis eiusdem uille de Bello tunc ibidem declaratam in presencia mea et aliorum plurimorum tunc ibidem presencium realiter adimpleuit. Et quia idem Vincencius post penitenciam predictam peractam taliter infirmabatur quod usque castrum predictum absque mortis sue periculo reduci non potuit, ipsum in domo sua propria apud Nedersfeld predictam custodiri feci ad effectum quod ipse interim uersus prefatum archiepisco-pum pro absolucionis beneficio ac erga dominum regem pro deliberacione sua habendis prosequi posset in forma iuris. Qui postmodum uidelicet xxuii⁰ die Septembris tunc proximo sequenti in domo sua predicta diem suum clausit extremum.

APPENDIX H

SELECTED DOCUMENTS CONCERNING APPEALS

1) *Request dated 1 Feb. 1322 from Archbishop Reynolds to chancery that a writ be issued superseding the capture of John Derset, vicar of all Saints, Catherington, Winchester diocese, who has appealed to Rome.*

(C.85/8/51)

Excellentissimo principi et domino suo domino Edwardo dei gracia regi Anglie illustri, domino Hibernie et duci Aquitanie Walterus permissione diuina Cantuariensis archiepiscopus, tocius Anglie primas, salutem in eo per quem reges regnant et principes dominantur.

Licet alias pro capcione Iohannis de Derset uicarii ecclesie omnium sanctorum de Kateringtone Wyntoniensis diocesis ad instanciam Thome Cosin rectoris ecclesie de Chalghton dicte diocesis auctoritate nostre curie Cantuariensis maioris excommunicacionis sentencia innodati uestre regie maiestati scripserimus supplicando, quia tamen per instrumenta sua coram nobis postmodum exhibita et examinata apparet causam pro qua excommunicatus extiterat in sacrosancta Romana curia esse pendentem, excellencie regie supplicamus quatinus a capcione dicti Iohannis pendente causa huiusmodi in curia memorata desistere dignetur regia celsitudo. Vestram conseruet dominus excellenciam ad populi sui regimen per diuturna.

Datum apud Lamheth kalendas Februarii anno domini M°CCC°xx° primo.
Dorse: Londonie.
　　　　Suthamptonie.

2) *Royal writ* scire facias et interim supersedeas *in connection with an appeal by an excommunicate, 8 Feb. 1397.*

(C.202/C.101/81 and dorse)

Ricardus dei gracia rex Anglie et Francie et dominus Hibernie uicecomiti Bedfordie salutem.

Licet nuper ad requisicionem uenerabilis patris Iohannis episcopi Lincolniensis per literas suas patentes nobis significantis Athelinam mulierem de Bydenham Lincolniensis diocesis propter manifestam contumaciam suam auctoritate ipsius episcopi ordinaria excommunicatam esse nec se uelle per censuram ecclesiasticam iusticiari per breue nostrum tibi precepimus quod predictam Athelinam per corpus suum secundum consuetudinem Anglie iusticiares donec sancte ecclesie tam de contemptu quam de iniuria ei illata ab ea esset satisfactum, quia tamen prefata Athelina a sentencia predicta tanquam ab iniqua ad curiam Cantuariensem legitime appellauit, sicut per instrumentum publicum super hoc confectum et in cancellaria nostra exhibitum plenius poterit apparere, et appellacionis sue negocium prosequitur ut dicitur cum effectu et nobis supplicauit sibi in hac parte remedium adhiberi, nos nolentes quod prefate Atheline per predictum breue nostrum uia precludatur quominus dicte appellacionis sue negocium prosequi possit in forma iuris, maxime cum huiusmodi breue nostrum de gracia nostra procedat et appellancium status integer esse debeat, tibi precipimus quod scire facias prefato episcopo quod sit coram nobis in cancellaria nostra a die pasche in xu dics proximos futuros ubicumque tunc fuerit. Quem diem prefate Atheline dedimus ibidem ad proponendum si quid pro se habeat uel dicere sciat quare capcioni corporis ipsius Atheline supersederi non debeat pendente placito appellacionis antedicte. Et quia Alanus Kyrketon de Bydenham et Thomas Bedford de comitatu tuo coram nobis in cancellaria nostra personaliter constituti manuceperunt uidelicet uterque eorum sub pena decem marcarum pro prefata Athelina de habendo ipsam tunc ibidem ad standum iuri in premissis et ad faciendum et recipiendum quod curia nostra considerauerit in hac parte, quas iidem manucaptores concesserunt de terris et catallis suis ad opus nostrum leuari si ipsam Athelinam in forma predicta non habuerunt, execucioni dicte breuis nostri de predicta Athelina per corpus suum secundum consuetudinem Anglie iusticianda interim supersedeas, et, si ipsam Athelinam ceperis, tunc ipsam Athelinam a prisona qua sic detinetur, si ea occasione et non alia detineatur in eadem, interim deliberari facias per manucaptionem supradictam. Et habeas ibi nomina illorum per quos prefato episcopo sic scire feceris et hoc breue.

Teste meipso apud Westmonasterium uiii die Februarii anno regni nostri uicesimo.

Dorse: Reginaldus Ragoun uicecomes.

Virtute istius breuis per Robertum Halsted et Willelmum Halsted probos et legitimos homines de balliua mea scire feci Iohanni episcopo Lincolniensi quod sit coram domino rege in cancellaria sua ad diem infracontentem ubicumque tunc fuerit ad faciendum quod istud breue exigit et requirit secundum tenorem eiusdem breuis.

[different hand] Ad quem diem predictus episcopus solempniter uocatus non uenit per quod consideratum est quod infrascripta Athelina eat inde sine die et recedat quieta de curia.

3) *Royal writ to the archbishop of Canterbury, requesting definite information about the alleged appeal and absolution of William Clerk of Dartmouth; 1 May 1393.*

(C.47/96/4/piece of that date).[1]

Ricardus dei gracia rex Anglie et Francie et dominus Hibernie uenerabili in Christo patri W. eadem gracia archiepiscopo Cantuariensis, tocius Anglie primati, salutem.

Cum nuper supplicante nobis Willelmo Clerk de Dertemuth Exoniensis diocesis quem ad denunciacionem uestram tanquam excommunicatum et claues ecclesie contempnentem per corpus suum secundum effectum cuiusdam sentencie diffinitiue et execucionis eiusdem in quadam causa testamentaria siue impedimenti ultime uoluntatis Willelmi Barowe eiusdem diocesis defuncti ad curiam uestram Cantuariensem legitime deuoluta que inter Willelmum Fitz Rauff militem et prefatum Willelmum Clerk in curia uestra predicta uertebatur secundum consuetudinem Anglie iusticiari precepimus donec sancte ecclesie tam de contemptu quam de iniuria ei illata ab eo esset satisfactum, ut, cum idem Willelmus Clerk a sentencia in ipsum sic lata tanquam ab iniqua ad sedem apostolicam legitime appellauerit et appellacionem suam ibidem prosequatur cum effectu beneficiumque absolucionis in forma iuris optinuerit in hac parte, uellemus execucioni breuis nostri de capiendo prefatum Willelmum Clerk ex causa predicta graciose supersederi iubere, et nos nolentes eidem Willemo Clerk iusticiam differri seu aliqualiter in hac parte indebite pregrauari uolentesque ex hac causa utrum idem Willelmus Clerk a sentencia predicta absolutus fuerit necne per uos plenius informari, uobis mandauerimus quod nos inde in cancellaria nostra sub sigillo uestro distincte et aperte sine dilacione redderetis cerciores, breue nostrum quod uobis inde uenit nobis remittentes. Super quo uos nobis in dicta cancellaria nostra certificatis quod utrum predictus Willelmus Clerk a sentencia predicta absolutus

---

[1] Clerk had been signified by the archbishop on 6 May 1390 (C.85/11/56) and a *significavit* was sent to the sheriff of Devon dated 12 October 1390 (C.47/96/4/piece of that date). On 28 November following, a writ issued from chancery whereby the writ for capture was superseded temporarily, until a hearing in King's Bench would determine if supersedence should be given pending the appeal which Clerk had claimed to have made to Rome; on the quindene of the following Easter he was acquitted and allowed supersedence pending appeal (*ibid.*). On 20 March 1393 the king, apparently in response to another request for a *supersedeas*, wrote to the archbishop inquiring whether or not Clerk had been absolved, to which the archbishop answered that he did not know (C.47/18/6/26, 27). Dissatisfied with this response the king sent the following letter to the archbishop and received an answer that he had not been absolved by the archbishop or by his authority; this is not suprising, since the appeal had been sent from the archbishop to the pope. Chancery should have directed this request to the papal court.

sit necne nesciuistis. Quam quidem certificacionem minus sufficientem et inualidam reputamus. Nolentesque proinde eidem Willelmo Clerk iusticiam in hac parte taliter prorogari, uobis mandamus quod nos in dicta cancellaria nostra utrum idem Willelmus Clerk a sentencia predicta absolutus sit necne sub sigillo uestro distincte et aperte ac sufficienter sine dilacione reddatis cerciores ut ulterius in hac parte fieri faciamus quod iuris fuit et consonum racioni, remittentes nobis hoc breue.

Teste meipso apud Westmonasterium primo die Maii anno regni nostri sextodecimo.

Roderh [chancery clerk]

Dorse: Domino nostro regi in cancellaria sua.

Infrascriptus Willelmus Clerk auctoritate nostra ordinaria fuit ad instanciam infrascripti domini Willelmi Fitz Rauf excommunicatus ut in breui continetur et citra per nos seu auctoritate nostra ab eadem excommunicacionis sentencia nequaquam fuerat absolutus.

Per Willelmum archiepiscopum Cantuariensem.

APPENDIX I

SELECTED DOCUMENTS CONCERNING ABSOLUTIONS

1) *Certification of absolution from the bishop of Coventry and Lichfield, 16 October 1338.*

(C.85/58/6)

Excellentissimo principi et domino suo domino Edwardo dei gracia regi Anglie illustri, domino Hibernie, et duci Aquitanie Rogerus eiusdem permissione Couentrensis et Lichfeldensis episcopus salutem in eo per quem reges regnant et principes dominantur.

Excellencie uestre notum facimus per presentes quod Iohannes Dunheued parochianus noster, qui ut excommunicatus et claues ecclesie contempnens uirtute mandati uestri regii ad significacionem nostram in prisona de Neugate Londonie, ut intelleximus, carcerali custodie mancipatur, de satisfaciendo ecclesie nobis inuenit ydoneam caucionem. Placeat igitur uestre dominacioni ulterius pro dicto Iohanne fieri precipere quod ad regiam celsitudinem noscitur pertinere. Quam in prosperis et iocundis conseruet altissimus per tempora feliciter successiua.

Datum Londonie xuii kalendas Nouembris anno domini M°CCC^mo tricesimo octauo.

2) *Certification of absolution from William Gray, bishop of Lincoln, 25 May 1433.*

(C.85/111/42)

Excellentissimo in Christo principi et domino nostro domino Henrico dei gracia regi Anglie et Francie et domino Hibernie illustri Willelmus permissione diuina Lincolniensis episcopus salutem in eo per quem reges regnant et principes dominantur.

Dominacionis uestre celsitudini inotescimus per presentes quod licet nos alias dominum Iohannem Saltby rectorem ecclesie parochialis sancti Andree uille Hertford nostre diocesis propter ipsius multiplicatas contumacias pariter et offensas in non comparendo coram nobis ad instanciam officii nostri contractas auctoritate nostra ordinaria excommunicauerimus dictamque excommunicacionis sentenciam crescentibus ipsius contumaciis cum inhibicione communionis christifidelium contra eundem aggrauari fecerimus necnon seruato processu legitimo pro ipsius corporis capcione scripserimus uestre regie maiestati. Nunc autem prefato domino Iohanni ad cor reuerso et gremium sancte matris ecclesie et eius mandatis redeunti et parenti ac absolucionem de huiusmodi excommunicacionis sentenciis humiliter et deuote petenti beneficium absolucionis huiusmodi impendimus in debita iuris forma. Vestram igitur sublimitatem regiam humiliter imploramus quatinus a capcione corporis dicti domini Iohannis occasione premissa supersedere dignetur celsitudo uestra regia memorata.

Datum sub sigillo nostro in hospicio nostro apud Vetus Templum Londonie xxu^to die Maii anno domini MCCCCxxxiii° et nostre translacionis anno tercio.

3) *Certification of absolution (7 Dec. 1291) from Ralph Walpole, bishop of Norwich, to chancery concerning Edmund de Hoo, rector of Redgrave and Risby, who had recently been absolved by the archdeacon of Westminster, commissary of the papal judge-delegate.*

(C.85/133/4)

Excellentissimo domino domino E. dei gracia illustri regi Anglie suus deuotus R. permissione diuina Norwycensis ecclesie minister salutem et quod potest deuocionis obsequium et oracionis suffragium uolentes iuxta iuris exigenciam testimonium perhibere ueritati ut conuenit.

Regie uestre serenitati humiliter duximus exponendum quod mandatum uenerabilis uiri domini .. archidiaconi Westmonasterii, domini .. prioris de Dunstapele iudicis principalis a sede apostolica delegati commissarii, recepimus sub hac forma:

> Venerabili patri in Christo domino R. dei gracia Norwycensi episcopo suus deuotus .. archidiaconus Westmonasterii, domini .. prioris de Dunstapele iudicis principalis a sede apostolica delegati commissarius, salutem, reuerenciam debitam pariter et honorem. Quoniam dominum Edmundum de Hoo rectorem ecclesie de Redgraue et de Ryseby a sentencia excommunicacionis in ipsum lata tam auctoritate curie Cantuariensis quam eciam auctoritate bone memorie domini W. Norwycensis episcopi uestri predecessoris ad instanciam magistri Ade de Lenn in forma iuris absoluimus, uobis auctoritate domini pape qua fungimur in hac parte firmiter iniungendo mandamus cum ea qua decet reuerencia quatinus ipsum Edmundum sic absolutum esse denuncietis puplice et solempniter per totam uestram diocesim ipsumque magistrum Adam quem dei timor a malo non reuocat et quem nos alias ad instanciam ipsius domini Edmundi excommunicauimus et adhuc non absque causa racionabili in hiis scriptis excommunicamus pro suis contumaciis pariter et offensa manifesta in singulis ecclesiis uestre diocesis prenotate, quocies et quando ex parte ipsius domini Edmundi de Hoo

fueritis requisiti, sic excommunicatum esse denuncietis uice nostra. Et de presenti execucione rite facta literis uestris patentibus harum seriem habentibus nos certificare dignemini.

Datum apud Westmonasterium xi kalendas Octobris anno gracie M°CC° nonogesimo primo.

Cuius auctoritate mandati ipsum Edmundum iuxta formam dicti mandati denunciauimus absolutum et fecimus denunciari. Hinc est quod uestre excellentissime regie maiestati innotescimus per presentes ipsum Edmundum in forma suprascripta esse absolutum.

Datum apud Lamburn uii idus Decembris anno domini supradicto.

4) *Certification by Archbishop Walden of an absolution which was granted with the consent of the excommunicate's adversaries, 12 March 1399.*

(C.85/12/8)

Excellentissimo principi et domino nostro domino Ricardo dei gracia Anglie et Francie regi illustri suus humilis et deuotus orator Rogerus permissione diuina Cantuariensis archiepiscopus, tocius Anglie primas, et apostolice sedis legatus utriusque uite prosperitatem in eo per quem reges regnant et principes dominantur.

Regie maiestati uestre insinuacione presencium intimamus quod Willelmus Credy laicus Lincolniensis diocesis a quacumque excommunicacionis sentencia, qua ipsum dudum ad instanciam dilectorum filiorum decani siue custodis et collegii libere capelle regie de Wyndesor Sarum diocesis nostris literis autenticis iusticia id poscente significauimus publice innodatum, de consensu eorundem decani siue custodis et collegii predicti, satisfaccione debita precedente, nostra auctoritate absolutus existit in consueta iuris forma. Que omnia et singula regie maiestati uestre antedicte si placeat innotescimus per presentes ut ulterius pro deliberacione corporis dicti Willelmi agere dignemini quod de laudabili consuetudine regni uestri Anglie in casu consimili fieri consueuit. In cuius rei testimonium sigillum nostrum presentibus est appensum.

Datum in manerio nostro de Maydeston duodecimo die mensis Marcii anno domini millesimo trecentesimo nonogesimo octauo et nostre consecracionis anno secundo.

5) *Certification of an absolution* ad cautelam *from a metropolitan in a case which came to his cognizance* per viam querelae, *18 July 1492.*

(C.85/23/24)

Excellentissimo in Christo principi et domino domino Henrico dei gracia regi Anglie et Francie, domino Hibernie illustrissimo, Iohannes permissione

diuina Cantuariensis archiepiscopus, tocius Anglie primas, et apostolice
sedis legatus salutem in eo per quem reges regnant et principes dominantur.

Vestre regie celsitudini tenore presencium intimamus quod, licet quidam
Willelmus Hill alias Bicon Exoniensis diocesis nostre prouincie Cantuariensis alias propter suam contumaciam fuerit et sit per quemdam magistrum Edmundum Ing uenerabilis confratris nostri domini Ricardi nuper
dei gracia Exoniensis episcopi commissarium se pretendentem maioris
excommunicacionis sentencia ad instanciam et promocionem cuiusdam
Elizabeth Helie alias Son dicte diocesis et prouincie canonice, ut asseritur,
innodatus et pro sic excommunicato publice denunciatus, in qua quidam
excommunicacionis sentencia per quadraginta dies et amplius animo
pertinaciter indurato, ut pretenditur, perseuerauerit, cuius occasione idem
uenerabilis confrater noster pro capcione corporis dicti excommunicati
celsitudini uestre regie scripsit, dilectus tamen nobis magister Humfridus
Hawardyn legum doctor decanus decanatus nostre de Arcubus Londonie
necnon officialitate curie nostre Catuariensis uacante commissarius generalis
et eiusdem curie presidens in quodam querele negocio quod coram eo in
dicta nostra curia Cantuariensi occasione prefate excommunicacionis
sentencie et aliorum premissorum inter prenarratum Willelmum partem
actricem et querelantem ex parte una et prefatam Elizabeth partem ream
et querelatam ex parte altera uertitur legitime procedens eundem Willelmum nunc penitencia ductum et ad gremium sancte matris ecclesie cor-
dialiter redire et beneficium absolucionis a dicta sentencia sibi impendi
effectualiter desiderantem, cum sancta mater ecclesia nulli uero penitenti
claudit gremium, iuris ordine per ipsum magistrum Humfridum in ea
parte in omnibus obseruato, a dicta excommunicacionis sentencia absoluit
seu saltem dictam excommunicacionis sentenciam ad cautelam relaxauit
atque eundem Willelmum sacramentis ecclesie et communioni fidelium
restituit iusticia id suadente. Vestre igitur celsitudini regie humili supplicamus affectu quatinus uicecomiti uestro in comitatu uestro Deuonie et
aliis uestris ministris pro ipsius Willelmi sic absoluti a carcerali custodia
qua detinetur liberacione scribere dignemini secundum regni uestri Anglie
consuetudinem in talibus hactinus obseruatam. Et uestram regiam celsitudinem conseruet in prosperis nostri clemencia saluatoris. In cuius rei
testimonium sigillum nostrum presentibus est appensum.

Datum in manerio nostro de Lamhith xuiii° die mensis Iulii anno domini
millesimo CCCC° nonogesimo secundo et nostre translacionis anno sexto.

Dorse: Concordat cum registro: Barett.
         Devonie.

6) *Certification of absolution sent to chancery by the prior of Christ Church, Canterbury, sede vacante, 23 June 1313.*

(C.85/7/63)

Excellentissimo principi domino suo domino E. dei gracia regi Anglie illustri, domino Hibernie, et duci Aquitanie Henricus prior ecclesie Christi Cantuarie, custos spiritualitatis archiepiscopatus Cantuariensis sede uacante salutem in eo per quem reges regnant et principes dominantur.

Excellencie regie intimamus quod Willelmus le Whyte de Barneby Norwicensis diocesis quem ad denunciacionem bone memorie quondam domini Roberti Cantuariensis archiepiscopi tanquam excommunicatum et claues ecclesie contempnentem per corpus suum secundum consuetudinem Anglie per uicecomitem uestrum Suffolkie iusticiari precepistis donec sancte ecclesie tam de contemptu quam de iniuria per ipsum ei illata ab eo daret debite satisfactionem, de contemptu ac iniuria per ipsum illatis deo et ecclesie satisfecit et est propterea ab huiusmodi excommunicacionis sentencia auctoritate nostra ordinaria canonice absolutus. Unde magestati regi supplicamus quatinus pro ipsius Willelmi liberacione dicto uicecomiti uestro dignemini uestras literas regias destinare. Valeat et crescat feliciter in Christo cum gaudio regia celsitudo.

Datum Cantuarie in uigilia natiuitatis beati Iohannis Baptiste anno domini millesimo CCC xiii°.

7) *Certification of absolution from the bishop of Hereford sent to chancery after the sheriff of Hereford had refused to honor a direct request from the bishop for the person's release, 18 July 1398.*

(C.85/91/24)

Excellentissimo in Christo principi ac domino suo domino R. dei gracia regi Anglie et Francie illustri suus capellanus et deuotus I. eadem gracia Herefordensis episcopus cum deuotarum oracionum suffragiis quicquid potest reuerencie et honoris.

Nouerit uestra celsitudo quod, cum alias ad requisicionem nostram quidam Iohannes Coke laicus nostre diocesis uigore cuiusdam breuis uestri scilicet Significauit captus fuerit et carceribus mancipatus iusticia exigente, idem tamen Iohannes ad cor reuertens ac sancte matris ecclesie uolens obedire mandatis coram nobis reddit se humilem nostris obedire mandatis. Quapropter scripsimus uicecomiti Herefordensi pro deliberacione eiusdem certificando quod ipse Iohannes sancte matris ecclesie mandatis atque nostris ad plenum paruit, prout exigit iuris ordo. Ex quo idem uicecomes uigore dicti breuis non habuit in mandato ulterius ipsum Iohannem carceribus detineri nisi donec sancte ecclesie tam de contemptu quam de iniuria sibi illata ab ipso Iohannes fuerit satisfactum. Idem tamen

14

uicecomes ipsum Iohannem a suis carceribus liberare recusat quousque ab eadem uestra celsitudine ad hoc habeat in mandato. Placeat igitur eidem uestre regie maiestati mandare eidem uicecomiti ut dictum Iohannem Coke, premisso breui non obstante, libere adire dimittat.

Datum in manerio nostro de Prestebury xuiii° die mensis Iulii anno domini millesimo trecentesimo nonogesimo octauo.

APPENDIX J

REGISTERS OF WRITS AND EXCOMMUNICATION

The formulary books of writs which chancery clerks used have been called since medieval times registers of writs. It is impossible to speak of *the* register of writs as if there existed an official prototype, of which all others were merely copies *iuxta typicum*. The earliest extant register was sent to Ireland in 1227. Like others which are clearly contemporary, it was quite small, only a few folios in length. A century and a half later registers of writs were to comprise whole books of several hundred folios. This growth is an essential feature of the story of the common law in those centuries.

As with so many other things, it was Maitland who first called attention to the nature and significance of these formularies in his brilliant essays of seventy-five years ago.[1] He drew attention to the unsatisfactory nature of the printed editions, since they merely reproduced a single register.[2] The need of a new edition which would treat the registers as expanding formulary books has long been acknowledged. A new edition of the early registers is now in preparation under the worthy aegis of the Selden Society.

In connection with the preparation of this present study an analysis of the writs concerning various aspects of the procedure for capturing excommunicates has been made. This analysis, based on an examination of 44 registers in the British Museum, indicates four unmistakably clear stages in the growth of the cluster of "excommunication writs." This appendix defines the contents of each of these stages and indicates the MSS belonging to each. Unless otherwise stated, all MSS are in the British Museum.

---

[1] F. W. Maitland, "The History of the Register of Original Writs," *Harvard Law Review* 3 (1889-1890) 97-115, 167-179, 212-225. This article was later reprinted in *The Collected Papers of Frederick William Maitland* (ed. H.A.L. Fisher; Cambridge, 1911) 2. 110-173. Holdsworth has outlined the contents of several early registers (*A History of English Law* 2 (London, 1909) 516-551).

[2] Editions appeared in 1531, 1553, 1595, 1634, and 1687. These later editions do not substantially differ from the Rastell edition of 1531. For the publishing history of the register see Maitland, *art. cit., Collected Papers* 2. 111.

FIRST STAGE

Contents:

Writ *de excommunicato capiendo*.

Registers:

1) Cotton MS. Julius D.II, f. 147ᵛ. The earliest extant register; it was sent to Ireland by Henry III in 1227.[3]
2) Cambridge Univ. Libr., MS. Ii.6.13; edited by Miss Elsa de Haas, "An Early Thirteenth-Century Register of Writs," *University of Toronto Law Journal* 7 (1947) 196-226. It is a register from the early years of Henry III, about the same date as the register sent to Ireland in 1227.[4]
3) Add. MS. 25,005, f. 73ᵛ. Before 1250, probably 1236 × 1238.[5]
4) Harl. MS. 746, f. 72ᵛᵃ.

Also, Add. MS. 35,179, ff. 81ʳ-82ᵛ, contains the above writ and in addition, though separated by other non-related writs, a writ *de excommunicatis incarceratis deliberatis* to be used when the bishop refused to accept caution and absolve the excommunicate.

SECOND STAGE

Contents:

In addition to the writ *de excommunicato capiendo* this stage contains, in general, writs concerning absolution and prohibitions. Although some variations exist from register to register, the registers of this stage have the following writs:

1) *De excommunicato capiendo*.
2) Concerning absolution:
   a) Writ to the bishop. Its tenor: although the captured excommunicate has requested absolution and has offered caution, you have refused to absolve him; we order you to admit his caution and absolve him.
   b) Writ to the sheriff in conjunction with the preceding. Tenor: go to the bishop or send "alium fidelem" to find out what the bishop proposes to do in this matter and then notify us.

[3] *Ibid.*, pp. 130-34.
[4] *Ibid.*, p. 135.
[5] H. G. Richardson, "Glanville Continued," *Law Quarterly Review* 34 (1938) 381.

c) Writ to the bishop. This was sent apparently upon the sheriff notifying chancery that the bishop would not admit caution and absolve the excommunicate. Tenor: We order you by our sheriff to receive caution and have the excommunicate delivered from prison; otherwise we shall order the sheriff to receive caution and deliver him.

d) Writ to the sheriff, not contained in all registers of this stage, directing him to go to the bishop and try to induce him to comply; if the bishop refuses, the sheriff is to deliver the excommunicate.

3) Concerning prohibitions. Contrary to a writ of prohibition the bishop has excommunicated and signified. Tenor of this writ sued by the excommunicate and sent to the sheriff: do not proceed to capture pending termination of the plea of attachment in the king's courts.

Registers:

Egerton MS. 656, ff. 25^r-26^r

Harl. MSS 409, ff. 12^r-13^r; 858, ff. 82^r-83^v; 1033, ff. 147^v-148^v; 1120, ff. 188^v-190^r; 3994, ff. 170^r-171^v

Lansdowne MSS 467, f. 54^{r-v}; 471, ff. 108^r-109^r; 564, ff. 40^v-41^r, 60^v-61^r (two registers)

Add. MSS 5762, ff. 10^r-11^r; 34,194, f. 14^{r-v}; 38,821, ff. 10^r-11^r.

Mr. Richardson has concluded that Add. Ms. 38,821 was "compiled under Henry III and revised in the early years of Edward I" and that Egerton MS. 656 is related to it but was "more extensively revised and supplemented under Edward I."[6]

Third Stage

Contents:

In general, this stage witnessed the addition of a writ *supersedeas pendente appellacione*. Allowing for minor variations, it can be said that the registers of this stage contain the following writs:

1) *De excommunicato capiendo*
2) *De excommunicato deliberando ad denunciacionem episcopi*
3) Concerning absolution
    a) Writ to the bishop. Tenor: we order you to receive caution and request the release of the excommunicate. This is the common form of the writ *de caucione admittenda*.

[6] *Ibid.*, p. 384, n. 13.

b) Writ to the sheriff in conjunction with the preceding. Tenor: we order you to try to induce the bishop to obey the order; if he refuses, deliver the excommunicate. In some examples the sheriff is ordered to appear in King's Bench if he fails to deliver the excommunicate after the bishop's refusal.

c) The bishop could seek a writ for the recapture of an excommunicate who had been delivered unjustly. This writ ordered the sheriff to recapture the excommunicate unless he was legitimately delivered.

4) Writ concerning prohibitions, as in the second stage.

5) Writ *supersedeas pendente appellacione*. The sheriff is told to supersede the writ *de excommunicato capiendo*, "donec de consilio nostro aliud duxerimus ordinandum," because the excommunicate has appealed.

Registers:

Cotton MS. Titus D. 23, ff. 33ᵛ-36ᵛ

Harl. MSS 858, ff. 132ᵛ-134ᵛ; 869, ff. 122ᵛ-123ᵛ; 927, ff. 24ᵛ-27ᵛ; 947, ff. 200ʳ-203ʳ; 1608, ff. 27ʳ-30ʳ; 1690, ff. 75ʳ-76ʳ; 3942, ff. 24ʳ-25ᵛ; 4351, ff. 23ᵛ-25ᵛ; 5213, ff. 18ʳ-19ᵛ

Lansdowne MSS 476, ff. 131ʳ-134ᵛ; 575, ff. 154ʳ-155ʳ; 652, ff. 256ʳ-257ᵛ

Add. MSS 5761, ff. 17ᵛ-18ᵛ; 11,557, ff. 18ᵛ-20ᵛ; 18,600, ff. 197ᵛ-200ʳ; 20,059, ff. 39ᵛ-42ᵛ; 22,174, ff. 108ʳ-110ᵛ; 25,142, ff. 94ʳ-95ʳ; 29,499, ff. 40ʳ-43ʳ

Pending a systematic study of each MS., no precise dating of these registers is possible. The writs in these registers, however, do represent the usage of chancery in the last years of the thirteenth century. This form of *supersedeas pendente appellacione* is first found in the case of Master William de Cardewell, probably in 1289 and certainly before 1290 (C.202/C.4/11; printed in Prynne, pp. 426-27).

FOURTH STAGE

Contents:

At this stage the principal addition is the writ *scire facias* in cases of appeals and the introduction of provisions for mainprise in these same cases. The writs commonly found in registers of this period are the following:

1) *De excommunicato capiendo*

2) *De excommunicato deliberando ad denunciacionem episcopi*

3) Concerning absolution. The same three writs which appeared in the third stage.

4) Concerning prohibitions. A separate writ is now being used in cases of clerics. Otherwise, essentially as in previous stages.
5) Concerning appeals.
   a) The same writ to sheriff as in the third stage.
   b) Combined writ to the sheriff:
      (i) *Scire facias*. Tenor: tell the instancer (or, in some registers, both the bishop and the instancer) to be in King's Bench on a specified day to show cause why the capture of the excommunicate should not be superseded pending appeal. In some registers this *scire facias* stands alone, for the obvious reason that in some cases the sheriff of the instancer was not the sheriff to whom the writ for capture had been sent.
      (ii) *Supersedeas*. Tenor: supersede in mainprise the capture of the excommunicate until the day on which he is to appear in King's Bench.
   c) Writ superseding capture because the instancer failed to come to King's Bench.

Other writs of only minor importance were added in some of the later registers of this final stage. The register in its printed editions is an example of a register of the late fourth stage.

Registers:

Harl. MSS 961, ff. 30^r-33^v; 1118, ff. 81^v-88^v
Royal MS. 11.A.IX, ff. 37^r-44^r
Stowe MS. 409, ff. 67^r-71^r
Add. MSS 22,162, ff. 45^r-50^r; 25,237, ff. 61^r-65^r; 34,901, ff. 64^v-66^v.

The earliest use of the *scire facias* writ which appears is in 1310 (C.202/C.10/141) and the earliest example of combining *scire facias* with interim supersedence in mainprise is in 1318 (C.202/C.14/193). The registers of the fourth stage, therefore, probably are all later than 1318.

SELECT BIBLIOGRAPHY

For more general works the reader is referred to the bibliographies appended to the relevant volumes of the *Oxford History of England*. It would seem unnecessarily repetitious to list here the bishops' registers which have been consulted; suffice it to say that every medieval bishop's register which is in print has been consulted and that the bibliographical data can be found in *Texts and Calendars: An Analytical Guide to Serial Publications* by E. L. C. Mullins (London, 1958). Likewise, only those MSS which have been actually quoted in this study will be listed below; for other MSS see the lists in Appendix J *supra*, pp. 211-15.

I. SOURCES

A. *Unprinted Material*

Cambridge University Library, *Ely Diocesan Records*
    Reg. Montacute.
London, *British Museum*
    Harl. MS. 667
    Harl. MS. 858
    Cotton MS. Julius D.II
    Royal MS. 10 D.X
    Cotton MS. Vitell. A.II
London, *Inner Temple Library*
    Petyt MS. 511.3
London, *Lambeth Palace Library*
    Reg. Courtenay
London, *Public Record Office*
    Miscellanea of the Chancery (C.47)
        Ecclesiastical Documents (bundles 15 to 21)
        Writs and Returns (bundles 89 to 146)
    Significations of Excommunication (C.85)
    Chancery Files, Tower Series (C.202)
Paris, *Bibliothèque Nationale*
    Latin MS. 3892

B. *Printed Material*

ACTON, John OF., *Constitutiones Legatinae sive Legitimae Regionis Anglicanae D. Othonis et D. Othoboni*. Oxford, 1679.
AMUNDESHAM, John., *Annales monasterii Sancti Albani*. Ed. H. T. Riley; 2 vols.; R. S., London, 1870-71.
Annales de Burton. Ed. H. R. Luard; *Annales Monastici*, vol. 1; R. S., London, 1864.
Annales de Wintonia. Ed. H. R. Luard; *Annales Monastici*, vol. 2; R. S., London, 1864.
ANTONINUS OF FLORENCE. *Tractatus utilis et necessarius de excommunicatione*. Printed in *Tract. univ. iur.* 14, ff. 366-387.

BRACTON, Henry de. *De legibus et consuetudinibus Angliae.* Ed. G. E. Woodbine; 4 vols.; New Haven, 1915-1942.

Bracton's Note Book. Ed. F. M. Maitland; 3 vols.; London, 1887.

BROOKE, Robert. *La Graunde Abridgement.* London, 1573.

Calendar of Chancery Rolls. Public Record Office, London, 1912.

Calendar of Chancery Warrants. Public Record Office, London, 1927.

Calendar of Documents relating to Ireland, preservde in H. M. Public Record Office, London. 5 vols.; Public Record Office, London, 1875-1886.

Calendar of the Charter Rolls. 6 vols.; Public Record Office, London, 1903-1927.

Calendar of the Close Rolls. vols.; Public Record Office, London, 1892- .

Calendar of the Patent Rolls. vols.; Public Record Office, London, 1901- .

Collectanea. Third Ser. Ed. Montague Burrows; Oxford Historical Soc., vol. 32, 1896.

Concilia, decreta, leges, constitutiones in re ecclesiarum orbis Britannici. Ed. Henry Spelman; 2 vols.; London, 1639-1664.

Concilia Magnae Britanniae et Hiberniae, A.D. 447-1718. Ed. D. Wilkins; 4 vols.; London, 1737.

Concilia Rotomagensis Provinciae. Ed. G. Bessin; Rouen, 1717.

Conciliorum oecumenicorum decreta. 2nd ed.; eds. J. Alberigo *et al.*; Freiburg, 1962.

Corpus Iuris Canonici. Eds. E. L. Richter and E. Friedberg; 2 vols.; Leipzig, 1879-1881.

Councils and Synods with other documents relating to the English Church, vol. 2, *A.D. 1205-1313.* Eds. F. M. Powicke and C. R. Cheney; 2 parts; Oxford, 1964.

Curia Regis Rolls. vols.; Public Record Office, London, 1922- .

CURIALIS. *Summa seu tractatus qui curialis dicitur.* Wahrmund, vol. 1, pt. 3.

De antiquis ecclesiae ritibus libri. Ed. Edmund Martène; 4 vols.; Antwerp, 1736-38.

Decretalis D. Gregorii papae IX suae integritati una cum glossis restitutae. Lyons, 1584.

Decretum aureum divi Gratiani cum glossa. Paris, 1501.

A Digest of the Charters Preserved in the Cartulary of the Priory of Dunstable. Ed. G. H. Fowler; Publications of the Bedfordshire Record Soc., vol. 10, 1926.

Documents Illustrative of English Church History. Eds. H. Gee and W. J. Hardy; London, 1896.

Documents Illustrative of English History in the Thirteenth and Fourteenth Centuries. Ed. H. Cole. London, 1844.

DROGHEDA, William of. *Summa aurea.* Wahrmund, vol. 2, pt. 2.

DUGDALE, William. *Monasticon Anglicanum.* 8 vols.; London, 1817-1830.

DURANDUS, William. *Speculum Iuris.* 3 vols.; Frankfurt, 1668.

Early Yorkshire Charters. Yorkshire Archaeological Soc., 10 vols., 1914-1955. Vols. 1-3 edited by W. Farrer; vols. 4-10 edited by C. T. Clay.

FANO, Martinus de. *De brachii secularis auxilio implorando per iudices ecclesiasticos.* Printed in *Tract. univ. iur.* 11. 2. pp. 409 ff.

FITZHERBERT, Anthony. *La Graunde Abridgement.* 2 vols.; London, 1565.

————, *The New Natura Brevium.* London, 1730.

Foedera, conventiones, litterae, etc. Ed. Thomas Rymer, re-ed. Adam Clark, 3 vols. in-6; Record Commission, London, 1816-1830.

FRÉDOL, Bérenger. *Le "Liber de excommunicatione" du Cardinal Bérenger-Frédol.* Ed. E. Vernay; Paris, 1912.

The Great Roll of the Pipe for the Third Year of the Reign of King John, Michaelmas 1201. Ed. Doris M. Stenton; Pipe Roll Soc., n.s., vol. 14, 1936.

The Great Roll of the Pipe for the Seventh Year of the Reign of King John, Michaelmas 1205. Ed. Sidney Smith; Pipe Roll Soc., n.s., vol. 19, 1941.

HALE, W. H. *A series of precedents and proceedings in criminal causes from 1475 to 1640;*

extracted from Act Books of Eecclesiastical Courts in the diocese of London, illustrative of the discipline of the Church of England. London, 1847.

HIGDEN, Ranulf. *Polychronicon.* Eds. C. Babbington and J. R. Lumby; 9 vols.; 1865-66.

Historical Papers and Letters from the Northern Registers. Ed. J. Raine; R.S., London, 1873.

HOSTIENSIS. *In V decretalium libros commentaria.* Venice, 1581.

———. *Summa domini Henrici Cardinalis Hostiensis.* Lyons, 1542.

INNOCENT IV. *In V libros decretalium commentaria.* Venice, 1578.

IOANNES ANDREAE, *In quinque decretalium libros novella commentaria.* 4 vols.; Venice, 1581.

The Laws of the Kings of England from Edmund to Henry I. Ed. A. J. Robertson; Cambridge, 1925.

Liber sextus decretalium D. Bonifacii VIII, Clementis papae V constitutiones, extravagantes tum viginti D. Iohannis papae XXII tum communes. Lyons, 1584.

LIEBERMANN, F., ed. *Die Gesetze der Angelsachsen.* 3 vols.; Halle, 1903-1916.

Literae Cantuarienses. Ed. J. B. Sheppard. 3 vols.; R. S., London, 1887-89.

LYNDWOOD, William. *Provinciale (seu Constitutiones Anglie),* Oxford, 1679.

Mediaeval Archives of the University of Oxford. Ed. H. E. Salter; Oxford Historical Soc., vols. 70 (1920) and 73 (1921).

Memorials of Beverley Minster. The Chapter Act-Book of the Collegiate Church of St. John of Beverley, A.D. 1287-1347. Ed. A. F. Leach; Surtees Soc., vols. 98 (1898) and 108 (1903).

MORE, St. Thomas. *The Apology.* English works; London, 1557.

———. *The Debellacyon of Salem and Bizance.* English works; London, 1557.

Natura brevium. London, 1528.

PARIS, Matthew of. *Chronica Majora.* Ed. H. R. Luard; 7 vols.; R. S., London, 1872-1883.

PARMA, Bernard of. *Summa decretalium.* Ed. E. A. Laspeyres; Regensburg, 1860.

PENNAFORT, Raymond of. *Summa sancti Raymundi de Peniafort.* Rome, 1602.

PLATEA, Franciscus de. *Tractatus R.P.D. Francisci de Platea de excommunicacione* in *Tract. univ. iur.* 14, ff. 347-363.

PLOWE, Nicholas de. *Tractatus de excommunicatione domini Nicolai Plouii.* Printed in *Tract. univ. iur.* 14, ff. 363-66.

PRYNNE, William. *The History of King John, King Henry III, and the most illustrious King Edward the I.* London, 1670.

Quellen zur Geschichte des römisch-kanonischen Processes im Mittelalter. Ed. Ludwig Wahrmund; 5 vols.; Innsbruck, Heidelberg, 1905-1931.

Registrum epistolarum fratris Johannis Peckham, archiepiscopi Cantuariensis. Ed. C. T. Martin; 3 vols., 1882-85.

Registrum omnium brevium. London, 1634.

Les Reports del cases en Ley [Year Books]. London, 1679.

ROLANDUS. *Die Summa Magistri Rolandi.* Ed. F. Tanner; Innsbruck, 1874.

Rolls from the Office of the Sheriff of Bedforshire and Buckinghamshire, 1332-1334. Ed. G. H. Fowler; Quarto Memoirs of the Bedforshire Historical Record Soc., vol. 3, 1929.

Rotuli curiae regis. Ed. Francis Palgrave; 2 vols.; London, 1835.

Rotuli litterarum clausarum in turri Londinensi asservati. Ed. T. D. Hardy; 2 vols.; London, 1833-1844.

Rotuli Parliamentorum. 7 vols. and index vol.; [London], 1783-1832.

Rotuli Parliamentorum Anglie hactenus inediti 1279-1373. Ed. H. G. Richardson and G. O. Sayles; Camden Third Ser., vol. 51, 1935.

Rotuli Roberti Grosseteste, Episcopi Lincolniensis, 1235-1253. Ed. F. N. Davis; Canterbury and York Soc., vol. 10, 1913.

RUFINUS. *Die Summa decretorum des Magister Rufinus.* Ed. Heinrich Singer; Paderborn, 1902.

Sacrorum conciliorum nova et amplissima collectio. Ed. J. D. Mansi and continued by J. B. Martin and L. Petit ; 53 vols. ; Florence, Venice, Paris, Leipzig, 1759-1927

Select Cases in King's Bench under Edward I. Ed. G. O. Sayles; Selden Soc.; vols. 55 (1936), 57 (1938), 58 (1939).

Select Cases of Procedure Without Writ Under Henry III. Eds. H. G. Richardson and G. O. Sayles; Selden Soc., vol. 60, 1941.

Select Charters and other Illustrations of English Constitutional History. Ed. William Stubbs; 9th ed.; Oxford, 1913.

The Statutes of the Realm. Eds. A. Luders, *et al.*; 11 vols. in 12; 1810-1828.

The Summa Parisiensis on the Decretum Gratiani. Ed. Terence P. McLaughlin; Toronto, 1952.

TOURNAI, Stephen of. *Die Summa des Stephanus Tornacensis über des Decretum Gratiani.* Ed. J. F. von Schulte; Giessen, 1891.

Le très ancien coutumier de Normandie. Ed. E. J. Tardif; Société de l'histoire de Normandie, Rouen, 1881.

WALSINGHAM, Thomas. *Historia Anglicana.* 2 vols.; R. S., London, 1863-64.

Year Books of Edward II. vol. 2, *The Eyre of Kent, 6 & 7 Edward II.* Ed. W. C. Boland; Selden Soc., vol. 27, 1912.

Year Books of the Reign of King Edward the Third. Year XIV. Ed. L. O. Pike; R. S., London, 1888. *Year XVI.* Ed. L. O. Pike; R. S., London, 1896-1900.

II. MODERN WORKS

ADAMS, Norma, "The Writ of Prohibition to Court Christian," *Minnesota Law Review* 20 (1936) 272-293.

AMANIEN, A. "Appel," *Dictionnaire du droit canonique* 1. 764-807.

BALDWIN, James F. "The Chancery of the Duchy of Lancaster," *BIHR* 4 (1926-27) 129-143.

BARLOW, Frank. *The English Church, 1000-1066.* London, 1963.

BASSET, Margery. "The Fleet Prison in the Middle Ages," *University of Toronto Law Journal* 5 (1943-44) 383-402.

———. "Newgage Prison in the Middle Ages," *Speculum* 18 (1943) 233-246.

BIGELOW, M. M. *History of Procedure in England.* London, 1880.

BÖHMER, Heinrich. *Kirche und Staat in England und in der Normandie im XI und XII Jahrhundert.* Leipzig, 1899.

CHENEY, C. R. "The Earliest English Diocesan Statutes," *EHR* 75 (1960) 1-29.

———. *English Bishops' Chanceries.* Manchester, 1950.

———. "Legislation of the Medieval English Church," *EHR* 50 193-224, 385-417.

———. "The Punishment of Felonious Clerks," *EHR* 51 (1936) 215-236.

———. "The so-called Statutes of John Pecham and Robert Winchelsey for the Province of Canterbury," *Journal of Ecclesiastical History* 12 (1961) 14-34.

CHEW, H. M. *The Ecclesiastical Tenants-in-Chief and Knight Service.* Oxford, 1932.

CHURCHILL, Irene J. *Canterbury Administration.* 2 vols.; London, 1933.

CLARKE, Maude. *Medieval Representation and Consent*. London, 1936.

DARLINGTON, R. R. "Ecclesiastical Reform in the Late Old English Period," *EHR* 51 (1936) 385-428.

————. *The Norman Conquest*. London, 1963.

DEIGHTON, H. S. "Clerical Taxation by Consent, 1279-1301," *EHR* 68 (1953) 161-192.

DIBBEN, L. B. "Chancellor and Keeper of the Seal under Henry III," *EHR* 27 (1912) 39-51.

DOUIE, Decima L. *Archbishop Pecham*. Oxford, 1952.

DICKENS, A. G. *Lollards and Protestants in the Diocese of York, 1509-1558*. Oxford, 1959.

DIDIER, Noël. "Henri de Suse en Angleterre (1236 ?-1244)," *Studi in Onore di Vincenzo Arangio-Ruiz* (Naples, [1953 ?]) 2. 333-351.

DUGGAN, Charles. *Twelfth-Century Decretal Collections*. London, 1963.

EHRLE, Franz. "Ein Bruchstück der Acten des Concils von Vienne," *Archiv für Literatur- und Kirchengeschichte des Mittelalters* 4 (1888) 361-470.

EKWALL, Eilert. *Studies on the Population of Medieval London*. Stockholm, 1956.

FLAHIFF, G. B. "The Use of Prohibitions by Clerics against Ecclesiastical Courts in England," *Mediaeval Studies* 3 (1941) 101-116.

————. "The Writ of Prohibition to Court Christian in the Thirteenth Century," *Mediaeval Studies* 6 (1944) 261-313; 7 (1945) 229-290.

FOREVILLE, Raymonde. *L'Église et la royauté en Angleterre sous Henri II Plantagenet (1154-1189)*. Paris, 1942.

FOWLER, R. C., "Secular Aid for Excommunications," *TRHS*, 3rd ser., 8 (1914) 113-117.

GABEL, Leona C. *Benefit of Clergy in the Later Middle Ages*. Smith College Studies in History, no. 14, Northampton, Mass., 1928-29.

GÉNESTAL, R. *Le Privilegium Fori en France du décret de Gratien à la fin du XIVe siècle*. 2 vols.; Bibliothèque de l'École des hautes études, Paris, Sciences religieuses, vols. 35 (1921) and 39 (1924).

GOEBEL, Julius, Jr. *Felony and Misdemeanor : A Study in the History of English Criminal Procedure*. Publications of the Foundation for Research in Legal History, Columbia Univ., New York, vol. 1, 1937.

GOMMENGINGER, Alfons, "Bedeutet die Exkommunikation Verlust der Kirchengliedschaft ?" *Zeitschrift für katholische Theologie* 73 (1951) 1-71.

GOTWALD, W. R. *Ecclesiastical Censure at the End of the Fifteenth Century*. Baltimore 1928.

GRAVES, E. B. "Circumspecte Agatis," *EHR* 43 (1928) 1-80.

Guide to the Contents of the Public Record Office. 2 vols.; London, 1963.

HAAS, Elsa de. "Concepts of the Nature of Bail in English and American Criminal Law," *University of Toronto Law Journal* 6 (1945-46) 385-400.

HARING, Nicholas M. "Peter Cantor's View on Ecclesiastical Excommunication and its Practical Consequence," *Mediaeval Studies* 11 (1949) 100-112.

HAVET, Julien. *L'Hérésie et le bras séculier au moyen âge jusqu'au treizeime siècle*. Paris, 1881.

HILL, Mary C. *The King's Messenger, 1199-1377*. London, 1961.

HILL, Rosalind M. T. "Public Penance: Some Problems of a Thirteenth-Century Bishop," *History* 36 (1951) 213-226.

————. "The Theory and Practice of Excommunication in Medieval England," *History* 42 (1957) 1-11.

HINSCHIUS, Paul. *Das Kirchenrecht der Katholiken und Protestanten in Deutschland*. 6 vols. in 7; Berlin, 1869-1897.

HOLDSWORTH, William S. *A History of English Law.*   vols.; London, 1903-   .

HUIZING, Peter. "The Earliest Development of Excommunication *Latae Sententiae* by Gratian and the Earliest Decretists," *Studia Gratiana* 3 (1955) 277-320.

HUNNISETT, R. F. *The Medieval Coroner.* Cambridge, 1961.

JENKINSON, C. H., and MILLS, M. H. "Rolls from a Sheriff's Office of the Fourteenth Century," *EHR* 43 (1928) 21-32.

JOHNSTONE, Hilda. "Archbishop Pecham and the Council of Lambeth of 1281," *Essays in Medieval History Presented to T. F. Tout* (eds. A. G. Little and F. M. Powicke; Manchester, 1925), pp. 171-188.

JONES, Douglas. *The Church in Chester, 1300-1540.* Chetham Soc., 3rd ser., vol. 7, 1957.

KANTOROWICZ, H. *Bractonian Problems.* Glasgow, 1941.

LAPSLEY, G. T. *The County Palatine of Durham.* New York, 1900.

LECLERCQ, Jean. "L'Interdit et l'excommunication d'après les lettres de Fulbert de Chartres," *Revue historique de droit français et étranger*, 4th ser., 1944, pp. 67-77.

LIEBERMANN, F. *Über die Leges Edwardi Confessoris.* Halle, 1896.

LUNT, William E. *Financial Relations of the Papacy with England to 1327.* Cambridge, Mass., 1937.

———. *Financial Relations of the Papacy with England,1327-1534.* Cambridge, Mass., 1962.

———. *Papal Revenues in the Middle Ages.* 2 vols.; New York, 1934.

LYTE, H. C. Maxwell. *Historical Notes on the Use of the Great Seal of England.* London, 1936.

MAITLAND, F. W. "The History of the Register of Original Writs," *Harvard Law Review* 3 (1899-1890) 97-115, 167-179, 212-225; reprinted in *The Collected Papers of Frederick William Maitland* (ed. H.A.L. Fisher; Cambridge, 1911) 2. 110-173.

MAKOWER, Felix. *The Constitutional History and Constitution of the Church of England.* Eng. trans.; London, 1895.

MILLS, Mabel H. "The Medieval Shire House (*Domus Vicecomitis*)," *Studies Presented to Sir Hilary Jenkinson* (ed. J. Conway Davies; London, 1957), pp. 254-271.

MOREL, Maurice. *L'Excommunication et le pouvoir civil en France du droit canonique classique au commencement du XVe siècle.* Paris, 1926.

MOREY, Adrian. *Bartholomew of Exeter, Bishop and Canonist.* Cambridge, 1937.

MORRIS, Colin. "A Consistory Court in the Middle Ages," *Journal of Ecclesiastial History* 14 (1963) 150-59.

MORRIS, W. A. *The Medieval English Sheriff to 1300.* Manchester, 1927.

———. "The Sheriff," *The English Government at Work*, 1327-1336 (eds. W. A. Morris et al.; Cambridge, Mass., 1947) 2. 41-108.

PAVLOFF, George G. *Papal Judge Delegates at the Time of the Corpus Iuris Canonici.* Catholic Univ. of America, Canon Law Studies, no. 426; Washington, 1963.

The Pilgrim Trust. Survey of Ecclesiastical Archives. Report of the Committee appointed by the Pilgrim Trustees in 1946 to carry out a Survey of the Provincial, Diocesan, Archidiaconal, and Capitular Archives of the Church of England. Unpublished typescript; 2 pts; [London], 1952.

POLLOCK, F. and MAITLAND, F. W. *The History of English Law before the Time of Edward I.* 2nd ed.; 2 vols.; Cambridge, 1911.

POWICKE, F. M. "The Chancery during the Minority of Henry III," *EHR* 27 (1912) 39-51.

PRICE, F. Douglas. "The Abuse of Excommunication and the Decline of Ecclesiastical Discipline under Queen Elizabeth," *EHR* 57 (1942) 106-115.

PUGH, R. B. "The King's Prisons before 1250." *TRHS*, 5th ser., 5 (1955) 1-22.

PURVIS, J. S. *Notarial Signs from the York Archiepiscopal Records*. London and York 1957.

RÉVILLE, A. *Le soulèvement des travailleurs d'Angleterre en 1381*. Paris, 1898.

RICHARDSON, H. G. "Azo, Drogheda, and Bracton," *EHR* 59 (1944) 22-47.

———. "Glanville Continued," *Law Quarterly Review* 54 (1938) 381-399.

———. "Heresy and the Lay Power under Richard II," *EHR* 51 (1936) 1-28.

RICHARDSON, H. G., and SAYLES, G. O., "The Clergy in the Easter Parliament, 1285," *EHR* 52 (1937) 220-234.

———. "The Early Statutes," *Law Quarterly Review* 50 (1934) 201-223, 540-571.

———. "Parliamentary Documents from Formularies," *BIHR* 11 (1933-34) 147-162.

RITCHIE, Carson I. S. *The Ecclesiastical Courts of York*. Arbroath, 1956.

ROSE-TROUP, Frances. *Exeter Vignettes*. History of Exeter Research Group, monograph no. 7; Manchester, 1942.

ROTHWELL, Harry. "Edward I and the Struggle for the Charters, 1297-1305," *Studies in Medieval History presented to Frederick Maurice Powicke* (eds., R. W. Hunt, W. A. Pantin, R. W. Southern; Oxford, 1948), pp. 319-332.

RUSSELL, Josiah C. "Mediaeval Midland and Northern Migration to London, 1100-1365," *Speculum* 34 (1959) 641-45.

RUSSO, François. "Pénitence et excommunication: Étude historique sur les rapports entre la théologie et le droit canon dans le domaine pénitentiel du IXe siècle," *Recherches de science religieuse* 33 (1946) 257-279, 431-461.

SALTER, H. E. *Snappe's Formulary*. Oxford Historical Society, vol. 80, 1924.

SALTMAN, Avrom. *Theobald, Archbishop of Canterbury*. London, 1956.

SALZMAN, L. F. "Sussex Excommunicates," *Sussex Archaeological Collections* 82 (1941) 124-140.

SAYERS, Jane E. "A Judge Delegate Formulary from Canterbury," *BIHR* 35 (1962) 198-211.

SCHULTE, J. F. VON. *Die Geschichte der Quellen und Literatur des canonischen Rechts*. 3 vols.; Stuttgart, 1875-1880.

SHEEHAN, Michael M. *The Will in Medieval England*. Toronto, 1963.

SKYUM-NIELSEN, Niels. *Blodbadet i Stockholm*. Copenhagen, 1964.

SOMERVILLE, Robert. *History of the Duchy of Lancaster*. vols.; London, 1953- .

STAMP, A. E. "Some Notes on the Court and Chancery of Henry III," *Historical Essays in Honour of James Tait* (eds. J. G. Edwards *et al.*; Manchester, 1933), pp. 305-311.

STUBBS, William. *The Constitutional History of England*. 3 vols.; Oxford, 1874-78.

———. *Report of the Ecclesiastical Courts Commission, 1883. Parliamentary Papers*, vol. 24, 1883, Historical Appendices 1 and 2.

STYLES, Dorothy. "The Early History of the King's Chapels in Staffordshire," *Transactions of the Birmingham Archaeological Soc.* 60 (1936) 56-95.

SUTCLIFFE, D., "The Financial Conditions of the See of Canterbury, 1279-1292," *Speculum* 10 (1935) 53-68.

THOMPSON, A. Hamilton. *The English Clergy and their Organization in the Later Middle Ages*. Oxford, 1947.

THOMSON, John A. F. *The Later Lollards, 1414-1520*. Oxford, 1965.

THRUPP, Sylvia L. *The Merchant Class of Medieval London, 1300-1500*. Chicago, 1948.

TOUT, T. F. "The Household of Chancery and its Disintegration," *Essays in History Presented to R. L. Poole* (ed. H. W. C. Davis; Oxford, 1927), pp. 46-85.

WALKER, Curtis H. "The Date of the Conqueror's Ordinance Separating the Ecclesiastical and Lay Courts," *EHR* 39 (1924) 399-400.

WESKE, Dorothy B. *Convocation of the Clergy*. London, 1937.

WILKINSON, B. "The Chancery," *The English Government at Work, 1327-1336* (eds. W. A. Morris, *et al.*; 3 vols.; Cambridge, Mass., 1940-1950), 1. 162-205.

———, *The Chancery under Edward III*. Manchester, 1929.

———. "A Letter of Edward III to his Chancellor and Treasurer," *EHR* 42 (1927) 248-251.

———. "The Seals of the Two Benches under Edward III," *EHR* 42 (1927) 397-401.

———. *Studies in the Constitutional History of the Thirteenth and Fourteenth Centuries*. 2nd ed.; Manchester, 1952.

WILLARD, J. F. "The Dating and Delivery of Letters Patent and Writs in the Fourteenth Century," *BIHR* 10 (1932) 1-11.

———. *Parliamentary Taxes on Personal Property, 1290 to 1334*. Cambridge, Mass., 1934.

WILLIAMS, Glanmor. *The Welsh Church from Conquest to Reformation*. Cardiff, 1962.

WOODCOCK, Brian L. *Medieval Ecclesiastical Courts in the Diocese of Canterbury*. London, 1952.

INDEX

The names of medieval authors are listed by Christian name; all others by surname.

Abbots, 62-63; power to excommunicate, 25; power to signify, 34.

Abergavenny, Monmouthshire, lord of, 115 n.

Ablyntone, Richard de, rector of Halford, 148 n.

Absolution, 212-14; *ad cautelam*, 118-20, 154, 207-08; and appeal, 118-20; canon law of, 137-44; in case of death, 139; certification of, 22, 145-48, 155, 155 n., 203-10; in Court of the Arches, 139; of excommunication *ab homine*, 138-39, and *latae sententiae*, 139; and oath of obedience, 140-41, 141 n.; and papacy, 139; and penance, 143-44; power of, 32 n.; and reconciliation, 137-55; and royal chancery, 145-55; and satisfaction, 141-43, 142 n.; simple form, 119, 140 nn.; from sin, 138; solemn form, 139 n., 140 n.; statistics on, 154-55; and 'sufficient caution,' 141-43, 150-154.

Ace, Maud, 108 n.

Acton, John of, *see* John of Acton.

Admoneston, William, magistrate, 99 n.

Aegidius de Fuscarariis, 142 n.

Albigensians, 16, 73 n.

Alexander III, pope, 118.

Alexander VI, pope, 44 n.

Alman, William, bailiff, 198-99.

Amersham, Bucks., 191-92.

Amwell, Herts., parish of, 191.

Anathema, 14 n.

Andreae, Ioannes, *see* Ioannes Andreae.

Anglesey, county of, (Wales), 114.

Antoninus of Florence, saint, 138 n.

Apostolic see, *see* Papacy.

Appeal, 116-36, 183-85, 201-04; and absolution, 118-20; canon law of, 116-20; and contumacy, 118; and ecclesiastical courts, 116-22; effect of, 117-18; to pope, 121; procedure of, 120-34; and royal chancery, 120, 122-36; tuitorial, 117 & n.; types of, 117; and writs of capture, 120-34.

Appelby, John de, dean of St. Paul's, London, 63 n.

Appelby, Robert, parson of Scawby, Lincs., 123 n.

Aragon, and secular constraint against excommunicates, 16-17.

Arcevesk, Reginald le, 38.

Archdeacon, courts of, 116-17; power to excommunicate, 25; power to signify, 28 n., 34.

Archidiaconus, 29-30.

Arnold, William, of Battle, Sussex, 199.

Articuli cleri (1316), 144, 154.

Arundel, Thomas, bishop of Ely, 56 n., 131 n.; archbishop of Canterbury, 64 n., 131-32 nn.

Ashford, Kent, 191.

Astley, Warwicks., 170.

Aubin, Richard, dean of Heacham and rector of Tatterford, Norfolk, 147.

Augustinians, 36 n., 62.

Auxon, Master P. de, vicar-general of the archbishop of Canterbury, 168.

Aylesbury, Bucks., 129 n.

Aylesford, Kent, 196.

Ayremyme, Richard de, keeper of the rolls, 92 n.

Bailiffs, 105-07.

Baker, Christina, *alias* Clerk, of Intwood, Norfolk, 130 n.

Baker, Nicholas, 145-46.

Baker, Richard, vicar of Aylesford, Kent, 196.

Ball, John, 63, 64 n.

Balshale, William, 64 n.

Balum, Reginald de, 64 n.

Bangor, diocese of, bishop of, 24 n., 114 n.; clergy of, 58 n.

Barbour, Richard, 164.

Bardney, Lincs., prior of, 56 n.

Barking, Essex, abbess of, 56 n.

Barnard, Thomas, 192.

Barnby, Suffolk, 209.

Barnstaple Priory, Devon, 40 n.

Barony, 28 n., 29.

Barow, William, of Walden, Herts., 191.

Barowe, William, 203.

Barrett, John, notary, 85 n., 208.

Barry, William, 126.

Bartholomew of Brescia, 46 n.

Bath and Wells, diocese of, 23 n., 27 n., 32 n., 35 n.,41-42 & n.,44 n.,51 n., 76 n.,85 n.,93; bishop of, 50 n., 82-83 nn., 101, 148; bishops of:
    John Droxford (1309-29), 42;
    John Stafford (1425-43), 35;
    Thomas Beckington (1443-65), 140 n.;
    John Clerk (1523-41), 190;
    keeper of the spirituality of, 168;
    official of the bishop, 79.

Battle, Sussex, 106, 107 n., 199-200.

Bavent, Hugh, 132 n.

Baxter, Richard, 65 n.

Bayham Abbey, Sussex, 36.

Baysio, Guido de, see Archidiaconus.

Beauchamp, Robert, 94 n.

Beckington, Thomas, bishop of Bath and Wells, 140 n.

Beckley, Sussex, 77, 166.

Beckote, John de, 132 n.

Bedford, Thomas, 202.

Bedfordshire, county of, 105.

Bedfordshire-Buckinghamshire, roll of the sheriff of, 96, 105.

Bedwyn, Wilts., 80.

Beggebury, John de, 169.

Belaugh, Norfolk, 188.

Belle, John, notary, 85 n., 175.

Belyn, John, rector of Mottistone, Isle of Wight, 106 n.

Benedictines, 62, 65.

Benett, Thomas, 192.

Bergh, William van, 65 n.

Berkeley, Glos., hospital at, 63.

Berkhampstead, Herts., 168.

Bermondsey, London, abbot of, 33; prior of, 56 n., 79 n.

Bernard of Parma, 118 n., 141 n.

Bernard of Pavia, 45 n., 48 n., 141 n.

Berwode, Thomas, vicar-general in spirituals, Exeter diocese, 192.

Bery, John, bailiff, 198-99.

Beseiule, John, 163.

Betson, John, citizen of London, 171.

Beverley, Yorks., 102.

— —, Minster, 21-22, 33-34; provost and chapter of, 101,176, 179 n., 180 n., 185-86.

Biddenham, Beds., 201-02.

Bilda, Roger de, 94.

Binham, Norfolk, prior of, 56 n.

Bishop, and certification of absolution, 145-48; courts of, 116-17; jurisdiction of, 35; power to excommunicate, 25; power to signify, 26-30, 79-91, 96, 101-02, 113-15, 162-67, 182-83; and secular arm, 70-71; subject to excommunication, 62; and supersedence, 147-48.

Bishop-elect, power to signify, 26.

Bishop's Tawton, Devon, 190.

Blida, Gilbert de, 140 n., 142 n.

Blida, Thomas de, 140 n., 142 n.

Bloyhou, William, master, 31 n., 38.

Bloyou, Michael, 39 n.

Bloyou, Ralph, 39 n.

Bobbingworth, Essex, 190.

Bohic, Henry, see Henry Bohic.

Bokeler, Gilbert, 143.

Bokeler, Roysa, 143.

Boniface VIII, pope, 39 n., 53, 58, 104 n., 151 n., 153.

Boniface of Savoy, archbishop of Canterbury, 134 n., 162.

Boore, Peter, 191.

Bordeaux, synods at (1214), 73 n.

Bourgchier, Thomas, cardinal, archbishop of Canterbury, 60, 84-85 nn.

Boveney, Bucks., 192.

Bowet, Henry, archbishop of York, 114.

Bowland, Master John, chancery clerk, 95 n.

Boyle, Joan, 50 n.

Boys, Robert, 121 n.

Bracton, Henry de, 27 n., 28, 31, 88-89 145, 151 & n.

Brakeleg, Ralph de, 195.

Braybrooke, Robert, bishop of London, 164.

Braynford, Richard, 121.

Brescia, Bartholomew of, see Bartholomew of Brescia.

Brewster, James, 192.

Briddey, Margaret van, 65 n.

Brightling, Sussex, church of, 77, 166.

Bristol, Calendaries, chaplain of, 63 n.; sheriff of, 110 n.

Bromele, Master Stephen de, 140.

Brompton, Thomas de, rector of Eyton, 140.

Broun, clerk of Petty Bag, 98 n.

Brown, John, 110 n., 191.

Browne, William, 191.

Bruning, Thomas, 140 n.

Brussell, William van, 65 n.

Brystowe, John, chaplain of Crutched Friars, London, 164.

Buckinghamshire, county of, 105; cheriff of, 109.

Buckland, Dorset, 130 n.

Buildwas Abbey, Salop., abbot of, 55 n.

Bullock, Richard, chaplain, 190.

Burbach, James, 84 n.

Burmyngham, John de., 147.

Burton John, dean of Lynn, 79.

Bury, Richard de, 181 n.

Bury St. Edmunds, Suffolk, Abbey, abbot of, 34, 111 n., 176, 180 n.

Bushmead, Beds., prior of, 56 n.

Byconyll, Master William, 170.

Byrst, Edmund, 190.

Caerleon, Monmouthshire, lordship of, 115 & n.

Caernarvonshire, 114.

Caldewell, William de, vicar of Stoke by Nayland, Suffolk, 126.

Calendaries, Bristol, the chaplain of, 63 n.

Camberwell, London, church of, 79 n.

Cambridge, castle at, 107 n., 108.

—, University of, chancellor of, 35, 177, 180 n.

Canterbury, city of, 143, 191; Christ Church, prior of, 50 n., 209; St. Augustine's Abbey, 32, 41 n.

—, diocese of, 24 n., 27 n., 31, 39, 41, 50 n., 75, 85 nn., 93-94, 156, 191-192;
archbishop of, 50-52 nn., 56 n., 59 n., 63-64 nn., 75, 82-83 nn., 90, 99-100, 107 n., 110-11, 115, 120-23 & nn., 125, 131 n., 139, 147 n., 152, 162-163, 167-68, 189-92, 195, 203;
archbishops of:
Theobald of Bec (1139-61), 21, 73;
Stephen Langton (1207-28), 22;
Boniface of Savoy (1245-70), 134 n., 162;
Robert Kilwardby (1273-78), 39;
John Pecham (1279-92), 36, 61 n., 67, 79 n., 83-84, 103, 119, 121, 143, 148-49 & n., 153-54 & n.;
Robert Winchelsey (1294-1313), 31, 53-54, 62 n., 83 n., 104 n., 151 n.;
Walter Reynolds (1313-27), 121 n., 201;

John Stratford (1333-48), 26 n., 55, 75 n., 76, 84, 144 n., 163-164;
William Whitlesey (1368-74), 63 n.;
Simon Sudbury (1375-81), 42, 63-64 nn., 114;
William Courtenay (1381-96), 64 n., 114, 172, 189;
Thomas Arundel (1396-97; 1399-1414), 64 n., 131-32 nn.;
Roger Walden (1397-99), 165, 207;
Henry Chichele (1414-43), 26 n., 78, 84 n., 103 n., 106 & n., 145-46 & n., 170;
John Stafford (1443-52), 83, 90 n., 170-71;
John Kemp (1452-54), 84-85 & n., 115;
Thomas Bourgchier (1454-86), 60, 84-85 nn.;
John Morton (1486-1500), 33, 85 n., 175;
Henry Dean (1501-03), 85 n.;
William Warham (1503-32), 57, 83, 85 n., 95, 98, 112 n., 122 n., 166, 171, 181 n., 193;
chancery of, 85;
court of (Arches), see Courts, ecclesiastical.

—, province of, 117, 119.

Canwell, Staffs., prior of, 65.

Capture, by sheriffs, 198-200; writs of, 17, 120-34.

Capwode, William, mainpernor, 184.

Carder, William, 191, 193-94.

Cardewell, William de, 214.

Cardiganshire, 114.

Carlisle, city of, 64.

—, diocese of, 24 n., 27 n., 41 n.; bishop of, 50 n., 62; John de Halton (1292-1324), 41 n., 134 n., 150 n.

Carmarthenshire, 114.

Carter, Andrew, of Cottingham, Yorks., 185.

Carter, John, 168.

Carthage, Fifth Council of (401), 73 n.

Cartwright, Thomas, 98 n.

Caru, Rose, 64 n.

Caru, William, esq., 64 n.

Cashel, archbishop of, 62; province of, synod of (1453), 142 n.

Castell, Griffin, chaplain, 172.

Catherington, Hants., All Saints Church, 201.

Causam quare non, 78-79.

Caution, 141-43, 150-54, 212-13.

Caux, *bailage* of, 20 n.

Celestine III, pope, 74 n.

Ceri (Kerry), march of, 114, 172.

Chalton, Hants., 201.

Chambre, Joan la, 133.

Chancery, bishop's, 79-85.

—, royal, and absolution, 145-55; and appeals, 122-36; courts of, 120; fees for writs, 97-98, 98 n.; and signification procedure, 72, 86-101, 110, 113; and signification by bishops of Ireland, 25 n.; *stylus* of excommunication & signification, 39-42; and supersedence, 123; and writs of capture and detention, 17.

—, sheriff's, 105.

Cheapside, London, 85 n.

Chelsea, London, parish of, 192.

Cheriton-Fitzpaine, Devon, rector of, 51 n.

Cherwode, Nicholas, 133 n.

Chester, archdeacon of, 29 n.

Chester, county palatine, 94, 112-13 & n.; diocese of, 157.

Cheyne, William, king's justice, 107 n.

Chichele, Henry, archbishop of Canterbury, 26 n., 78, 84 n., 103 n., 106 & n., 145-46 & n., 170.

Chichester dicese of 24 n., 27 n., 36-37, 44 n., 50 n., 52, 106 & n.;
bishop of, 56 n., 77, 129 n., 166;
bishops of:
John Climping (1254-62), 54;
Simon Sydenham (1431-38), 84.

—, synod at, 102 n.

Chirchegate, Joan, 164.

Cirencester, Glos., abbot and convent of, 132 n.

Cistercians, 36, 62, 111.

Clegh, William, 51 n.

Clement III, pope, 139 n., 141 n.

Clement V, pope, 62 n.

Clerk, John, bishop of Bath and Wells, 190.

Clerk, William, 107 n., 125 n., 203-04.

Clerke, Roland, 166.

Clifford, Herefs., prior of, 57.

Climping, John, bishop of Chichester, 54.

Close Rolls, 127.

Cluniacs, 41 n.

Clyderowe, Richard, 51 n.

Clyffe, Dorset, 52 n.

Coates, Cambs., rector of, 56 n.

Cok, John le, of Maidstone, Kent, 169.

Coke, John, 209-10.

Colchester, Essex, 192; archdeacon of, 177, 180 n.; St. John's Abbey, 163-64; prior of, 56 n.

Colvill, Thomas, 51 n.

Colyn, Simon, 190.

Colyns, Nicholas, 191.

Contumacy, 43-53, 137, 193; and appeals, 118; and ecclesiastical courts, 43 & n., 45-46, 49, 60-61; and excommunication, 18 & n., 28, 47-53; and *missio in possessionem*, 47-49; mode of incurrence, 45-46; and offense, 46-47; and secular arm, 43-44; and signification, 49-53, 72, 74, 77-79.

Coo, William, 95.

Cook, Adam, of Cottingham, Yorks., 185.

Cooper, J., 85 n.

Copleston, Henry, keeper of king's jail, Exeter, 111 n.

Corbet, William, gentleman, 173.

Corbridge, Thomas, archbishop of York, 80, 148 n.

Cornwall, sheriff of, 93.

Cosin, Thomas, rector of Chalton, Hants., 201.

Costard, William, 128 n.

Cosyn, Robert, 191.

Cottingham, Yorks., 185.

Councils.
General:
Lyons (1245), 118;
Lyons (1274), 58;
Vienne (1311-12), 31, 153;
Constance (1414-18), 60;
English:
Winchester (*ca.* 1076), 18, 28, 48 n.;
Oxford (1222), 102, 171 n.;
London (1257), 103;
Merton (1258), 103;
Westminster (1258), 103;
Lambeth (1261), 103;
Reading (1279), 103;
Lambeth (1281), 61 n., 103;
Other:
Carthage (401), 73 n.;
Tribur (895), 45 n.;
Caen (1047), 19 n.;
Lillebonne (1080), 19;
Melun (1216), 16 n.

Counties Palatine, signification procedure, 112-15.

Courtenay, William, bishop of London, 64 n.; archbishop of Canterbury, 42 n., 64 n., 114, 172, 189.

Courteys, Richard, of Battle, Sussex, 199.

Courts, ecclesiastical, of apostolic see, 117, 121-22, 123 n., 124; and appeal, 116-22; of archbisop, and appeal to pope, 121; of archdeacon, 116-17; of bishop, 116-17; and contumacy, 43 & n., 45-46, 49, 60-61; fees for writs, 98 & n.; inferior & superior, 116-117; of metropolitan, 117; officers of, 63; provisions of William the Conqueror, 17-18; and signification procedure, 72-79.
  Individual:
    Canterbury (Arches), 49 n., 51 n., 63 n., 75 n., 78 n., 80-81, 84, 98, 100, 112 n., 117, 121-24, 127, 129, 132 n., 134, 139, 143 n., 145 n., 163, 166, 175, 189; dean of, 125 n., 147 n., 175, 189;
    Coventry and Lichfield, 140;
    Hereford, 138, 140;
    Lincoln, 85 n.;
    York, 99 n., 114, 117, 123 n., 146 n.
—, hundred, 17, 18 n., 28.
—, royal, chancery, and appeal, 120; King's Bench, 34, 51 n., 56 n., 64 n., 105, 111 n., 123, 127-33, 136, 203 n., 214-15.
—, shire, 19 n.

Coventry and Lichfield, diocese of, 23 n., 26, 44 n., 64 n., 75, 93; bishop of, 50 n., 57 n., 64 n., 65 & n., 94, 115 n., 146 n., 170, 189, 205; Walter Langton (1296-1321), 26; court of, see Courts, ecclesiastical.

Cras, William, 168.

Credy, William, 207.

Crestien, Robert, 167.

Cropedy, Oxon., 64 n.

Croydon, Surrey, 111.

Crue, Richard, 94.

Crux Easton, Northants., rector of, 106 n.

Cryne, John, 175.

Cudworth, Thomas, 190.

Cum desideres, papal decretal (1187 × 91), 141 n.

Cum non ob homine, papal decretal (1191 × 98), 74 n.

Cum olim, papal decretal (1207), 46 n., 141 n.

Cumberland, sheriff of, 100; sheriff's clerk, 105.

Curia Regis Rolls, 39, 44 n., 88 n.

Curialis, 16 n.

Curteys, Alice, 101.

Curteys, Robert, 101.

Damiani, Peter, see Peter Damiani.

Danheney, Robert, vicar of Stonesby, Leics., 57 n.

Darley, William, 130 n., 131 n.

Dartmouth, Devon, 107 n., 125 n., 203.

David, Griffin ap, 172.

Dawes, Joan, 50 n.

Day, Lady, 142 n.

Dean, Henry, archbishop of Canterbury, 85 n.

Decretals of Gregory IX, 29, 45 n., 116 n.

Decretum of Gratian, 45 n., 47, 72, 73 n., 75 n.

Dengie, Essex, 196.

Denmark, and secular constraint against excommunicates, 17.

Derbyshire, 189.

Derset, John de, vicar, 121 n., 201.

Devon, county of, 190; justice of the peace in, 111 n.; sheriff of, 38, 83 n., 93, 107 n., 111 nn., 203 n.

Disherison, 73; defined, 21 n.; and excommunication, 21.

Dispenser, Henry, bishop of Norwich, 188.

Distraint, 109 & n.; and excommunication, 21; and subsidies, 57.

Ditton, Master William de, 32 n.

Dogery, Stephen, bailiff, 198-99.

Dorone, William, 171.

Dover Castle, Kent, constable of, 92.

Drayton, Nicholas, 189.

Drewe, Isabel, 146 n.

Drewe, Robert, mainpernor, 173.

Drogheda, William of, see William of Drogheda.

Droxford, John, bishop of Bath and Wells, 42.

Druval, Robert, bailiff of Becs., 105 n.

Dublin, archbishop of, 181 n.

Duemyngyg, 84 n.

Dunheved, John, 205.

Dunstable Priory, Beds., 206.

Durandus, William, see William Durandus.

Durham, county palatine of, 95, 112-14; city, cathedral, prior of, 34.

—, diocese of, 24 n.; bishop of, 113-14; Thomas Langley (1406-37), 114, 180 n.

Durham, Thomas, 51 n., 189.

Duxford, Cambs., 94 n.; rector of, 56 n.

East Farleigh, Kent, 152.

East Woodhay, Hants., 106 n.

Edward I, king of England, 26-27, 53-55, 59 & n., 62 n., 90 n., 114 n., 123-36 nn., 213.

Edward II, king of England, 154.

Edward III, king of England, 26, 55, 58, 97, 124.

Edward VI, king of England, statute of, 156.

Ekindon, Robert de, deacon, 105 n.

Elizabeth I, queen of England, 95-96 nn., 113 n.; statute of, 156.

Ellerton, William, 57 n.

Ely, archdeacon of, 34.

—, diocese of, 24 n., 27 n., 32 n., 44 n., 75, 94, 108;
    bishop of, 43 n., 155, 180 n.;
    bishops of:
        Simon Montacute (1337-45), 55;
        Thomas de Lisle (1345-61), 94 n.;
        Thomas Arundel (1374-88), 56 n., 131 n.

Elys, Richard, 63 n.

Engall, T (?)., notary, 172.

Ernesfast, Henry, 133.

Essex, county of, sheriff of, 64 n., 95, 108-09 & n.

Evesham Abbey, Worcs., abbot of, 34, 55 n., 63, 177, 180 n.

Ex parte, papal decretal (1205), 46, 141 n.

Excommunication, and appeal, 117-34; and contumacy, 18 & n., 28, 47-53; and disherison, 21; and distraint, 21; exemptions, 61 & nn.; for failure to execute a writ, 102-04; invalidity of, 15; and outlawry, 13 & n.; 21 & n.; publicity of, 75-76.

—, form of, 13 n.

—, kinds: a iure, 15; ab homine, 15, 47, 138-39; ferendae sententiae, 15; latae sententiae, 15, 139.

—, nature and effects of, 13-15.

—, power and jurisdiction, 25, 35-36; of collectors of papal tenth, 32; by legatine authority, 32.

—, and secular power: in Aragon, 16-17; in Denmark, 17; in France, 16; in Germany, 16; in Normandy, 19-20; origins and early growth in England, 17-23.

—, significations of, see Significations.

Exeter, city of, 42, 111, 192; cathedral at, 111 n., 121 n., 192; king's jail at, 111 n.; St. George's parish, 192.

—, diocese of, 24 n., 36-38, 50 n., 52 & n., 55 n., 60, 93, 140 n., 156;
    bishop of, 51 n., 58, 100, 190, 192;
    bishops of:
        Peter Quinel (1280-91), 37-38, 39 n., 78-89 nn.;
        George Nevill (1458-65), 26;
        Hugh Oldham (1505-19), 111-12 nn.

Eyvill, John de, 109.

Fano, Michael de, 29.

Farbon, John, 131 n.

Fauconberg, Eustace of, bishop of London, 145 n.

Feey, Richard, mainpernor, 173.

Ferby, Nicholas, 121 n.

Fiddington, Somerset, 140 n.

Fidejussors, 141-42.

Fine Rolls, 57 n.

Fisher (Fyssher), Simon, mainpernor, 184.

Fitz Rauff, William, knight, 203-04.

Flaxley Abbey, Glos., abbot of, 55 n.

Flintshire, 113 n.

Foghelston, Henry de, 32 n., 54 n.

Foke, Walter, 111 n.

Foliot, Hugh, bishop of Hereford, 73 n.

Folkingham, Lincs., 163.

Forde Abbey, Dorset, 36.

Fordham, Cambs., prior of, 56 n.

Forum, internal, 14.

France, and secular constraint against excommunicates, 16, 86 n., 109, 120; against heretics, 86 n.

Frederick II, emperor, 16 n.

Frédol, Berenger, 119.

Fresel, Master William, 27 n.

Freton, John de, 180 n.

Fryth, John, 192, 194.

Fulbourn, Cambs., 132 n.; chaplain of, 108.

Furness Abbey, Lancs., monks of, 152 n.

Fuscarariis, Aegidius de, see Aegidius de Fuscarariis.

Fynch, William, sheriff of Sussex, 107 n.

Fynche, Vincent, 106-08 & nn., 198-200.

Gage and pledge, 21.

Gascoyn, Ireton, 65 n.

Gascoyn, Katherine, 65 n.

Gassyngham, William, 50 n.

Gateman, William, bailiff, 198-99.

George II, king of England, 113 n.

George III, king of England, statute of, 157 n.

Germany, and secular constraint against excommunicates, 16.

Giffard, Walter, archbishop of York, 101, 110.

Gilbert, Dr. Thomas, 168.

Glanvill, 22.

Glossa ordinaria, on the *Decretum*, 47; on the *Decretals*, 45 n., 46, 48 n., 75 n., 118 n., 141 n.; on *Liber Sextus*, 118-19 nn.; on Clementine letter, 75 n.

Gloucester, St. Oswald's Priory, 41.

Gloucestershire, sheriff of, 109-10 & n.

Goadby Marwood, Leics., parson of, 57 n.

Goldham, William de, 162 n.

Gratian, *Decretum*, 45 n., 47, 72-75 & nn.

Gravamina, papal, 31; clerical, 61, 87-89, 103-04, 122-23, 134 n., 149-54 *passim*.

Gravesend, Richard, bishop of London, 121.

Gray, William, bishop of Lincoln, 205.

Great Curse, 102-03, 149.

Greenfield, William, archbishop of York, 148 n.

Gregory IX, pope, *Decretals* of, 29, 45 n., 116 n.

Gregory X, pope, 58.

Grene, T., 85 n.

Grenehelde, Humphrey atte, 152.

Grenlefe, William (*alias* John), 190.

Grevell, Agnes, 191.

Greyndore, Robert, esq., 170.

Griffits, Henry, 115 n.

Grosseteste, Robert, bishop of Lincoln 61 n., 103, 105 n.

Guido de Baysio, *see* Archidiaconus.

Guildford, Surrey, castle at, 106-07 & n.

Gurum, Thomas, 168.

Gurum, Walter, cleric, 168.

Gyles, William, of Battle, Sussex, 199.

Gylys, Anne, 50 n.

Hailsham, Sussex, 36-37 nn.

Hakum, Robert, 109, 145 n.

Hallum, Robert, rector of Northfleet, 165.

Halsted, Robert, 202.

Halsted, William, 202.

Halton, John de, bishop of Carlisle, 41 n., 134 n., 150 n.

Hamelton, William de, king's clerk, 39 n.

Hampshire, sheriff of, 55, 106 n.; sheriff's bailiff, 100.

Hare, Master Thomas, official principal of Norwich consistory, 174.

Harysay, Robert, 191.

Hatfield, Essex, prior of, 56 n.

Hauhisia, Anna de, 109, 122.

Hauxton, Cambs., vicar of, 56 n.

Hawardyn, Master Humphrey, official of the Arches, 121 n.; dean of the Arches, 175, 208.

Hawe, Richard, 130 n.

Hay, William in the, 43 n.

Heacham, Norfolk, dean of, 147.

Hedde, Thomas, 192.

Hedenham, Norfolk, parson of, 127 n.

Helie (*alias* Son), Elizabeth, 208.

Henley, Thomas, 107, 130 n.

Henricus de Segusia, *see* Hostiensis.

Henry I, king of England, 179 n.

Henry II, king of England, 21, 179 n.

Henry III, king of England, 22-23, 27, 32, 86 n., 101, 120, 161, 212-13.

Henry IV, king of England, 58, 129 n.

Henry VI, king of England, 101, 106 n.

Henry VIII, king of England, 17, 58, 112 n.; statutes of, 156.

Henry Bohic, 30 n.

Herbere, John, baker, 184.

Herd, Christine, 51 n.

Hereford, archdeaconry of, 57; cathedral of, dean and chapter of, 51 n.; city of, 64.

—, diocese of, 24 n., 27 n., 41 n., 44 n., 50 n., 55 n., 93, 157;

    bishop of, 51 n., 73 n., 79 n., 82 n., 90, 92, 114-15 & n., 132 n., 138-39, 148, 190;

    bishops of:

        Hugh Foliot (1219-34), 73n.;

        John Trefnant (1389-1404), 132 n., 148;

        Thomas Milling (1472-92), 79 n.;

    court of, *see* Courts, ecclesiastical.

Hereford, Master Nicholas, 63, 189, 193.

Heresy, 68-71, 189-94.

Herle, Sir William, 29 n.

Hertfordshire, 108; sheriff of, 95, 109, 209.

Hervy, John, 52 n.

Heryng, John, 85 n., 167.

Hildesleye, John de, magistrate, 92 n.

Hill (*alias* Bicon), William, 208.

Hindolveston, Norfolk, 173.

Hoddesdon, John, 191.

Hodere, Petronilla, 131 n.
Hogons, William, mainpernor, 173.
Holand, Adam de, 131 n.
Hólar, Iceland, bishop of, 62.
Honorius, archdeacon of Richmond, 97.
Hoo, Edmund de, rector of Risby, 32 n., 77, 110, 126 n., 206-07.
Hope, Nicholas atte, bailiff, 198-99.
Hospital of Jerusalem, 32, 59.
Hostiensis, 14, 23, 28 n., 45-46 nn., 118, 138 n., 140-44 nn.
Hounslow, Middlesex, Trinitarian house at, 111 n.
Huett, Andrew, 192, 194.
Huguccio, 45 n., 47, 138 n.
Humphrey, duke of Gloucester, 106 n.
Hunne, Richard, 192.
Hunte, Nicholas, 173-74.
Huntingdonshire, sheriff of, 95.
Hyllyng, Ralph, 51 n.
Hylton, Richard, 50 n.

Iceland, Hólar, bishop of, 62.
Incorrigibility, 74.
Ing, Master Edmund, 208.
Innocent III, pope, 46, 48 n., 117-18, 139 n.; decretal of, 141 n.
Innocent IV, pope, 20 n., 34 n., 45-46 & nn., 74 n., 109 n., 118-19; decretal of, 139-40 & nn., 143.
Intwood, Norfolk, 130 n.
Ioannes Andreae, 75, 118-19 nn., 142 n., 144 n.
Ioannes Teutonicus, 47.
Ipswich (Yepeswych), Nicholas, 189.
Ireland, 22, 25 n., 62 n., 73 n., 161, 211-12; bishops of, and signification, 25 n; justiciar of, 161.
Italy, and secular constraint against excommunicates, 16.
Ive, John, 129 n.

Jails, see prison.
James I, king of England, 95 n.
James, Richard, of Battle, Sussex, 199.
Jeys, William, mainpernor, 184.
Joce, John, 170-71.
John of Acton, 49 n.
Judge, ecclesiastical, and power to excommunicate, 25; and power to signify, 28 n.

Judge-delegate, 206-07; and issuance of writs, 33; and power to signify, 30-31.
Jurisdiction, 35-42; disputed, 36-42; exempt, 33-34; probate, 171-72.

Kays, Henry, clerk of Hanaper, 98 n.
Keeper of the spirituality, 168-69; and power to signify, 27-82.
Kemp, John, cardinal, archbishop of Canterbury, 84-85 & n., 115.
Kent, county of, sheriff of, 64 n., 93, 95, 111, 152, 196; eyre of, 26-27, 40.
Kerry, see Ceri.
Kildesby, William de, prebendary of Beverley Minster, 185.
Kilwardby, Robert, archbishop of Canterbury, 39.
King's Bench, see Courts.
Kingston-upon-Hull, Yorks., 125.
Kirtling, Cambs., 107 n.
Knights Hospitallers, 32, 59; Templar, 59, 60.
Knolle, Richard de la, 151 n.
Knossington, Leics., 133 n.
Knyght, Adam, and Alice, 189.
Knyght, Hugh, 52, 190.
Knyght, Robert, 133 n.
Kyng, John, rector of Fiddington, Somerset, 140 n., 148 n.
Kyrk, William atte, 132 n.
Kyrketon, Alan, of Biddenham, Beds., 202.
Kyrkham, Robert, clerk of Hanaper, 98 n.

Lakenham, Norwich, rector of, 57 n.
Lambeth, 84-85.
Lancaster, county and duchy of, 113; sheriff of, 94.
Langeley, Alexander de, 81 n.
Langeley, Richard de, 81 n.
Langford, Margery, 51 n.
Langford, vicar of, 166.
Langley, Thomas, bishop of Durham, 114, 180 n.
Langregg, Robert, of Battle, Sussex, 199.
Langton, Stephen, archbishop of Canterbury, 22.
Langton, Walter, bishop of Coventry and Lichfield, 26.
Launde, Anna de la, 52 n.
Layborn, Joan, 190.
Layborn, Margaret, 190.

Lecmufeld, Robert, 170.

Leges Edwardi Confessoris (Pseudo-Edward), 16 n., 28, 48 n.

Leicestershire, county of, 189; sheriff of, 147.

Leigh, Devon, hamlet of, 51 n.

Leiston Abbey, Suffolk, abbot of, 58.

Lenn, Master Adam de, 206.

Lesnes Abbey, Kent, abbot of, 56 n.

Lewes, Sussex, archdeacon of, 77, 166; prior of, 54.

Leycester, R. de, 27 n.

Lichfield, dean of, 26.

Lichfield, Staffs., 43 n.; canon of, 121 n.; diocese of, *see* Coventry and Lichfield.

Liddeford, chaplain of, 88.

Ligham, Peter, 181 n.

Limerick and Waterford, bishop of, 62.

Lincoln, city of, 101, 131 n., 147; cathedral, 63, 127 n., 140 n.

—, diocese of, 23 n., 27 n., 32, 44 n., 51-52 nn., 57, 71, 85 n., 94, 123 n., 156, 163, 166;
archdeacon of Lincoln, 34, 63, 177, 180 n.;
bishop of, 44 n., 52 n., 63 n., 79, 85, 92, 97 n., 131-32 nn., 140 n., 146 n., 150 n., 180 n., 190-92, 205;
bishops of:
Robert Grosseteste (1235-53), 61 n., 103, 105 n.;
Oliver Sutton (1280-99), 64 n., 79, 180 n.;
Philip Repingdon (1405-19), 132 n.;
William Gray (1431-36), 205;
John Longland (1521-47), 190;
court of, *see* Courts, ecclesiastical;
sheriffs of, 150 n., 187.

Lincoln, John of, 131 n.

Lincolnshire, 95; sheriff of, 52 n., 128 n.

Lisle, Thomas de, bishop of Ely, 94 n.

Lismore, bishop of, 62.

Little Missenden, Bucks., 191.

Llandaff, Wales, diocese of, 24 n., 27 n., 56 n., 93, 107, 115; bishop of, 113, 122, 127; chancellor of, 56 n.

Lohout, Philip, 162 n.

Lollards, 69, 190.

London, city and county of, 64, 93-95, 101, 112-13, 117, 131 n., 143, 147, 189-90;
churches:
St. Gregory-by-St. Paul, 64 n.;

St. Margaret, 192;
St. Martin-le-Grand, royal free chapel, dean of, 34, 62 n., 177, 180 n.;
St. Mary-le-Bow, 117;
St. Paul's Cathedral, 32 n., 34, 35 n., 63, 177, 180 n.;
mayor and bailiffs, 147, 194-95;
merchants, 130 n.;
prisons:
Fleet, 145, 147 n.;
Newgate, 99-100, 107, 147, 151 n., 205;
sheriff of, 64 n., 86, 93, 95, 99-100, 105, 107 & nn., 129, 131 n., 151 n., 175, 192, 194-95; and execution of writs, 93-95.

—, diocese of, 23, 27 n., 32 n., 44 n., 55 n., 58, 64 n., 71, 75, 86, 94, 107 n., 129 n., 133 n., 146 n., 163, 189;
archdeacon of, 80;
bishop of, 58, 63-65 & nn., 80, 85, 107, 155, 162, 164;
bishops of:
Eustace de Fauconberg (1221-28), 145 n.;
Richard Gravesend (1280-1303), 121;
William Courtney (1375-81), 64 n.;
Robert Braybrooke (1382-1404), 164;
Cuthbert Tunstall (1522-30), 190;
John Stokesley (1530-39), 194;
consistory of, 52 n.

London, John, bailiff, 198-99.

Longland, John, bishop of Lincoln, 190.

Loste, John atte, 163.

Lucca, merchants of, 142 n.

Lumbard, James, 65 n.

Lupus, William, archdeacon of Lincoln, 63 n.

Lygham, Master Peter, official of court of Canterbury, 166.

Lyndwood, Master William, 30, 47 n., 51 n., 73, 75-78, 80 n., 87 n., 90-91 & n., 103 n., 123 n., 134-36, 142 nn., 144-45 & n., 149 n.

Lyngen, John, 50 n.

Lyons, archbishop of, 62.

Lytelwylle, Alice, 125 n.

Lytelwylle, William, 125 n.

Lyttelyngton, Richard, 165.

Lyw, Walter de, 39 n.

Macworth, John, dean of Lincoln cathedral, 63 n.

Magna Carta, 73 n.

Magna Derset, Warwicks., 189.

Maidstone, Kent, 192; jail at, 64 n.

Mainpernors, see Mainprise.

Mainprise, 127-30, 136, 173-74, 183-85, 202, 214-15.

Malinges, Matthew de, 111 n.

Malmesbury, John, 127.

Malore, Reginald, lord of Tachbrook, 64 n.

Man, Thomas, vicar-general in spirituals, London diocese, 192.

Marchaunt, John, 101 n.

Marches of Wales, see Wales.

Marisco, Master Robert de, 27 n., 161.

Marlowe, Thomas, 32 n.

Marriage, 51 & n., 163.

Marsa, Raymond de, 80.

Martival, Roger, bishop of Salisbury, 80.

Matthew of Paris, 61 n.

Maunsel, William, sheriff of Warwicks., 149 n.

Mawreward, Master John, 172.

May, Thomas, 191.

Mayse, Roger, 51 n.

Medford, Richard, 35, 132 n., 180-81 nn.

Mells, Somerset, parish of, 51 n.

Melton, chancery clerk, 95 n.

Melton Ross, Lincs., 190.

Menusse, William, chaplain, 107 n., 129 n.

Merionethshire, 114.

Merton, Surrey, 87 n.

Messenger, Christina, 94.

Metropolitan, 207-08; courts of, 117; and excommunication, 36; and signification, 25, 27, 82.

Michelham Abbey, Sussex, 36 n.

Middlesex, sheriff of, 93, 95.

Midelton, Thomas de, chancery clerk, 95 n.

Miller, William, 80.

Milling, Thomas, bishop of Hereford, 79 n.

Milton, reeve of, 64 n.

Milward, Richard, 65 n.

Milward, Stephen, 110 n.

Missio in possessionem, 17 19.

Modbury, Devon, monk of, 50 n.

Mompeson, Henry, 85 n.

Montacute, Simon, bishop of Ely, 55.

Montfort, Simon de, 73 n.

Montibus, Robert de, 151 n.

Moor Hall, Sussex, manor of, 129.

More, John atte, 51 n.

More, Thomas, saint, 52 n., 71, 132   n.

Mortimer, Master Hugh de, official of the archbishop of Canterbury, 27 n., 167.

Morton, John, cardinal, archbishop of Canterbury, 33, 85 n., 175.

Mottistone, Isle of Wight, rector of, 106 n.

Multon, Thomas, 50 n.

Murden, James, 192.

Murimouth, Adam de, vicar-general of Canterbury, 84.

Netherfield, Sussex, 106-07 & n.

Neuport, Richard de, 26.

Nevill, George, bishop of Exeter, 26.

Neville, George, knight, of Abergavenny, 115 n.

Newark, Henry, archbishop of York, 26, 148 n.

Newbridge, James de, 81 n.

Newbridge, Sarah de, 81 n.

Newbridge, William de, 81 n.

Newburg, William, 51 n.

Newehay, John, vicar of Astley, Warwicks., 170.

Newlyn, Cornwall, vicar of, 51 n.

Newman, Robert, rector of Great Ryburgh, Norfolk, 174.

Newport, Devon, St. John the Baptist chapel, 190.

Nicholas III, pope, 58-59 & n.

Nogaret, Raymonde de, 59.

Norfolk, archdeacon of, 34, 177, 180 n.; sheriff of, 95, 111 n., 126-27 & n., 130 n., 148, 151 n.

Normandy, duchy of, 19-20, 73 n., 109 n., Normans, 113, 157.

North Crawley, Bucks., 145 n.

Northfleet, Kent, rector of, 165.

Northfolk, Joan, 132 n.

Northfolk, John, 132 n.

Northamptonshire, sheriff of, 52 n.; lollards of, 190.

Norton Bavant, Wilts., parson of, 130 n.

Norwich, city, prison at, 147.

, diocese of, 21 n., 00 n., 50 n., 00 n., 00, 64 n., 75, 79, 95, 124 n., 127 n., 129 n., 175; bishop of, 58, 83, 88 n., 126, 146 n., 148, 188, 206; bishops of: Ralph Walpole (1289-99), 206; Henry Dispenser (1370-1406), 188; consistory of, 121 n., 123 n.; vicar-general of, 151 n.

Notley Abbey, Bucks., abbot of, 56 n.
Nottingham, 133 n.
Nottinghamshire, 133 n., 189; sheriff of, 52 n., 94, 109, 130 n., 148 n.
Nowers, Agnes, 133 n.
Noyl, William, 131 n.
Nutley, Sussex, 106.

Obedience, and absolution, 140-41.
Offense, 46-47.
Oldham, Hugh, bishop of Exeter, 111-12 nn.
Ordainers, 31.
Ottobon, Fieschi, cardinal, legate, 54.
Outlawry, and excommunication, 13 & n., 21 & n.
Oxford, 22, 113.
—, University of, 34-35, 51 n.; chancellor of, 34-35, 51 nn., 64 n., 177, 180-83 & nn., 189.

Pampylyon, Thomas, 155.
Panfield, Essex, prior of, 56 n.
Papacy, and absolution, 139; and appeal, 121; courts of the apostolic see, 117, 121-22, 123 n., 124; gravamina, 31, 61; power to excommunicate, 32; power to signify, 30-33.
Paris, Matthew of, see Matthew of Paris.
Park, John, rector of Withington, Glos., 86 n.
Parliament, Commons, 89, 98.
—, of Michaelmas 1279, 61 n.
Parma, Bernard of, see Bernard of Parma.
Pastoralis, papal decretal (1204), 117.
Patteshull, Thomas, 190.
Pavia, Bernard of, see Bernard of Pavia.
Payn, William, 163.
Peasants' Rising, 57.
Pecham, John, archbishop of Canterbury, 36, 61 n., 67, 79 n., 83-84, 103, 119, 121, 143, 148-49 & n., 153-54 & n.
Pembrokeshire, 113 n.
Penallt, Mon., rector of, 107.
Penance, 143-144.
Penkridge, Staffs., royal free chapel, dean, 34, 177, 181 n.
Pennafort, Raymond of, see Rayond of Pennafort.
Persyvale, John, 146 n.
Pertenhall, Richard de, under-sheriff of Beds., 105 n.
Peter Damiani, saint, 44 n.
Peters, Stephen, mayor of city of London, 194.

Petty Bag, clerk of, 98 n.
Petyt, John, chaplain of Fulbourn, Cambs., 108, 132 n.
Peyur, Lawrence, 109.
Philip II, king of France, 20 n.
Pistor, Walter, 111 n.
Pokelington, Christina de, 149 n.
Polpayne, Nicholas, 51 n.
Pond, Thomas atte, 107 n., 180 n.
Pontissara, John, bishop of Winchester, 153 n.
Poundstock, Cornwall, 38.
Poyntell, Robert, vicar of Ticehurst, Sussex, 129.
Prelates, lesser, and power to signify, 33-35.
Premonstratensians, 36, 62.
Prentiss (Prentys), John, 164.
Preston, Lancs., dean of, 79.
Prisons, royal, 108; release from, 145-49, 209-10, 212-14.
Probate, 171-72.
Prohibition, writs of, 88-89, 144, 212-15.
Pseudo-Edward, see Leges Edwardi Confessoris.
Putte, Isabel atte, 51 n.

Quinel, Peter, bishop of Exeter, 37-38, 39 n., 78 n.
Quoniam frequenter, papal decretal (1209), 46.

Radenover, Master Simon de, 27 n.
Ragoun, Reginald, sheriff, 202.
Rammesdene, John, 109 n.
Ramsey Abbey, Hunts., 62.
Rand, Lincs., church of, 99.
Rave, Robert, 192.
Raymond of Pennafort, 45 n., 118-19 & n., 138 n.
Reading Abbey, Berks., abbot of, 56 n.
Redeland, Thomas, 121.
Redgrave, Suffolk, rector of, 206.
Reigate, Surrey, 106.
Remigny, Thomas de, 88.
Rennes, William of, see William of Rennes.
Repingdon, Philip, bishop of Lincoln, 132 n.
Retford, Notts., dean of, 140 n.
Rewley Abbey, Oxon., abbot of, 110.
Reynolds, Walter, archbishop of Canterbury, 121 n., 201.
Richard II, king of England, 34-35, 57-58, 69 n., 115, 131, 182, 203 n.
Richard, duke of York, 115 n.

Richardson, Richard, Trinitarian priest, 111 n.

Richmond, Yorks., archdeacon of, 33-34, 97, 177, 181 n.

Risby, Suffolk, rector of, 110.

Rochester, diocese of, 24 n., 27 n., 144; bishop of, 57, 100.

Roderham, chancery clerk, 95 n.

Rogger, John, 50 n.

Roggers, John, 140 n.

Rolle, notary, 85 n.

Romeyn, John le, archbishop of York, 94, 148 n.

Romney, Kent, 131 n.

Rothewell, John, 132 n.

Rouen, province of, suffragan bishops of, 20 n., 143 n.

Rowe, John, justice of the peace, 111 n.

Rox, John, 52 n., 190.

Royston Priory, Herts., prior of, 56 n.

Ruffus, Hamo, 88 n.

Rufinus, *Summa*, 47 n.

Rumburgh Priory, Suffolk, prior of, 56 n.

Russchale, John, chaplain, 170.

Russell, Philip, Frater, 107 n.

Rutlandshire, sheriff of, 61 n., 100-01, 195.

Ryburgh, Great, Norfolk, 174.

St. Albans Abbey, Herts., abbot of, 29 n., 32-34, 81 n., 178, 181 n.

Sy. Asaph, diocese of, 23, 44 n.; clergy of, 58 n.

St. Buryan, Cornwall, dean of, 55 n.

St. Davids, diocese of, 24 n., 44 n., 55 n., 93.

S. Jacu (Jacet), prior of, 56 n.

St. Neots Priory, Hunts., prior of, 56 n.

St. Osyth Abbey, Essex, abbot of, 56 n.

S. Valery-sur-Somme, abbot of, 56 n.

Salisbury, cathedral, dean of, 62 n.

—, diocese of, 24 n., 32, 52, 93-94, 132 n.; bishop of, 54 n., 64 n., 80, 85, 125, 148, 165; bishops of:
    Robert Wickhampton (1271-01), 80 n.;
    Roger Martival (1315-30), 80.

Salop, archdeacon of, 79 n.

Saltby, John, rector of Hertford, 205.

Sampson, William, knight, 143.

Saundir, William, 85 n.

Savoy, Boniface of, archbishop of Canterbury, 134 n., 162.

Savoy (de Sabaudia), Peter of, 62 n.

Sawley Abbey, Yorks., 62-63; abbot of, 63 n., 127-28 nn.

Scawby, Lincs., parson of, 123 n.

Scotland, and secular constraint against excommunicates, 25 n.

Scryvyner, William, 191-92.

Secular arm, and appeals, 122-23, 134-136; and clerical subsidies, 53-61; and contumacy, 43-44; and heresy, 68-71; under William the Conqueror, 43.

Sées, abbot of, 56 n.

Seftford, William, parson of Norton Bavant, Wilts., 130 n.

Segusia, Henricus de, *see* Hostiensis.

Seis, Simon de, 150 n.

Seman, Master Thomas, 145 n.

Sempringham, order of, 123 n.

Sequestration, 54.

Sheriff, and capture, 198-200; and delivery from jail, 148-49; and execution of writs, 92-95, 102-11.

Shoreham, deanery of, 165.

Shrewsbury, Salop, 190; abbot of, 56 n.; collectors at, 57 n.; royal free chapel, dean, 34, 178, 181 n.

Shropham, Robert, chaplain, 107 n.

Sidbrooke, Lincs., 132 n.

Significations of excommunication: earliest evidence, 23-24, 162; form of, 80-84, 90; selected examples, 162-75.

Silkestede, Thomas, 33.

Silkstone, Yorks., 190.

Skarle, chancery clerk, 95 n.

Smith, John, 166-67.

Smith, William le, 64 n.

Smithfield, Cumberland, 192.

Smyth, David, 190.

Smyth, Thomas, 131 n.

Solerio, Master Peter de, 27 n.

Somerset, sheriff of, 101.

Southampton, *see* Hampshire.

Southwell, Notts., Minster, 85 n.; 115 n.; 143.

Sparke, William, of London, 175.

Spencer, John, 79 n.

Spencer, Richard, 85 n.

Spigurnel, Henry de, royal justice, 26-27.

Stafford, John, bishop of Bath and Wells, chancellor of England, 35; archbishop of Canterbury, 83, 90 n., 170-71.

Stafford, Staffs., archdeacon of, 122; royal free chapel, dean, 34, 178, 181 n.

Staffordshire, county of, 50 n.; sheriff of, 120, 147.

Stamford Priory, Northants., prioress of, 56 n.

Stanegrave, John, 110.

Stanford, Norfolk, 188.

Stapelegh, William, of Battle, Sussex, 199.

Stapilford, Richard, chaplain of Crutched Friars, London, 164.

Statutes: Constitutions of Clarendon (1166), 61-62 nn., 69 n., 104; First Statute of Westminster (1275), 128 n.; Statute of Provisors (1351), 89; Statute of Praemunire (1353), 89.

Staunton, Hervey de, royal justice, 40.

Stedgrave, John, of East Woodhay, Hants., 106 n.

Stoke by Nayland, Suffolk, vicar of, 126.

Stoke Edith, Herefs., parish of, 50 n.

Stokesley, John, bishop of London, 194.

Stone, William, 191.

Stonesby, Leics., vicar of, 57 n.

Stonhouse, Richard de, 142 n.

Stowe (Stowte), John, 125 n.

Strata Florida Abbey, Cardigan, abbot of, 55 n.

Stratford, John, archbishop of Canterbury, 26 n., 55, 75 n., 76, 84, 144 n., 163-64.

Studley, Wilts., parish church of, 76 n.

Style, Adam atte, 51 n.

Subsidies, clerical, 187-88; and distraint, 57; and secular arm, 53-61.

Sudbury, Simon, archbishop of Canterbury, 42, 63-64 nn., 114.

Suffolk, sheriff of, 95, 126 n., 148.

Sumercot, Master Lawrence, 27 n.

Supersedence, 120-33, 201-04, 213-15.

Supplication against the Ordinaries (1532), by the Commons, 98.

Surrey, county of, 108; sheriff of, 109 n., 111.

Suspension, 54.

Sussex, county of, 108; sheriff of, 100, 106-07 & nn., 109 n., 198.

Suthwerk, Alan de, 151 n.

Sutton, Oliver, bishop of Lincoln, 64 n., 79, 180 n.

Sutton, Roger de, king's clerk, 98 n.

Swavesey, Cambs., prior of, 56 n.; rector of, 56 n.

Swayn, Roger, alias Taylour of Beds., 52 n.

Swetyng, William, 192.

Swynesford, William de, knight, 168.

Sydenham, Simon, bishop of Chichester, 84.

Symond, Thomas, 129 n.

Synods: Chichester II, 102 n.; Durham III, 102 n.; Ely, 102 n.; Exeter II, 102 n.; Le Mans, 73 n.; Lincoln, 102 n.; Merton, Oxon., 149; Norwich, 102 n.; Salisbury II, 102 n.; Wells, 39 n.; York, 102 n.

Tachbrook, Warwicks., 64 n.

Tadcaster, Yorks., hospital, 63.

Taillour, John, 163.

Tatterford, Norfolk, rector of, 147.

Tattersett, Norfolk, 188.

Taunton, Somerset, archdeacon, 178, 181 n.

Taylour, William, 43 n.

Techett, Roger, rector of Lakenham, Norwich, 57 n.

Tenterden, Kent, 191, 193.

Tettenhall, Staffs., royal free chapel, dean of, 34, 178, 181 n.

Theobald of Bec, archbishop of Canterbury, 21, 73.

Theselere, Roger le, 100.

Thorpland, Norfolk, 175.

Thremhall House, Essex, vicar of, 56 n.

Thurrock, Essex, prebendary of, 34-35, 132 n., 178, 180-81 nn.

Ticehurst, Sussex, vicar of, 129.

Tiler, John, bailiff, 198-99.

Tillesworth, William, 191.

Tilty Abbey, Essex, abbot of, 56 n.

Tinctor, Geoffrey, of Berkhampstead, Herts., 168.

Tiptree, Essex, prior of, 50 n.

Tithes, 166-67.

Tollesbury, Essex, 108.

Tollet, Richard, canon of Exeter, 121 n.

Tomlyn, Richard, 50 n.

Towghton, John, 77-78 & n., 166.

Trefnant, John, bishop of Hereford, 132 n., 148.

Trevelian, John, 140 n.

Trinitarians, 111 n.

Trissel, Alexander, parson of Goadby-Marwood, 57 n.

Troy, Theobald de, proctor, 185.

Tuae Fraternitatas, papal decretal (1206), 48 n.

Tuke, Nicholas, 129 n.

Tunstall, Cuthbert, bishop of London, 190.
Turner's Hill, Sussex, 106.
Twyte, William, 63 n.
Tylly, Richard, 51 n.
Tylney, John, 63 n.
Tyndall (*alias* Hochyn), John, 190.
Tyndalle, Philip, 146 n.

Usk, Monmouthshire, lordship of, 114-15 & nn., 236.
Uvedale, William, sheriff of Sussex, 106, 198-200.

Veer, Walter, sheriff of Southampton, 106 n.
Venerabilibus, papal decretal (1254), 46 n., 139 n., 143 n.
Vicar-general, power to signify, 28.
Voyse, Richard, 76 n.

Waddingham, Agnes, 41 n.
Wadyngham, Robert, parson, 196.
Walcote, Lambert de, 163.
Walden, Herts., 191.
Walden, Roger, archbishop of Canterbury, 165, 207.
Wales, 23 n., 56 n., 112, 114-15; signification procedure, 112-15.
Walpole, Ralph, bishop of Norwich, 206.
Walshman, William, 168-69.
Walsingham, Thomas, 181 n.
Walter, Edward, 192.
Waltham Abbey, Essex, abbot of, 34, 178, 181 n.
Ware, Herts., parish of, 191; priory, prior of, 56 n.
Warham, William, archbishop of Canterbury, 57, 83, 85 n., 95, 98, 112 n., 122 n., 166, 171, 181 n., 193.
Warwick, prison at, 148; St. Margaret's Church, canon of, 108, 149 n.
Warwickshire, sheriff of, 64 n., 108, 147-149.
Warter, William, 146 n.
Waterman, Robert, 108 n.
Webbe, William, 106 n.
Wedde, Nicholas, of Battle, Sussex, 199.
Wellington, prior of, 56 n.
Wells, archdeaconry of, 84.
Wells, Somerset, city of, 64; cathedral cemetary, 168.
—, diocese, *see* Bath and Wells.

Wendling Abbey, Norfolk, abbot of, 56 n.
Werland, Devon, chapel at, 111 n.
West Torrington, Robert of, 86, 99.
Westminster, abbey, abbot of, 34-35, 85, 133, 146 n., 178, 182-84 & n., 196; archdeacon of, 32 n., 206.
—, palace of, 99.
Westmoreland, county of, sheriff of, 94, 100.
Weston, Richard de, 51 n.
Wetherden, Suffolk, 188.
Whatlington, Sussex, rector of, 50 n.
Wheatacre, Norfolk, vicar of, 129 n.
Whelwryght, John, chaplain, 190.
Whelwryght, Thomas, chaplain, 190.
Whitlesey, William, archbishop of Canterbury, 63 n.
Whyte, William le, of Barnby, Suffolk, 209.
Wickham, Cambs., rector of, 56 n.
Wickhampton, Robert, bishop of Salisbury, 32 n.
Wickwane, William, archbishop of York, 26, 104 n.
William I, the Conqueror, king of England, 17-21, 28, 43, 48, 102.
William Durandus, 45 n., 48, 49 n., 124 n., 126 n., 139-40 nn., 142-44 & n.
William of Drogheda, 49.
William of Pagula, 45 n., 144 n.
William of Rennes, 138 n.
Wilmyngton, Bartholomew, 129.
Wilton Abbey, Wilts., abbess of, 56 n.
Wiltshire, 42, 93; sheriff of, 108.
Winchelsey, Robert, archbishop of Canterbury, 31, 53-54, 62 n., 83 n., 104 n., 151 n.
Winchester, diocese of, 23 n., 44 n., 75, 94, 102 n., 106 n., 140;
    bishop of, 54-55 & nn., 60, 79 n., 148;
    bishops of:
        John Pontissara (1282-1304), 153 n.;
        Henry Woodlock (1316-19), 54-55 nn., 60 n., 78-79 nn.;
    rectors of, 100.
Windsor, Berks., royal free chapel, 207.
Witham, John de, 163.
Withebroc, Master H. de, 27 n.
Withington, Glos., rector of, 86.
Wodburn, Robert, bishop of Hólar, 62.
Wolsey, Thomas, cardinal, archbishop of York, 33, 58, 85, 123 n., 171, 190.
Wombleton, Yorks., 101 n.

Wood, William atte, 133, 183-85.

Woodlock, Henry, bishop of Winchester, 54-55 nn., 60 n., 78-79 nn.

Worcester, cathedral, prior of, 84.

—, diocese of, 24 n., 27 n., 39, 41, 55 n., 62 n., 77; bishop of, 65, 82 n., 86, 90, 142 n., 148, 195; consistory of, 63 n.

Wreklesham, William de, 111 n.

Writs, 22; and absolved excommunicates, 147; of capture, 17, 120-34; *de cursu*, 86-112; delivery of, 99-102; of delivery, 145, 147; of detention, 17; execution of, 92-95, 102-11; failure to execute, 102-04; fees, 97-98; issuance, 91-97; multiple, 94-95, 110; of prohibition, 88-89, 144, 212-15; registers of, 211-15; shrieval, 105.

—,

    de caucione admittenda, 150-54, 213;

    de excommunicatis incarceratis deliberatis, 212;

    de excommunicato capiendo, 53, 57, 66, 82-83, 86-112; and appeal, 120; and contumacy, 44; counteraction, 125; and heresy, 68, 70; issuance by judges-delegate, 33; subjects of, 61-71; supersedence by chancery, 123;

    de excommunicato deliberando, 213-14;

    de heretico comburendo, 69-70, 189, 191-194;

    de vi laica amovenda, 83;

    interim supersedeas, 127, 130-31, 133 n.;

    scire facias, 89, 128, 131, 133 n., 214-15;

    supersedeas, 214-15;

    supersedeas pendente appellacione, 213-15.

Wrowe, Hughtred, 114.

Wyggeton, John de, knight, 100, 195-196.

Wygot, John, 51 n.

Wynbusshe, chancery clerk, 95 n.

Wyngate, John de, 162.

Wynnesbury, Henry, 51 n.

Wynselaw, William, chaplain, 108.

Yale, Wales, lordship of, 114 n.

Yonge, John, bailiff, 106 n.

Yonge, Thomas, bailiff, 198-99.

York, city of, 64, 78 n., 117; castle of, 190; cathedral, dean and chapter of, 27, 131 n., 143 n.; Holy Trinity priory, 125 n.; prison at, 149 n.

—, county of, 22; cursitor for, 95 n.; sheriff of, 93-94, 98, 101, 109-10, 179 n.

—, diocese of, 23 n., 26, 41, 49 n., 93, 95, 156; archbishop of, 54, 62-63, 80, 86, 101, 110, 114, 125 n., 127 n., 140 n., 143 n., 146 n., 148, 179, 181 n., 190;

    archbishops of:

        Walter Giffard (1266-79), 101, 110;

        William Wickwane (1279-85), 26, 104 n.;

        John le Romeyn (1286-96), 94, 148 n.;

        Henry Newark (1298-99), 26, 148 n.;

        Thomas Corbridge (1300-04), 80, 148 n.;

        William Greenfield (1306-15), 148 n.;

        Henry Bowet (1407-23), 114;

        Thomas Wolsey (1514-30), 33, 58, 123 n., 171, 190;

    court of, *see* Courts, ecclesiastical.

PB-6882-3
75-72T
C